THE INTERNATIONAL RELATIONS
OF MANCHURIA

THE UNIVERSITY OF CHICAGO PRESS
CHICAGO, ILLINOIS

THE BAKER & TAYLOR COMPANY
NEW YORK

THE MACMILLAN COMPANY OF CANADA, LIMITED
TORONTO

THE CAMBRIDGE UNIVERSITY PRESS
LONDON

THE MARUZEN-KABUSHIKI-KAISHA
TOKYO, OSAKA, KYOTO, FUKUOKA, SENDAI

THE COMMERCIAL PRESS, LIMITED
SHANGHAI

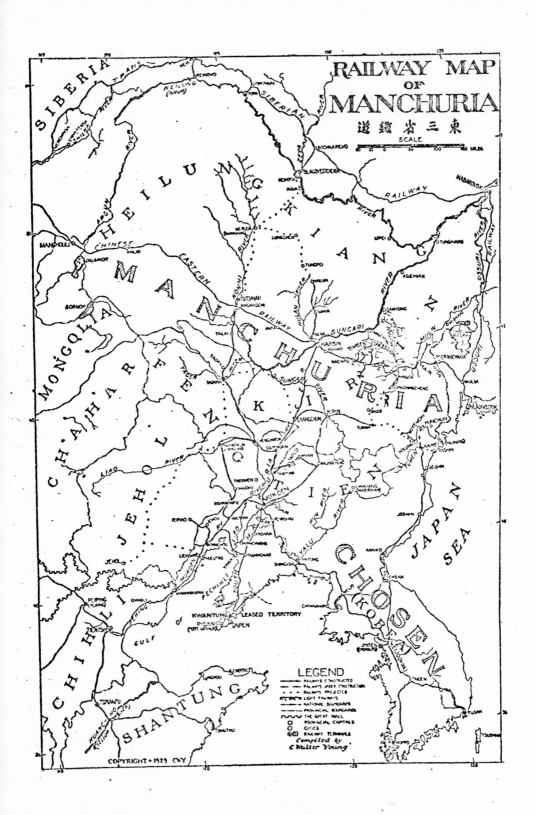

RAILWAY MAP OF MANCHURIA

東三省鐵道

SCALE

LEGEND
RAILWAYS CONSTRUCTED
RAILWAYS UNDER CONSTRUCTION
RAILWAYS PROJECTED
LIGHT RAILWAYS
NATIONAL BOUNDARIES
PROVINCIAL BOUNDARIES
THE GREAT WALL
PROVINCIAL CAPITALS
CITIES
RAILWAY TERMINALS
Compiled by
C Walter Young

COPYRIGHT · 1929 CWY

The International Relations of Manchuria

A Digest and Analysis of Treaties, Agreements, and Negotiations Concerning the Three Eastern Provinces of China

PREPARED FOR THE 1929 CONFERENCE OF
THE INSTITUTE OF PACIFIC RELATIONS IN
KYOTO, JAPAN

By

C. WALTER YOUNG

*Assistant Professor of Political Science,
The George Washington University,
Washington, D. C. (1929);
Visiting Lecturer in Far Eastern History,
Harvard University Summer School, 1928*

Published for the
AMERICAN COUNCIL
INSTITUTE OF PACIFIC RELATIONS
by
THE UNIVERSITY OF CHICAGO PRESS
CHICAGO, ILLINOIS

COMPOSED AND PRINTED BY QUINN & BODEN COMPANY, INC.

RAHWAY, N. J., U. S. A.

To the Memory

of

My Mother.

HILDA BREDBERG YOUNG

This Work is Affectionately Inscribed

FOREWORD

THIS is one of a series of publications which the Research Committee of the American Council of the Institute of Pacific Relations, under the chairmanship of Professor James T. Shotwell, has prepared for the forthcoming Conference of the Institute at Kyoto. The situation in the Three Eastern Provinces of China will be the principal concern of one of the four major round tables at Kyoto. The American Council offers the following study of treaty relations as part of the material background necessary for profitable discussion. The presentation of this material, however, for consideration in the program does not imply that either the Institute itself or the American Council assumes responsibility for statements of facts or opinion contained in the texts. These remain as much the personal expression of the author as would be the case had the contribution been communicated orally.

—- E. C. CARTER.

New York.

PREFACE

IN this volume the complicated facts with regard to a region which served as the battle-field in the Russo-Japanese war (1904-1905), and which, since then, has furnished the most crucial of the international issues in the Far East, are stated in detail in an objective and accurate manner. It is, therefore, eminently proper that at the present time this factual material should be made available. The Institute of Pacific Relations, which holds its Third Biennial Conference in Kyoto, Japan, during October and November, 1929, is to be congratulated that it has been able to secure for the preparation of this volume one who has made a special and first-hand study of all the aspects of the problem of Manchuria. The circumstance that a bare recital of the facts of the situation has required more than two hundred pages of print is sufficient to show how complex that situation is. But, notwithstanding this complexity, the general features of the Manchurian problem, as an international one, can be readily and briefly stated.

All of the nations which have commercial and financial dealings of any considerable degree of importance with China have had an interest which they have exhibited either in the attempt to obtain in that region special or exclusive privileges of railway or other forms of financial exploitation, or, as has been especially the case of the United States, to have applied the principle of equal opportunity for all, that is, what is commonly called the "Open Door." However, the three nations which have been especially concerned with the development and the political status of Manchuria have been China, Russia and Japan.

China has, of course, been concerned because she regards Manchuria as an integral part of her national domain; because Manchuria has furnished the road for the invasion, in the past, of her older eighteen provinces; because Manchuria, at the present time, provides a place of settlement under her own sovereignty for millions of her surplus population; and because Manchuria is, for China, a source of agricultural products and an area of opportunity for forest and mining enterprises.

Russia has been concerned with Manchuria primarily because of her desire to obtain a footing upon the Pacific better than that supplied by her possessions north of the Amur river, with harbors ice-bound a large part of every year. Especially in connection with the Chinese Eastern Railway are the present interests of Russia entangled with the interests of China and of the other powers in Manchuria.

Japan has been concerned with Manchuria because she looks to that country for a supply of badly needed raw mat rials, such as food and coal, and because she has been unwilling to have as strong a power as Russia so close to her own home islands and to her dependency, Chosen. Since the Russo-Japanese war the special Russian interests have been confined to North Manchuria, and Japanese ambitions—political and economic—to South Manchuria, including the Kwantung (Liaotung) peninsula.

Politically, or internationally, the problem confronting China as well as, in lesser degree, the other powers, has been to prevent Russia and Japan from transmuting their economic and financial interests in Manchuria into political interests or rights which would furnish those countries with a basis for a claim upon their part to exercise forms of political jurisdiction which would be in contravention of the sovereign rights of China.

Japan, in common with the other powers having treaty relations with China, i.e., the so-called treaty powers, has repeatedly recognized the sovereignty of China over all of Manchuria, and has declared in the most formal manner her firm intention to respect China's sovereign jurisdictional rights therein. In fact, however, Japan has claimed and exercised certain political jurisdictional rights in Manchuria, as in the South Manchuria Railway zone. So far as these rights have been founded upon treaty concessions obtained from China, it cannot be said that China's sovereignty has been infringed; but the situation has been rendered doubly complex by reason of the fact that China, in the matter of exercise of some of these jurisdictional rights, has denied that they can properly be drawn from the treaty provisions to which Japan has referred, and, as to other of these rights, points to the fact that they are based upon the Sino-Japanese treaties and agreements of 1915 which were entered into under circumstances which have led China to declare that these treaties and agreements ought to be deemed without binding force.

Aside, however, from any claims of treaty rights, Japan asserts that, on the basis of these treaties and agreements, she has developed economic interests in Manchuria which are vital to her own national existence, and because of this fact, she has made it clear that, whatever concessions she may make to China under pressure from China or from other powers, she is determined not to surrender, in any essential respects, her existing treaty rights or economic interests in Manchuria. She has, indeed, gone beyond this, and has declared her intention not to permit action upon the part of China, even though within China's right as the territorial sovereign, such as waging civil war, which will seriously endanger or prejudice Japan's economic or other vested proprietary rights in Manchuria.

Here the issue tends to become a delicate international one, for it will not be surprising should China, while recognizing the right of a sovereign state to protect its own political existence, take the position that this right does not justify a state in interfering with the exercise by another state of its sovereign rights within its own territory, unless the acts of such other state are in violation of treaty undertakings or are aimed directly and with primary purpose against the security or vested interests of the interfering state. It would seem, then, that, if this position is taken, a state is unfortunately circumstanced when it has interests which it deems to be vital to its own national existence but which are located in the territory and under the political jurisdiction of another state.

It seems likely that, at the coming Conference at Kyoto, the above situation, as influenced by the facts which are detailed in the present volume, will receive considerable and, perhaps, major attention. If the discussions are carried on in the spirit which characterized those of the two former conferences, it will be fortunate if this is the case, for it may be expected that, as a result, the entire Manchurian problem will receive a clarification which will render easier its peaceful and satisfactory settlement.

In any event, the present work will be a great permanent value to anyone who wishes to be well informed as to a situation which, in the immediate years to come, is certain to be one of international importance.

WESTEL W. WILLOUGHBY.

The Johns Hopkins University.

AUTHOR'S PREFACE

THE preparation of the present volume was undertaken in response to a request of the American Council of the Institute of Pacific Relations. To serve their purpose and that of the Kyoto Conference of the Institute, meeting in Japan in late autumn of 1929, it was desirable that the volume should be primarily a reference work, systematically arranged, suitable at once for ready reference to any important subject or category and for conveying a connected account of events in the modern *International Relations of Manchuria*. To fulfill these requirements thorough documentation was necessary, while frequent direct quotation was both desirable and unavoidable, however unliterary the resulting style. Objectivity was essential. A degree of realism was required.

Special pains have been taken to serve each of these ends, ends which occasionally have been found to militate against each other. If a foreign loan contract agreement for industrial purposes hypothecates revenues of one country, and, on the face of the agreement, is intended for industrial purposes, but, if, on the other hand, the loan is in reality not for industrial purposes at all, but to finance a civil war, though that purpose is not mentioned in the agreement, what should be said of it? To quote the agreement would be objectivity, perhaps; to detail its real purpose would be realism. To reconcile objectivity and realism has occasionally been attempted in this work; but, more usually, rather than sacrifice objectivity, realism has been left for inference by the critical reader. Where the nature of a particular issue in controversy requires definite decision on essential points, the writer has, with reluctance and with deference to more rational views, passed some judgment. The appendices, too, however opinionative, are based on the facts noted in context, in fact, on all materials available to the writer.

The selection of materials and the task of making a digest of particular documents naturally involves the problem of discretion. The criteria influencing this discretion, however, have been the historic and practical importance of the materials and of the contents of particular documents. No conscious effort has been made to use this discretion in a manner unfairly to influence the reader in his judgment as to the merits of a particular controversy or contention. A certain amount of redundancy will be noticed in several sections, as in those dealing with the Chinese Eastern Railway since 1919, a repetition and monotony which may be explained, if not condoned, by the writer's effort to facilitate a quick grasp of isolated subjects, especially when the volume is to be used purely for reference purposes. It is hoped, however, that the study may have permanent value not only for reference, but for intensive study, purposes.

Peculiarly enough, the *International Relations of Manchuria* fall very naturally into the exact periods of division which may well be taken to characterize the modern foreign relations of China generally, i.e., (1) The First Period, from 1895 to 1905, (2) The Second Period, from 1905 to 1915, (3) The Third Period, from 1915 to 1921, and (4) The Fourth Period, from 1921 to the present. Within each of these periods an attempt has been made to subdivide the categories in such a way as to make it readily possible to carry through the narrative concerning a particular subject from period to period. In the interest of presenting the reader with a connected account of general events throughout the four periods, a concise and somewhat interpretative summary has been prefixed to each of the four period divisions. An endeavor has also been made to enable the reader to form a rapid but reliable judgment on the position of each of the powers in interest, especially of China, Japan and Russia. No special category has been devoted to the position of China because Manchuria is China, and, wherever Manchuria is concerned, China is concerned.

An Introductory Chapter has been prepared in view of the important developments in connection with the Chinese Eastern Railway during 1929. Several appendices have been added further to elucidate the main text, to supply requisite information on the authenticity of controverted or officially unpublished international agreements, and to include an account of facts which do not naturally fall within the categories of the body of the work.

The purpose of this digest and analysis of important treaties, agreements and official negotiations concerning Manchuria required that the work should be "shod in the clumsy bootery of footnotes." These footnotes, in the main, give the exact sources of the documents and materials upon which principal reliance has been placed. The official texts of documents have been used in all cases except where, because of their non-availability, quasi-official or unofficial sources have had to be relied on and are, therefore, designated. As to the general treaty compilations used, it is evident that principal use has been made of the Honorable John Van Antwerp MacMurray's monumental collection: *Treaties and Agreements with and concerning China* (1894-1919), in two volumes. Because it is believed that that work is at once an example of very superior scholarship and the most accessible and useful general treaty collection for the period covered, references have usually been made solely to *MacMurray*, except where, in rare cases, it has been necessary to supplement those volumes with references drawn from other sources, usually the official publications of the various foreign offices concerned. Parenthetically, it may be said that the incomparable accuracy of Mr. MacMurray's volumes frequently reveals errors of dates and phraseology in the publications of several foreign offices, including *United States Foreign Relations*. For these reasons it has been deemed sufficient to refer to *MacMurray*, which source may be used for further reference to official, quasi-official and unofficial sources mentioned therein. Where references have been given in footnotes to sources other than *MacMurray*, it may generally be concluded that the documents are not found in that unusually comprehensive compilation, or that, for reasons of accuracy or alternative reference, it has been deemed advisable to refer to other sources. For the entire period after 1919 reliance has naturally had to be placed on materials found elsewhere. In frequent instances, mentioned in the footnotes, the writer has drawn upon information supplied directly from official agencies or garnered by him on the field in Manchuria, usually at the time that the events depicted were actually taking place there.

As to the difficult problem of transliterating into English the numerous Chinese, Japanese and Russian proper names used, an effort has been made to conform to commonly accepted standards. As to Chinese geographical names, the romanization adopted by the Chinese Postal Administration has been followed, except where it has been thought advisable, for special reasons, to conform to the "Wade System," or to accepted alterations of that system. Diacritical marks have generally been omitted in place names, and frequently in names of Chinese officials referred to, except, perhaps, where an occasional apostrophe has been inserted to caution the unwary reader against too much assurance in pronouncing Chinese proper names. This might well be done also for place names, except that that would lead to confusion, and it is perhaps more important to locate them (with the use of the map especially prepared to serve this volume) than to pronounce them properly—even if it be granted that the clumsy diacritical marks used for romanizing Chinese names might be some assistance in pronunciation. Where archaic spelling has been used in documents, as occasionally in

MacMurray and usually for justifiable reasons therein, an effort has been made to adopt a standard spelling. The syllable "ou," pronounced in *Kuan-hua* ("Mandarin" Chinese) like long "o," has generally been used for "ow," for example, as also "hsin" for "sin," and "hua" for "hwa." Place names in Chosen (formerly Korea) are usually given in Japanese, with occasional additional pronunciation in Chinese, as "Huining" (Chinese) for "Kainei" (Japanese), in each case where they occur, it is believed, being justified by special circumstances.

The Index at the end of the volume is not intended to be comprehensive, but rather especially practical for the purposes of the present study. The tables of Contents before each major part are intentionally suggestive, while the Index is intended to supplement the tables of Contents. No comprehensive bibliography has been included because that would encumber the volume, and, at all events, citations are always made in the footnotes to complete titles, where the date of publication is included if the same is thought to be of special importance.

The author is under particular obligation to Dr. Westel W. Willoughby for his generous "Preface" and for his labor in reading the galley proofs at a time when, far removed from his office and library, he was supposed to be casting for bass in Ontario, Canada. To Mr. Bruno Lasker, of the staff of The Inquiry (New York), has fallen the usually thankless task of preparing the manuscript for the printer, and arranging the Index. It is a pleasure also to acknowledge the unstinting service of Miss M. Alice Matthews, Librarian, and Miss C. K. Van Nest, Reference Assistant, of the Library of the Carnegie Endowment for International Peace, Washington, who have placed otherwise inaccessible materials at the disposal of the author. To them, to Mr. E. C. Carter, Secretary-Treasurer of the American Council of the Institute of Pacific Relations, to the New York office staff, and to those others who have been helpful, perhaps in criticism and corrections, the writer owes a debt of gratitude. The responsibility, both for interpretations and errors, does not, however, rest upon the American Council in any sense, but upon the writer himself.

C. WALTER YOUNG.

Washington, D. C.
September 1, 1929.

EPITOME OF CONTENTS

Detailed tables of content will be found at the opening of each major section—viz. for Part I, page 1; Part II, page 45; Part III, page 127; Part IV, page 191; and for the Appendices, page 253.

INTRODUCTORY CHAPTER

The Sino-Russian Crisis of 1929 over the Chinese Eastern Railway

THE CRISIS which developed between China and Russia over the interpretation and application of the Sino-Russian agreements of 1924, which arose during 1929, was the most serious situation with regard to the international relations of Manchuria which has occurred since the Washington Conference. It is evident that the several incidents connected therewith will have far-reaching effects not only on the future management and perhaps the status of the Chinese Eastern Railway itself, but on the broader aspects of the relations of the two countries most concerned. The interests of third parties are likewise involved, in one way or another, in the issues in dispute, as well as in the prospects for peaceful settlement.

On May 27, 1929, local Chinese authorities at Harbin, Manchuria, under the orders of General Chang Ching-hui, Governor of the Harbin Special District, forcibly entered the Soviet Russian Consulate in that city for the avowed purpose of obtaining documentary and circumstantial evidence of reported violations by the Soviet Government and Soviet nationals in the management of the Chinese Eastern Railway of the Sino-Russian agreements of 1924. The Sino-Russian (Peking-Moscow) agreement on general principles for the settlement of questions between China and Soviet Russia, dated May 31, 1924, and the Sino-Russian (Mukden-Moscow) agreement for provisional management of the Chinese Eastern Railway and in regard to other matters, dated September 20, 1924, had each provided in identical terms (Article 6 of the Peking agreement, and Article 5 of the Mukden agreement) that propaganda directed against the political and social systems of either party would in future be interdicted. The following phraseology was used in the agreements:

"The Governments of the two Contracting Parties mutually pledge themselves not to permit within their respective territories the existence and/or activities of any organizations or groups whose aim is to struggle by acts of violence against the Governments of either Contracting Party.

"The Governments of the two Contracting Parties further pledge themselves not to engage in propaganda directed against the political and social systems of either Contracting Party."

Against the action of the local Chinese authorities in entering the Soviet Consulate at Harbin on May 27, the Soviet Government immediately entered a protest. The Chinese Government at Nanking, however, later took the position that the action of the local authorities had been justified. In an open manifesto issued subsequently for communication to interested foreign powers the Chinese Government, on July 21, declared:

"On May 27, Communist leaders in Manchuria held a meeting for the purpose of spreading the program of Communism of the Third Internationale at the Soviet Consulate in Harbin. During the raid on the consulate by authorities of the northeastern provinces documents relative to secret plottings for destruction of the unification of China, organization of an assassins' corps for Nanking and Manchuria, and other important centers, as well as the organization of a secret army for the destruction of the Chinese Eastern Railway, were seized, together with other Red propaganda designed to prolong internal strife in China.

"Most of the culprits arrested were important members of the staffs of the Chinese Eastern Railway, the Soviet Union of railway employees, the Soviet Mercantile Marine, the Soviet Far Eastern Petroleum Syndicate and other Soviet commercial organizations in the Far East."

In the meantime Soviet news organs published the statement that the alleged Communist meeting held in the Soviet Consulate in Harbin was actually a small group of non-consular officials meeting in the basement of the consulate, and that the individuals apprehended in the consulate's offices, and against whom charges of complicity in dissemination of propaganda were directed, were in the consulate on ordinary business, not of a character to compromise the position of the Soviet Consulate itself.

On July 10/11, 1929, local Chinese authorities under the orders of General Chang Ching-hui, Governor of the Harbin Special District, a subordinate of Marshal Chang Hsueh-liang, military governor of the Three Eastern Provinces, entered the Harbin central offices of the Chinese Eastern Railway and placed a large number of Soviet officials of the railway management under arrest. Of these some were deported to the frontier under guard. Other Soviet nationals in the railway's management were placed under careful surveillance, including Mr. Emshanoff, Manager of the railway, and certain Russian members of the Board of Directors of the railway. Mr. Emshanoff and certain members of the Board of Directors shortly thereafter departed for Moscow where they arrived on July 21. The Chinese authorities, immediately following the arrest of the Soviet officials in the railway's management, took over complete control of the central offices of the railway in Harbin, under the direction of the Chinese President of the Board of Directors, and made an effort to assume complete control of the railway throughout the entire system. The Chinese Foreign Minister (Dr. C. T. Wang), in a signed public declaration of July 25, later admitted, to quote his words, that "in order to put an end to the source of trouble and to preserve peace and order, the local authorities were compelled to take temporary control of the Chinese Eastern Railway and to close down the above-mentioned Soviet organizations." The subsequent employment by the Chinese management of "White" Russians in technical positions in the railway's offices, and the refusal of certain Soviet nationals, members of the Soviet Union of railway employees (*Dorcom*), to return to their posts, complicated the situation. The Harbin and district branch offices of the *Dorcom* had been closed by order of the local Chinese authorities.

Concentration of both Chinese and Russian troops on either side of the Sino-Russian frontier at the terminals of the Chinese Eastern Railway (Manchouli, on Chinese territory at the western terminus of the railway, and Suifen, on Chinese territory at the eastern terminus of the railway, adjoining Pogranitchnaya on Russian territory), as well as along the Amur river boundary (as at and opposite Blagovestchensk) followed immediately upon the July 10/11 incidents and the Russian ultimatum of July 13.

On July 13 the Soviet Government, acting through the Vice Commissar for Foreign Affairs (L. M. Karakhan, former Soviet Ambassador to Peking and an acting Commissar of the Soviet Foreign Office in 1919 and 1920), presented to the Chinese *Chargé d'Affaires* (Liao S. K. Liao), for transmission to his home government at Nanking, a protest including an ultimatum with regard to the action of the Chinese authorities in seizing control of the Chinese Eastern Railway on July 10/11. The communication, after deploring the alleged violation of the Sino-Russian agreements of 1924 by Chinese authorities, proposed the calling of a conference immediately for the purpose of settling all questions connected with the Chinese Eastern Railway, and demanded the release immediately of all Soviet nationals who had been arrested by action of the local Chinese authorities, as well as the cancellation of all arbitrary orders regarding the Chinese Eastern Railway, i.e., to bring about a return to the *status quo* before the July 10/11 seizures. Failing compliance with these demands within three days the Soviet Government reserved the right to take such steps as might be necessary to safeguard their interests in the Chinese Eastern Railway.

After a delay in transmission of the lengthy Russian communication, and apparently before the entire telegraphic communication had been received at Nanking, the Chinese Government (Nanking) replied on July 16/17, within the time limit set in the Soviet ultimatum. While repudiating the possible interpretation of the reply as containing counter demands, the Chinese note to the Soviet Commissariat for Foreign Affairs stated that the action of the local authorities in taking control of the Chinese Eastern Railway was in conformity with the Sino-Russian agreements of 1924, that the Soviet Russians in the management of the railway and other Soviet nationals in Harbin had violated these agreements by disseminating propaganda subversive of the political and social institutions of China, and that the Soviet Government had not fulfilled the terms of the agreements of 1924 pertaining to joint Sino-Russian management of the Chinese Eastern Railway. The Chinese Government offered to settle the dispute through negotiations with Moscow. The note contained what, in fact, amounted to counter demands, namely, that the Soviet Government immediately release Chinese nationals imprisoned in Russia, and that adequate protection be given for Chinese nationals in Russian territory against political aggression and repression. The Chinese reply did not give any indication of willingness to permit a return to the *status quo ante* with respect to the joint management of the Chinese Eastern Railway.

The Chinese reply was received in Moscow on July 17. Almost simultaneously the Soviet Government handed the Chinese *Chargé d'Affaires* his passports and severed diplomatic relations with China —relations which had been hanging by a rather slender thread since Ambassador Karakhan was forced to leave Peking following the forcible entry of Chinese police into the premises of the Soviet Embassy on April 6, 1927. In a communication presented to the Chinese *Chargé*, immediately upon the receipt of the reply from Nanking, the Soviet Government declared that the Nanking reply to the Soviet protest and ultimatum of July 13 was unsatisfactory, failing as it did to indicate a willingness to reinstate the condition of joint management of the Chinese Eastern Railway which had prevailed before July 10/11. It declared further that the Chinese Government would be held responsible for eventualities for non-compliance with Russia's proposition for direct settlement by negotiation. Simultaneously, the Russian Government announced the withdrawal of all Soviet diplomatic and consular officers from China, the recall of Soviet nationals in the management and employ of the Chinese Eastern Railway, and the suspension of railway communications between the Trans-Siberian and the Chinese Eastern Railways.

The official news organ, *Izvestia*, drew attention to what it characterized as the "empty charges by means of which the Chinese Government is trying to evade giving a proper explanation of its unlawful action with regard to the Chinese Eastern Railway." *Izvestia* further declared that "the Soviet Government decided to break off relations only when it became impossible to tolerate the existing situation longer. The Union of Soviet Socialist Republics is aware that the breach for which the Chinese Government is solely responsible, undermines the position not only of the ruling group but also to a certain extent the national elements in China in their struggle against unequal treaties."

On July 19 the Nanking Government, through action of the State Council, declared that diplomatic relations had been severed between the two governments and suspended official communications with the Soviet diplomatic and consular authorities in China, while simultaneously ordering the withdrawal of Chinese diplomatic and consular officials from Russian territory. The State Council thereupon drew up a draft of a manifesto in order to state the position of the Nanking Government to outside powers. The text of the manifesto, which was signed by the heads of the five *yuan*, and was released for publication abroad on July 21, declared that the Soviet Government had repudiated their declarations of 1919 and 1920 which had promised a return of the Chinese Eastern Railway to China, and had repeatedly violated the 1924 agreements both with respect to the management of the railway and in regard to interdiction of officially sanctioned propaganda, that the raid of the Chinese local authorities on the Harbin Consulate on May 27 had produced incriminating documentary evidence which would shortly be published, and that the local authorities had taken appropriate steps concerning the administration of the Chinese Eastern Railway and the Soviet organizations connected therewith. The manifesto declared that the Soviet officials in the management of the railway had continued to take part in anti-Chinese propaganda and had permitted the use of railway revenues for propaganda purposes. While imbued with the spirit of the Pact of Paris, the manifesto declared, China was prepared to take appropriate measures for self-defence. It placed upon the Soviet Government the responsibility for suspending communications between the Trans-Siberian and the Chinese Eastern Railways. The manifesto deplored the Russian ultimatum of July 13 and the second note severing diplomatic relations between the two countries, declaring that these facts complicated the possibility of an amicable settlement. Countering the *Izvestia's* assertion that the Nanking note of July 16/17 had replied with "empty charges," the manifesto declared that the Soviet communication severing diplomatic relations contained nothing but "empty phrases."

Both the Chinese and Russian Governments in these interchanges of notes and in their unilateral declarations alleged adverse violation of the Sino-Russian agreements of 1924. In the meantime Chinese and Russian troop concentration at strategic border points was evident. In an interview with foreign press correspondents at Moscow, given on July 19, the acting head of the Council of People's Commissars (Jan E. Rudzutak, Commissar for Transport), who in the absence of the Chairman of the Council (A. Rykoff) was the head of the Soviet Government, declared that, while the Russian Government was compelled to take steps to protect the frontier, particularly because of the presence of "White" Russian guards in the Chinese railway police along the Chinese Eastern, the Soviet Government had no intention to order Soviet troops to cross the frontier into Chinese territory. Commissar Rudzutak was represented as stating that the financial interests of the Soviet Government in the Chinese Eastern Railway were of less import than the observance of the Pact of Paris, which on the day before had been invoked by the American Government, but not in any communication to the Soviet Government.

The attempt to invoke the Pact of Paris (Briand-Kellogg treaty), for which ratifications were later exchanged and deposited at Washington on July 24, turned the attention of the world to the interests of outside powers involved in the controversy over the Chinese Eastern Railway, but particularly to the prospect for forestalling hostilities between China and Russia. The Chinese and Russian Governments had both signed and ratified the Pact of Paris. China was a member of the League of Nations; Russia was not. After preliminary conversations held on July 18 with the diplomatic representatives of Japan, China, Great Britain and France, the

American Secretary of State (Henry L. Stimson) announced on July 19 that the cooperation of Japan, Great Britain and France had been enlisted in an effort to prevent hostilities between China and Russia through calling the attention of China and Russia to the application in principle of the Pact of Paris, then not yet legally binding upon the signatories. The Secretary of State requested the Chinese Minister (Dr. C. C. Wu) to communicate to his government the reminder that China was a signatory of the Pact of Paris, and that it was the earnest desire of the United States and the cooperating powers that China and Russia settle the dispute over the Chinese Eastern Railway and related questions by diplomatic means without resort to arms. The Secretary of State made no specific suggestion as to what means should be resorted to for the settlement of the issues involved.

The Chinese Minister, speaking on his own authority on July 21, announced that "although the Kellogg pact is not yet formally in effect, China has abided and will abide by its terms." On the following day (July 22) the Chinese Legation received the formal reply of the Nanking Government. Simultaneously, following a meeting of the Nanking State Council, the Chinese Government announced that "the National Government continues its policy of peaceful negotiations for amicable settlement of the Chinese Eastern Railway issue, but in the event of Moscow's deliberate violation of the Kellogg pact, the National Government, in accordance with Articles 12, 16 and 17 [of the League Covenant], will place the matter in the hands of the Council of the League of Nations for investigation and settlement." On July 22 the Chinese Minister at Washington conveyed to the Secretary of State the reply of the Nanking Government, declaring verbally for the press that the reply contained assurances that the Chinese Government would abide by the terms of the Pact of Paris, and would not resort to force except in self-defence. On the occasion of that official call upon the Secretary of State the latter called attention to the necessity of arranging for a return to the *status quo ante,* i.e., to the form of joint management of the Chinese Eastern Railway as a prerequisite for settlement by such means as arbitration. A reinstatement of Soviet nationals, not necessarily the *same* ones as had been ejected from the management of the railway, was to be inferred in any actual return to the *status quo ante.* Minister Wu made the assertion, afterwards expanded in press interviews, that the action of the Chinese was not tantamount to seizure of the Chinese Eastern Railway, but was only directed toward the ousting of specific

Russian individuals from the management of the line. This statement, it will be noted, was not in complete harmony with that made by the Nanking Foreign Minister (Dr. C. T. Wang) in which he admitted (July 25) that "in order to put an end to the source of trouble and to preserve peace and order, the local authorities were compelled to take temporary control of the Chinese Eastern Railway and to close down the above-mentioned Soviet organizations." Moreover, the Minister of Communications (Sun Fo) was on more than one occasion represented as stating that the Ministry had made definite plans to take over control of the Chinese Eastern Railway, and later that the Ministry had actually taken over control.

In view of the fact that the Russian Government had no diplomatic representative at Washington, due to the non-recognition of the Soviet Government by the United States, the French Ambassador (Paul Claudel) and Secretary Stimson conferred on the proper course to follow in the circumstances. The French Ambassador was given the suggestion that, if the French Government were in complete harmony with the American Government as to the manner of procedure, and in accord with the American Government as to the desirability of common action to the end of securing statements from China and Russia committing themselves to resort only to pacific means for settlement of the dispute, then it would be highly desirable to secure Russia's reply through the French Government. The French Ambassador, apparently in entire accord with the Secretary of State, communicated this conversation to Paris. Immediately thereupon, the Foreign Minister (Aristide Briand) called the Chinese Minister and the Russian Ambassador at Paris into conference. The latter communicated with Moscow. There was, in fact, therefore, no official note of the French Government directly to Moscow, the intent of the French Government being communicated verbally to the Russian Ambassador. Upon receipt of the communication from Paris the Soviet Foreign Office issued an official *communiqué* on July 22 which stated that the Moscow Government had rejected the French offer of "mediation" on the ground that the Chinese Government had not established a "judicial basis" for negotiations. The same *communiqué*, however, asserted that the Soviet Government intended to secure an amicable settlement of the dispute. The exact character of the conversations between M. Briand and the Russian Ambassador in Paris has not been published. The fact that reports from Moscow, following the receipt of the Russian Ambassador's communication at the Foreign Office, asserted that the Soviet Foreign Office denied that the American Government had in any way participated and that the French Government acted entirely on their own responsibility, and even that the Pact of Paris was not mentioned in the Russian Ambassador's communication to Moscow, is, except for the last point, readily to be understood. The American Government had not recognized the Soviet Government. Official communication between them was, therefore, impossible, and, from the American point of view, undesirable. The French Government, therefore, naturally acted on their own responsibility in communicating with Moscow. Whether the Russian Ambassador's communication to the Soviet Foreign Office made mention of the Pact of Paris must remain an interesting dubiety. As to the alleged rejection of the French offer of "mediation," there is equally no evidence that any specific offer of actual mediation, as usually understood in international practice, was made. Secretary Stimson later was represented as declaring that, in the nature of the case, the French Government in communicating with Russia acted on their own responsibility.

Although Secretary Stimson had conferred with the Japanese Ambassador (K. Debuchi) about noon of July 18, on the same day as he conferred with the diplomatic representatives of France, Great Britain and China, and although the reports of that conversation and of the invocation of the Pact of Paris by the United States were published in Tokyo newspapers shortly thereafter, the Japanese Foreign Office continued to deny official knowledge of any such action on the part of the United States. The situation created the presumption, supported by vernacular editorials, that the Japanese Government had been in some way slighted and intentionally overlooked. Nor is it difficult to understand why the Japanese press sought to create that inference, in view of the current feeling in Japan that in certain matters, especially such as concern Japan's interests in Manchuria, the Japanese Government have a prior right not only to be consulted, but to take the initiative themselves. That Secretary Stimson conferred with the Japanese Ambassador on the same day as he conferred with the other diplomatic representatives, i.e., on July 18, is evident. That Ambassador Debuchi communicated with the Japanese Foreign Office shortly thereafter is also reasonably certain. The absence of Premier Hamaguchi from Tokyo at the time the latter message was received supported the generally cautious action of the Foreign Office in such matters in their reports to the press. In fact, the Japanese Government, as represented by Ambassador Debuchi at Washington, was in complete accord with the action taken by the United States in invoking the cooperation of the powers concerned to prevent hostilities between China and Russia. On July 25 the *New York Times* published a plausible explanation of the more or less inconsequential misunderstanding.

THE INVOCATION OF THE PACT OF PARIS

With respect to the application of the Pact of Paris to the Chinese Eastern Railway crisis during July, 1929, it may be said, therefore, that, while the Chinese and Russian Governments made unilateral declarations committing themselves not to resort to war except in self-defence, no official reply from the Soviet Government was either received or obtainable by the United States. It is not clear if the Russian Ambassador actually even mentioned the Pact of Paris in his communication with the Moscow Government. However that may be, the fact that the French Government, in the person of M. Briand, was an initiator along with the United States of the Pact of Paris, whether the pact itself was mentioned in the Russian Ambassador's communication or not, was perhaps a matter carrying considerable weight with the Soviet Foreign Office which, by virtue of its other acts in support of the Pact of Paris, might have been expected to respect the pact. It would perhaps be as easy to minimize the importance of the attempt to invoke the Pact of Paris in the Chinese Eastern Railway crisis as to exaggerate it. Whatever the effect on the specific diplomatic acts of the Chinese and Russian Governments, it is perhaps tenable to assert that the so-called moral effect of the existence of the pact, although not yet legally binding upon the signatories, was not overlooked by either China or Russia. The Pact of Paris offered, in fact, a scapegoat for both governments, who found themselves in a delicate situation from which neither China nor Russia was eager to retire without grace—or "face." It may not be an untenable assertion that neither the Chinese nor the Russian Governments were particularly eager for armed conflict over the issue of the Chinese Eastern Railway. Particularly did the Soviet Government at the early stages of the controversy manifest this attitude by encouraging the Moscow press to refrain from coloring the situation, or even presenting the facts. Both governments, from motives of internal policy, had reason in appearing diplomatically and otherwise brave. The Chinese Government perhaps misjudged the opposition—in Moscow and in other capitals. Both manifested throughout the period of the crisis that, if there were to be any settlement of the question of the Chinese Eastern Railway, that settlement would have to be the outcome of direct negotiations between the two governments. Moreover, it did not appear that any foreign government was inclined officially to suggest either to China or Russia that settlement of the dispute through participation of third parties be initiated. The German Government had offered their good offices with respect to taking charge of diplomatic and consular properties of the two governments, but apparently were unwilling to do more than to act as the medium of official communication between China and Russia in direct negotiations. To that end preliminary conferences were held in Manchuria between representatives of the two governments. The existence of the Pact of Paris served to reenforce the possibilities for settlement which were inherent in the nature of the dispute itself, in all likelihood, without war.

THE PROBLEM OF THE CHINESE EASTERN RAILWAY

The problems involved in the amicable settlement of such complicated legal and political issues as are inherent in the Chinese Eastern Railway question, aside from the complications resulting from the severing of diplomatic relations between Russia and China in July of 1929 and the events connected therewith, are such that they are not to be readily resolved and regularized either by direct negotiation or through the participation of third parties. A solution which, on the one hand, would safeguard the vested proprietary interests of the Russian Government in the Chinese Eastern Railway, and which, on the other, would satisfy the claims of the Chinese Government to unqualified sovereign rights over the railway and the zone which it traverses, is difficult in the extreme to secure. Furthermore, there are the claims to certain interests in the railway which the French Government since 1918 has asserted in behalf of the French bondholders of the Russo-Asiatic Bank which, as the Russo-Chinese Bank, practically financed the construction of the Chinese Eastern Railway. Direct negotiation between China and Russia, furthermore, would have to take account of the complicated political issues germane to the question of the Chinese Eastern Railway, as well as the larger phases of the relations of the two governments, as for example, the propaganda phase. The recent relations of the Chinese and Russian Governments, especially since 1927, have been such as seriously to compromise any otherwise mutually satisfactory settlement in connection with the railway question itself. To these political questions between China and Russia must be added the concern of the Japanese Government in any ultimate arrangement with respect to the operation of the Chinese Eastern Railway. The Chinese Eastern Railway, along with the Japanese-controlled South Manchuria Railway, are essential links in the communications between Japan and Europe. The interests of Japan, whether in North or in South Manchuria, both vested and intangible, are involved, even more than the question of through communications with Europe. Japan, more than any other outside party, is concerned with the maintenance of an efficient transportation system over the Chinese Eastern Railway because of the not unimportant dependence of the South Manchuria Railway upon freight traffic from that line. The possibility of disruption to traffic on the Chinese Eastern Railway and the greater menace of political settlement in North Manchuria naturally are of much concern to the Tokyo Government. Moreover, present negotiations between Mukden and Tokyo, and pending concessions, such as for certain railways in Kirin province, are more or less directly involved in the position which the Japanese Government assume toward the participants in the controversy over the Chinese Eastern Railway. The likelihood that the Chinese and Russian Governments through direct negotiations will seek to settle the question without considering the interests of "third parties," as they sought to do in the agreements of 1924, may be fraught with unpleasant potentialities not only for the French bondholders in the former Russo-Asiatic Bank, but for the otherwise interested Japanese. In any event, the prospect for an immediate and final settlement of the Chinese Eastern Railway controversy, and the problems related thereto, either by the action of third parties or by direct negotiations between China and Russia, are not promising.[1]

[1] The diplomatic and documentary history of the Chinese Eastern Railway is dealt with in considerable detail in the several sections of the present volume. The following specific references are of particular importance for an appreciation of the historical background of the present controversy between China and Russia over the railway and over related matters:
The contractual bases and early history: Chap. III, Secs. a, b and c.
Scope of political jurisdiction: Chap. V, Secs. a, b and c.
Transfer of a part of the southern section to Japan: Chap. XVI, Secs. a, b and c.
Russian rights and the railway after Portsmouth: Chap. XXIV, Secs. a and b.
Relation of Russia to the railway, 1915-1921: Chap. XLIII, Sec. a.
The problem of the railway after the Washington Conference: Chap. LII, Secs. a and b.
The Sino-Russian agreements of 1924: Chap. LII, Sec. d.
The Ivanoff incident and Chinese troop transportation: Chap. LII, Sec. e.
The status of the railway after 1925: Chap. LII, Sec. f.

PART I

THE FIRST PERIOD: 1895-1905

CONTENTS

PART I. THE FIRST PERIOD: 1895-1905

SUMMARY OF THE FIRST PERIOD

WHILE Russian expansion into Manchuria during 1895 to 1905 was at once a phase and the culmination of a more extensive general expansion movement which brought Russian pioneers and resultant political and economic interests into Siberia, down the Amur river, and to the north Pacific littoral, it was the development of Russian interests in Manchuria that had the most influence on the course of international relations in the Far East. The period following the war between China and Japan (1894-1895) and that between Russia and Japan (1904-1905) might with considerable justification be characterized as the "Russian period in Manchuria." The political and military weakness of China having been made manifest in the war with Japan, there occurred in China a chain of events against which the contemporary activities of Russia in Manchuria should be considered. The development of "spheres of interest" in the Yangtze valley, in Shantung, and in southern China (through bilateral agreements of guarantee, through declarations of non-alienation of particular areas on the part of China, and through acquisition of prior rights to finance railway and industrial enterprises in delimited areas), the acquisition of leased territories by Germany, Great Britain and France, during 1898, the new obligations placed on China in the Boxer Protocol of 1901, were all evidences in other parts of China of activities not dissimilar in some respects to those of the Russians in Manchuria.

Japan possessed tangible interests and special treaty rights in Manchuria even before Russia. Japan had acquired in the treaty of Shimonoseki (1895) certain interests as shown by the territory ceded by China, including the Liaotung peninsula in Manchuria, but, due to the interposition of Russia, France and Germany, Japan was forced to relinquish the territory thus acquired, and by so doing sacrificed such tangible interests as she had acquired as a result of the Sino-Japanese war. Except for a rapidly developing trade, in particular with Newchwang, Japan's tangible interests were confined thereafter, until the war with Russia, to Korea.

3

The development of Russia's interests in Manchuria and the acquisition of special treaty rights and politico-commercial concessions from 1895 to 1904 were in great measure the result of the construction of the Trans-Siberian railway, long a cherished project of Tsar Alexander III, which was carried through to completion under Tsar Nicholas II. Serge (later Count) Witte, Minister of Finance, was especially responsible for the short-cut of the Trans-Siberian across north Manchuria which obviated certain construction difficulties of the northern Amur route and furnished a more direct means of access to Vladivostok. The Russian Government took the initiative in floating for the Peking Government the first loan to enable China to pay the initial instalment of the war indemnity to Japan, this being accomplished through the Franco-Russian "Chinese 4 Per Cent. Gold Loan of 1895." A military alliance directed against Japan was concluded between Russia and China in June (May), 1896, when Li Hung-chang was in St. Petersburg attending the coronation of Tsar Nicholas II.

By the Sino-Russian convention of March, 1898, the Russian Government acquired the lease of the southern portion of the Liaotung peninsula for a period of twenty-five years. The lease included Port Arthur which was acquired in order to give Russia an ice-free naval base on the Gulf of Pechihli with direct access to the Chinese coastal seas and the Pacific. Dalny, on the bay of Talien, was actually built in pursuance of an imperial ukase of August, 1899, which created it as a "free port."

The Russian program of development of her national commercial and political interests in Manchuria was carried on principally through the medium of the Russo-Chinese Bank and its offspring, the Chinese Eastern Railway Company. The former was a Russian financial organization chartered in 1895 and under the control of the Russian Minister of Finance, having an initial capital supplied in the main by French banking groups in Paris. This bank was the initial medium through which the Russian Government obtained railway concessions in Manchuria, notably the contract agreement of September 8, 1896, for the construction and operation of the north Manchurian short-cut of the Trans-Siberian railway to be built by the Chinese Eastern Railway Company, a Russian institution formed for the purpose. Having obtained in the Liaotung lease convention the right to extend the railway south to the Liaotung peninsula the Chinese Eastern Railway acquired the concession for this South Manchurian branch line from Harbin to

Dalny and Port Arthur in the formal contract agreement of July 6, 1898:

Within the Liaotung leased territory Russian jurisdiction was defined in the convention as almost complete, the right to fortify the territory and to exclude foreign warships from Port Arthur being specifically granted to Russia. Within the Chinese Eastern Railway zone (both sections) the railway company contended that the agreement of 1896 conferred the "absolute and exclusive right of administration" of its lands and asserted that judicial jurisdiction in both civil and criminal cases over Chinese subjects in Heilungkiang and Kirin provinces, in all cases "directly or indirectly" touching the interests of persons employed by the railway, was obtained by two specially established Chinese bureaus in Harbin in relation to which the Russian engineer-in-chief of the railway had broad jurisdictional rights. China later contested this interpretation.

No specific provision in any Sino-Russian agreement from 1895 to 1904 conferred on the Russian Government or the Chinese Eastern Railway authorities the right to provide for "railway guards" in the railway zone. The Russian statutes of the railway, however, did specify the right of police protection. The right was assumed from the provision (Article 6) in the railway agreements which Russia interpreted so as to give the railway company broad administrative jurisdiction over its lands. Ambiguity, however, naturally led to contested jurisdiction in 1908 and 1909. The lease convention and the railway agreements combined to give Russia a preferential position with respect to administration of the Chinese Maritime Customs and specifically provided for preferential land frontier freight rates in favor of Russian goods.

A qualified recognition of a Russian "sphere of interest" in Manchuria was secured from Great Britain in the Anglo-Russian exchange of notes of 1899 by which Great Britain agreed not to seek or to support her nationals in seeking from the Chinese Government railway concessions north of the Great Wall. The German Government, moreover, interpreted the Anglo-German agreement of October 16, 1900, as having no application to Manchuria, thus taking a position of not questioning the Russian assertion of her declared rights in Manchuria. During and following the Boxer Rising the Russian position in Manchuria was strengthened by the introduction of Russian military troops and railway guards and by the assumption of administrative authority both within and outside of the railway zone. The Sino-Russian convention of 1902 which provided for evacuation of important cities occupied by Russian troops in 1900 and following had little material effect on the military position of Russia in Manchuria.

Inasmuch as none of the powers, except France and one British corporation, had special treaty rights or other commercial concessions in Manchuria similar to those acquired by Russia, these other powers, especially Great Britain, the United States, and Japan, sought to secure the adherence of Russia to the diplomatic formula of the "open door" policy, thus to prevent the absorption of Chinese territory and the encroachment upon Chinese administrative rights, and to maintain equality of opportunity for the commerce and industry of all nationals in Manchuria. All the powers concerned, including Russia, nominally committed themselves at one time or other from 1899 to 1900 to a policy of (1) refraining from impairing the territorial and administrative integrity of China, and of (2) insuring equality of opportunity for commerce and industry in Manchuria. Russian acceptance of that policy, however, was modified by failure to make commitments on certain subjects contained in the first "open door" note of John Hay, American Secretary of State. Russia's position in Manchuria was the major influence in bringing to fruition the first Anglo-Japanese alliance of 1902, which in turn was countered by the Franco-Russian declaration and agreement with reference to Manchuria made immediately thereafter.

The period of Russian supremacy in Manchuria from 1895 to 1905 was one in which Russia obtained, besides the Liaotung leased territory, a series of railway concessions including principally the Chinese Eastern Railway with an administrative zone in which Russian jurisdiction was paramount wherever the Russian officials chose to exercise it. These administrative rights in the railway zone were later acquired by Japan in the treaty of Portsmouth (1905) for the southern section (below Changchun) of the railway but were retained by Russia for the northern and main line of the Chinese Eastern Railway. But before 1905 Russia was in control of the only railways then existent in Manchuria. These commanded the principal arteries of trade both in northern and southern Manchuria. These acquisitions were supported by administrative rights in connection with the customs, native and maritime, and by preferential land frontier freight rates on the railways. To support these politico-commercial concessions Russia had obtained the military alliance with China in 1896, had reenforced them by acquiring a strategic position in the Liaotung leased territory in 1898, and had brought into Manchuria troops and railway guards in especially large numbers after 1900. At no time since 1905 has Manchuria been so nearly on the verge of practical absorption as during the closing years of the Russian period before 1905.

A. THE POSITION OF JAPAN: 1895-1896

CHAPTER I

Manchuria and the Outcome of the Sino-Japanese War
(1894-1895)

a. THE TREATY OF SHIMONOSEKI, APRIL 17, 1895. By virtue of the treaty of Shimonoseki, April 17, 1895, which concluded the Sino-Japanese war, China ceded (Article 2) to Japan "in perpetuity and full sovereignty" the southern portion of the province of Fengtien, Manchuria, including a zone generally south of a line drawn from a point on the Yalu river west to Yingkou, and including the islands adjacent to that region. Other territorial cessions included Formosa and islands of the Pescadores group. China recognized (Article 1) the complete independence of Korea, and agreed (Article 4) to pay a war indemnity of 200,000,000 Kuping taels, the same to be paid in eight instalments, the first of which (50,000,000 Kuping taels) within six months, the last within seven years after the exchange of ratifications of the treaty. Ratifications were to be exchanged by May 8, 1895.[1]

b. RETROCESSION OF THE LIAOTUNG PENINSULA, 1895. Before the exchange of ratifications (May 8, 1895) the three powers, Russia, France and Germany on April 23 made representations to the Japanese Government in Tokyo to the effect that the cession of the Liaotung peninsula by Japan would constitute a menace to the peace of the Far East and therefore was highly inadvisable. Motivated by this tripartite intervention, Japan by imperial proclamation on May 10, 1895, two days after the formal exchange of ratifications of the treaty, announced that negotiations were under way with the Chinese Government for a return of the Liaotung peninsular districts to China.[2] Previous to the formal convention between Japan and China to effect the retrocession of the Liaotung districts, the governments of France, Germany and Russia presented identic notes to the Japanese Government on

[1] Sino-Japanese *Treaty of Peace* (Shimonoseki), April 17, 1895. (With Separate Articles and Convention to Prolong Armistice.) MacMurray, Vol. I, p. 18.
[2] Japanese *Imperial Proclamation regarding Retrocession of Liaotung Peninsula*, May 10, 1895. MacMurray, Vol. I, p. 52.

October 18, 1895, acknowledging the declarations of the Japanese Government regarding *inter alia* the reduction of the additional indemnity which Japan had desired in compensation for the return of the Liaotung to China.[3] In consequence of her declarations to these three powers, and in pursuance of the imperial proclamation of May 10, the Japanese Government signed on November 8, 1895, the formal convention to effect the return of the entire portion of southern Fengtien province which had been ceded to Japan in the treaty of Shimonoseki, in compensation for which China agreed to pay Japan an additional indemnity of 30,000,000 Kuping taels, evacuation by the Japanese troops to be completed within three months after the payment of this indemnity.[4] The terms of the treaty of peace with China (Shimonoseki) were thus altered principally by cancelling the cession of territory in Manchuria to Japan, and by increasing the indemnity to be paid by China to a total of 230,000,000 Kuping taels. A portion of the territory which by virtue of the tripartite intervention of the powers was returned to China was acquired by Russia in 1898 under a twenty-five year lease.[5]

Japan thus acquired permanently no special rights or privileges in Manchuria in consequence of the war with China in 1894-1895. Except for the unqualified acceptance by the Japanese Government of the declaration of policy contained in the first "open door" note of John Hay, United States Secretary of State, in 1899, and their commitments in the Anglo-Japanese treaty of alliance of 1902, and certain lesser general agreements, Japan entered into no international agreements from 1895 to 1904 by which she acquired any special rights in Manchuria.[6]

[3] Multi-Power (France, Germany and Russia) *Identic Note to Japanese Minister for Foreign Affairs regarding Retrocession of Liaotung Peninsula,* October 18, 1895. MacMurray, Vol. I, p. 53.

[4] Sino-Japanese *Convention for the Retrocession of the Southern Portion of the Province of Fengtien to China* (i.e., the Liaotung Peninsula), November 8, 1895. MacMurray, Vol. I, p. 50.

[5] See Chap. IV, Sec. a, for the Sino-Russian Lease Convention.

[6] See, Chap. X, Sec. a, for characterization of the later Japanese position after the development of Russian interests in Manchuria, regarding acceptance of the "open door" policy in China, and pertaining to Russia's relations with China in Manchuria.

B. THE POSITION OF RUSSIA: 1895-1905

CHAPTER II

The Russian Loan to China

a. FRANCO-RUSSIAN LOAN OF 1895 TO CHINA. While nego-tiations were in progress for the return of the Liaotung penin-sular areas to China, and for the fixing of the additional indemnity to be required of China in consequence of that retrocession, the Russian Government undertook to raise a loan for China. This was done through the agency of a Franco-Russian banking syndi-cate which on July 6, 1895, signed a contract with the Chinese Government for the "Chinese 4 Per Cent. Gold Loan of 1895" in the amount of 400,000,000 francs (100,000,000 gold roubles), the same to be guaranteed (Article 9) "by the duties levied by the Maritime Customs of China, and by the deposit of customs bonds." The Russian Government undertook (Article 9) to guarantee the payment of the loan to China in the event of possible suspension or delay on the part of the syndicate.[7] Assurance to this effect was given in the protocol of exchange of declarations concerning the "Chinese 4 Per Cent. Gold Loan of 1895" signed by repre-sentatives of the Russian and Chinese governments on the same date.[8] Also on that date the Russian Government undertook to guarantee to the lending syndicate the due payment by the Chinese government of interest and amortization of the loan.[9]

[7] China—Franco-Russian Syndicate *Contract for the Chinese Four Per Cent. Gold Loan of 1895*, July 6, 1895. MacMurray, Vol. I, p. 35.

[8] Sino-Russian *Protocol of Exchange of Declarations concerning the Chinese Four Per Cent. Gold Loan of 1895*, July 6, 1895. MacMurray, Vol. I, p. 40. Article 3 provided that "in case the service of the loan should, for any reason whatever, happen to suffer abeyance or delay, the Imperial Government of Russia, in accord with the Imperial Government of China, takes the obligation toward the contracting banks and firms, to make up for its part and place at their disposal in good time, as fast as they fall due, all sums required for the payment of coupons and redeemed bonds of the present loan, save that the Chinese Government will afterwards furnish the Russian Government with additional security. The manner of such additional security will be made the subject of a special agreement to be established between the two governments by their plenipotentiaries at Peking."

[9] Russian Government *Guarantee of Chinese Four Per Cent. Gold Loan of 1895*, July 6, 1895. MacMurray, Vol. I, p. 42. The Russian Government herein (Article 2) declared that "in case for any reason the payments on the loan should fail to be made or should be delayed," that government would "make up on its part and to place at the disposal of the contracting parties to the loan, in due time and as fast as the payments fall due, all the sums necessary for the payment of the coupons and redeemed bonds of the present loan."

CHAPTER III

The Russo-Chinese Bank and Russian Railways

a. ORGANIZATION AND FUNCTIONS OF THE RUSSO-CHINESE BANK. The Russo-Chinese Bank was formed in St. Petersburg under a charter, approved by the Russian Minister of Finance on December 22, 1895, with an initial capital (Section 4) of 6,000,-000 gold roubles derived especially from French sources. The management of the bank, created as a joint stock company, was entrusted to a Board of Directors elected by the shareholders, their nominations to be confirmed (Section 27) by the Russian Minister of Finance. "The object of the Russo-Chinese Bank was (is) exclusively to develop the commercial relations with the East-Asiatic countries" (Section 14) and, to this end, in addition to ordinary banking operations, was entrusted with broad powers to collect duties in China and to develop communications by construction of railways and telegraph lines.[10] To the capital of the Russo-Chinese Bank the Chinese Government, by an alleged agreement with Russia of August 28, 1896, undertook (Article 1) to contribute 5,000,000 Kuping taels, by which the Chinese Government was privileged to participate in the profits of the bank.[11] The Russo-Chinese Bank was merged with the Banque du Nord on July 30/August 12, 1910, to form the Russo-Asiatic Bank (Banque Russo-Asiatique).

[10] Russian *Charter of the Russo-Chinese Bank*, December 22, 1895. *Manchuria Treaties and Agreements*, p. 17.

[11] Sino-Russian *Alleged Agreement regarding Russo-Chinese Bank*, August 28, 1896. MacMurray, Vol. I, p. 78. Concerning the financing of the Russo-Chinese Bank and the Chinese Eastern Railway Company the following facts, obtained from Russian sources, are of importance: At the time of the organization of the Russo-Chinese Bank the Russian Government paid the bank 5,000,000 gold roubles, in return for which the bank issued to the Russian State Bank a receipt to the effect that the equivalent in shares to the amount of 5,000,000 gold roubles was received. This would indicate that the actual shares belonged to the Russian Government. Share certificates, however, do not seem to have been issued at all, while the Russian Government appears to have obtained and later possessed the temporary share control power which, in the absence of anything more definite, may be an incontestable claim to possession of the bank itself. The loans which were received from French sources were loans to the Russian Government itself, in return for which the latter gave Russian Government Bonds, apparently not of a character to give the French investors any particular legal claim to the Russo-Chinese Bank's assets. In 1897 it appears that the only issue of obligations of 4 per cent. railway bonds, to the nominal amount of 15,000,000 gold roubles, was effected. Of this amount, 7,200,000 gold roubles were acquired in bonds by the Russian State Savings Banks. Here, again, it appears that the purely Russian investment in the railway was of significance. Data is not available for the Russian outlays for the Chinese Eastern Railway from 1906 to 1911, but it appears that the Russian Government invested in the construction and operation of the Chinese Eastern Railway up to January 1, 1906, the sum of 428,600,000 gold roubles. During the period from 1911 to 1917 it is estimated that additional disbursements were made by the Russian Government for operation and other expenses to the amount of 50,000,000 gold roubles.

b. The Chinese Eastern Railway Agreements (Main Line) of 1896. Following the creation of the Russo-Chinese Bank, the Russian Government utilized this agency to acquire concessions for railway construction in Manchuria, the first being the trans-Manchuria short-cut of the Trans-Siberian. By virtue of the Sino-Russian treaty of alliance of June 3, 1896 (May 22, Russian date), the Chinese Government consented (Article 4) to the construction by Russia of a railway across Heilungkiang and Kirin provinces in the direction of Vladivostok "in order to facilitate the access of the Russian land troops to the menaced points" in case of war with Japan.[12]

Shortly after the conclusion of this treaty of alliance the Russo-Chinese Bank concluded with the Chinese Government (September 8, 1896) a contract agreement for the construction and operation of the Chinese Eastern Railway to be built across Manchuria by the Chinese Eastern Railway Company which was to be charged with construction and operation. The Chinese Government agreed to pay the sum of 5,000,000 Kuping taels to the Bank to be repaid (Article 12) to China on the day of the completion of the line and the opening of traffic. The statutes of the Company were to conform to Russian law; the president of the Company was to be named by the Chinese Government, though principal control was vested in a General Manager. Over the "lands actually necessary for the construction, operation, and protection of the line" the Company was to have (Article 6) *"the absolute and exclusive right of administration."*[13] No interference was to be permitted (Article 8) with regard to the movement of Russian troops or munitions over the railway. Merchandise proceeding in either direction over the railway between Russian and Chinese territory was to be permitted (Article 10) a third reduction from the usual Chinese Maritime Customs charges. The *"complete and exclusive right to operate the line"* was granted (Article 12) by the Chinese Government to the Chinese Eastern Railway Company. China was given the right (Article 12) to

[12] See Appendix A for the Sino-Russian (Li-Lobanoff) *Secret Treaty of Alliance of 1896.* Printed in MacMurray, Vol. I, p. 81. Telegraphic summary of the same presented by the Chinese Delegation to the Washington Conference in *Conference on the Limitation of Armament*, p. 1414.

[13] Sino-Russian (China—Russo-Chinese Bank) *Contract for the Construction and Operation of the Chinese Eastern Railway*, September 8, 1896. MacMurray, Vol. I, p. 74. Article 1. "The Russo-Chinese Bank will establish for the construction and operation of this railway (to connect Chita with the Russian South Ussuri Railway) a company under the name of the Chinese Eastern Railway Company." See Chap. XXIV, Sec. b, for the subsequent (1908-1914) controversy over the interpretation of the important Article 6.

recover the line thirty-six years from the opening of the entire line to traffic, or after eighty years without payment.

Following this railway contract agreement, the Imperial Government of Russia sanctioned (December 4/16, 1896) the statutes of the Chinese Eastern Railway Company.[14] These statutes confirmed the terms of the contract of September 8, 1896, between the Russo-Chinese Bank and the Chinese Government, and imposed special obligations on the railway company to construct telegraph lines, to permit free carriage of Russian mails, and to meet the requirements of the Russian Government regarding capitalization. While the duty of the Chinese Government to adopt measures to insure the safety of the railway was recognized, the statutes provided (Section 8) that "the preservation of law and order on the lands assigned to the railway and its appurtenances shall be confided to police agents appointed by the Company." It was provided (Section 29) in the statutes that after the expiration of eighty years the Chinese Government would become owners of the Chinese Eastern Railway without payment. If, however, recovery should be desired before that time it was provided (Section 30) that on the expiration of thirty-six years from the date of completion of the line and the opening of traffic the Chinese Government might obtain possession by "refunding to the Company in full all the outlays made on it, and on payment for everything done for the requirements of the railway, such payments to be made with accrued interest."

c. THE CHINESE EASTERN RAILWAY AGREEMENT (SOUTHERN BRANCH), 1898. The right to extend the Chinese Eastern Railway to southern Manchuria and the Gulf of Pechihli was acquired by Russia in the convention with China of March 27, 1898, for the lease of the southern part of the Liaotung peninsula.[15] Besides granting (Articles 1-3) the lease of the territory including Port Arthur and Talien (Dalny, later Dairen) to Russia for a period of twenty-five years, the Chinese Government agreed (Article 8) "that the concessions granted by it in 1896 to the Chinese Eastern Railway Company" should be "extended to the connecting branch" of the main line (northern) to be built to Talienwan as well and/or to one other point on the littoral of the peninsula, the provisions of the contract agreement of September 8, 1896, to apply likewise to these branch lines. China's

[14] Russian *Statutes of the Chinese Eastern Railway Company*, December 4-16, 1896. MacMurray, Vol. I, p. 84.

[15] Sino-Russian *Convention for the Lease of the Liaotung Peninsula*, March 27, 1898. MacMurray, Vol. I, p. 119.

consent to the construction of these branch railways should "never under any form serve as a pretext for the seizure of Chinese territory or for an encroachment on the sovereign rights of China." [16]

The formal agreement for the construction of this, the South Manchurian Branch of the Chinese Eastern Railway from a point on the main line of the Chinese Eastern Railway (northern) to Dalny and Port Arthur in the Liaotung peninsula was signed by the Chinese Eastern Railway (for Russia) and the Chinese Government on July 6, 1898. [17] The provisions of the contract agreement of September 8, 1896, for the construction and operation of the main line were made to apply likewise to this southern branch. By virtue of this agreement, therefore, the Chinese Eastern Railway Company (for Russia) acquired the right to connect the Trans-Siberian railway and the main line of the Chinese Eastern Railway (trans-Manchurian) with an ice-free port on the littoral of the Liaotung peninsula, together with *"the complete and exclusive right to operate the line"* through the territory, including *"the absolute and exclusive right of administration"* over the lands necessary for the use of the railway. China's rights of recovery in relation to the Southern Manchuria Branch line were the same as for the main line.

d. The Kirin-Changchun Railway Agreement, 1902. Two additional Sino-Russian railway agreements, the second being of special importance, were concluded in 1902 through the medium of the Chinese Eastern Railway Company pertaining to branch and connecting lines of the Chinese Eastern Railway. The first was a preliminary agreement of July 11, 1902, for the construction and management of a railway from Changchun (on the Southern Manchurian Branch of the Chinese Eastern Railway) east to Kirin (Article 1) "with the express object of encouraging the trade of the city of Kirin." [18] In the case of this Kirin Branch Railway, however, the provisions of the contract agreement of September 8, 1896, were declared to have no application, general control over management of the line to be vested in a Supervising Commission (Chinese) though the Chinese Eastern Railway

---

[16] *Ibid.*, pp. 120-121, Article 8. "Consent to the construction of the railway on the basis indicated shall never under any form serve as a pretext for the seizure of Chinese territory or for an encroachment on the sovereign rights of China."

[17] Sino-Russian (China-Chinese Eastern Railway) *Agreement concerning the Southern Branch of the Chinese Eastern Railway,* July 6, 1898. MacMurray, Vol. I, p. 154.

[18] Sino-Russian (China-Chinese Eastern Railway) *Preliminary Agreement for the Kirin-Changchun Railway,* July 11, 1902. MacMurray, Vol. I, p. 629.

Company was given complete charge of operation, as in the jurisdiction over land regulations and in the fixing of traffic rates.
China was empowered to buy back the Kirin Branch Railway after
the expiration of thirty-six years by the payment of the original
capital stock plus the debts incurred.   Criminal and civil jurisdiction over the Chinese inhabitants within the zone of the railway was retained by the local Chinese authorities.   This railway, however, was never completed by the Russians.

   e. Restoration of the Shanhaikwan-Hsinmintun Railway to China, 1902.   This second railway agreement of 1902
was contained in the Sino-Russian convention of April 8, 1902,
which provided also for the manner of evacuation of Russian
troops in Manchuria following the Boxer Rising in 1900, and
included the provisions by which Russia agreed to restore territories outside of Russia's treaty jurisdiction to the administration
of the Chinese Government.   In the convention Russia agreed
(Article 4) "to restore to the owners the railway Shanhaikwan-
Newchwang-Sinminting [Hsinmintun], which, since the end of
September, 1900, has been occupied and guarded by Russian
troops." [19]   China agreed to protect the line, and not to permit
other powers to participate in its protection, construction or operation.   Russia specifically recognized the validity of the private
British corporation contract for the construction of that line, as
well as the Anglo-Russian agreement of April 28, 1899, by which
these two powers had agreed that the Great Wall (abutting at the
sea at Shanhaikwan) was to be the dividing line to the north of
which Great Britain would not apply for (nor in behalf of her
nationals) railway concessions, to the south of which Russia
would not on her part (nor in behalf of her nationals) apply
for railway concessions.

   The provisions of the Sino-British railway contract agreement
for the construction of the Shanhaikwan-Hsinmintun railway were
thus specifically recognized as an exception to the application of
the Anglo-Russian agreement of April 28, 1899.   But it was also
provided (Article 4) that any extension or branch of this railway which China might propose to construct was to be undertaken only after these questions had been made "the subject of
mutual discussion between the Russian and Chinese Governments."
Russia thus acquired the right to be consulted with regard to the

   [19] Sino-Russian *Convention with regard to Manchuria,* April 8, 1902.   MacMurray,
Vol. I, p. 326.   For the relation of this convention to British railway interests in Manchuria during this period see Chap. VII, Secs. a and b.

future construction of *any or all* extensions or branches of the Shanhaikwan-Newchwang-Hsinmintun railway in southern Manchuria, in apparent conflict with the British rights acquired in the Sino-British railway loan agreement of October 10, 1898, which Russia in this same convention of 1902 nevertheless categorically recognized. Furthermore, Russia had previously received a pledge from China in a note from the Tsungli Yamen to the Russian Minister at Peking, dated June 1, 1899 (shortly after the Anglo-Russian exchange of notes of April 28), to the effect that if China proposed to use foreign capital or assistance for the construction of railways north of the Great Wall the proposal should "be first made to the Russian Government or to the Russian syndicate to construct the railway, and on no consideration will any other Government or a syndicate of any other nationality be allowed to construct the railway."

In summary, as to the British right to construct the Shanhaikwan-Newchwang-Hsinmintun railway itself, there would appear to have been no possibility of varying interpretation, the right being specifically recognized by the Russian Government in both the Anglo-Russian agreement of April 28, 1899, and in the Sino-Russian convention of April 8, 1902. As to the right to construct extensions or branch lines, however, it would appear that the Chinese Government granted exclusive privileges to a private British concern and to the Russian Government, the latter in the pledge to the Russian Minister in Peking on June 1, 1899, and in the Sino-Russian convention of April 8, 1902, which were, as exclusive grants, mutually irreconcilable.

CHAPTER IV

RUSSIAN ACQUISITION OF THE LIAOTUNG PENINSULA

a. CONVENTION AND AGREEMENT FOR THE LEASE OF THE LIAOTUNG PENINSULA, 1898. By the Sino-Russian convention of March 27, 1898, negotiated in Peking, Russia acquired (Article 1) the lease for a period (Article 3) of twenty-five years of Port Arthur and Talienwan "for the purpose of ensuring (Article 1) that the Russian naval forces shall possess an entirely secure base on the littoral of northern China."[20] Contiguous waters were likewise leased and a territory to include the southern part of the Liaotung

[20] Sino-Russian *Convention for the Lease of the Liaotung Peninsula*, March 27, 1898. MacMurray, Vol. I, p. 119. Article 3. "The term of the lease shall be twenty-five years from the date of the signature of the present agreement and may be prolonged subsequently by mutual consent of both Governments."

peninsula was included (Article 2) "to secure the proper defense of the area on the land side." A neutral zone was designated between the leased territory and the Chinese portion of Fengtien province within which (Article 5) "the civil administration will be entirely in the hands of the Chinese authorities," though Chinese troops were to be admitted only with the consent of the Russian authorities. Within the leased territory it was provided (Article 4) that "the entire military command of the land and naval forces and equally the supreme civil administration will be entirely given over to the Russian authorities." No Chinese troops were to be allowed within the leased territory, while Chinese subjects accused of crime were to be entitled to the privilege of trial and punishment by local Chinese authorities. Port Arthur was created (Article 6) an exclusive military (naval) port open solely to Russian and Chinese vessels, the war and merchant vessels of other states being absolutely prohibited from entry. Talienwan (later Dalny), however, was declared open to foreign commerce. The right of fortifying the leased territory was declared to be (Article 7) within the exclusive province of the Russian Government. The right of the Chinese Eastern Railway Company to construct a branch railway from the main line of the Chinese Eastern Railway to Talienwan was also granted (Article 8).[21]

In the additional agreement of May 7, 1898, the exact boundaries of the Liaotung leased territory and of the neutral zone were defined.[22] Chinchow, a city within the leased territory, was upon China's request declared to be (Article 4) under the administration and police of the Chinese, though Chinese troops in the city were to be replaced by Russian troops. Within the neutral zone the Chinese Government agreed to grant to Russia, if to any foreign power, special communication and industrial concessions.

CHAPTER V

Russian Jurisdiction in Manchuria

a. JURISDICTION WITHIN THE LIAOTUNG LEASED TERRITORY. No single Sino-Russian agreement of this period gives any adequate statement of the extent of Russian jurisdiction within the Liaotung

[21] *Ibid.*, pp. 120-121. Article 8 included the provision that "all the stipulations of the contract concluded by the Chinese Government with the Russo-Chinese Bank on August 27 (September 8), 1896, shall apply scrupulously to these supplementary branches." See Chap. III, Secs. b and c.

[22] Sino-Russian Additional *Agreement Defining the Boundaries of the Leased and Neutralized Territory in the Liaotung Peninsula*, May 7, 1898. MacMurray, Vol. I, p. 127.

leased territory, the neutral zone, or the railway zone of the main and southern branch lines of the Chinese Eastern Railway. In addition to the lease and railway conventions and agreements previously considered several special Sino-Russian agreements pertaining to jurisdiction over Chinese subjects and relating to municipal administration in the railway zones were concluded.

Within the Liaotung leased territory the lease convention (March 27, 1898) provided (Article 4) that "the entire military command of the land and naval forces and equally the supreme civil administration will be entirely given over to the Russian authorities." [23] Chinese military land forces were forbidden to enter the territory, though Port Arthur was declared open to the war vessels of China and Russia alone. The right to fortify the leased territory was granted to Russia. Chinese subjects accused of crime within the leased territory were to be given over (Article 4) to the local Chinese authorities for trial and punishment. Over Russian subjects within the leased territory the Russian Government was to have jurisdiction. Within the city of Chinchou an exception was made, in the additional agreement of May 7, 1898, defining the boundaries of the leased territory and the neutral zone, enabling (Article 4) the administration and police of the city to be retained by the Chinese authorities, though Chinese troops in the city were to be replaced by Russians. [24]

Within the neutral zone complete civil administrative authority was given (Article 5) by the lease convention to the Chinese authorities, though Chinese troops were to be admitted only with the consent of the Russian authorities.

√ b. JURISDICTION WITHIN THE RAILWAY ZONE. *Within the railway zone* (main and southern branch lines) the Sino-Russian contract agreement of September 8, 1896, for the construction and operation of the Chinese Eastern Railway provided (Article 6) that over "the lands actually necessary for the construction, operation, and protection of the line" the Company was to have "the absolute and exclusive right of administration." The French text of the agreement provided, in other words, that over the lands actually necessary for the business of the railway *"La Société aura le droit absolu et exclusif de l'administration de ses terrains."* The importance of the wording in the French text became apparent in 1908-1909 when the construction of this article became a matter of controversy between Russia and China. The

[23] MacMurray, Vol. I, p. 119. See Chap. IV, Sec. a.
[24] MacMurray, Vol. I, p. 127. See Chap. IV, Sec. a.

Russian Government construed this article after 1896 as conferring the general rights of administration, and of civil and criminal jurisdiction, in the lands adjoining the railway line itself. The Chinese Government, after 1908, took issue with this interpretation calling attention to the provision in Article 5 of the same contract agreement of 1896 which established that "the Chinese Government will take measures to assure the safety of the railway and of the persons in its service against any attack," and also that "criminal cases, lawsuits, etc., upon the territory of the railway, must be settled by the local authorities in accordance with the stipulations of the treaties." [25] In this connection it is not unimportant to note that the statutes of the railway company, sanctioned by the Russian Government on December 4/16, 1896, reaffirmed (Article 8) the duty of the Chinese Government (as conceded in Article 5 of the contract agreement of 1896) to provide for the safety of the railway through protection of the railway "against any extraneous attacks," though the same article in the statutes declared that "the preservation of law and order on the lands assigned to the railway and its appurtenances shall be confided to police agents appointed by the Company." [26] This provision, however, was a unilateral assertion of jurisdiction, and was not approved by China.

Over Russian subjects in Manchuria, both within and outside the railway zone, the Russian Government enjoyed extraterritorial rights by virtue of provisions of early treaties having application beyond the confines of Manchuria. On August 2, 1901, Tsar Nicholas II by imperial ukase ordained the establishment of justices of the peace, subordinate to the nearest Russian district courts, these justices to have jurisdiction exclusively in civil and criminal cases in which both parties were Russians. In mixed cases jurisdiction was declared to be with "other authorities," among whom the Russian Consul in Newchwang was designated.[27]

Over Chinese subjects employed by the railway and in "all cases arising in Kirin Province if these cases directly or indirectly touch the interests of the Chinese Eastern Railway Company, and also directly or indirectly touch the interests of persons working on the Chinese Eastern Railway, and also the interests of contractors of every sort for the supply of labor and work, and of artisans" a Principal Department of Foreign and Railway Affairs, to be estab-

[25] MacMurray, Vol. I, p. 74. See Chap. III, Sec. b.
[26] MacMurray, Vol. I, p. 86.
[27] Russian *Imperial Ukase regarding Jurisdiction in the Chinese Eastern Railway Zone,* August 2, 1901. MacMurray, Vol. I, p. 88.

lished in Harbin (Kirin province), was to have jurisdiction, this to be exercised in all cases referred to the Department in conjunction with the Russian engineer-in-chief. This Department was created by a Sino-Russian agreement of May 31, 1899, between the Tartar General of Kirin and the engineer-in-chief of the railway.[28] The department was to be a Chinese office whose membership was to be designated by the Tartar General (*chiang chun*) of Kirin, after consultation with the Russian engineer-in-chief, the advice of the latter to be decisive. Only in cases in which Chinese unskilled laborers employed by the railway were involved was jurisdiction to be with the local Chinese authorities, while "exceptional cases," within this category, might be referred to the department for disposal, perhaps decision. Responsibility for the execution of the judgment of the department in all cases was placed in the hands of the local Chinese authorities. By virtue of this local agreement, therefore, a Russian official of the Chinese Eastern Railway obtained broad powers over settlement of controversies involving Chinese subjects in both civil and criminal matters in which the railway was "directly or indirectly" concerned. The above agreement was confirmed and supplemented by the Sino-Russian agreement (Provincial Government of Kirin and the Chinese Eastern Railway) of July 5/18, 1901.[29] This agreement extended the jurisdiction of the Department of Foreign and Railway Affairs at Harbin to include (Article 2) "other Chinese, temporarily or permanently residing in the leased zone of the railway, even if the nature of their occupation does not have any direct relation to the railway" in all cases "directly or indirectly" affecting the interests of the railway. A Sino-Russian agreement, similar in most sections to the ones just described, but having application to Heilungkiang province, was made between the acting Tartar General of Heilungkiang and the Russian engineer-in-chief of the railway on January 1/14, 1902.[30] The Principal Heilungkiang Bureau at Harbin was created with functions similar to the Principal Department of Foreign and Railway Affairs of Kirin province, also established at Harbin. In addition, however, this agreement was made binding upon all per-

[28] Sino-Russian (Tartar General of Kirin province—Russian Engineer-in-Chief of the Chinese Eastern Railway) *Agreement regarding Jurisdiction over Chinese in the Railway Zone,* May 31, 1899. MacMurray, Vol. I, p. 277.

[29] Sino-Russian (Kirin Provincial Government—Chinese Eastern Railway) *Agreement regarding Jurisdiction over Chinese Subjects in the Railway Zone,* July 5/18, 1901. MacMurray, Vol. I, p. 274.

[30] Sino-Russian (Heilungkiang Provincial Government—Chinese Eastern Railway) *Agreement regarding Jurisdiction over Chinese Subjects in the Railway Zone,* January 1/14, 1902. MacMurray, Vol. I, p. 321.

sons (Article 2), Chinese, Manchus or Mongols, within the whole area of Heilungkiang province, jurisdiction of the bureau being extended to all cases "directly or indirectly" affecting the interests of the railway outside the railway zone but within the province.

Considerable space has been given to these several Sino-Russian local arrangements of 1899, 1901 and 1902 because they were of a nature to raise a strong presumption that the later contentions of the Russian Government, that the railway actually possessed broad jurisdictional authority, even in criminal and civil cases involving Chinese subjects, were sound. It is evident that they are in direct contraversion of the provision in Article 5 of the original railway contract agreement of 1896 to the effect that "criminal cases, lawsuits, etc., upon the territory of the railway, must be settled by the local authorities in accordance with the stipulations of the treaties." The Chinese Government during 1908 and 1909, while protesting the right of the railway authorities to establish a municipal council in Harbin and elsewhere along the railway line, also protested the assumption of jurisdiction by the Russians over Chinese subjects involved in civil and criminal cases. The *intent* of the Chinese Government, as well as the specific provisions of these several agreements, would seem to be a factor of considerable importance in the interpretation of the exact character of jurisdictional rights conferred on the Russians. Moreover, it would seem to be important to interpret each single provision of the several agreements in conjunction with other clauses of the same agreements to ascertain the general tenor of the commitments made. The *local* character of the agreements of 1899, 1901 and 1902 is also a factor of significance in resorting to them as against the fundamental provisions of the original contract agreement of 1896 which was negotiated by the Peking Government. Parenthetically, it should be noted that these provisions in the latter agreements did not apply to the province of Fengtien (Sheng-king or Mukden) through which the southern branch of the Chinese Eastern Railway ran to Dalny and Port Arthur in the Liaotung leased territory.[31]

c. POLICE AND RAILWAY GUARDS IN THE RAILWAY ZONE. Previous to 1905 the Russians were by implication from a clause (Article 4) in the Sino-Russian treaty of alliance of June (May, Russian date), 1896, and by direct grant (Article 8) in the Sino-Russian railway contract agreement of September 8, 1896, entitled

---

[31] For jurisdiction in the Liaotung leased territory see Chap. V, Sec. a. For the subsequent controversy over Russian jurisdiction in the railway zone see Chap. XXIV, Sec. b.

to send military troops into Manchuria but these latter were not "for any pretext" to stop on the way "longer than is strictly necessary." [32]   It would seem, therefore, that the right to police the railway line and zone with "railway guards" or police could in no wise be inferred from any general authority to station troops in the railway zone.   On the other hand, the Sino-Russian agreements of this period placed no limitations on the actual number of Russian troops which might be transported *over* the Chinese Eastern Railway in Manchuria.

Furthermore, difficulties arise in connection with ascertaining the right of the Russians to station railway guards in Manchuria in view of the fact that in none of these agreements with China is there any single provision specifically conferring the right or even using the term "railway guards."   Such rights as the Russians possessed to police the railway were those which might reasonably be inferred from the general grants of authority over administration of the railway.   There would seem to be no questioning the right of the railway authorities to provide for the policing of the "lands actually necessary for the construction, operation, and protection of the line" if "the absolute and exclusive right of administration of its lands" were to be interpreted so as to mean general political administration.   But that interpretation was contested by China in 1908 and 1909 on the ground that the term "administration" referred to *business administration*, not political administration, and that, while the company was to be conceded the right to have general charge of the lands and buildings actually necessary

[32] See Appendix A and Chap. III, Sec. b.

In connection with the assertions of the Russian political and railway authorities with regard to their scope of jurisdiction within the Chinese Eastern Railway area it is pertinent to call attention to the attempts of the Russian Government in 1901 to secure the acceptance on the part of China of a specific proposal in the form of an agreement in twelve articles which contained provisions directed to the end of increasing Russian jurisdiction in the railway area. Rumors were prevalent in the early months of 1901 that China had conceded the Russian demands and that the same were incorporated in a secret treaty of February, 1901. MacMurray, Vol. I, p. 330.

There appears to be ample evidence to substantiate the assertion that the Russian Government, through their Minister in Peking, did present such proposals to the Chinese Government in February, 1901, and that the Chinese Government sought to secure an alteration of the same. These proposals were especially directed toward securing Chinese sanction for the maintenance of a Russian railway guard along the Chinese Eastern Railway and, further, for the maintenance of regular military troops in the same area. Moreover, China was to quarter no troops along the railway; no foreign military or naval instructors, except Russians, were to be employed by China "in the various provinces of northern China;" and Russia was to be given special mining and other concessions in Manchuria, Mongolia and Hsinkiang. It appears, however, that in response to the refusal of Li Hung-chang to accept these demands the Russian Government withdrew them. (*British Documents on the Origins of the Great War*, 1898-1914. Vol. II, pp. 38-39, 47, 51-57.)

to conduct the business of the railway, that did not confer the right of police. The Chinese Government in 1908 and 1909 drew attention to the fact that Article 5 of the original railway agreement of 1896 empowered the Chinese Government to "take measures to assure the safety of the railway and of the persons in its service against any attack." Russia conceded this right to provide for protection against "external attack" but declared that for purposes of *internal* and, therefore, ordinary police administration the right was possessed by the Russian authorities to be exercised through the railway administration.

If the phrase, "absolute and exclusive right of administration of its lands," were to be interpreted as conferring the right to execute administrative regulations in whatever field within the zone by the use of police or railway guards, these two provisions would seem to have been intrinsically mutually irreconcilable. In any case it is obvious that Article 5 conveyed a blanket power upon the Chinese authorities to police the railway and maintain law and order in the railway zone, a power which would naturally have appertained to the Chinese Government unless there were a specific waiver of specific sovereign rights in the railway area in favor of the railway company.

The careless wording of Article 6 (careless in acceptance on the part of China of that wording) naturally led to a contest over jurisdictional rights between Russia and China, a difference of interpretation which became especially apparent during 1908 and 1909 when the Chinese Government protested the establishment by the Russian authorities of a municipal council in Harbin, directly under the supervision of the railway authorities regarding the more important matters affecting municipal administration. China contended at that time that the "absolute and exclusive right of administration" granted to the company in Article 6 was by that same article confined to "the lands actually necessary for the construction, operation, and protection of the line," and that the right did not extend to one of granting police authority or general rights of municipal administration which were retained by the Chinese Government to be exercised by the local officials. China at that time also contested the right assumed by the Russians in the railway administration to prosecute criminal offenders and to adjudicate civil cases arising on the railway lands, the Chinese case resting upon the wording of Article 5 which had specified that "the Chinese Government will take measures to assure the safety of the railway and of the persons in its service against any attack" and "criminal cases, lawsuits, etc., upon the territory of the railway, must be settled by the local authorities in accordance with the stipulations of the treaties." [33] The future importance of this question of actual jurisdictional rights conferred in the original railway contract of 1896 for the Chinese Eastern Railway is apparent in the fact that this same contract agreement is the legal basis for such jurisdictional rights as were conferred upon Japan over the South Manchuria Railway zone in the treaty of Portsmouth, as sanctioned by China. At the Washington Conference the Chinese Delegation asserted that "the precedent of a Russian guard has no legal ground."

CHAPTER VI

Status of Customs Administration

a. CUSTOMS IN THE LIAOTUNG LEASED TERRITORY. "Within the leased territory on the Liaotung Peninsula Russia may fix the Customs Tariff to suit herself, and China may levy and collect duties at the boundaries on all goods going from the leased territory to the interior or from the interior to the leased territory." By this provision (Article 5) of the Sino-Russian agreement of July 6, 1898, concerning the construction and operation of the southern branch of the Chinese Eastern Railway Russia obtained unqualified jurisdiction over the matter of customs, both native and maritime, within the leased territory. [34] Russian goods brought "from the railway stations within the Russian boundaries" to the leased territory were exempt from all customs duties (including *likin*) in Manchuria, and likewise, all goods sent from the leased territory to Russia. The latter category of goods, however, were by Russian ukase made subject to Russian duty. [35] Only goods consigned for through transit from abroad via a Liaotung port to the interior of Manchuria were thus made subject to the jurisdiction of the Chinese Maritime Customs, while it was further provided that if and when a Chinese customs office were established at Dalny (formerly Talien) the collection of the customs duties on goods consigned to the interior should be entrusted to the Chinese Eastern Railway Company to act in behalf of the Chinese Imperial Board of

[33] See Chap. XXIV, Secs. a and b for the controversy over Russian jurisdiction in the Chinese Eastern Railway area during 1907 to 1914. For the issue at the Washington Conference see Chap. L, Sec. d and Chap. LII, Sec. a.

[34] MacMurray, Vol. I, p. 154. See Chap. III, Sec. c.

[35] Russian *Imperial Order regarding Establishment of Dalny as a Free Port*, August 11, 1899. MacMurray, Vol. I, p. 121. Note the distinction between "open port" and "free port."

Revenue. Goods shipped by rail from the interior of China (i.e., Manchuria or elsewhere but outside the railway zone) to the leased territory or from the leased territory to the interior were to pay export and import duties to the Chinese Maritime Customs.[36]

b. CUSTOMS IN THE RAILWAY ZONE. "Merchandise imported from Russia into China by the railway, and likewise merchandise exported from China into Russia by the same route, will respectively pay the import and export duty of the Chinese Maritime Customs, *less one-third*." By this provision (Article 10 *infra*) of the original railway contract of September 8, 1896, the principle of preferential customs tariffs for a specific territory (land frontier tariff) was introduced in Manchuria.[37] Where goods from Russia were consigned to places outside the railway zone there was to be an additional customs charge of one-half the import duty in lieu of *likin*. These customs charges were to be collected at the frontier between Manchuria and Russian territory.[38]

In summary, with regard to collection of customs in Manchuria, as provided in the Sino-Russian agreements of 1896 to 1905, it may be said that Russia obtained exclusive jurisdiction over the matter of customs collection with respect to the Liaotung leased territory, and obtained a land frontier reduction of one-third from the usual Chinese Maritime Customs rates, for all Russian goods destined for the zone of the Chinese Eastern Railway in Manchuria. In addition, no stations of the Chinese Maritime Customs were established in the Liaotung leased territory during the period of Russian possession (1898-1905).

[36] The creation of Dalny as a "free port" and the difference of opinion between China and Russia regarding the conditions under which a branch of the Chinese Maritime Customs would be established resulted in the non-establishment of a station for customs collection in Dalny for goods consigned to the interior. No other Chinese customs stations were established on the borders of the Liaotung leased territory during the period of Russian possession from 1899 to 1905. (*U. S. Foreign Relations*, 1903-1904, p. 48; British *Parliamentary Debates*, 4th Series, 1903, No. 124, p. 1025.)

[37] MacMurray, Vol. I, p. 77. See Chap. III, Sec. b.

[38] The charter of the Russo-Chinese Bank (December 22, 1895) had provided that the functions of the bank were to include the collection of customs duties in the Chinese Empire. See Chap. III, Sec. a.

C. THE POSITION OF OTHER POWERS: 1895-1905

CHAPTER VII

The Position of Great Britain

a. BRITISH RAILWAY RIGHTS IN MANCHURIA. On June 7, 1898, a private British bank, The Hongkong and Shanghai Banking Corporation, Ltd., signed with the Chinese Administrator General of the Imperial Railways of North China (Peking) a preliminary loan agreement for the construction of an extension of the Peking-Tientsin-Shanhaikwan railway lines into Manchuria.[39] The formal loan agreement for the financing and construction of this new line, the Shanhaikwan-Newchwang railway, was signed on October 10, 1898, by the Chinese Administrator General of the Imperial Railways of North China and the agent of the Hongkong and Shanghai Banking Corporation (in behalf of the British firm of Jardine, Matheson, and Company, the two representing as joint agents the British and Chinese Corporation, Ltd.) [40] By this loan agreement the British and Chinese Corporation, Ltd., obtained the right (transferable to any British firm) to finance and construct the Shanhaikwan-Newchwang railway, this to be an extension from Chunghouso (north of Shanhaikwan) of the Peking-Tientsin-Shanhaikwan lines to be built to Hsinmintun (Hsinminting) and to Newchwang (Ying-tzu or Yingkou, being below Newchwang). The Corporation bound itself to offer to the Chinese Government for this and related purposes a sterling loan of £2,300,000, with interest at 5 per cent. per annum, the loan bonds to be issued at 90 per cent. for subscription in London, the term of the loan to be forty-five years, the security being the lines themselves and their earnings, as well as the earnings of the Peking-Shanhaikwan line. The railway was to be constructed within a period of three years (i.e., by October 10, 1901). The chief engineer of these railways was to be a British subject, the staff to be principally trained Europeans. These railways were to be constructed as a part of the Im-

[39] Sino-British (China-British Syndicate) *Preliminary Loan Agreement for Peking-Newchwang Railway*, June 7, 1898. MacMurray, Vol. I, p. 179.
[40] Sino-British (China-British and Chinese Corporation, Ltd.) *Loan Agreement for the Shankhaikwan-Newchwang Railway*, October 10, 1898. MacMurray, Vol. I, p. 173.

perial Chinese Government lines over which, in case of war or famine, Chinese Government troops or grain might be transported without charge. It was further provided (Article 4) that the principal and interest of the loan were guaranteed by the Imperial Government of China, and that:

"This arrangement, which differs from other contracts in that the Administrator-General retains control of the railway lines so long as the principal and interest of this loan are regularly paid, has been agreed to in consequence of the friendly relations which have long existed between the Contracting Parties."

The right to finance the construction of extensions or branch line was granted (Article 3) to the British and Chinese Corporation, Ltd., in the following provision:

"Should it be decided hereafter to construct branch lines or extensions connecting with the lines herein named, their construction shall be undertaken by the Railway Administration, and should the funds of the Railway Administration be insufficient for that purpose, it shall apply to the Corporation for the same." [41]

b. BRITISH OFFICIAL WAIVER OF RAILWAY RIGHTS. Such British railway concessions as had been acquired in Manchuria prior to 1899 were entirely of a private nature in which the British Government was not a participant. Less than a year following the acquisition by the private British firm (British and Chinese Corporation, Ltd.) of the right to finance and construct the Shanhaikwan-Newchwang railway, the British Government in an exchange of notes with the Russian Government on April 28, 1899, agreed not to seek, or to support British nationals in seeking, further railway concessions north of the Great Wall, that is, none in Manchuria. [42] While mutually declaring their respect for the sovereign rights of China and existing treaties, they agreed that:

"1. Great Britain engages not to seek for her own account, or on behalf of British subjects or of others, any railway concessions to the north of the Great Wall of China, and not to obstruct, directly or indirectly, applications for railway concessions in that region supported by the Russian Government.

"2. Russia, on her part, engages not to seek for her own account, or on behalf of Russian subjects, or of others, any railway concessions in the basin of the Yangtze, and not to obstruct, directly or indirectly, applica-

[41] *Ibid.*, p. 174.
[42] Anglo-Russian *Exchange of Notes with regard to Railway Interests in China*, April 28, 1899. MacMurray, Vol. I, p. 204.

tions for railway concessions in that region supported by the British Government."

The exchange of notes, however, clearly *recognized the prior rights acquired by the British and Chinese Corporation, Ltd.,* on June 7, 1898, by declaring (1) that the Anglo-Russian agreement was "not to infringe in any way the rights acquired under the said Loan Contract," but (2) that the Shanhaikwan-Newchwang railway must "remain a Chinese line, under the control of the Chinese Government, and cannot be mortgaged or alienated to a non-Chinese Company." Both countries agreed that the branch line from Hsiaoheishan to Hsinmintun was to "be constructed by China herself."

CHAPTER VIII

The Position of France

a. FRENCH RAILWAY RIGHTS IN MANCHURIA.   Neither the French Government nor French nationals acquired in Manchuria prior to 1905 any special railway rights (or other special treaty rights) as distinct from those which were included within the interests of the Russo-Chinese Bank or the rights of the Russian-controlled Chinese Eastern Railway lines.   French bankers, participating in the Franco-Russian syndicate which arranged for the "Chinese 4 Per Cent. Gold Loan" to the Chinese Government of July 6, 1895 (400,000,000 francs or 100,000,000 gold roubles), guaranteed by the returns of the Chinese Maritime Customs, acquired no special railway rights in Manchuria by virtue of this loan itself.[43]   Various French banks, however, supplied (by loans direct to the Russian Government) a part of the initial capital for the Russo-Chinese Bank which was chartered under Russian law on December 22, 1895.[44]   But inasmuch as the bank itself was a Russian organization, incorporated under Russian law, and under the control of the Russian Ministry of Finance, neither the French Government nor French nationals acquired any rights in Manchuria as a result of the railway contracts negotiated by the bank *except such as were recoverable from the Russian Government itself.*[45] The Russian Government apparently retained stock control power

[43] For an analysis of the Franco-Russian contract with China for the "Chinese 4 Per Cent. Gold Loan of 1895" see Chap. II, Sec. a.
[44] For the charter of the Russo-Chinese Bank (December 22, 1895) see Chap. III, Sec. a.
[45] For the statutes of the Chinese Eastern Railway Company see Chap. III, Sec. b. The Russo-Chinese Bank was merged with the Banque du Nord on July 30/August 12, 1910, to become the Russo-Asiatic Bank (Banque Russo-Asiatique).

in the Russo-Chinese Bank, and, through the bank, also in the Chinese Eastern Railway.

French interests in Manchuria were officially recognized by Russia in general terms, and a joint policy of cooperation between the two governments was announced in the Franco-Russian declaration to the powers of May 16, 1902. By virtue of this declaration "the two allied Governments" reserved to themselves the right to consult together "as to the means to be adopted for securing those interests" in any case "in which either the aggressive action of third Powers, or the recurrence of disturbances in China jeopardising the integrity and free development of that Power, might become a menace to their own interests." [46]

CHAPTER IX

The Position of the United States

a. AMERICAN OPPOSITION TO PREFERENTIAL RIGHTS. During the period between 1895 and 1905 the United States entered into no formal treaty with special application to Manchuria. In addition to treaty rights which were obtained in the general treaties and conventions of the United States with China, the United States Government, however, did make formal declarations of its own policy with respect to Manchuria on several occasions, notably in 1899 and 1900, and additionally secured from the powers having special interests in Manchuria (Russia, Japan, Great Britain, France and also Germany and Italy) declarations of policy and certain specific commitments pertaining to (1) the guarantee to the nationals of all powers of equality of opportunity for trade applicable to Manchuria, and (2) the guarantee of the "sovereignty" and the territorial and administrative integrity of China in Manchuria. As none of the American agreements secured for the United States any special rights in Manchuria not enjoyed by all other powers, and as the international agreements arising out of American initiative (as the commitments in reply to the first "Hay note" of 1899 pertaining to the "open door" policy) sought to maintain the *status quo* or to guarantee equality of opportunity for trade and preserve the integrity of China in Manchuria, these agreements, particularly the specific commitments of the various powers concerned, are considered in a subsequent section. [47]

[46] See Chap. XIV, Sec. a, for the Franco-Russian declaration of 1902.
[47] See Chap. XV, Secs. a and b, for the enunciation of American policy by John Hay, Secretary of State, during 1899 and 1900 especially.

CHAPTER X

The Position of Japan

a. JAPANESE OPPOSITION TO PREFERENTIAL RIGHTS AFTER 1896. After Japan had been deprived of the Liaotung peninsula and additional territory ceded by China in the treaty of Shimonoseki, 1895, the retrocession having been forced on Japan by the tripartite intervention of Russia, Germany and France, the Japanese Government from 1896 to 1904 consistently opposed the acquisition by other powers of preferential rights in Manchuria. Besides securing from Russia in several agreements an arrangement for mutual assistance to Korea and concessions to Japan for communications and trade privileges, in any required loans, in return for which Japan conceded to Russia certain similarly defined privileges in Korea, the Japanese Government during the period of 1899 to 1904 conducted extensive negotiations with Russia to secure the integrity of Manchuria, to guarantee the *status quo*, and to obtain a self-denying ordinance from Russia with respect to commercial privileges in Manchuria.[48]   The Japanese Government, through Viscount Aoki on December 26, 1899, replied unconditionally accepting the declaration of policy as contained in the first "open door" note of November 13, 1899, of John Hay, Secretary of State of the United States.[49]   Japanese declarations with regard to Manchuria during the period from 1896 to 1904 were in entire accord with the declarations of policy of the United States.

[48] Russo-Japanese (Lobanoff-Yamagata) *Arrangement relative to Affairs in Korea,* June 9, 1896. *Korea Treaties and Agreements,* p. 23; also p. 24.
[49] See Chap. XV, Sec. a.

D. TREATIES AND AGREEMENTS OF ALLIANCE, CO-OPERATION AND GUARANTEE: 1895-1905

CHAPTER XI

Sino-Russian Agreements

a. SINO-RUSSIAN TREATY OF ALLIANCE OF JUNE (MAY), 1896. When Li Hung-chang was in St. Petersburg attending the coronation ceremonies of Tsar Nicholas II he signed a treaty of alliance with Prince Lobanoff-Rostovsky, Minister for Foreign Affairs, under date of June 3 (May 22, old Russian style), 1896, by which the two countries agreed to support each other by means of conducting war against Japan should that country perform any act of "aggression" against either.[50] No official version of this treaty of alliance was made public until the Chinese Delegation to the Washington Conference on Limitation of Armament submitted for the conference a telegraphic summary of the document, which authenticated, in the main, the provisions as published by Li Ching-mai, son of Li Hung-chang, in 1910. As then published in 1910, when the treaty was about to expire, it contained the following provisions:

"Article 1.—Every aggression directed by Japan, whether against Russian territory in Eastern Asia, or against the territory of China or that of Korea, shall be regarded as necessarily bringing about the immediate application of the present treaty.

"In this case the two High Contracting Parties engage to support each other reciprocally by all the land and sea forces of which they can dispose at that moment, and to assist each other as much as possible for the victualling of their respective forces."

The remaining articles of the treaty of alliance provided (Article 6) that the treaty should remain in force for fifteen years after 1896, with the possibility of renewal on mutual agreement

[50] Sino-Russian *Treaty of Alliance*, June (May), 1896. Unofficial text printed in MacMurray, Vol. I, p. 81. Telegraphic Summary of the treaty presented by the Chinese Delegation to the Washington Conference (1921-1922) printed in *Conference on the Limitation of Armaments*, p. 1414. This telegraphic summary serves to support the substantial accuracy of the treaty as printed in MacMurray. For a discussion of the authenticity and publicity of this Sino-Russian treaty of alliance of 1896 see Appendix A.

within six months before the date of termination; that (Article 3) all Chinese ports were to be open to Russian warships during the period of war; that (Article 4) "in order to facilitate the access of the Russian land troops to the menaced points, and to ensure their means of subsistence, the Chinese Government consents to the construction of a railway line across the Chinese provinces of the Amur (Heilungkiang) and Kirin in the direction of Vladivostok," the granting of this contract to be a prerequisite to the coming into force of the treaty; that (Article 5) Russian troops might be transported over the railway both in time of war and in peace without restriction as to numbers; and, finally that (Article 2) neither party to the alliance was to conclude peace without the consent of the other party in case of such war against Japan. This Sino-Russian treaty of alliance would have expired some time in 1911 if the terms of Article 6 had been adhered to, and in the absence of renewal.

b. Sino-Russian Convention pertaining to Evacuation of Manchuria, 1902. Following the Boxer Rising in 1900 and the disturbances consequent upon the same in Manchuria with the occupation of principal Chinese cities in the Three Eastern Provinces outside the Chinese Eastern Railway zone, the Chinese and Russian Governments signed and ratified the Convention with regard to Manchuria of April 8, 1902.[51] Besides providing for the manner of evacuation of Russian troops in each of the three provinces of Manchuria, and containing other previsions pertaining to railway rights, the convention contained specific recognition on the part of Russia of China's sovereign and administrative rights. The convention was thus a bilateral agreement of guarantee of China's jurisdictional rights in Manchuria. The document declared that Russia "agrees (Article 1) to the reestablishment of the authority of the Chinese Government in that region, which remains an integral part of the Chinese Empire, and restores to the Chinese Government the right to exercise therein governmental and administrative authority, as it existed previous to the occupation by Russian troops of that region." The restoration of these rights, however, was made (Article 2) conditional upon the observance by China of all the provisions pertaining to Russian administrative and legal jurisdiction contained in the original railway contract agreement of September 8, 1896.[52]

[51] Sino-Russian Convention with regard to Manchuria, April 8, 1902. MacMurray, Vol. I, p. 326.
[52] Ibid., pp. 327-328.

CHAPTER XII

Anglo-Russian Agreement of 1899

a. ANGLO-RUSSIAN EXCHANGE OF NOTES OF 1899. Great Britain and Russia made an agreement by virtue of an exchange of notes of April 28, 1899, whereby the two powers recognized the Great Wall (abutting on the Gulf of Pechihli at Shanhaikwan) as the limit south of which Russia would not apply for railway concessions.[53] While mutually declaring their respect for the sovereign rights of China and existing treaties, Great Britain conceded to Russia the territory north of the Great Wall, i.e., including Manchuria, as a sphere within which the former recognized the Russian rights with respect to railway construction in the following terms:

"1. Great Britain engages not to seek for her own account, or on behalf of British subjects or of others, any railway concessions to the north of the Great Wall of China, and not to obstruct, directly or indirectly, applications for railway concessions in that region supported by the Russian Government."

"2. Russia, on her part, engages not to seek for her own account, or on behalf of Russian subjects, or of others, any railway concessions in the basin of the Yangtze, and not to obstruct, directly or indirectly, applications for railway concessions in that region supported by the British Government."

This exchange of notes, however, clearly recognized the prior rights of the private British and Chinese Corporation, Ltd. (as acquired by the latter on June 7, 1898) by declaring (1) that the Anglo-Russian agreement was "not to infringe in any way the rights acquired under the said Loan Contract," but (2) that the Shanhaikwan-Newchwang railway must "remain a Chinese line, under the control of the Chinese Government, and cannot be mortgaged or alienated to a non-Chinese company."[54]

CHAPTER XIII

Anglo-Japanese Alliance of 1902

a. THE FIRST ANGLO-JAPANESE ALLIANCE, 1902. During the period from 1902 to 1911 inclusive the governments of Japan and

---

[53] Anglo-Russian *Exchange of Notes with regard to Railway Interests in China,* April 28, 1899. MacMurray, Vol. I, p. 204.

[54] *Ibid.,* p. 205. For the character of the British waiver of railway rights in Manchuria see Chap. VII, Sec. b.

Great Britain concluded three agreements of formal alliance, dated January 30, 1902, August 12, 1905, and July 13, 1911. Of these the first was limited in its application to the interests of the respective countries in China and Korea. By virtue of this first Anglo-Japanese alliance of January 30, 1902 (signed by Count Hayashi, Japanese envoy at the Court of St. James, and Lord Lansdowne, British Secretary of State for Foreign Affairs), the two powers, declaring their desire to "maintain the *status quo*" of the Far East, and "specially interested in maintaining the independence and territorial integrity of the Empire of China and the Empire of Corea, and in securing equal opportunities in those countries for the commerce and industry of all nations," agreed (Article 1) that, unmotivated by any aggressive tendencies in either country, Great Britain had "special interests" (undefined) in China, while Japan, "in addition to the interests which she possesses in China, is interested in a peculiar degree politically as well as commercially and industrially in Corea," for the safeguarding of which either country was at liberty to "take such measures as may be indispensable" including actual "intervention." In case of war arising from a defence of these interests by one power it was agreed (Article 2) that the other should "maintain a strict neutrality, and use its efforts to prevent other Powers from joining in hostilities against its ally." If any other power should join in hostilities against that ally, the other agreed (Article 3) to "come to its assistance" and to conduct war and make peace in common. Each agreed (Article 4) not to enter into separate agreements prejudicial to the interests of its ally. The alliance (Article 6) was to come into effect immediately on signature and to remain in force for five years.[55] This first Anglo-Japanese alliance of 1902 was renewed, with significant alterations, in 1905, and again in 1911.

CHAPTER XIV

Franco-Russian Agreement of 1902

a. FRANCO-RUSSIAN AGREEMENT OF 1902. The existence of a Franco-Russian treaty of alliance of 1891, and of a military convention of the following year, both entered into in particular because of the situation in Europe, was the formal background for

[55] Anglo-Japanese *Agreement relative to China and Korea*, January 30, 1902, MacMurray, Vol. I, p. 324. For the second Anglo-Japanese Alliance (1905) see Chap. XXXIII, Sec. a.

Franco-Russian cooperation in Manchuria from 1895 to 1904. French loans to Russia for internal purposes, the participation of French finance in the Franco-Russian "Chinese 4 Per Cent. Gold Loan" of 1895, and in the capitalization of the Russo-Chinese Bank which had its principal *raison d'être* in Manchuria, combined with the formal alliance of the two powers to produce concerted action in Manchuria in 1902. When the terms of the first Anglo-Japanese alliance of 1902 were officially transmitted to the governments of France and Russia these two powers replied in a joint declaration of policy and agreement for cooperation to secure their special interests in China (applicable especially to Manchuria). By virtue of this Franco-Russian declaration and agreement of March 16, 1902, these two powers took cognizance of the existence of the Anglo-Japanese alliance, and declared adherence to the principles of preserving the *status quo,* preserving the independence of China and Korea, and of guaranteeing equality of opportunity for the commerce and industry of all nations.[56] But while declaring adherence to these principles of policy they asserted the right to take such steps as would be necessary to maintain their "special interests in the Far East." To this end they announced that France and Russia reserved to themselves the right to consult with each other "as to the means to be adopted for securing those interests" in any case where those interests were jeopardized by the action of third parties. The particular bearing of this joint declaration upon Manchuria was made evident by a Russian *communiqué officiel,* dated St. Petersburg, March 7/20, 1902, in which special attention was called to Russian railway rights in Manchuria in connection with the ice-free Port Arthur.[57]

CHAPTER XV

Enunciation and Application of the "Open Door" Policy in 1899 and After

a. THE FIRST AMERICAN "OPEN DOOR" NOTES OF 1899 AND ACCEPTANCES. Following upon the acquisition in 1896-1899 by Russia, Germany, France and Great Britain of "spheres of interest" in various parts of China by means of bilateral conventions with China granting leased territories and prior rights of development of particular "spheres of interest" (as loans for the con-

---

[56] MacMurray, Vol. I, p. 325.
[57] *Ibid.,* p. 326.

struction of railways outside the leased territories), and by means of declarations of non-alienation of particular areas obtained by Great Britain, France and Japan, as well as by the added guarantees to respect these "spheres of interest" obtained in bilateral power agreements, John Hay, the United States Secretary of State, enunciated the "open door" policy with reference to China in September, 1899.[58]

This enunciation of the official "open door" policy by Mr. Hay in 1899 was contained in circular notes (differing in minor details) of September 6 conveying instructions to the respective American ambassadors at London, Berlin and St. Petersburg to convey to the foreign offices of Great Britain, Germany and Russia the American declaration of policy with respect to China and inviting adherence to such a policy on the part of these powers.[59]   Similar communications were conveyed to Japan through the American Minister in Tokyo on November 13, and also to Italy on November 17, and France on November 21, 1899.   The American note to Great Britain of September 6, as presented to Lord Salisbury in London on September 22, declared that the United States "will in no way commit itself to any recognition of the exclusive rights of any power within or control over any portion of the Chinese Empire, under such agreements as have been recently made" and consequently that the American Government could not "conceal its apprehensions that there is danger of complications arising between the treaty powers which might imperil the rights insured to the United States by its treaties with China."[60]   The declaration continued:

"It is the sincere desire of my Government that the interests of its citizens may not be prejudiced through exclusive treatment by any of the controlling powers with their respective "spheres of interests" in China, and it hopes to retain there an open market for all the world's commerce, remove dangerous sources of international irritation, and thereby hasten united action of the powers at Pekin to promote administrative reforms so greatly needed for strengthening the Imperial Government and maintaining the integrity of China, in which it believes the whole western world is alike concerned."

The American note to Great Britain of September 6, 1899, specifically declared that, while the British Government had by agreements with Russia and Germany conceded the possession of so-called "spheres of influence or interest," at the same time that

[58] *U. S. Foreign Relations,* 1899, pp. 128-143.   See also Moore's *International Law Digest,* Vol. V, pp. 534-549.
[59] MacMurray, Vol. I, pp. 221-234.
[60] MacMurray, Vol. I, p. 225.   *U. S. Foreign Relations,* 1899, p. 133.

Government had "sought to maintain what is commonly called the 'open-door' policy, to secure to the commerce and navigation of all nations equality of treatment within such 'spheres.'" Consequently the note, besides containing the American declaration of policy, both with respect to insuring equality of opportunity for commerce and industry of all nations in China and with regard to "maintaining the integrity of China," continued by inviting Great Britain to adhere to a specific declaration in three categories mentioned in the note, as follows:

"1. That it will in no wise interfere with any treaty port or any vested interest within any so-called "sphere of interest" or leased territory it may have in China.

"2. That the Chinese treaty tariff of the time being shall apply to all merchandise landed or shipped to all such ports as are within such "spheres of interest" (unless they be "free ports"), no matter to what nationality it may belong, and that duties so leviable shall be collected by the Chinese Government.

"3. That it will levy no higher harbor dues on vessels of another nationality frequenting any port in such "sphere" than shall be levied on vessels of its own nationality, and no higher railroad charges over lines built, controlled, or operated within its "sphere" on merchandise belonging to citizens or subjects of other nationalities transported through such "sphere" than shall be levied on similar merchandise belonging to its own nationals transported over equal distances."

In the communication of September 6, 1899, to the German Government there was no mention of the fact that, as declared to Great Britain, the United States was committed to a policy of "maintaining the integrity of China."[61] With regard to insuring equality of opportunity for trade, however, the American declaration to Germany was similar, and the German Government was invited to adhere to the same declaration conveyed to Great Britain. Similarly, the American note to Russia of the same date concerned itself with equality of opportunity for trade and invited a declaration from Russia on the three categories as contained in the note to Great Britain and Germany.[62] In the note to Japan of November 13, 1899, the United States asserted its "sincere desire to insure to the commerce and industry of the United States and of all other nations perfect equality of treatment within the limits of the Chinese Empire for their trade and navigation, especially within

[61] MacMurray, Vol. I, p. 223. *U. S. Foreign Relations,* 1899, p. 129.
[62] MacMurray, Vol. I, p. 232. *U. S. Foreign Relations,* 1899, p. 140.

the so-called 'spheres of influence or interest'" and requested adherence of the Government of Japan to the same three categories above mentioned.[63]   The communication to the Italian Government on November 17, 1899, was practically identical.[64]   To France an initial communication had been sent on September 6, 1899, informing the French Government that circular notes had been sent to Great Britain, Germany and Russia on that date inviting them to "make formal declaration of an 'open door' policy in the territories held by them in China."[65]   But it was not until November 21, 1899, that the United States invited France to adhere to the declaration in three categories above mentioned.[66]

After written exchanges of communications and verbal conversations between the American envoys and the foreign offices in the posts to which they were accredited, each of the powers addressed replied with varying degrees of precision to the original declaration and request of the American Secretary of State.   Great Britain replied on November 30, 1899, in complete agreement with the Hay declarations under the three categories declaring them applicable to Weihaiwei, but refraining from including Kowloon within the scope of their application.[67]   Germany replied on February 19, 1900, declaring the intention not to depart from the established policy of guaranteeing "absolute equality of treatment of all nations with regard to trade, navigation, and commerce."[68]   France, after objecting to the term "spheres of influence" on the ground that it was a misnomer, replied on December 16, 1899, with the declaration of intention "to apply in the territories which are leased to it, equal treatment to the citizens and subjects of all nations, especially in the matter of customs duties and navigation dues, as well as transportation tariffs on railways."[69] Japan, on December 26, 1899, and Italy, on January 7, 1900, replied without reservation, the former using the phrase "adheres willingly" to the Hay declaration, the latter with the expression "will have no hesitation to give their assent to so just and fair a proposal of the United States."[70]   Russia replied on December 18/30, 1899, to the Hay communication, the reply being neither a general statement of acceptance of the American declaration of policy nor a

[63] MacMurray, Vol. I, p. 230.   U. S. Foreign Relations, 1899, p. 138.
[64] MacMurray, Vol. I, p. 229.   U. S. Foreign Relations, 1899, p. 136.
[65] MacMurray, Vol. I, p. 221.   U. S. Foreign Relations, 1899, p. 128.
[66] MacMurray, Vol. I, p. 222.   U. S. Foreign Relations, 1899, p. 128.
[67] MacMurray, Vol. I, p. 228.   U. S. Foreign Relations, 1899, p. 136.
[68] MacMurray, Vol. I, p. 224.   U. S. Foreign Relations, 1899, p. 131.
[69] MacMurray, Vol. I, p. 222.   U. S. Foreign Relations, 1899, p. 128.
[70] MacMurray, Vol. I, p. 230.   U. S. Foreign Relations, 1899, pp. 138, 139.

specific reply to each of the three categories above mentioned.[71] While declaring that the Russian Government had "already demonstrated its firm intention to follow the policy of the 'open door,' " there was no declaration to the effect that it would be followed in the future, except as applied to customs charges and collection. The Russian reply contained no general statement of adherence to a policy of guaranteeing equality of opportunity for commerce and industry, nor any assurance that within the Russian "sphere of interest" or leased territory vested rights of other powers would be respected. The reply was likewise silent on the subject of harbor dues and railway charges, although equality of opportunity with respect to each of which in the respective "spheres" of the other powers, though not specifically guaranteed, might be inferred from the statements of adherence to the general policy contained in all of the other replies. All powers made their adherences conditional upon general acceptance of similar declarations.

To complete and make definitive the "open door" policy as outlined in the first Hay note of September 6, 1899, the American Secretary of State sent instructions *mutatis mutandis* to the several envoys of the United States in the countries concerned, dated March 20, 1900, requiring them to transmit to the governments to which they were accredited copies of all the replies of the powers which were to be represented to these powers as formal guarantees that they had given assent in such a manner as to be "final and definitive." [72] This statement of the United States of March 20, 1900, did not specifically, by repetition or reference, declare just what was "final and definitive" in the commitments of the powers, leaving to interpretation of any one government a freedom evidently permissible under the interpretation of treaties and agreements which would follow from the fact that each acceptance was conditional upon the acceptances of all the others. The Secretary of State merely enclosed the copies of the various replies received.

b. The Second American "Open Door" Declaration of 1900. During the Boxer Rising in China in the summer of 1900 Secretary Hay dispatched to the envoys of his government in Great Britain, France, Germany, Russia, Italy, Japan and Austria-Hungary a circular telegram of July 3, with instructions to convey to the respective governments a further declaration of American policy with regard to China.[73] Besides reasserting the established

[71] MacMurray, Vol. I, p. 234. *U. S. Foreign Relations,* 1899, p. 141.
[72] MacMurray, Vol. I, p. 235. *U. S. Foreign Relations,* 1899, p. 142.
[73] *U. S. Foreign Relations,* 1900, pp. 229, 304.

American policy with respect to China the note specifically declared adherence of the United States to (1) the policy of guaranteeing equality of opportunity for commerce and industry in China, and (2) the policy of preserving the territorial and administrative integrity of China, in the following terms:

"The policy of the Government of the United States is to seek a solution which may bring about permanent safety and peace to China, preserve Chinese territorial and administrative entity, protect all rights guaranteed to friendly powers by treaty and international law, and safeguard for the world the principal of equal and impartial trade with all parts of the Chinese Empire."

To this circular telegram to the powers, which did not request replies, several powers independently made specific or general replies expressing similar views as to their policies in China. For example, the Japanese Minister for Foreign Affairs expressed through the American Minister at Tokyo views in accord with those of the United States Government, while the Japanese Ministry for Foreign Affairs officially made a general assertion (September 31, 1900) to the same effect.[74] Similar declarations as to policy in China, including statements of adherence to the two postulates of the general policy above characterized, were made by each of several powers in various ways during the period from 1899 to 1904, the principal examples of these being included in the next section.

c. COMMITMENTS OF THE POWERS TO OBSERVE COMMERCIAL EQUALITY AND THE INTEGRITY OF CHINA. Each of the principal powers, in addition to the United States, powers with interests in North China and Manchuria, committed itself with varying degrees of precision to the policy of respecting the sovereignty of China and the treaty rights of the various powers, and of preserving the territorial and administrative integrity of China in a total of fully a dozen treaties, agreements, or declarations made during the period from 1896 to 1904. By the Anglo-Russian exchange of notes of April 28, 1899, these two countries declared that they had no intention "to infringe in any way the sovereign rights of China or existing treaties." [75] In the Anglo-German agreement of

[74] U. S. Foreign Relations, 1900, p. 364. Secretary of State Bryan declared to the Japanese Government in the American communication of March 13, 1915, that in 1900, in reply to the circular telegram of July 3, 1900, of Secretary Hay, the "Minister for Foreign Affairs of the Imperial Japanese Government expressed through the American Minister at Tokyo views in accord with those of the United States Government." (U. S. Foreign Relations, 1915, p. 106.)

[75] Anglo-Russian Exchange of Notes with regard to Railway Interests in China, MacMurray, Vol. I, p. 204.

October 16, 1900, these two powers pledged themselves alike to the policy of maintaining equality of opportunity for trade "for all Chinese territory as far as they can exercise influence" and to the declaration that both would not take advantage of the crisis in China in 1900 to obtain for themselves advantages in Chinese dominions, and will direct their policy towards maintaining undiminished the territorial condition of the Chinese Empire." [76]

When this agreement had been conveyed to France that government replied on October 31, 1900, that "as to the integrity of China, the Government of the Republic is the more ready to assert that principle, having made it, and having on several occasions declared it, the basis of its policy in the crisis for which the joint efforts of the Powers are seeking to find a satisfactory solution." [77] Russia similarly replied on October 15/28, 1900, declaring that "the maintenance of the integrity of the Celestial Empire" was "the fundamental principle of its policy in China." [78] But Russia further asserted that "the *status quo* established in China by the existing treaties" must be recognized. The United States replied by recalling the commitments of the powers in reply to the first Hay note of September 6, 1899, and reasserting the same policy as further expanded to include that of guaranteeing the territorial and administrative integrity of China contained in the second Hay note of July 3, 1900. [79] The note declared that the United States

[76] Anglo-German *Agreement relative to China*, October 16, 1900. MacMurray, Vol. I, p. 263.

Qualifying the commitments of these two powers to the maintenance of a policy of the "open door" in Manchuria are the reservations which it is now clear were made by the German negotiator, and accepted by the British negotiator, at the time this Anglo-German agreement of October 16, 1900, was signed. The famous speech of Count von Bülow in the Reichstag on March 15, 1901, is well known. At that time he said in substance, as reported in the London *Times* (March 16, 1901):

"The Anglo-German Agreement has no reference to Manchuria ['Hear, hear,' and sensation]. . . . I can now add that during the negotiations which led to the conclusion of this Agreement, we left no room for any doubt that we did not take it as applying to Manchuria. . . . As regards the future of Manchuria—really, gentlemen, I can imagine nothing which we regard with more indifference. ['Hear, hear,' on the right.]"

Another version of Count von Bülow's statement may now be found in a recent British Foreign Office publication:

"That agreement was in no sense concerned with Manchuria. . . . There were no German interests of importance in Manchuria, and the fate of that province was a matter of absolute indifference to Germany." (*British Documents on the Origins of the Great War*, 1898-1914, Vol. II, pp. 26-28.)

This recent publication of the British Foreign Office shows clearly that the British Government had admitted in the negotiations the reservations proposed by the German negotiators, and that the phrase "as far as they can exercise influence" was inserted by Germany to exclude Manchuria from the application of the terms of the agreement.

[77] MacMurray, Vol. I, p. 264.

[78] *Ibid.*, p. 265.

[79] *Ibid.*, p. 265.

at that time had "had the gratification of learning that all the Powers held similar views" with respect to the policy "regarding impartial trade and the integrity of the Chinese Empire." Finally, Japan similarly gave unqualified adherence to the policy of maintaining the integrity of Chinese territory and of equality of opportunity for trade by stating simply that they accepted "the principles embodied" in the Anglo-German agreement of October 16, 1900.[80]

Japan and Great Britain further declared themselves in the Anglo-Japanese alliance of January 30, 1902, "actuated solely by a desire to maintain the *status quo* and general peace in the Extreme East," and "specially interested in maintaining the independence and territorial integrity of the Empire of China" (and of Korea), as well as being interested "in securing equal opportunities in those countries for the commerce and industry of all nations." [81] When this agreement was conveyed to the governments of Russia and France they replied with the joint declaration of March 16, 1902, as being both in entire agreement with the policy thus asserted, adding that these principles were those "which they have themselves, on several occasions, declared to form the basis of their policy, and which still remain so." [82] But Russia made it known immediately thereafter by an official statement that while Russia insisted "on the independence and integrity of China" she desired the maintenance of the *status quo* but no interference with extension of her acquired railway rights in Manchuria.[83]

Russia further recognized in the Sino-Russian convention of April 8, 1902, the right of China to exercise in Manchuria "governmental and administrative authority, as it existed previous to the occupation by Russian troops" in 1900, and declared Manchuria to be "an integral part of the Chinese Empire." [84] But even during the years 1896-1898 the various railway agreements between Russia and China, as that of March 27, 1898, for the lease of the Liaotung, declared that these should "never under any form serve as a pretext for the seizure of Chinese territory or for an encroachment on the sovereign rights of China." [85]

[80] MacMurray, Vol. I, p. 265.
[81] *Ibid.*, p. 324.
[82] *Ibid.*, p. 325.
[83] *Ibid.*, p. 326.
[84] *Ibid.*, p. 327.
[85] *Ibid.*, p. 121. See Chap. XXXVII, Sec. a for subsequent commitments to the "open door" policy.
On February 1, 1902, when it was apparent that the Russian Government were seeking from China further concessions with regard to Manchuria as a condition for evacuation of that territory by Russian troops, John Hay, American Secretary of State, sent a memorandum to the Chinese Minister and to the representatives of

Summarily, it may therefore be stated that each of the principal powers having interests in Manchuria during the period from 1896 to 1904, including the United States, Great Britain, Germany, France, Russia and Japan, declared themselves in one form or another, some in treaties, others in unilateral declarations, and some in both, as committed both to the policy of guaranteeing equality of opportunity for commerce and industry in China and to that of maintaining the territorial and administrative integrity, or at least the "sovereignty" of China. These treaties and declarations, when unqualified, applied likewise to Manchuria, which was recognized even by Russia as an integral part of the Chinese Empire.

the powers at Washington (including those of France, Germany, Great Britain, Japan and Russia) in which he declared that the reported agreement (of Russia and China) with regard to establishment of a commercial monopoly for Russia in Manchuria could "but be viewed with the gravest concern by the Government of the United States." He declared that "it constitutes a monopoly, which is a distinct breach of the stipulations of treaties concluded between China and foreign powers, and thereby seriously affects the rights of American citizens; it restricts their rightful trade and exposes it to being discriminated against, impairing the sovereign rights of China in this part of the Empire, and seriously interferes with her ability to meet her international obligations." He declared further that "the attainment by one power of such exclusive privileges for a commercial organization (referring to the Russo-Chinese Bank) of its nationality conflicts with the assurances repeatedly conveyed to this Government by the Imperial Russian ministry of foreign affairs of the Imperial Government's intention to follow the policy of the open door in China, as advocated by the Government of the United States and accepted by all the treaty powers having commercial interests in that Empire." (*U. S. Foreign Relations*, 1902, pp. 276-277.)

PART II
THE SECOND PERIOD: 1905-1915

CONTENTS

CONTENTS

PART II. THE SECOND PERIOD: 1905-1915

SUMMARY OF THE SECOND PERIOD

THE Russian period of paramountcy over all Manchuria (1896-1905) ended with the defeat of the Russian armies in the war with Japan (1904-1905), the treaty of Portsmouth (1905) transferring to Japan both the Liaotung leased territory (thereafter termed *Kwantung*) and the Russian railway rights in South Manchuria, i.e., the southern section of the Chinese Eastern Railway from Changchun to Port Arthur and Dalny (thereafter known as *Dairen*). Russian interests in Manchuria have been confined since then to North Manchuria, which term is used variously, especially for convenience, to delimit the territory lying roughly north of a line drawn east and west through Changchun, or to denote a territory slightly farther north. Russia retained the northern section (from Changchun to Harbin) of the southern branch line of the Chinese Eastern Railway and also the main line across northern Manchuria, retaining therein those jurisdictional rights and contract privileges obtained through the Russo-Chinese Bank in 1896 and following. After 1905 neither the Russian Government nor the Chinese Eastern Railway, which was still under Russian control, obtained any new and significant railway concessions in Manchuria, the period following 1905 being for the Russians one of assertion of the right to police the railway areas and to establish municipal administration in the railway settlements, rights contested, more or less successfully, by China. With respect to mining and lumbering rights, also, the period was one in which, generally speaking, the Chinese Government succeeded in placing limitations upon Russian rights of exploitation.

The period following the Russo-Japanese war was, however, one in which the former belligerents came to recognize the identity or the similarity of certain of their respective interests in North and South Manchuria. The efforts of American and British private financial firms to construct for the Chinese Government certain railways in Manchuria, especially the Hsinmintun-Fakumen and the Chinchow-Aigun railways, brought the Japanese and Russian Governments together in opposition to a program which might prejudice their almost unqualified railway monopolies in North and South Manchuria. Japan and Russia, therefore, entered into a series of political conventions and treaties of cooperation through which they undertook to guarantee their respective "spheres of interest" in Manchuria, agreeing on a general line of division between these spheres. Significant among the bilateral agreements of this period relating to Manchuria are the Russo-Japanese agreements of 1907, 1910, 1912 and later of 1916.

Japan, who had acquired tangible interests and treaty rights in Manchuria at the close of the Sino-Japanese war (1894-1895), had been compelled to retrocede the annexed Liaotung peninsular areas to China. Success in the war with Russia, however, enabled Japan to reacquire a portion of the Liaotung area, this time in the form of the unexpired Russian lease. Japan likewise acquired the transfer from Russia of the southern section of the Chinese Eastern Railway from Changchun to Port Arthur and Dalny (Dairen), both of these transfers being, under the Portsmouth treaty, conditional upon consent to be obtained from China. This consent was obtained from China in the Sino-Japanese treaty of Peking (December 22, 1905), wherein Japan agreed to observe the terms of the original Sino-Russian agreements with respect to the same. Although the treaty of Portsmouth had bound the signatories to return the whole of Manchuria (except the Liaotung [Kwantung] leased territory) to Chinese administration, the other terms of that treaty operated to qualify the general statement, especially in view of the fact that Japan acquired the rights of administration which Russia had possessed with reference to the southern section of the Chinese Eastern Railway. Moreover, the right of Japan to police the South Manchuria Railway was specifically stated in the treaty of Portsmouth to which the Chinese Government gave their consent in the treaty of Peking. The treaty of Portsmouth also bound the signatories to use their railway holdings solely for commercial purposes (except in the case of those in the Kwantung leased territory).

In an additional agreement attached to the treaty of Peking (1905) China gave to Japan the right to retain and rebuild the Antung-Mukden military railway and also the right to exploit the Yalu timber reserves. Moreover, the Japanese Government has subsequently asserted, especially in connection with their protest against the construction of the Hsinmintun-Fakumen railway by British capital, that the Chinese Government consented, in the negotiations attending the treaty of Peking in 1905, not to construct "any main line in the neighborhood of and parallel to" the South Manchuria Railway. On the strength of this assertion the Japanese Government has so far successfully prevented the construction of railways in South Manchuria with foreign financial backing other than Japanese. The Chinchow-Aigun railway project, however, failed because of opposition also by Russia, while this project and the Knox program for the neutralization of the Manchurian railways under Chinese ownership and control failed of acceptance by the powers generally. Great Britain, being allied with Japan under the treaty of 1905, renewed in 1911, refrained from opposing the claims which Japan and Russia asserted in connection with their declared "spheres of interest" in Manchuria.

It was during this post-war period to 1915 that Japan laid the foundation for her subsequent paramount position in Manchurian economics and diplomacy. Following the treaty of Portsmouth, which was the cornerstone of Japan's superstructure in Manchuria, the Japanese Government negotiated with China a series of railway loan agreements which led eventually to Japanese control of the Kirin-Changchun and the Kirin-Tunhua railways in Kirin province, and gave Japanese financiers or the South Manchuria Railway Company prior rights to finance several railways projected in Fengtien province and Jehol. By virtue of a series of Sino-Japanese industrial agreements during this period the South Manchuria Railway Company acquired control of the Fushun and Yentai collieries, while Japanese finance was enabled to participate in several other important mining and lumbering projects in South Manchuria, including the Penhsihu collieries and the Yalu river lumbering industry. Although legally permitted to participate in the exploitation of mines along the Antung-Mukden railway, no foreign financiers, other than Japanese, invested in mining in this region of South Manchuria during the period before 1915. During and since this period the industrial and mining exploitation of South Manchuria has been exclusively in the hands of Japanese and Chinese.

During and after 1906 the Japanese Government established the Government General of Kwantung province to administer the leased territory acquired from Russia and to provide for the protection of the railway area with "railway guards." The authority to station "railway guards" along the South Manchuria Railway was inferentially conceded by China through its ratification of the treaty of Peking (1905), though the Chinese Government subsequently contested the character of the jurisdiction exercised by these Japanese "railway guards" and "consular police." The South Manchuria Railway Company was established by Japanese imperial authority in 1906. It was formed as a joint stock company in which one-half of the original shares were owned by the Japanese Government which appointed the principal officers of the company. The company was given broad administrative powers in the area of the railway and was authorized to develop subsidiary industries, including mining. By virtue of this authorization the South Manchuria Railway Company became the most important industrial agency in South Manchuria, operating the railway system (including for a time the Chosen Government Railways) and the Fushun and Yentai collieries, and undertaking additionally a generous program of education, health and police administration throughout the railway area, and especially in Dairen, where the head offices of the South Manchuria Railway Company are located.

This period saw the first efforts of an international financial group to advance loans for the development of Manchurian industries, though with but mild success. The Chinese currency and Manchurian industrial loan of 1911, offered by the "Four Power Consortium" (composed of French, German, British and American bankers), succeeded in placing at the disposal of the Chinese Government a sum estimated at only £400,000, though the loan agreement itself called for a total of £10,000,000 of which £1,000,000 was to be used for industrial development, especially of an investigational character, in Manchuria. When the Japanese and Russian financial groups were included, thus to form the "Six Power Consortium," these two groups reserved to themselves the right to offer loans for Manchuria inasmuch as they claimed "special interests" in the Three Eastern Provinces. The American group withdrew from the "Six Power Consortium" in 1913, and though the British, French and Japanese groups remained, this international banking group never succeeded thereafter in offering loans to the Chinese Government for either administrative reorganization or industrial development in Manchuria.

The more important bilateral treaties and agreements of this period which concern Manchuria were (1) the Anglo-Japanese treaties of alliance of 1905 and 1911, in force until the Washington Conference; (2) the Russo-Japanese treaties and agreements of 1907, 1910, and 1912, which were political conventions in which they undertook to respect or to support the claims of each other to "special interests" in the areas declared to be their "spheres of interest" in Manchuria; and (3) the Root-Takahira agreement of 1908 between the United States and Japan, by which they agreed to respect the *status quo* in China, the Far East and the Pacific area, while at the same time adhering to the policy of preserving the territorial and administrative integrity of China and of maintaining equality of opportunity for the commerce and industry of all nations in China. The period from 1905 to 1915 exhibited in Manchuria the inevitable conflict between the policy of the "open door" and the assertion of treaty rights which, while legally valid and enforceable in themselves, constituted, in fact, limitations of the general assertion of policy characterized as the "open door."

CHAPTER XVI

Manchuria and the Outcome of the Russo-Japanese War (1904-1905)

a. THE TREATY OF PORTSMOUTH, SEPTEMBER 5, 1905. By virtue of the treaty of Portsmouth, September 5, 1905, which terminated the Russo-Japanese war, Japan acquired from Russia, subject to the consent of the Chinese Government (secured in December, 1905), the Russian territorial holdings (i.e., the Liaotung leased territory) and other rights, including the southern section of the Chinese Eastern Railway, from near Changchun (i.e., Kuanch'eng-tzu) to Port Arthur, together with the coal mines in that area which had belonged to or were worked by the Russians for the benefit of the railway.[1] The more important provisions of the treaty are included in the following articles:

"Article 5. The Imperial Russian Government transfer and assign to the Imperial Government of Japan, with the consent of the Government of China, the lease of Port Arthur, Talien and adjacent territory and territorial waters and all rights, privileges and concessions connected with or forming part of such lease and they also transfer and assign to the Imperial Government of Japan all public works and properties in the territory affected by the above mentioned lease.

"The two High Contracting Parties mutually engage to obtain the consent of the Chinese Government mentioned in the foregoing stipulation.

"Article 6. The Imperial Russian Government engage to transfer and assign to the Imperial Government of Japan, without compensation and with the consent of the Chinese Government, the railway between Changchun (Kuanch'eng-tzu) and Port Arthur and all its branches, together with all rights, privileges and properties appertaining thereto in that region, as well as all coal mines in the said region belonging to or worked for the benefit of the railway.

"The two High Contracting Parties mutually engage to obtain the consent of the Government of China mentioned in the foregoing stipulation."

With respect to the Liaotung leased territory, thus acquired by Japan, the treaty specifically excluded (Article 3) that area from

[1] Russo-Japanese *Treaty of Peace* (Portsmouth), September 5, 1905. MacMurray, Vol. I, p. 522.

54

the application of the provisions with respect to evacuation of troops, and further provided (Article 7) that the prohibitions with respect to the use for strategic purposes of the railways acquired by Japan were not to apply to the leased territory. Both powers agreed (Article 3) "to evacuate completely and simultaneously Manchuria except the territory affected by the lease of the Liaotung Peninsula," evacuation to be completed (Article 1 of Annex) within eighteen months after the treaty went into effect. The right "to maintain guards to protect their respective railway lines in Manchuria" was reserved by the two countries to themselves, the number of such guards (Article 1 of the Annex) not to exceed fifteen per kilometre, the specific number within that maximum to be arranged between them.

The administrative rights of China in Manchuria (the administrative integrity), and the right of China to adopt without obstruction "general measures common to all countries" for "the development of the commerce and industry of Manchuria," were guaranteed both by Japan and Russia, while Russia declared that her concessions were not "in impairment of Chinese sovereignty or inconsistent with the principle of equal opportunity." These self-imposed limitations upon the treaty rights of Japan and Russia were included in the following important provisions of the treaty of peace:

"Article 3. Japan and Russia mutually engage to restore entirely and completely to the exclusive administration of China all portions of Manchuria now in occupation or under the control of the Japanese and Russian troops" [with the exception of the Liaotung leased territory].

"The Imperial Government of Russia declare that they have not in Manchuria any territorial advantages or preferential or exclusive concessions in impairment of Chinese sovereignty or inconsistent with the principle of equal opportunity."

"Article 4. Japan and Russia reciprocally engage not to obstruct any general measures common to all countries, which China may take for the development of the commerce and industry of Manchuria."

"Article 7. Japan and Russia engage to exploit their respective railways in Manchuria exclusively for commercial and industrial purposes and in no wise for strategic purposes" with the exception of the railways in the Liaotung leased territory."

The remaining provisions of the treaty of Portsmouth pertain to Korea and the island of Saghalien, and to the subject of fishing rights for Japanese subjects along the coast of the Russian possessions in the Japan, Okhotsk and Behring Seas. Russia acknowledged (Article 2) "that Japan possesses in Korea paramount political, military and economical interests," and engaged "neither to obstruct nor interfere with the measures of guidance, protection and control which the Imperial Government of Japan may find it necessary to take in Korea." Most favored nation treatment was accorded Russian subjects in Korea and both parties agreed (Article 2) to abstain from military measures on the Russo-Korean frontier which might menace the security of Russian or Korean territory. Ratifications of the treaty of Portsmouth were exchanged at Washington on November 25, 1905.[2]

b. WITHDRAWAL OF TROOPS FROM MANCHURIA: RAILWAY GUARDS. The treaty of Portsmouth itself had provided (Article 3) for the complete and simultaneous evacuation by Japanese and Russian troops of all Manchurian territory except that within the Liaotung lease, the same to be accomplished (Article 1 of the Annex) within eighteen months after the treaty came into operation, i.e., within eighteen months after the final official announcement of the exchange of ratifications, which latter took place at Washington on November 25, 1905. But the treaty specifically authorized (Article 1 of the Annex) the employment of railway guards to protect their respective railway lines in Manchuria, the same *not to exceed* fifteen per kilometre.[3] On October 30, 1905, the respective military authorities in Manchuria concluded a protocol which set April 15 (April 2), 1907, as the final date for the complete withdrawal of the troops of the two countries from Manchuria, the Liaotung leased territory excepted by the treaty itself.[4] The following dates were agreed upon as the final dates before which certain portions of the occupied territory were to be evacuated by both armies: December 31 (December 18), 1905, June 1 (May 19), 1906, August 1 (July 19), 1906. Neither power was to have more than 250,000 combatants in Manchuria after April 15 (April 2), 1906, or more than 75,000 after October 15 (October 2), 1906. All were to be evacuated by April 15 (April 2), 1907.

This protocol of evacuation, as well as the treaty of Portsmouth itself, provided (Article 1, Sec. 5) for the employment of railway guards by each country "to protect their respective railways in Manchuria," the same to be "on the average" of fifteen

[2] MacMurray, Vol. I, p. 525; also *Additional Articles* comprising the *Annex* to the treaty of Portsmouth.
[3] MacMurray, Vol. I, p. 526.
[4] *Protocol concerning Withdrawal of Japanese and Russian Armies from Manchuria,* October 30, 1905. MacMurray, Vol. I, p. 527.

per kilometre. The manner of transfer of the railways to Japan was only partly provided for in this protocol, the determination of the extreme northern point of the railways to be transferred to Japan being left to diplomatic negotiations. The Chinese Government on December 22, 1905, by virtue of a provision in the additional agreement to treaty with Japan of that date, i.e., by direct implication from a general recognition (Article 2) of Japan's right to withdraw the railway guards conditionally, consented to the employment of such railway guards along the railways acquired by Japan from Russia.[5] In the so-called additional protocols alleged to have been attached to the same treaty, and of the same date, China is alleged to have made a similar commitment with regard to the purposes for which the railway guards were to be used.[6]

c. SINO-JAPANESE TREATY AND AGREEMENTS OF PEKING, DECEMBER 22, 1905. *The Treaty of December 22, 1905.* The transfer both of the Liaotung leased territory and of the former Russian railway right in South Manchuria to Japan, as provided for in the treaty of Portsmouth, was conditional upon the consent of China. To validate these transfers to Japan, therefore, it was necessary to secure that consent in a formal treaty or agreement with China. China's consent was obtained in two bilateral agreements (a formal treaty and an agreement of the same date) dated Peking, December 22, 1905.[7] To these the Japanese Government has asserted that protocols in additional articles, signed by the negotiators for both countries, were also mutually agreed upon. These latter protocols were for a time kept secret though later communicated by the Japanese Government to the British Government, although no official text of these temporarily "secret protocols" has ever been made public.[8] Inasmuch as all three of these treaties and agreements of December 22, 1905, between China and Japan have had far-reaching importance subsequently in their bearing on the international relations of Manchuria they should be taken, along with the treaty of Portsmouth, as the fundamental formal bases for Japan's position in Manchuria after 1905.

[5] MacMurray, Vol. I, p. 551. See Chap. XVI, Sec. c.
[6] MacMurray, Vol. I, p. 555. See Appendix B, bearing on authenticity of the attached protocols. See also Chap. XVI, Sec. c.
[7] Sino-Japanese *Treaty of Peking and Additional Agreement relating to Manchuria*, December 22, 1905. MacMurray, Vol. I, p. 549.
[8] *Summary of Alleged Secret Protocols to Sino-Japanese Treaty*, December 22, 1905. MacMurray, Vol. I, p. 554. See Appendix B.

The Sino-Japanese treaty of Peking of December 22, 1905, signed by Baron Komura and Yuan Shih-k'ai, included but three brief articles which contained China's sanction to the terms of transfer of former Russian rights to Japan as contained in the treaty of Portsmouth, and contained a provision that the Japanese Government was to conform to the original agreements between China and Russia with regard to acquired rights in the Liaotung leased territory and in connection with railways.   The following language was used to effect these transfers and determine Japanese treaty rights:

"Article 1.   The Imperial Chinese Government consent to all the transfers and assignments made by Russia to Japan by Articles V and VI of the Treaty of Peace above mentioned."

"Article 2.   The Imperial Japanese Government engage that in regard to the leased territory as well as in the matter of railway construction and exploitation, they will, so far as circumstances permit, conform to the original agreements concluded between China and Russia.   In case any question arises in the future on these subjects, the Japanese Government will decide it in consultation with the Chinese Government." [9]

Ratifications of t' e treaty were exchanged at Peking, January 23, 1906, the treaty coming into effect on the date of signature.

Additional Agreement of December 22, 1905.   To the formal treaty of Peking of December 22, 1905, was attached an additional agreement of the same date "with a view to regulate, for their guidance, certain questions in which they are both interested in Manchuria." [10]   By virtue of this additional agreement with China, Japan obtained (Article 1) the consent of China to the opening of sixteen cities and towns in Manchuria to international residence and trade (Fenghuangcheng, Liaoyang, Hsinmintun, Tiehling, Tangkangtzu and Fakumen in Fengtien province; Changchun, Kirin, Harbin, Ninguta, Hunchun and Sanhsing in Kirin province; and Tsitsihar, Hailar, Aigun and Manchouli in Heilungkiang province).   The Japanese Government agreed to withdraw both their troops and railway guards (Article 2) "in the event of Russia agreeing to the withdrawal of her railway guards," the same to be conditional upon the reestablishment of tranquillity in Manchuria and when "China shall have become herself capable of affording full protection to the lives and property of foreigners." Chinese troops sent to suppress banditry in areas evacuated or

[9] MacMurray, Vol. I, p. 549.
[10] MacMurray, Vol. I, p. 551.

even in areas from which Japanese troops had not yet been evacuated were not to proceed within twenty *li* (Chinese) from the boundary of the territory where Japanese troops were stationed (Article 3).

Article 6 contained the important provision by which the Japanese Government were conceded the right "to maintain and work the military railway line constructed between Antung and Mukden and to improve the said line so as to make it fit for the conveyance of commercial and industrial goods of all nations." The right to reconstruct and to control the Antung-Mukden railway was thus conceded to Japan for a period of fifteen years "from the date of the completion of the improvements above provided for," the improvements to be completed within two years after an initial twelve months required for the withdrawal of the troops. It was further provided that at the expiration of that period (i.e., in 1923-1924) the railway should be sold to China "at a price to be determined by appraisement of all its properties by a foreign expert who will be selected by both parties." Minor rights in connection with supervision of the improvements of the line and pertaining to general supervision of the business of the line were given to a Chinese Commissioner.[11]

Additional articles of the agreement provided that all railway construction materials "for the railways in South Manchuria" should be exempt from all duties, taxes and *likin* (internal transit tax), that other matters pertaining to interlineal traffic arrangements were to be arranged by separate negotiations, and that reciprocal most favored nation treatment should be extended to all matters contained in the treaty and in the agreement, and specifically also to the matter of frontier trade between Manchuria and Korea. A final important provision of the additional agreement of December 22, 1905, was that (Article 10) by which the Chinese Government agreed to the formation of a joint-stock company of Chinese and Japanese capitalists for exploiting the forests in the regions on the right bank of the Yalu river, the

[11] A final agreement for the construction of the Antung-Mukden line was not arranged until August 19, 1909. MacMurray, Vol. I, p. 797. See Chap. XIX, Sec. c, for further consideration of the Antung-Mukden Railway. According to the initial Sino-Japanese agreement of December 22, 1905, the Chinese Government was to have the right of recovery of the line by purchase during 1923-1924. This, however, was altered by the Sino-Japanese treaties and exchanges of notes of 1915 by virtue of which the Japanese were to remain in possession of the Antung-Mukden line until the year 2007, the term of the railway agreement having been extended to 99 years. Sino-Japanese *Treaty respecting South Manchuria and Eastern Inner Mongolia*, May 25, 1915. MacMurray, Vol. II, p. 1220. See Chap. XXXVIII, Sec. a for consideration of these treaties and agreements of 1915.

nationals of the two countries who became shareholders to share equally in the profits of the undertaking, the details for organization of the company to be later arranged.[12]

Alleged "Protocols" of December 22, 1905. To the formal treaty of Peking of December 22, 1905, and the additional agreement of the same date were attached certain memoranda of the proceedings of the Peking conference which the Japanese Government have interpreted as containing commitments made by China which are binding and enforceable.[13] The Japanese Government, for example, in 1907 protested the construction of the Hsinmintun-Fakumen railway by Pauling and Company, a British firm, on the ground that the concession to that company by the Chinese Government was in violation of the arrangement in the form of the attached protocols which the two countries had agreed upon on December 22, 1905. Inasmuch as no official and complete statement of these temporarily secret "protocols" has ever been published the analysis which follows is of such portions of those "protocols" alleged to "possess the character of executory agreements," these also from an unofficial version.[14]

The most important provision of these alleged secret "protocols" (those which were temporarily kept secret and later referred to by the Japanese Government) was that by which the Chinese Government is said to have agreed (Article 3) not to construct any main line "in the neighborhood of and parallel to" the South Manchuria Railway, or any branch line "which might be prejudicial to the interest of the above-mentioned railway."[15]

The article follows:

"Article 3. The Chinese Government engage, for the purpose of protecting the interests of the South Manchurian Railway, not to construct, prior to the recovery by them of said railway, any main line in the neighborhood

[12] MacMurray, Vol. I, p. 553. The *Agreement for a Chinese-Japanese Joint-Stock Company for the Exploitation of the Yalu Timber* was signed by representatives of the governments of China and Japan on May 14, 1908. MacMurray, Vol. I, p. 731. See Chap. XX, Sec. b, for consideration of the Yalu timber concession.

[13] For one version of a *Summary of Alleged Secret Protocols to the Sino-Japanese Treaty of December 22, 1905,* see MacMurray, Vol. I, p. 554. The subject of the authenticity and enforceability of these alleged "protocols," together with their subsequent importance, is considered at some length in Appendix B.

[14] MacMurray, Vol. I, p. 554.

[15] MacMurray, Vol. I, p. 554. A somewhat different translation of this Japanese version of the alleged "protocols" attached to the treaty and additional agreement of December 22, 1905, was given by Dr. K. Asakawa in 1908, as follows: "The Chinese Government, with a view to protecting the interest of the South Manchurian Railway, agrees not to construct in its neighborhood, before the recovery of that railway, a trunk line in parallel thereto or a branch line detrimental to the interest of that railway." (*Yale Review,* August, 1908, p. 206.)

of and parallel to that railway, or any branch line which might be prejudical to the interest of the above-mentioned railway."

With regard to railway construction in Manchuria the "protocols" as later published unofficially, also contained a provision (Article 1) that the Kirin-Changchun railway should be constructed by China "with capital to be raised by herself," but, in case of necessity, to borrow from Japan the insufficient capital through a loan contract to be subsequently arranged, the term of the loan to be twenty-five years, redeemable in yearly instalments. The Hsinmintun-Mukden line, which had been constructed as a military line by Japan, was to be sold to China (Article 2) for a fair price. Reconstruction of the line was to be undertaken by China with funds borrowed from Japan to reconstruct a portion of it, the amount of the loan to be approximately one-half of the cost, the loan contract to be subsequently arranged, the term of the loan to be eighteen years, payable in yearly instalments.

Other articles of the protocol provided that the Japanese Government were to take steps to prevent (Articles 11-14) the railways guards and other Japanese subjects from unreasonably, and without proper authority from China, interfering with local Chinese administration "or to proceed without permission beyond the limits of the railway." China consented (Article 9) to the opening of the Sungari river to navigation by Japanese, if without objection of Russia. Fair reparation was to be made (Article 12) for damage incurred by Chinese subjects or the Chinese Government on account of destruction or appropriations by Japanese subjects during the period of military occupation. The revenue of the Maritime Customs collected at Yingkou (Newchwang) was to be deposited with the Yokohama Specie Bank (Article 16) to be delivered to the local Chinese authorities on the completion of evacuation.

CHAPTER XVII

Organization of the South Manchuria Railway Company

a. ORGANIZATION OF THE SOUTH MANCHURIA RAILWAY COMPANY. Before the date for the completion of evacuation by the Japanese military of Manchuria and of the railways acquired from Russia it was necessary to perfect or approve some public or private company or organization to receive and to operate the lines thus acquired. The Japanese Government, after having given some consideration to other projects for managing the railways in Manchuria, finally decided to organize a joint stock company to take charge of all Japanese-owned or operated railways in Manchuria, the company thus formed to be directly under the control of the Japanese Government through the ownership of one-half of the shares of the capital stock by the government and through the power given to the government to appoint the principal officers.[16] By an Imperial Ordinance (No. 142) of June 7, 1906, the Japanese Government sanctioned the organization of the South Manchuria Railway Joint Stock Company "for the purpose of engaging in railway traffic in Manchuria."[17]   Subsequently, on August 1, 1906, a Government Order, in pursuance of the additional agreement of December 22, 1905, with the Chinese Government, entrusted the company with control over seven railways in Manchuria, of which the principal ones were the main line of the South Manchuria Railway from Dairen to Changchun and the Antung-Mukden line, the line connecting the Manchurian railways with those of Korea.[18]   The branch lines included those to Port Arthur, Yingkou (Newchwang), Fushun and Yentai.[19]   The articles of incorporation of the South Manchuria Railway were published simultaneously during August, 1906.[20]

The articles of incorporation of the South Manchuria Railway Company provided (Article 21) that the shareholders of the company were to be limited to the Governments of Japan and China, and the subjects of the two countries only.   The original capital being fixed at 200,000,000 yen, distributed in 1,000,000 shares, it was provided that the Japanese Government was to turn over its acquired railway and mining properties in Manchuria as equivalent to their share of the original capital, i.e., to a total fixed value of 100,000,000 yen (500,000 shares), or one-half of all the shares of the capital stock.[21]

---

[16] Japanese Government *Order regarding South Manchuria Railway Company,* August 1, 1906. MacMurray, Vol. I, p. 557.

[17] Japanese *Imperial Ordinance Sanctioning Organization of South Manchuria Railway Company,* June 7, 1906 (No. 142). MacMurray, Vol. I, p. 555.

[18] MacMurray, Vol. I, p. 557.

[19] *Ibid.*   The Tashihchiao-Yinkou branch of the South Manchuria Railway was not definitely conceded by China to belong to the South Manchuria Railway system until after protracted negotiations, which were finally ended by its acquisition by Japan in the Sino-Japanese agreement of September 4, 1909. (MacMurray, Vol. I, p. 790.)

[20] *Articles of Incorporation of the South Manchuria Railway Joint Stock Company.* MacMurray, Vol. I, p. 559.

[21] MacMurray, Vol. I, p. 559.

Although the original capital of the South Manchuria Railway Company was fixed at 200,000,000 yen distributed in 1,000,000 shares of 200 yen each, this capital was later

The Japanese Government undertook to guarantee the payment of interest on debentures issued for reconstruction of the railway and for consolidation, as well as to guarantee the repayment of the principal. The management of the Company was entrusted to various officers, among whom the president, vice president and directors were the most important. The president and vice president (Article 35) were to be appointed "by the Government subject to Imperial sanction," i.e., not subordinated to the Ministry of Communications, but to the Prime Minister, both to serve for five year terms. The directors were to be appointed also by the Government for four years but only "from among those who own fifty shares or more," i.e., to a minimum amount of 10,000 yen. Direct control by the Japanese Government of the South Manchuria Railway Company was further assured through the provisions (Articles 52-57) for complete assumption of control by the Government at its discretion, and for requiring the Imperial Diet to approve special expenditures and guarantees relating to the railway. Broad powers were conferred on the railway company to engage in subsidiary enterprises in Manchuria including mining, especially the operation of the coal mines at Fushun and Yentai, water transportation, electrical enterprises, sale on commission of the principal goods carried by the railways, warehousing, real estate

increased until now the capital is 440,000,000 yen, of which one-half is held by the Japanese Government, as originally. Although both the Chinese Government and private Chinese are legally permitted to purchase and hold shares in the railway it is evident that the Chinese Government at the outset indicated their unwillingness to subscribe, and it appears that very few, if any, shares are actually owned by Chinese individuals. Three blocks of shares were issued for private subscription in Japan before 1918, totalling 80,000,000 yen worth of new shares, which, with the unsubscribed capital, gave a total capitalization of 300,000,000 yen. The total capitalization was increased in 1920 to the present 440,000,000 yen, of which shares one-half are owned by the Japanese Government. The company has resorted to several foreign loans to finance the railway, these being taken up in the London market in the following debenture issues: July 19, 1907, £4,000,000 at 97, with interest at 5 per cent. for 25 years; June 1, 1908, £2,000,000 at 98, with interest at 5 per cent. for three years (repaid in 1911); December 16, 1908, £2,000,000 at 97½, with interest at 5 per cent., for 34 years; January 3, 1911, £6,000,000 at 98, with interest at 4½ per cent., for 25 years. This gave an outstanding total of foreign loans of £12,000,000. On December 1, 1920, the Japanese Government assumed the responsibility of paying the interest and capital on the loans taken up in London. After 1911 the home market was resorted to for loan issues, especially from 1917 to 1921, debentures being issued, for example, in 1917 to the value of over 10,000,000 yen. It is thus apparent that while no South Manchuria Railway loans have been floated in the American market, this is not the case with respect to the British market, British financiers having offered a total of £14,000,000 to the South Manchuria Railway before 1912. In 1923 a fifth loan of £4,000,000 was obtained in London. (Bank of Chosen *Economic History of Manchuria*, pp. 94-96; *South Manchuria Railway: Its Origin, Development, etc.* S. M. R. publication, 1922, pp. 9-15. *Report on Progress in Manchuria: 1907-1928*, p. 71. S. M. R. Publications, 1929.)

transactions within the railway zone, and "in addition, any business for which Government permission has been given." [22]

Summarily, it may be said that the South Manchuria Railway was formed as a government-controlled enterprise, subject to the direction of the Japanese Government (Prime Minister and the Diet) in numerous matters, and managed by officers the principal of whom (president, vice president and the directors) were appointed by the Government. The railway was further made subject to the general supervision of the Kwantung Government especially for police purposes. In fact, power to police the railway was specifically given the Kwantung Government General. The Japanese Government initially owned one-half of the shares of the capital stock, the remainder being sold principally to Japanese subjects, being prohibited to foreigners, though not to Chinese. The company itself was given broad civil administrative powers, as the authority to collect taxes within the railway area, and to establish a form of local government (settlement councils). By virtue of authorization contained in an Imperial Ordinance (No. 90) of July 31, 1917, the South Manchuria Railway Company also operated the Chosen (Korean) State Railways until 1925. [23]

CHAPTER XVIII

Organization of the Kwantung Government

a. ORGANIZATION OF THE GOVERNMENT GENERAL OF KWANTUNG. In order to establish a Japanese administrative system for the newly acquired Liaotung leased territory (henceforth referred to as Kwantung leased territory, or Kwantung province) the Japanese Government promulgated an ordinance establishing the Government General of Kwantung (*Kwanto Totoku Fu.*) [24] By treaty with China the Japanese Government had agreed on December 22, 1905, to "conform to the original agreements concluded between China and Russia" concerning the leased territory (and also in the matter of railway construction) "so far as circumstances permit," and in case of any question arising in future pertaining thereto the Japanese Government was to "decide it in

[22] *Japanese Government Order regarding South Manchuria Railway Company,* August 1, 1906. MacMurray, Vol. I, p. 558.

[23] Japanese *Imperial Ordinance* of July 31, 1917 (No. 90), MacMurray, Vol. I, p. 563. See Chap. XLI, Sec. a.

[24] Japanese *Imperial Ordinance Providing for Organization of the Government General of Kwantung,* July-August, 1906 (No. 196). MacMurray, Vol. I, p. 565.

consultation with the Chinese Government." [25] This provision may be taken as tantamount to a recognition by China of the application to Japan of the former Sino-Russian treaties, agreements and conventions pertaining to the leased territory. The treaty of Portsmouth with Russia had made no mention of the future application of these Sino-Russian treaties and agreements to either the leased territory or the railways acquired by Japan, merely effecting the transfer of possession, subject to the consent of China.

By an Imperial Ordinance (No. 196), as published in the Japanese *Official Gazette* on August 1, 1906, the organic act for the establishment of the Government General of Kwantung province was promulgated. [26] A Governor General (*Totoku*) was established as administrative head of the Kwantung government charged with the authority to protect and supervise the railway lines in South Manchuria and with general civil administrative power in the leased territory. The Governor General was to be of *Shinnin* rank (i.e., appointed directly by the Emperor) and a general or lieutenant general of the Japanese army. He was thus subject to the Prime Minister for appointment, had to be chosen from the army, but was responsible directly to the Minister for Foreign Affairs in foreign relations (Article 4 as amended in 1917), and in promotion and dismissal of officials of *sonin* rank (appointed by the Cabinet and reported to the emperor) responsible to both, while subject to the Minister of War (Article 6) in matters of military administration, and to the General Staff (Article 6) with reference to plans of operation and mobilization. The Governor General was made commander of the Kwantung Garrison and charged with the defense of the area subject in this respect to the Minister of War and the Chief of the General Staff. For ordinary civil administrative purposes the Governor General was given authority to issue ordinances, including penal regulations of a limited character, and, in exceptional cases of emergency, special ordinances and regulations beyond that jurisdiction subject in this category to imperial sanction or disapproval. Two departments, a Civil Administration Department and a Military Department, were provided for, the former to be subdivided into four bureaus, one of which was to be a Bureau of Police with

[25] Sino-Japanese *Treaty of Peking*, December 22, 1905. MacMurray, Vol. I, p. 549. See Chap. XVI, Sec. a.

[26] MacMurray, Vol. I, p. 565. Other Imperial Ordinances in English translation (Nos. 197 to 204, all of 1906) pertaining to the organization of the Kwantung Government General are printed in *U. S. Foreign Relations*, 1906, Pt. II, p. 1050 ff.

jurisdiction to be determined by the Governor General.   On January 10, 1908, by an Imperial Ordinance (No. 2) the Bureau of Foreign Affairs, under a Director, was added to the divisions of the civil administration.[27]   The ordinary police then might be used as consular police in the railway area.   Several "secretaries" of *sonin* rank were also provided for in 1908, these to be the chiefs of the bureaus above mentioned, and additionally to include the Japanese consular officers in Manchuria.

Originally, therefore, the Japanese administrative system estab-lished in Kwantung province to displace the purely military régime *(Sotoku Fu)* provided for complete fusion of civil and administra-tive functions in one officer, the Governor General, who was required to be a high officer of the army.   Thus the Governor General of Kwantung province continued from July-August, 1906, to April, 1919, with a military head having divided responsibility to the home government but in complete charge of civil administration in the Kwantung leased territory and police jurisdiction over the South Manchuria Railway area.   He had general supervisory power over the railway, and at the same time had command of the Japanese army stationed in South Manchuria.   By Imperial Ordi-nance (No. 82) of July 31, 1917, a slight clarification was made in the jurisdiction of the Governor General when (Article 2) he was authorized to "exercise jurisdiction over Kwantung Province" and "have control of the protection and supervision of the rail-way lines in South Manchuria" and "have charge of the operation of the South Manchuria Railway Company." [28]   The Governor General was then (Article 4) placed in "command of the army under his jurisdiction" and given control over "all political affairs under the supervision of the Minister President of the Cabinet" though under the Minister for Foreign Affairs "in matters respect-ing diplomacy."

The fusion of military and civil functions under one officer, the Governor General, was abolished in 1919 when an Imperial Ordi-nance (No. 94) of April 12 established instead of the Government General *(Totoku Fu)* the Kwantung Government *(Kwanto cho)*, to have at its head a Governor *(Chokan)* with civil jurisdiction over the province and authority to police the railway lines in South Manchuria, as well as the power "to supervise the business" of the

[27] MacMurray, Vol. I, p. 566.
[28] Japanese *Imperial Ordinance regarding Organization of the Kwantung Govern-ment General,* July 31, 1917 (No. 82).   MacMurray, Vol. I, p. 569.

South Manchuria Railway.[29]   At that time the Japanese consuls
in Manchuria were made "secretaries" in the Kwantung Government, while the consul general at Mukden was given three important posts in the Kwantung Government to be held simultaneously
with his consular and diplomatic office at Mukden.[30]   This alteration thus removed the command of the Japanese troops (Kwantung Garrison) from the Governor of the province, but left the
latter in complete charge of ordinary police, including the police
along the South Manchuria Railway.   The official organization of
the Kwantung Government has been altered in minor particulars
twice since 1919, once during June, 1921, and the other time during
December, 1923.[31]

CHAPTER XIX

Sino-Japanese Railway Agreements (1905-1915)

a. RETURN OF THE HSINMINTUN-MUKDEN RAILWAY TO
CHINA.   During the course of the Russo-Japanese war the Japanese
military authorities had constructed a military railway from
Mukden to Hsinmintun, a light rail line to the left bank of the
west fork of the Liao river.   This line, as rebuilt subsequently,
became the last link in the railway which is now known as the
Peking-Mukden line, the section from Tientsin to Shanhaikwan,
and those from Shanhaikwan to Hsinmintun (on the right bank
of the Liao river) having been constructed by a British syndicate
and by the Chinese Government.   The rights acquired by the British
syndicate in 1898 to construct the line to Hsinmintun from Shanhaikwan were specifically excepted, and therefore validated, in a
provision in the Anglo-Russian exchange of notes of April 28,
1899.   Great Britain and Russia had agreed therein that the continuation of the Peking-Tientsin-Shanhaikwan railways from
Hsiaoheishan to Hsinmintun should be undertaken "by China herself." [32]   The continuation of the line from Hsinmintun to Mukden

---

[29] Japanese *Imperial Ordinance regarding Organization of the Government of
Kwantung*, April 12, 1919 (No. 94).   MacMurray, Vol. I, p. 569.   See Chap. XLI,
Sec. a.

[30] See Chap. XLI, Sec. a.

[31] See Chap. XLI, Sec. a.

[32] See Chap. VII, Sec. a, for the Hongkong and Shanghai Banking Corporation,
Ltd., contract agreement of June 7, 1898, for the construction of an extension of the
Peking-Tientsin-Shanhaikwan railway to Hsinmintun.   See Chap. VII, Sec. b, for the
character of the British official waiver of railway rights in Manchuria in the Anglo-
Russian exchange of notes of April 28, 1899, which, however, recognized the prior
rights acquired by the British syndicate in 1898.   See Chap. III, Sec. e, for the restora-
tion by the Russian army to China, after the Boxer Rising, of the Shanhaikwan-
Hsinmintun railway as provided for in the Sino-Russian convention of April 8, 1902.

had been impeded on account of that same exchange of notes between Great Britain and Russia. The Russians had occupied the section from Hsinmintun to Shanhaikwan during the Boxer Rising and had agreed in 1902 to return that section to Chinese control. The section from Hsinmintun to Mukden was thus left for construction by the Japanese military in the field during the war with Russia.

Japan had agreed in December 22, 1905—if the authenticity of the protocols attached to the treaty and additional agreement be accepted—to restore this railway from Hsinmintun to Mukden to China, the line to be rebuilt by the Chinese Government with funds of their own, unless it were necessary to borrow additional capital, in which case China agreed to borrow from Japan the required amount presumed to be one-half of the total reconstruction outlay.[33]

In the spring of 1907 the Chinese Government approached the Japanese Foreign Office and the South Manchuria Railway Company in an effort to secure the return of the Hsinmintun-Mukden line to China. The transfer was effected by a Sino-Japanese convention of April 15, 1907 (also pertaining to the Kirin-Changchun railway), in which China agreed (Article 1) to purchase the line constructed by Japan for the sum of 1,660,000 yen, to reconstruct the line (Article 1) with funds one-half of which should be borrowed from the South Manchuria Railway Company, the status of the new railway to be changed so as to be identical with those lines which China had herself constructed, the loan for the line to extend for eighteen years (i.e., after August, 1909, no repayment in full to be permitted before the expiration of that period), i.e., until 1927, the security to be the real property and the earnings of the line itself.[34] In case the Chinese Government should fail to meet the payments of principal and interest of the loan (Article 3) the line itself should "be handed over to the temporary control of the Company" (South Manchuria Railway) until the deficits were paid. A Japanese engineer-in-chief was to be employed during the currency of the loan, as well as a Japanese accountant; all earnings of the railway were to be deposited in

[33] See Chap. XVI, Sec. c. It is evident that the alleged secret "protocols" attached to the Sino-Japanese treaty and additional agreement of December 22, 1905, are not mentioned in any of the subsequent agreements or loan contracts pertaining to the Hsinmintun-Mukden line, the Kirin-Changchun line or other branch lines in Manchuria.

[34] Sino-Japanese *Convention regarding the Hsinmintun-Mukden and Kirin-Changchun Railways*, April 15, 1907. MacMurray, Vol. I, p. 627.

Japanese banks; the line was to be built to connect with the South Manchuria Railway; while the details as to the interest and character of the loan contract should be arranged in a subsequent contract agreement with the South Manchuria Railway. On May 27, 1907, the respective railway representatives of the two countries signed the formal agreement effecting the transfer of the Hsinmintun-Mukden line to China.[35] The date for transferring the properties of the railway to China was fixed as June 1, 1907.

In a Sino-Japanese supplementary loan agreement of November 12, 1908, the amount of the funds which were to be borrowed from Japan (South Manchuria Railway Company) was fixed (Article 1) at 320,000 yen.[36] The interest rate was fixed (Article 2) at 5 per cent. *per annum*, and the provision with reference to the employment of a Japanese chief engineer was repeated (Article 4). The loan was to be met by a sinking fund created by monthly deposits in some Japanese bank to the credit of the South Manchuria Railway Company. The detailed agreement for the loan contract itself was signed by a South Manchuria Railway representative and a Chinese official of the Board of Posts and Communications on August 18, 1909.[37] This final loan contract agreement repeated the former provisions for the loan which was to run for eighteen years (Article 2) and to be paid in thirty-six instalments. The loan contract agreement was to be ratified by Imperial Edict in China, the text was written in Chinese and Japanese only, and it was provided that any disagreement as to the text should be decided by an arbitrator. It appears that the loan was paid in instalments as they became due and that the loan agreement, therefore, was to

[35] Sino-Japanese *Agreement for the Transfer by Japan of the Hsinmintun-Mukden Railway*, May 27, 1907. MacMurray, Vol. I, p. 632.

[36] Sino-Japanese *Supplementary Agreement for a Loan for the Hsinmintun-Mukden and Kirin-Changchun Railways*, November 12, 1908. MacMurray, Vol. I, p. 767. The facts recorded above indicate, therefore, that the present Peking-Mukden Railway was actually constructed in several sections, each under separate contract or construction arrangements. The British and Chinese Corporation, Ltd., contracted for and built the line from near Shanhaikwan to Newchwang *via* Koupangtzu; the Hsiaoheishan-Hsinmintun section was built by the Chinese under their own responsibility; the Hsinmintun-Mukden section was built by the Japanese military in the field in the Russo-Japanese war, and was in 1907 transferred to China. Subsequently the entire system has been under the Peking-Mukden railway administration subordinated to the Ministry of Communications in Peking, the same being a Chinese Government Railway. As indicated above, the Japanese loan on the Hsinmintun-Mukden section appears to have been redeemed in full, only 35,559 yen being still outstanding by 1925. A large portion of the British and Chinese Corporation, Ltd., loan of 1898 for the Shanhaikwan-Newchwang section and that to Hsinmintun remains still outstanding, £1,092,500 being the portion of the British loan unredeemed as of December 31, 1924. (*The China Year Book*, 1928, p. 290.)

[37] Sino-Japanese *Detailed Agreement for the Hsinmintun-Mukden Railway Loan*, August 18, 1909. MacMurray, Vol. I, p. 782.

terminate in 1927, the Hsinmintun-Mukden line having thus become an integral part of the Peking-Mukden Railway, and
a section of the Chinese Government Railways. The Japanese
Government on September 4, 1909, agreed to the extension of
the Peking-Mukden line to the walled city of Mukden thus permitting the crossing of the South Manchuria Railway.

/ b. SINO-JAPANESE AGREEMENTS REGARDING THE KIRIN-
CHANGCHUN RAILWAY. A preliminary contract agreement for the
construction of a line from the southern branch (Harbin to Dalny)
of the Chinese Eastern Railway to Kirin city had been signed by
representatives of the Chinese Eastern Railway for Russia and by
the Chinese Government on July 11, 1902, during the period of
Russian possession of the Liaotung (Kwantung) leased territory
and the connecting railway.[38] The line, according to that preliminary agreement, was to be built by the Chinese Eastern Railway
Company, China to be permitted to buy back the line after a period
of thirty-six years. As the line was to be strictly a commercial line
to develop the trade of Kirin city (Chuan Ch'ang) it was to have a
status different from the Chinese Eastern Railway itself. Construction of this line was not begun immediately, however, and the
matter was left for attention following the Russo-Japanese war
and the treaty settlement of 1905.

As in the case of the Hsinmintun-Mukden line, this projected
railway from Changchun to Kirin is mentioned in the summary of
the alleged "secret protocols" of December 22, 1905, China being
empowered to build such a line with her own capital, but to use
Japanese capital in case insufficient funds were available at home.[39]
In the convention for the purchase of the Hsinmintun-Mukden
railway from Japan, dated April 15, 1907, it was also provided
that the Chinese Government was to borrow from the South Manchuria Railway Company one-half of the funds necessary for the
construction of a line, some eighty miles in length, from Changchun
to Kirin.[40] The loan was to extend for a period of twenty-five years,
with the real property and the earnings of the line as security. An
important provision of this convention, having significant bearing
on future events, was that contained in Article 3 which stated that
"If the Kirin-Changchun line should hereafter build branch lines
or an extension, the construction of such lines shall rest of right

[38] See Chap. III, Sec. d.
[39] See Chap. XVI, Sec. c, and Chap. XIX, Sec. a.
[40] Sino-Japanese *Convention regarding the Hsinmintun-Mukden and Kirin-
Changchun Railways,* April 15, 1907. MacMurray, Vol. I, p. 627.

with the Chinese Government, but, if there should be a lack of capital, application shall be made to the [South Manchuria Railway] Company for an arrangement."

In a supplementary agreement of November 12, 1908 (also concerned with the Hsinmintun-Mukden loan arrangements), it was provided that the amount to be borrowed by China from the South Manchuria Railway Company for the construction of the Kirin-Changchun railway was to be 2,150,000 yen, with interest at 5 per cent.[41] The engineer-in-chief and the accountants of the line were to be Japanese (Article 6). On the same date as the final loan agreement for the Hsinmintun-Mukden line was signed, i.e., August 18, 1909, the representatives of the two countries (The South Manchuria Railway for Japan) also signed a detailed agreement for the loan for the construction of the Kirin-Changchun line.[42] The loan, as mentioned above, was to run for 25 years from the date of offering of the loan to China (Article 3), to be repaid in forty instalments of various amounts, the same to be met through traffic receipts deposited with the Yokohama Specie Bank.

For purposes of clarification of the status of the Kirin-Changchun railway during the period from 1905 to 1915 it may be said that the line was not profitable, and that the loan instalments soon were in arrears. By virtue of the Sino-Japanese treaty of May 25, 1915, respecting South Manchuria and Eastern Inner Mongolia the Chinese Government agreed "speedily to make a fundamental revision of the Kirin-Changchun Railway loan agreement." [43] On October 5, 1913, the Chinese Government had conceded to Japan the right to finance a branch or extension of the Kirin-Changchun line from Kirin to Hailungcheng *in case foreign capital were required*, a provision not dissimilar to that contained in the agreement of April 15, 1907, above mentioned.[44] In 1917, by a new loan agreement with Japan the management of the Kirin-Changchun line was taken over by the South Manchuria Railway Company, the amount in arrears (nearly 2,000,000 yen) being deducted from the new loan of 6,500,000 yen then newly attached

[41] Sino-Japanese *Supplementary Agreement for a Loan to the Hsinmintun-Mukden and Kirin-Changchun Railways,* November 12, 1908. MacMurray, Vol. I, p. 767.
[42] Sino-Japanese *Detailed Agreement for the Kirin-Changchun Railway Loan,* August 18, 1909. MacMurray, Vol. I, p. 785.
[43] Sino-Japanese *Exchange of Notes respecting Railways and Taxes in South Manchuria and Eastern Inner Mongolia,* May 25, 1915. MacMurray, Vol. II, p. 1220. See Chap. XXXVIII, Sec. a, for the Sino-Japanese treaties and exchanges of notes of May 25, 1915, respecting Manchuria.
[44] Sino-Japanese *Exchange of Notes in regard to the Construction of Certain Railways in Manchuria,* October 5, 1913. MacMurray, Vol. II, p. 1054. See Chap. XIX, Sec. d.

to the railway.   The term of the loan is for thirty years, i.e., to mature in 1947, but may be redeemed in full before that time.[45]

/ c. Reconstruction of the Antung-Mukden Railway. During the course of the Russo-Japanese war the Japanese military authorities had built a light military line of narrow gauge from the Korean border to Mukden, a distance of nearly 200 miles.   The Russian Government, therefore, had never possessed the line and did not transfer it to Japanese control in the treaty of Portsmouth.   This railway was placed under Japanese control by the Sino-Japanese additional agreement attached to the treaty of Peking of December 22, 1905.[46]   China agreed at that time (Article 6) that the Japanese Government had "the right to maintain and work the military railway line constructed between Antung and Mukden and to improve the said line so as to make it fit for the conveyance of commercial and industrial goods of all nations." This right was to extend for fifteen years "from the date of the completion of the improvements above provided for."   The work of improvement was to be "completed within two years, exclusive of a period of twelve months during which it will have to be delayed owing to the necessity of using the existing line for the withdrawal of troops."   By virtue of this agreement, therefore, the term for Japanese control was to terminate in 1923-1924, the specific date (49th years of Kuang Hsü) having been fixed (Article 6) in the agreement.   The improvements of the line were to be undertaken by the Japanese in consultation with a commissioner appointed by China.

The actual reconstruction of the Antung-Mukden railway was delayed by the Japanese for various reasons, the two year period, plus the additional year allowed for removal of Japanese troops (thus a total of three years after December 22, 1905) having expired in 1908, though the line had not been reconstructed.   Technically the limits of the period of reconstruction had been fixed in the agreement of December 22, 1905, therefore, as expiring in 1908.   On August 19, 1909, i.e., after the date originally set for the completion of reconstruction of the line, and after the Japanese Government had sent an ultimatum to Peking, dated August 6, 1909, representatives of the two governments signed a memorandum which provided (Article 2) that the surveys which had been

[45] Sino-Japanese *Agreement for a Loan for the Kirin-Changchun Railway,* October 12, 1917.   MacMurray, Vol. II, p. 1390.   See Chap. XXXIX, Sec. c, for attention to the Kirin-Changchun Railway during the period from 1915 to 1921.
[46] MacMurray, Vol. I, p. 551.   See Chap. XVI, Sec. c.

made were to be the basis for future construction, reconstruction to be undertaken at once after that date.[47] The line was to be standard gauge (Article 1) and Chinese local officials were to be instructed (Article 5) not to impede further the reconstruction of the line. As a matter of fact the reconstruction of the Antung-Mukden railway was not completed until November, 1911, at a total estimated cost to Japan of about 22,000,000 yen. To repeat, according to the original agreement of December 22, 1905, the term for which the Japanese were to "maintain and work" the Antung-Mukden railway was to expire in 1923-24 (the 49th year of Kuang Hsü). In 1915, however, by virtue of the Sino-Japanese treaty of May 25, respecting South Manchuria and Eastern Inner Mongolia,[48] China agreed that the term for Japanese control of the Antung-Mukden railway should be extended to ninety-nine years.[49] By an exchange of notes of the same date it was provided that the term of the Antung-Mukden railway should expire in the year 2007 (96th year of the Chinese Republic).

d. SINO-JAPANESE AGREEMENTS IN REGARD TO NEW RAIL-WAYS IN MANCHURIA. In addition to the Sino-Japanese agreements and loan contracts pertaining to the three principal lines dealt with in the last preceding sections (Hsinmintun-Mukden railway, Kirin-Changchun railway, and the Antung-Mukden railway) the representatives of China and Japan negotiated several other agreements having special bearing on Japan's rights to construct, to finance, or to impede the construction of, certain new projected lines in Manchuria. If the alleged "protocols" attached to the Sino-Japanese treaty and additional agreement of December 22, 1905, be considered as valid and enforceable it is important to recall that at that time the Japanese Government obtained the right to interdict the construction by China of any main line "in the neighborhood of and parallel to" the South Manchuria Railway, and also any branch line "which might be prejudicial to the interest of the above-mentioned railway."[50] In the convention of April 15, 1907, for the purchase by China of the Hsinmintun-Mukden railway it was provided that (Article 3) "if the Kirin-Changchun line should hereafter build branch lines or an extension, the construction of such lines shall rest of right with the Chinese Govern-

[47] Sino-Japanese *Memorandum concerning the Reconstruction of the Antung-Mukden Railway*, August 19, 1909. MacMurray, Vol. I, p. 787.
[48] Sino-Japanese *Treaty respecting South Manchuria and Eastern Inner Mongolia*, May 25, 1915. MacMurray, Vol. II, p. 1220.
[49] MacMurray, Vol. II, p. 1221. See Chap. XXXIX, Sec. a.
[50] See Chap. XVI, Sec. c.

ment, but, if there should be a lack of capital, application shall
be made to the [South Manchuria Railway] Company for an
arrangement." [51]

No further provision appears in the Sino-Japanese agreements
during the period from 1905 to 1915 which might be interpreted
as a general grant to interdict the construction of lines "parallel"
to the South Manchuria Railway in Manchuria. By virtue of an
exchange of notes of October 5, 1913, however, the Japanese
Government obtained from China a provisional agreement to
finance the construction of three railways projected as branch or
connecting lines of the South Manchuria Railway (Ssupingkai-
Chengchiatun-Taonan railway, Kaiyuan-Hailungcheng railway,
and Changchun-Taonan railway), and additionally the right to
finance two other lines (Taonan-Jehol railway and Kirin-Hailungcheng railway, this latter to connect, therefore, with the Kirin-
Changchun line). [52] Immediately thereafter this Sino-Japanese
understanding was generally referred to as "The Five Manchurian
and Mongolian Railways Agreement." Later, however, due to
the fact that the Ssupingkai-Chengchiatun-Taonan railway project
was excluded from this group and dealt with separately, the agreement came to be known as "The Four Manchurian and Mongolian
Railways Agreement," a term which is still current. In the subsequent specific loan contract agreements for the construction of
certain of these lines another was added, i.e., a line from a point
(undetermined) on the Taonan-Jehol line to a seaport (on the
Gulf of Pechihli).

In anticipation of the specific loan contract agreements entered
into by representatives of Japan and China during the period
from 1915 to 1921 it may be desirable here to summarize briefly
the future of each of these five projected railways to finance which
the Japanese originally obtained in 1913 the option. Of the three
lines projected to connect with the South Manchuria Railway,
one, the Changchun-Taonan railway has never been constructed,
another, the Kaiyuan-Hailungcheng railway, has been constructed
only in part, i.e., from Kaiyuan to Taolu, and from Hailungcheng
to Hsian, while the third, and the most important, the Ssupingkai-
Chengchiatun-Taonan system has been constructed in two sections,
the first from Ssupingkai to Chengchiatun (with a further extension west to Paiyintalai (Tungliao), this in pursuance of a Sino-

[51] See Chap. XIX, Sec. b.
[52] Sino-Japanese *Exchange of Notes in regard to the Construction of Certain Railways in Manchuria*, October 5, 1913. MacMurray, Vol. II, p. 1054. Also noted in
The Japan Year Book, 1914, p. 570; *The China Year Book*, 1919, p. 216, *etc.*

Japanese loan and construction agreement of December 27, 1915.[53] The other section from Chengchiatun to Taonan was constructed in pursuance of the same agreement which contained the provision (Article 20) that in case foreign capital was needed for its construction it would be obtained from Japan. The extension of the Ssupingkai-Chengchiatun-Taonan railways to Angangchi and Tsitsihar, across the Chinese Eastern Railway, is of still later date, having been completed to Angangchi in 1926, and to Tsitsihar in 1928.

Turning to the other two lines projected in the agreement of October 5, 1913, and to a branch projected from one of them, it may be said, in anticipation of more detailed attention in a later section, that the Taonan-Jehol railway has never been built, nor the projected branch from a point on that line to a seaport, although a Japanese syndicate (Industrial Bank of Japan et al) was given the right to finance the same, should foreign capital be required, by virtue of the Sino-Japanese preliminary loan agreement of September 28, 1918.[54] The Kirin-Hailungcheng railway has been built by the Chinese themselves against the protest of the Japanese Government.[55]

An important railway line which was projected for construction during this period before 1915 was one which would connect Kirin city with Korea, i.e., to pass through the Yenchi (Chientao) district to connect with the Korean railways from Huining (*Kainei* in Japanese). This line has not yet been constructed although the section from Kirin to Tunhua was completed during 1927, the same having been financed by the Japanese, though the line has essentially the same status as the Kirin-Changchun railway. Originally, the right to participate in the financing of such a line from Kirin to Huining, which the Chinese Government then agreed to construct, was granted to Japan under terms to be identical with those for the Kirin-Changchun line as provided in the agreement then effective for the latter, namely, that of April 15, 1907.[56] The provision, because of its later importance, is given here in full:

"Article 6. The Government of China shall undertake to extend the Kirin-Changchun Railway to the southern boundary of Yenchi, and to connect

[53] Sino-Japanese (China-Yokohama Specie Bank) *Agreement for the Building of the Ssupingkai-Chengchiatun Railway*, December 27, 1915. MacMurray, Vol. II, p. 1249. See Chap. XXXIX, Sec. b.

[54] Sino-Japanese (China-Industrial Bank of Japan et al.) *Preliminary Agreement for a Loan for Railways in Manchuria and Mongolia*, September 28, 1918. MacMurray, Vol. II, p. 1448.

[55] See Appendix F.

[56] See Chap. XIX, Sec. b.

it at Hoiryong (Huining) with a Korean railway, and such extension shall be effected upon the same terms as the Kirin-Changchun Railway. The date of commencing the work of the proposed extension shall be determined by the Government of China, considering the actual requirements of the situation, and upon consultation with the Government of Japan." [57]

It appears that no further Sino-Japanese agreements were made pertaining to such a line from Kirin to Korea during the period from 1905 to 1915, the exchange of notes of May 25, 1915, however, by the blanket provision that "if foreign capital is required [for railway construction in South Manchuria] China may negotiate for a loan with Japanese capitalists first," having bearing on the future of the project. The preliminary loan contract for the financing of construction of the Kirin-Huining (Kirin-Kainei) line was not entered into by Chinese and Japanese representatives until June 18, 1918. [58]

The interdiction by Japan during 1907 to 1909 of the construction by a British syndicate of the Hsinmintun-Fakumen railway, which led to the granting of the concession for that line to Japanese interests, pertains especially to the British position in Manchuria during 1905 to 1915 and will be considered in that place. [59] The failure of the Chinchow-Aigun railway project during 1909 and 1910 is for similar reasons treated along with the American and British positions in Manchuria during this period. [60]

CHAPTER XX

Sino-Japanese Mining and Lumbering Agreements (1905-1915)

√   a. SINO-JAPANESE MINING AGREEMENTS RESPECTING MANCHURIA. Of the various minerals found in South Manchuria coal and iron, but especially the former, are of special importance. During the period of control of the entire system of the Chinese Eastern Railway by Russia, i.e., from 1896 to 1905, the Russians acquired various mining privileges in Manchuria, including rights to operate certain of the coal mines in the Fushun and Yentai areas,

[57] Sino-Japanese *Agreement relating to the Chientao Region,* September 4, 1909. MacMurray, Vol. I, p. 796.
[58] Sino-Japanese (China-Industrial Bank of Japan *et al.*) *Preliminary Agreement for a Loan for the Construction of the Kirin-Huining Railway,* June 18, 1918. Mac-Murray, Vol. II, p. 1430. See Chap. XXXIX, Sec. d.
[59] See Chap. XXX, Sec. a, for the British position and the Hsinmintun-Fakumen railway project.
[60] See Chap. XXXI, Sec. a, for the American and British positions and the Chinchow-Aigun project.

east and south of Mukden. These rights at Fushun, however, were not specifically granted in any of the Sino-Russian treaties or agreements of the period, but were presumed to be derivable from the general grant to the Chinese Eastern Railway Company, contained in the Sino-Russian agreement concerning the southern branch of the Chinese Eastern Railway, dated July 6, 1898. The only clause appertaining thereto is Article 4 by which the Railway Company was given authority "to cut timber and mine coal for the use of the railway" and "to be allowed in the regions traversed by this branch line to mine such coal as may be needed for the construction or operation of the railway."[61] By virtue of this provision the Russian administration of the Chinese Eastern Railway had begun to mine coal at Fushun interpreting their mining rights with considerable latitude. In the original contract agreement for the construction and operation of the main line of the Chinese Eastern Railway, that of September 8, 1896, there was no specific mention of mining rights at all, though a clause (Article 6) stipulating that "lands actually necessary for the construction, operation and protection of the line" and lands "in the vicinity of the line necessary for procuring" construction materials would be turned over to the Company freely "if these lands are the property of the State."[62] Private lands also might be acquired for the above purpose, but only upon cash payment or through rental. Whether the Chinese Eastern Railway on the eve of the Russo-Japanese war or during the war actually owned or legally possessed each of the several concessions operated by them at Fushun is a mooted question.

Such mining rights as the Russians possessed in connection with the southern branch of the Chinese Eastern Railway were transferred to Japan by virtue of the treaty of Portsmouth of September 5, 1905, subject to the consent of China. All "rights, privileges and properties" appertaining to the Chinese Eastern Railway from Changchun to Port Arthur, together with its branches, "as well as all coal mines in the said region belonging to or worked for the benefit of the railway," were transferred (Article 6) to Japan by the treaty of peace with Russia.[63] The Chinese Government

[61] Sino-Russian (China-Chinese Eastern Railway) *Agreement concerning the Southern Branch of the Chinese Eastern Railway*, July 6, 1898. MacMurray, Vol. I, p. 154. See Chap. III, Sec. c.

[62] Sino-Russian (China-Russo-Chinese Bank) *Contract for the Construction and Operation of the Chinese Eastern Railway*, September 8, 1898. MacMurray, Vol. I, p. 74. See Chap. III, Sec. b.

[63] Russo-Japanese *Treaty of Peace*, September 5, 1905. MacMurray, Vol. I, p. 522. See Chap. XVI, Sec. a.

validated (Article 1) these transfers by signing the treaty of Peking of December 22, 1905.[64] Thus, all the coal mining concessions at Fushun or elsewhere (within the meaning of the clause) which actually belonged to or were "worked for the benefit of the railway" were transferred to Japan. The same treaty with China, however, provided (Article 2) that the Japanese Government would, in the matter of railway construction and exploitation, be bound "so far as circumstances permit," to "conform to the original agreements concluded between China and Russia." A reasonable interpretation of this article would require that the rights and titles transferred by Russia to Japan in 1905 should be valid rights and clear titles. The coal mines at Yentai had been worked by private Russians under local arrangements.

The controversy between China and Japan over the working by the Japanese of certain coal mines at Fushun, which during the Russian régime were actually worked by private Chinese owners, or were worked by the Chinese Eastern Railway authorities in some instances with questionable titles, or by private Russians, was adjusted in a Sino-Japanese agreement of September 4, 1909.[65] In regard to the coal mines at Fushun and Yentai the two governments agreed (Article 3) that (a) "the Chinese Government recognizes the right of the Japanese Government to work the said coal mines," (b) that "the Japanese Government, respecting the full sovereignty of China, engages to pay to the Chinese Government tax upon coals produced in those mines" at a rate to be fixed separately, (c) that "the Chinese Government agrees that in the matter of the exportation of coals produced in the said mines, the lowest tariff of export duty for coals of any other mines shall be applied," and (d) that "the extent of the said coal mines, as well as all detailed regulations, shall be separately arranged by commissioners specially appointed for that purpose." In pursuance of this latter provision the representatives of the two governments signed on May 12, 1911, detailed regulations which fixed (Article 1) the amount of the mining tax to be paid the Chinese Government by Japan (South Manchuria Railway Company) as 5 per cent. of the value of the coal at the pits.[66] This applied to both the Fushun and Yentai collieries. Export taxes were also fixed in these regulations,

[64] Sino-Japanese *Treaty and Additional Agreement relating to Manchuria*, December 22, 1905. MacMurray, Vol. I, p. 549. See Chap. XVI, Sec. c.

[65] Sino-Japanese *Agreement concerning Mines and Railways in Manchuria*, September 4, 1909. MacMurray, Vol. I, p. 790.

[66] Sino-Japanese *Detailed Regulations for Fushun and Yentai Mines*, May 12, 1911. MacMurray, Vol. I, p. 792.

and an additional 50,000 yen *per annum* was to be paid, in lieu of *likin,* to the Chinese Government. When the South Manchuria Railway required private Chinese lands within the boundaries of the mines for exploitation purposes the same were to be acquired only after an agreement with the Chinese authorities.

The Penhsihu collieries, on the Antung-Mukden line southeast of Mukden, were worked by the Japanese firm of Okura and Company after the war with Russia, large investments having been made previous to the agreement with China of May 22, 1910, by which the mines were to be thereafter operated by the Penhsihu Coal Mining Company, Ltd., registered as a Sino-Japanese company.[67] Okura and Company, which from 1905 to 1909 had expended an estimated total of $1,000,000 (Chinese *Peiyang*) on the mining properties, was to contribute the same properties to the new company which amount was to be the Japanese share of the total capital of $2,000,000. The equivalent of $350,000 was to be paid the Chinese Government for the privilege of continuing, through the newly organized company, the operation of the mines, which sum was to be paid in the form of shares in the enterprise, thus leaving $650,000 in shares to be subscribed by the Chinese. Profits were to be divided equally between the Chinese and Japanese private owners. The amount of taxes, including *likin,* to be paid was fixed in the agreement. After the expiration of thirty years, the duration of the company's rights, the arrangement with the Chinese Government was to come to a close and the company to go into voluntary liquidation to permit recovery by the Chinese Government.

General agreements for the operation of mines, especially mines along the Antung-Mukden railway, were entered into by the representatives of China and Japan during 1907 and 1909. The Viceroy of Manchuria and the Japanese Consul General at Mukden signed in 1907 a memorandum prohibiting unauthorized prospecting by Japanese subjects between Antung and Mukden.[68] In 1909, it was provided in a Sino-Japanese agreement of September 4 that the mines along the Antung-Mukden railway and the main line of the South Manchuria Railway, excepting those at Fushun and Yentai, were to be exploited as joint Sino-Japanese enterprises.[69]

[67] Sino-Japanese *Agreement for Penhsihu Coal Mining Company, Ltd.,* May 22, 1910. MacMurray, Vol. I, p. 793.

[68] Sino-Japanese *Memorandum concerning Mines along Antung-Mukden Railway,* 1907. MacMurray, Vol. I, p. 791.

[69] Sino-Japanese *Agreement concerning Mines and Railways in Manchuria,* September 4, 1909. MacMurray, Vol. I, p. 790. In the course of subsequent correspond-

/ b. Sino-Japanese Lumbering Agreements Respecting
Manchuria. Kirin province has rich standing timber reserves of
which one of the most important in South Manchuria is that circumscribing the upper reaches of the Yalu river and also the Tumen
river, the Yalu forming part of the southern boundary of south-
eastern Manchuria. The Russian concessions acquired in the Yalu
area before the Russo-Japanese war, however, were acquired from
the Korean Government and were technically limited to the jurisdiction of that government.[70] In connection with the construction and
operation of the Chinese Eastern Railway the Russian authorities
felled timber in the area traversed by the line, especially in North
Manchuria along the main line, in pursuance of the railway agreements.[71] As none of these timbering rights of the Chinese Eastern
Railway concerned themselves with the Yalu region, there were no
vested rights in the Yalu region transferred to Japan in the treaty
of Portsmouth and the treaty of Peking which followed. Only such
timbering rights as appertained to the Chinese Eastern Railway
Company within the area traversed by the southern branch of the
line (from Harbin to Port Arthur) were transferred to Japan.
These rights were confined solely to the authority to cut timber
"for the use of the railway" itself (Article 4), as provided in the
Sino-Russian agreement of July 6, 1898.[72]

ence between the Chinese Foreign Office, under date of November 18, 1909, the
Chinese Government stated to the Government of the United States that "the reference in the said agreement to joint Chinese-Japanese exploitation of mines along the
two railways mentioned does not involve a monopoly of the rights and privileges
of opening mines in the designated territory, nor confer any exclusive rights to
mines therein upon Japanese subjects, but that mines in the territory mentioned may
with the consent of the Chinese Government be exploited by third parties also."
Under date of November 25, 1909, the Japanese Ministry for Foreign Affairs likewise advised the American Embassy that "the provisions of the agreement of September 4 last, in reference to joint exploitation of mines along the said railways do
not and were not intended in any way or to any extent to involve a monopoly of
the right to discover, open, and operate mines in Manchuria, to the exclusion of
American citizens, or any other persons." (U. S. Foreign Relations, 1909, pp. 116-124.)
See Chap. XL, Sec. a, for later Sino-Japanese agreements relating to mining.

[70] As early as 1896 the Korean Government had granted to Russian concessionaires
the right to exploit the timber wealth of the Yalu river area. This concession had
been acquired in 1898 by Alexander Mikhailovich Bezobrazoff, a State Councillor
in the Civil Service of the Russian Tsar. Bezobrazoff interested the Tsar himself
in the Yalu concession, the latter having become interested to the degree of invest-
ing a large amount of his private capital in the enterprise. The Tsar's interest in
this concession continued down until the outbreak of the war with Japan. (For a
discussion of this timber concession, held by "The Royal Timber Company," see
General Kuropatkin, The Russian Army and the Japanese War, 2 Vols., Vol. II,
p. 306 of the Appendices.)

[71] See Chap. III, Secs. b. and c.

[72] Sino-Russian (China-Chinese Eastern Railway) Agreement concerning the Southern Branch of the Chinese Eastern Railway, July 6, 1898. MacMurray, Vol. I, p.
154.

During the Russo-Japanese war the Japanese military authorities appropriated the receipts derived from the tax on timber rafts on the Yalu river, and with the coming of peace following 1905 the question of the extent and character of Japanese rights to exploit the timber areas along the Yalu river and its branches was awaiting settlement with China. In the additional agreement attached to the treaty of Peking of December 22, 1905, the Chinese Government had agreed (Article 10) to the formation of a joint stock company "for the exploitation of the forests in the regions on the right bank of the River Yalu," the details to be arranged later.[73] Japanese and Chinese shareholders were to share equally in the enterprise. The exact area to be thus exploited was determined in the final agreement for the formation of this Sino-Japanese joint stock company, signed on May 14, 1908.[74] By virtue of this agreement the valley of the Hun river was excluded from the jurisdiction of the new company, except that private Chinese lumbermen in the latter area might apply to the company for loans to assist their industry and were to sell their product to the company. The area reserved for exploitation by the Sino-Japanese Timber Company was later defined to include the "right bank of the Yalu, extending from Maoershan (Linkiang) to Erhshih-tzu-taoku (as far as the 24th tributary of the Yalu) and measuring 60 *li* inland from the main stream." The company was capitalized at $3,000,000 (Chinese), each country to contribute half. The term of the contract agreement was to continue for twenty-five years with the privilege of renewal if the Chinese Government desired it. The company was to be jointly managed by Chinese and Japanese. It was further provided (Article 10) that 5 per cent. of the net profits should be paid annually to the Chinese Government. In the subsequent regulations of September 11, 1908, signed by Chinese and Japanese officials, it was provided that the original capital ($3,000,000) contributed by the two governments was to be withdrawn when the same was absorbed by private individuals, members and shareholders of the new company.[75] The Chinese Viceroy and Governor of Fengtien Province were to appoint the superintendent of the company, and also one manager, the other manager to be chosen by the Japanese. Preferential Chinese tax

[73] Sino-Japanese *Treaty and Additional Agreement relating to Manchuria*, December 22, 1905. MacMurray, Vol. I, p. 549.

[74] Sino-Japanese *Agreement for a Chinese-Japanese Joint Stock Lumber Company for the Exploitation of the Yalu Timber*, May 14, 1908. MacMurray, Vol. I, p. 731.

[75] Sino-Japanese *Regulations for Sino-Japanese Yalu Timber Company*, September 11, 1908. MacMurray, Vol. I, p. 733.

rates were to apply to the company and the timber cut (Article 14), only Chinese laborers were to be employed in timber cutting and rafting the logs (Article 20), while all local timber companies operating in conflict with the agreement and regulations were forthwith dissolved (Article 17). The Sino-Japanese Timber Company came into operation immediately thereafter. The company is chiefly Japanese and the Chinese interests are principally connected with officials in the Mukden Government.[76]

CHAPTER XXI

Sino-Japanese Agreements Relating to Cables and Telegraphs (1905-1915)

a. SINO-JAPANESE CABLE AND TELEGRAPH COMMUNICATIONS AGREEMENTS. During the Russian period of occupation of Manchuria from 1896 to 1905 the Russians had constructed a submarine cable across the Gulf of Pechihli from Port Arthur to Chefoo in Shantung province, apparently without specific authorization from China. This cable was cut during the course of the war with Japan. To relay a submarine cable between the Kwantung leased territory and Chefoo the Japanese Government secured permission from the Chinese Government in a convention of October 12, 1908, which dealt also with telegraph lines in Manchuria.[77] This convention provided (Article 1) that a submarine cable between Kwantung province and Chefoo would be laid by the two governments, the Japanese to lay and maintain the cable from Kwantung to within seven and a half miles of Chefoo, each country to operate its section of the cable, the Chinese end of the cable to be "connected up direct to the Japanese Post Office at Chefoo" to facilitate its use by the Japanese Government. The Japanese Government was to interdict the retransmission of messages to other parts of China from Chefoo and undertook (Article 1) "under the reserve of most favored nation treatment for the future, not to land submarine cables or to construct telegraph or telephone land-lines or to establish any kind of wireless communications in China, outside her leased or railway territories, without in every case first having obtained the consent of the Chinese Government." In conformity with the provisions of this convention the two governments signed

[76] See Chap. XL, Sec. a., for later Sino-Japanese timbering agreements.
[77] Sino-Japanese *Convention concerning the Telegraph Cable between Kwantung and Chefoo, etc.*, October 12, 1908. MacMurray, Vol. I, p. 760.

an agreement of November 7, 1908, which determined the number of hours daily during which the Japanese telegraph office in Chefoo might use the cable, provided also that the cable should be connected with the Manchurian telegraph lines, and fixed the rates together with the fees to be collected by the respective countries.[78]

Before the Russian period of occupation of the leased territory, and of the railway connecting therewith, the Russian Government had negotiated several wire telegraph agreements with China which (as in Article 6 of that of September 8, 1896) gave the Chinese Eastern Railway the right to construct and operate telegraph lines for the needs of the railway.[79] During the Russo-Japanese war the Japanese military constructed land telegraphs for the use of the armies in the field, as well as telephone lines, the latter being transferred to private Japanese management after the war, in the absence of an agreement with China on the subject.

In the submarine cable convention of October 12, 1908, the subject of land telegraphs in Manchuria to connect with the cable was also considered.[80] All land telegraphs then operated by the Japanese in Manchuria, outside the leased territory and the railway area, were transferred (Article 2) to China, subject to the payment of 50,000 yen. Japan, however, retained the telegraph lines in the railway area. China agreed to place at the disposal of the Japanese Government for a period of fifteen years (Article 3) two special telegraph wires from designated "open marts or treaty ports in Manchuria" (Antung, Newchwang, Liaoyang, Mukden, Tiehling and Changchun) to the railway area, these to be maintained by the Chinese Government up to the railway territory. These special wires were to be operated by Japanese clerks "in the employ of the Japanese Government," the Japanese to be given offices in the Chinese telegraph buildings to facilitate the use of these wires. The Japanese Government further agreed (Article 7) "to pay to the Chinese Government an annual sum of 3,000 yen as a royalty on all messages forwarded over the Japanese Manchurian telegraph lines."

In conformity with this convention the two governments signed an agreement of November 7, 1908, in which it was provided (Article 1) that China should connect her telegraph offices at Antung, Newchwang, Liaoyang, Mukden, Tiehling and Changchun with the

[78] Sino-Japanese *Agreement concerning the Working of the Chefoo-Kwantung Cable*, November 7, 1908. MacMurray, Vol. I, p. 762.

[79] Sino-Russian *Contract for the Construction and Operation of the Chinese Eastern Railway*, September 8, 1896. MacMurray, Vol. I, p. 74.

[80] MacMurray, Vol. I, p. 760.

respective telegraph offices of Japan within the "railway zone" at these places.[81]   A royalty was to be paid to China "on the telegraphic traffic handled by the Japanese offices in Manchuria"; messages handled by the Japanese offices destined for places outside the railway area were to be credited to the Chinese lines; messages handled by the Chinese offices destined for the railway area were to be credited to the Japanese lines.   Japan undertook "not to establish competition, by low rates or other means, against China," the provision not to apply, however (Article 2), to "traffic forwarded exclusively over the Japanese lines."   With the exception of the special provision for the use of two wires from the treaty ports mentioned (these being actually along the South Manchuria Railway or its connecting lines), the Japanese thus forfeited in these agreements the lines previously operated during the war outside of the acquired railway area.   The Japanese telegraph lines in Manchuria, on which they agreed to pay royalties to China (Article 1 of the agreement of November 7, 1908), were thus to be confined exclusively to the railway area and the Kwantung leased territory. Russia had transferred her telegraph lines in North Manchuria (outside the C.E.R. zone) the year before.

CHAPTER XXII

Status of Customs Administration in South Manchuria
(1905-1915)

a. CUSTOMS ADMINISTRATION IN THE KWANTUNG LEASED TERRITORY.   The treaty of Portsmouth and the subsequent treaty of Peking, both of 1905, transferred the lease of the Liaotung (Kwantung) territory to Japan.   Japan by virtue of these treaties acquired, with the consent of China obtained, the former Russian rights in the leased territory which included, among others, the right which Russia had acquired to administer the customs, i.e., the right within the leased territory itself to "fix the Customs Tariff to suit herself." [82]   China had had the qualified right reserved to her to "levy" and collect duties at the boundaries on all goods going from the leased territory to the interior or from the interior to the leased territory."   Russia had also possessed the right of exemption

<hr />

[81] Sino-Japanese *Agreement concerning the Working of the Japanese and Chinese Telegraph Lines in Manchuria*, November 7, 1908.   MacMurray, Vol. I, p. 765.   See Chap. L, Sec. e.

[82] See Chap. VI, Sec. a.

from all customs duties of Russian goods brought "from the railway stations within the Russian boundaries" to the leased territory, and, likewise from all customs duties of Russian goods sent from the leased territory to Russia.[83] Goods consigned for through traffic from abroad *via* a Liaotung port to the interior of Manchuria were to be subject to the jurisdiction of the Chinese Maritime Customs. It had also been provided that if and when a Chinese customs office were established at Dalny (later Dairen), the collection of the customs duties on goods consigned to the interior should be entrusted to the Chinese Eastern Railway Company to act in behalf of the Chinese Imperial Board of Revenue.[84] But during the Russian occupation of the leased territory no office of the Chinese Maritime Customs was established in the area. Dalny had been created as a "free port" by Russian Imperial Ukase on August 11, 1899, and hence no duties were to be collected at that port on goods destined for the leased territory.[85] No office of the Chinese Maritime Customs was established there during the Russian occupation of the leased territory.

Following the Russo-Japanese war, although goods imported from abroad through Newchwang (north of Dairen on the Gulf of Pechihli) were required to pay the usual Chinese customs duties, the port having been opened to trade and a Chinese customs house established there, goods were permitted to enter Dairen, destined either for the leased territory or for the interior of Manchuria, free of duty, no customs house of the Chinese Maritime Customs having been established there until July 1, 1907, in pursuance of an agreement of May 30, 1907, made between Japan and China for the establishment of a Chinese Maritime Customs office at the port.[86] The customs house was opened at once for the collection of duties on goods destined beyond the Kwantung leased territory only, Dairen itself, together with the leased territory, being established a duty-free zone. The opening of the "ports" in North Manchuria

[83] See Chap. VI, Sec. a.
[84] See Chap. VI, Sec. a.
[85] MacMurray, Vol. I, p. 121.
[86] Sino-Japanese *Agreement for the Establishment of a Maritime Customs Office at Dairen, etc.,* May 30, 1907. MacMurray, Vol. I, p. 634. For the opening of branch stations of the Dairen customs office see: British *Diplomatic and Consular Reports, Trade of Dairen (Dalny),* 1907, Annual Series, No. 4013, p. 8. This report, however, is in error as to Port Arthur which was not then opened to foreign trade. As a matter of fact, Port Arthur is unimportant as a commercial city, being important rather as the head of the Kwantung Government and as a strategic *point d'appui* of the leased territory, although it is no longer a naval base, as frequently it is thought to be.
For the reasons for the delay connected with the establishment of a customs station at Dairen see: *U. S. Foreign Relations,* 1907, Pt. I, p. 130; 1908, p. 128.

with established Chinese customs offices was delayed for some time, Manchouli and Suifenho not being opened until February, 1908.

The manner of collection of customs duties at Dairen to be paid into the Chinese treasury and the status of the exempted leased territory were established by the Sino-Japanese agreement of May 30, 1907.[87] Following the Russian precedent of requiring that an agency of that nationality should actually collect the customs at Dalny for transmission to the Chinese Imperial Board of Revenue, and in conformity with the precedent established by the German Government at Kiaochow, the function of actual collection of the maritime customs duties at Dairen was entrusted (Article 1) to a local customs office, technically under the Inspector General of Customs of China, but in the charge of a Commissioner who was to be of Japanese nationality, who was to have a Japanese staff.[88] Certain of these arrangements were modelled after the German practice at Kiaochow, one of which was specifically mentioned in the agreement (Article 6). Goods brought by sea to Dairen and destined for the leased territory were to be passed (Article 5) without duty, while goods thus arriving and destined for points beyond the leased territory were to pay the prevailing Chinese maritime customs duties. Chinese merchandise brought from the interior of China into the leased territory and shipped from Dairen "to other places" were (Article 6) to be charged an export duty, as also goods manufactured in the leased territory from materials brought there from the interior of China. Detailed provisions for other specific kinds of goods imported were provided. The agreement being declared of a provisional nature, it terminated with the clause (Article 18) that, "in view of the possibility that with the development of commercial activity in the Japanese leased territory new requirements may arise which are not to be foreseen, it is understood that the present Agreement bears a provisional character," subject to amendment as occasion may require. It appears that no revision of this agreement has been made.[89]

b. CUSTOMS ADMINISTRATION PERTAINING TO THE JAPANESE RAILWAY AREAS. During the Russian period of possession of the Chinese Eastern Railway in South Manchuria (1898 to 1905) the Russians had secured from China a preferential land frontier customs tariff rate for all goods brought from Russia to China over

[87] MacMurray, Vol. I, p. 634.
[88] MacMurray, Vol. I, p. 635.
[89] On June 26, 1907, the Japanese Government (i.e., by ordinance of the Government General of Kwantung) established provisional customs regulations for Kwantung leased territory. MacMurray, Vol. I, p. 638.

the Chinese Eastern Railway. Such Russian goods were to be charged the regular import and export tariffs *less one-third*. An additional charge of one-half the import duty was to be charged for goods destined to the interior, outside the railway area, this in lieu of *likin*.[90] Such land frontier customs preferences were and are prevalent in other parts of China.

After the establishment of branch offices of the Chinese Maritime Customs at Dairen and Antung (the latter near the mouth of the Yalu river) the Chinese Government issued regulations for the collection of duties at these ports, providing that foreign goods in transit having paid the regular duties at these ports (or at Tientsin or Newchwang) were to receive special certificates to permit their free entry into the other "open ports" in Manchuria.[91] After considerable delay the Chinese Government opened to foreign trade certain "ports" mentioned in the additional agreement attached to the treaty of Peking (December 22, 1905) between Japan and China, and also Antung and Mukden, likewise specially designated therein for opening.[92] By virtue of a Sino-Japanese convention of November 2, 1911, goods imported from Chosen (Korea) *via* Antung and destined for Manchuria were to be charged the customs duties at Antung, with provisions for exemption of goods destined for the Kwantung leased territory.[93] Detailed regulations for the same, i.e., through traffic over the Yalu river bridge from Chosen to Manchuria, were issued by the Chinese Government on March 31, 1912.[94]

The Japanese Government obtained from China on May 29, 1913, a *reduction of one-third* from the customs tariffs on all dutiable goods transported to Manchuria from Chosen (Korea) over the South Manchuria Railway and the Chosen State Railways, the reduction also to apply to export duties on dutiable goods car-

---

[90] See Chap. VI, Sec. b.

[91] MacMurray, Vol. I, p. 683. China, in the Sino-Japanese additional agreement attached to the treaty of Peking of December 22, 1905, had agreed to open to foreign residence and trade 16 "ports" in Manchuria, and in addition to these, Antung and Mukden. (MacMurray, Vol. I, p. 551.) Mukden and Tatungkow had been designated for opening in the Sino-Japanese supplementary treaty of commerce and navigation of October 8, 1903. (MacMurray, Vol. I, p. 411.) Mukden and Antung were likewise designated for opening in the Sino-American treaty of commerce of October 8, 1903. (MacMurray, Vol. I, p. 423.)

[92] In pursuance of the Sino-Japanese treaty of 1905 the Chinese Government had opened by the middle of 1907 practically all the ports designated. Delay occurred especially in North Manchuria. (*U. S. Foreign Relations*, 1907, Pt. I, p. 131.)

[93] Sino-Japanese *Convention relating to Railway Connections at Antung*, November 2, 1911. MacMurray, Vol. I, p. 914.

[94] MacMurray, Vol. II, p. 950.

ried by rail from Manchuria to Chosen.[95]   Transit dues on such goods destined for Manchuria were to be one-half the maritime customs charges (i.e., one-half of the two-thirds charged).   Goods imported via the Yalu river at Antung and then destined for Manchuria were not to receive the one-third reduction which was accorded only to goods carried by rail from Chosen to Manchuria. These provisions gave a distinct land frontier customs tariff advantage to Japanese goods carried through Chosen similar to, in fact modelled after, the provision (noted above) giving preference to Russia for goods transported into Manchuria over the Chinese Eastern Railway.[96]

CHAPTER XXIII

Japanese Jurisdiction in Manchuria (1905-1915)

a. JURISDICTION WITHIN THE KWANTUNG LEASED TERRITORY. In view of the fact that by virtue of the treaty of Portsmouth (September 5, 1905) and the treaty of Peking (December 22, 1905) the Japanese Government obtained from Russia, sanctioned by China, the transfer of all the Russian acquired rights to the Kwantung (Liaotung) leased territory, it would be superfluous here to recount in detail all the provisions of the original Sino-Russian agreements (the lease convention and the railway agreements) pertaining thereto.[97]   Suffice it to say that *within the Kwantung leased territory* Japan acquired all the rights of administration that appertain to sovereignty, except the ultimate right of recovery by China upon the termination of the lease, and such minor provisions as were specifically excepted for Chinese jurisdiction in the original Sino-Russian lease convention of March 27, 1898. "The entire military command of the land and naval forces and equally the supreme civil administration" was entirely conceded (Article 4) to the Russians by that convention, and, hence, passed to the Japanese after the Russo-Japanese war. Only within the city of Chinchou in the leased territory were the Chinese authorities to retain the right of administration and police. *Within the neutral zone* complete

---

[95] Sino-Japanese *Agreement concerning Special Duty Reduction Treatment of Goods Imported into Manchuria from or through Chosen, and Exported from Manchuria to or through Chosen, by rail via Antung,* May 29, 1913. MacMurray, Vol. II, p. 1039. The importance of this provision is suggested by the fact that in consequence of this reduction Dairen "sustained a heavy blow by the reduction of the customs duties on the Manchuria-Korea frontier." (British *Diplomatic and Consular Reports, Japan: Trade of Dairen,* 1914, Annual Series, No. 5508, p. 5.)

[96] See Chap. VI, Sec. b. and Chap. XXVII, Sec. a.

[97] See Chap. XVI, Secs. a and c; also Chap. V, Sec. a.

civil administrative authority had been given (Article 5 of the lease convention) to the Chinese authorities, though Chinese troops were to be admitted only with the consent of the Russians, hence, after 1905, with the consent of the Japanese.

b. JURISDICTION WITHIN THE SOUTH MANCHURIA RAILWAY ZONE AND ELSEWHERE. Japanese jurisdiction within the South Manchuria Railway zone (the term "zone" being interpreted here as the lands legally acquired and "actually necessary for the construction, operation, and protection of the line") is determined by the original Sino-Russian agreements providing for Russian jurisdiction within that area, by Sino-Japanese agreements relative to this jurisdiction following the Russo-Japanese war, and by the general treaty rights of Japan in Manchuria, including consular jurisdiction. The entire subject of Japanese jurisdiction in the South Manchuria Railway zone is, therefore, a highly complicated and somewhat controversial question, not capable of exhaustive attention here.

As to Japanese administrative rights actually exercised within the railway zone it may be said that they are practically all-inclusive, including some of the usual rights of administration which appertain to a sovereign power in its territory, such as taxation, police and the right to possess and to transfer real property. The right to provide for the defence of the railway is limited by the restrictions imposed upon the Japanese Government with regard to the number of troops which can be stationed along the line of the railway, the treaty of Portsmouth (Article 1 of the Annex) having authorized no more than fifteen per kilometre, while the protocol of evacuation (October 30, 1905) had authorized the employment by Japan and Russia of railway guards "to protect their respective railways in Manchuria" which were to be "on the average" of fifteen per kilometre.[98] The right to exercise the functions of ordinary police within the area of the railway zone is a more complicated question which, in the absence of other commitments of the Chinese Government, would rest entirely upon the original Sino-Russian railway contract agreement of 1896 which is the contractual basis for the Chinese Eastern Railway, applicable also to the southern section after 1898, and now in part the South Manchuria Railway. But since 1905, the Chinese Government has acquiesced in the exercise by Japan of ordinary rights of municipal and local administration actually within the South Manchuria Railway zone, and through the local provincial authorities of Manchuria (at Mukden) have

[98] See Chap. XVI, Sec. a and b.

entered in agreements providing for a limitation of the police powers which were thus presumed to be legally possessed.[99]

Over Japanese subjects in the South Manchuria Railway zone, as in Manchuria generally, the Japanese possess (as do other nationals whose treaties in regard to the subject still confer the right) the right of extraterritoriality and of consular jurisdiction, as provided in the general commercial treaties between China and Japan.[100]   It should be emphasized that Japanese jurisdiction over their own nationals extends, therefore, beyond the railway area itself, and it follows that Japanese "consular police" attached to the Japanese consulates in Manchuria have authority beyond that possessed by the "railway guards," or ordinary police. Moreover, by virtue of the authority given to Japan to establish Japanese "settlements" in the various open ports in Manchuria other specific rights of jurisdiction have been conferred.

The difficult question as to jurisdiction over Koreans (Japanese nationals after the annexation of Korea in 1910) in Manchuria, many of whom reside especially in the southern part of Kirin province adjoining the Chosen border, was for a restricted area dealt with in the Sino-Japanese agreement relating to the Chientao

[99] See Chap. V, Sec. b, Chap. XVI, Sec. b, and Chap. XXIV, Secs. a and b. It is interesting to note that while the United States emphatically protested the exercise by Russia of broad administrative authority in Harbin and the Chinese Eastern Railway area, no such protest was directed to Japan with reference to the South Manchuria Railway and the exercise by that company of administrative powers of a political nature in that railway zone. The fact that the Kwantung Government General exercised police powers in the railway zone, and not the company officials, merely raises the question: Where did that power come from? This inconsistency of American policy did not go unnoticed by the Russian Minister in Peking who inquired of the American Minister as to the neglect of the American Government to make representations to Japan as they had to Russia over the Harbin situation. The United States Department of State contented itself with the declaration that "the department has received no complaints from Americans resident along the South Manchuria Railway of any infringement of their extraterritorial rights nor of any exercise by the company of political powers" (completely ignoring the fact that the stationing of police officers is a political power in itself). (*U. S. Foreign Relations,* 1910, pp. 227-228.)   The American Government took the view that the Chinese Eastern Railway, being avowedly a *commercial* organization, could not exercise political powers, but that the South Manchuria Railway was "practically a government railway" and, presumably, might therefore exercise political powers. As a matter of fact, it is highly doubtful if the difference in status and functions between the Chinese Eastern Railway Company, as it existed in 1908, and the South Manchuria Railway Company was one of kind rather than of degree of government connection and participation. Japan acquired in the treaty of Portsmouth only the rights which Russia had actually possessed in the Chinese Eastern Railway (southern branch).

[100] The matter of Japanese extraterritorial rights and consular jurisdiction in Manchuria has been raised during recent years by the Chinese Government and is related to the subjects discussed in 1927-1929 in the negotiations pertaining to revision of the Sino-Japanese treaties of commerce of 1896 and 1903.

region, signed on September 4, 1909.[101] By virtue of this agreement the Tumen river was recognized as part of the boundary between China and Korea, and China agreed to open four cities in Chientao district to residence and trade, thus permitting the Japanese Government to establish consulates or branch offices of consulates at those places. The limits of the area in the Chientao region within which Koreans were permitted to reside and work agricultural lands were defined in a map drawn for the purpose. Korean subjects (Article 4) were to "submit to the laws of China" within this district and be amenable to Chinese local jurisdiction, but to enjoy treatment equal to the Chinese; civil and criminal cases concerning these Koreans were to be heard and decided by Chinese authorities under Chinese law, but a Japanese consular officer (Article 4) or other authorized official should be allowed freely to attend the court, notice of hearing to be given the Japanese consulates concerned in all cases concerning the lives of persons. Japanese consular officers were given the right to apply to the Chinese authorities for a trial *de novo* by "officials specially selected," if it appeared to them that a judgment or award had been in disregard of law. Korean subjects thus obtained the right of residence for agricultural purposes in the area, and the right (Article 5) to own such lands as already possessed. Free and unrestricted movement across the Sino-Korean border (except when carrying firearms) was granted the Koreans residing in Chientao district. On April 5, 1910, the Japanese Government issued a statement of the law and procedure to be applied by Japanese consular officers for cases within their jurisdiction in Chientao (Kanto).[101]

The annexation of Korea by Japan on August 21, 1910, made the Koreans actually Japanese nationals and, hence, would have altered the status of all Korean subjects who were residing in Manchuria at that time, entitling them, in the absence of other Sino-Japanese agreements to the contrary, to the protection and rights of extraterritoriality and consular jurisdiction. As a matter of fact, however, "the Chientao agreement was recognized by both Japan and China as still operative, and the Chinese judicial authorities in Chientao continued to exercise jurisdiction over Koreans residing in that territory as theretofore until the conclusion of the treaty

[101] Sino-Japanese *Agreement relating to the Chientao Region*, September 4, 1909. MacMurray, Vol. I, p. 796.
[102] MacMurray, Vol. I, p. 797.

relating to South Manchuria and Inner Mongolia of May 25, 1915." [103]

[103] *U. S. Foreign Relations,* 1915, p. 205. See also Chap. XXXVIII, Sec. a, relating to Sino-Japanese treaties and exchanges of notes of May 25, 1915. This Sino-Japanese agreement of 1909 relative to Koreans in Chientao did not finally settle difficult questions of jurisdiction where Koreans were involved. Conflicts arose thereafter as to the interpretation of the agreement, while the practice frequently differed from the letter of the law, especially after 1915. The boundary question itself, however, was settled in the agreement of 1909. Japan does not claim that Chientao is Japanese territory. The latter, however, has for some years past, and notably in 1927, attempted to secure the opening of Linkiang (Maoerhshan) to trade and to secure permission for a Japanese consular office to be established there. This the Chinese have always opposed. Whatever the law on the subject, it is a fact that many Koreans have become naturalized as Chinese subjects in Kirin province in an effort to obtain for themselves greater security against Chinese oppression in the matter of their land leases and taxes.

B. THE POSITION OF RUSSIA: 1905-1915

CHAPTER XXIV

The Russian Position in Manchuria After Portsmouth
(1905-1915)

a. RUSSIAN RAILWAY RIGHTS AND JURISDICTION IN MAN-
CHURIA IN 1905. By virtue of the treaty of Portsmouth (September 5, 1905) Russia lost only those treaty rights with China which she had obtained in South Manchuria, i.e., the lease of the Liaotung (later Kwantung) territory, which she had acquired in 1898, and the railway rights south of Changchun. Russia thus retained all the railway and other treaty rights which she had obtained during the period from 1895 to 1905 bearing on Manchuria north of Changchun, which, for purposes of convenience, may be referred to as North Manchuria.[104] The railway rights, therefore, appertained to the Chinese Eastern Railway which was to remain in the possession of the Chinese Eastern Railway Company (principally under Russian jurisdiction and management) until thirty-six years from the date of completion of the line, if at that time the Chinese Government desired to buy back the line, or until eighty years after completion, if China desired to recover the railway without payment.[105] The same rights of recovery by China were attached to the southern section of the railway from Harbin to Changchun (i.e., to Kuan-ch'eng-tzu). The extent of Russian jurisdiction within the zone of the Chinese Eastern Railway, therefore, was legally the same in 1905 and 1906 as it had been during the period from 1896 to 1905. The Russian authorities assumed that the original con-

---

[104] The term "North Manchuria" may be used, as it is in this section, to refer to that part of Manchuria which lies generally north of a line drawn east and west from Changchun, the junction point of the southern branch of the Chinese Eastern Railway and the South Manchuria Railway, i.e., to follow approximately the forty-fourth parallel. During this period from 1905 to 1915, however, the terms "North Manchuria" and "South Manchuria" come to have a more definite, though not necessarily legal or generally applicable, connotation, the distinction being drawn in certain of the Russo-Japanese treaties and conventions of this period. See Chap. XXXV, Sec. a.

[105] See Chap. III, Secs. b and c for the original Chinese Eastern Railway agreements of 1896 and 1898. See Sec. 16 a for the treaty of Portsmouth; See Chap. V, Secs. b and c for Russian jurisdiction in the railway area and the right to police the line.

tract of 1896 conferred practically complete civil administrative rights (as taxation, police jurisdiction, and the right to possess and dispose of real property), and, likewise, civil and criminal jurisdiction over certain Chinese nationals, and involving all cases either "directly or indirectly" affecting the interests of the railway. This interpretation of the 1896 agreement was, after January, 1908, contested by China.[106]

b. RUSSIAN JURISDICTION IN HARBIN MUNCIPALITY AND THE RAILWAY ZONE. The period following the Russo-Japanese war saw the development of two questions of interpretation of the original Sino-Russian railway agreements, these being one concerning the extent and character of the right of Russia to police the Chinese Eastern Railway with "railway guards," and another concerning the extent and character of Russian rights of administration in the railway zone, especially in the Harbin municipality. With regard to the latter issue it arose over a question raised by the Chinese Government as to the extent of Russia's right to establish a municipal administration in Harbin and over the general question of jurisdiction in other railway towns. In January, 1908, the Russians established a municipal council in Harbin on the ground that the original railway contract (1896) conferred on the railway the absolute and exclusive administration of its lands. The Chinese Government, however, calling attention to the Chinese text, protested this assertion of right in February, 1908, declaring that:

"The words, 'land required by the company,' as used in Article VI of the agreement, mean only the land actually required for the use of the railway. Thereon the company may erect any buildings and may establish a telegraph line, worked by the company, for the company's use; but as regards the matter of protection of the land and maintenance of the peace thereon, the authority for that rests in the hands of Chinese officials, as witness Article V of the same agreement, which plainly stipulates that 'the Chinese Government will take measures for the protection of the line and the men employed thereon'; and, further, 'all crimes and law suits arising

106 See Chap. V, Secs. b and c. By virtue of a Sino-Russian contract agreement of August 30, 1907, pertaining to the subject of expropriation of lands in Heilungkiang province for the use of the Chinese Eastern Railway, it was specifically provided that "the whole quantity of land required for the railway has been included in this agreement" and that "the Chinese Eastern Railway will never make any further expropriations." (MacMurray, Vol. I, p. 663.) On the same date a similar contract agreement was made to apply to the section of the railway in Kirin province. (MacMurray, Vol. I, p. 667.) These two agreements, therefore, set a definite limit upon the lands which might be expropriated for inclusion within the railway zone. No such expropriation agreement appears to exist for the territory traversed by the South Manchuria Railway.

on the land of the company will be dealt with by the local officials in accordance with the treaty.' From this it may be seen that the authority to administer the land rests entirely with China. There can be no doubt about it whatever. Therefore the action of the railway company in instituting municipal administrations at any of the various places on the line is evidently a usurpation of China's sovereignty, and it is absolutely impossible for the board of foreign affairs to recognize their rights in so doing." [107]

After the Chinese Government made this protest the two governments, following considerable negotiations, entered into an agreement of May 10, 1909, pertaining to municipal administration in the whole railway area, including Harbin. This agreement provided that (Article 1) "as a matter of fundamental principle the sovereign rights of China are recognized on the lands of the railway company," but that (Article 3) "the existing agreements of the railway company remain in full force." [108] Instead of retaining complete control for the Russians of municipal administration in the towns and cities of the railway zone, including Harbin, the agreement provided that henceforth such rights of municipal administration were to be possessed by the "inhabitants of these com-

[107] *U. S. Foreign Relations*, 1910, p. 203. The United States Government refused to accept this preliminary agreement of May 10, 1910, as binding upon American nationals and instructed the American Consul not to admit that the railway administration under Russian direction had the power to require of foreign residents in the Harbin municipality compliance with local regulations contrary to the general treaty provisions establishing extraterritorial rights of foreigners in China. The American Government declared on August 6, 1909, that: "The preliminary arrangement, while eliminating some of the objectionable features of the former regulations and providing for a share in the supervision of the municipal organization by an official representative of China, still vests in the manager of the Chinese Eastern Railway Co. at Harbin and the board of directors at St. Petersburg virtual control over all important acts of the municipality, and it is further provided that pending the elaboration of a detailed scheme of administration the former intolerable regulations shall remain in full force. No provision is made for securing the approval of municipal regulations either by the local consuls or by the diplomatic representatives of the interested powers in Peking. The arrangement thus conflicts with some of our most important rights, and this Government therefore finds it impossible to recognize it as in any way binding upon the United States or its citizens." (*U. S. Foreign Relations*, 1910, p. 213.) Again on November 6, 1909, in a *note verbale* to the Russian Embassy the American Government declared that: "The claim of the Chinese Eastern Railway Co. that China has granted to it the municipal power necessary to the government of all cities and towns built upon the railway's leased land is not considered by the Government of the United States to be justified by the language of the original contract of 1896 between the Chinese Government and the Russo-Chinese Bank, which is the concession under which the Chinese Eastern Railway was built and exists to-day. The administration by the railway company of its leased lands provided for in Article VI of the contract can refer only to such business administration as may be necessary to the "construction, exploitation, and protection" of the railway, these being the objects expressly mentioned in the article for which these lands were granted by China." (*U. S. Foreign Relations*, 1910, p. 219.)
[108] Sino-Russian *Preliminary Agreement in regard to Municipal Administration in the Chinese Eastern Railway Zone*, May 10, 1909. MacMurray, Vol. II, p. 1185.

mercial centers" (Article 6) who were to "elect delegates by vote," who in turn should choose an Executive Committee charged with the powers and duties of municipal administration.　Chinese subjects were to enjoy (Article 7) equal rights with foreigners in all respects, as in voting for the municipal officers, the right to vote being limited (Article 8) to owners of real estate of a fixed value or to those who paid rental and taxes.　The Executive Committee and the assembly of delegates, were specifically empowered to deal with local questions of public utilities and to have charge of "the management of municipal affairs," a "right of control and personal revision" being granted to the Chinese president of the Harbin Bureau of Foreign Affairs (*Chiao Shê Chu*) and the director of the railway, this to be overridden only by a three-fourths vote of the assembly.　"Important questions, having reference to the public interest or the finances of the municipalities" were (Article 15) to be referred to the President of the Chinese Eastern Railway (a Chinese) *who would attend to them in consultation with the management of the railway.*　The railway retained the right to administer its stations, workshops, etc., which were exempted from the land tax.　The agreement was to be (Article 17) but the "basis for determining detailed regulations in regard to the municipalities and police."

At the same time as this preliminary agreement was signed between China and Russia the two governments, through an exchange of notes, laid down the fundamental principles on which the municipal administration agreement was to be made, Russia acknowledging that "the leased territory of the Manchurian Railway is Chinese territory, and Chinese sovereignty therein is now fully recognized," and declaring that the Russian Government would henceforth "fully respect within the limits of the leased territory the rights and privileges which the subjects of other Powers enjoy under the treaties between China and the other Powers.[109]

This preliminary agreement, especially because of its application to Harbin, though approved by Japan, failed to secure the approval of certain treaty powers necessary to apply it to their own nationals, and the respective consuls of those countries were instructed not to observe the agreement.　Nor did the local Chinese officials agree with the interpretation placed upon it by the Russians.　During 1914 and following, however, the various governments, including France, Great Britain, Japan, Belgium, the Netherlands and Spain, adhered to a draft agreement negotiated by the British consul at Harbin and the local Russian authorities on April 17/30, 1914,

[109] MacMurray, Vol. II, p. 1186.

which provided that, under certain conditions, the nationals of each of these powers would pay the same taxes as collected from Russian subjects in the municipal area of Harbin and at other settlements in the railway zone.[110]

The matter of Russia's right to patrol the railway zone with "railway guards" was left open for subsequent attention, Russia retaining her "railway guards" in the zone of the Chinese Eastern Railway.[111] No additional right to Russia to station "railway guards" along the Chinese Eastern Railway had been conceded by China after the Russo-Japanese war, as had been conceded to Japan by the treaty of Peking and by the additional agreement of December 22, 1905, attached thereto.[112] If the right to station "railway guards" for limited purposes were to be conceded to Russia, it was *limited* to the number of fifteen per kilometre by the treaty of Portsmouth with Japan, not *granted* to Russia by the treaty. At the Washington Conference the Chinese Delegation declared that there was no legal justification for the maintenance of "a Russian guard" along the railway.[113]

CHAPTER XXV

Sino-Russian Railway Agreements (1905-1915)

a. SINO-RUSSIAN RAILWAY AGREEMENTS. During the period from 1905 to 1915 neither the Russian Government nor the Chinese Eastern Railway Company negotiated any single important railway agreement with China bearing on the construction of new lines or branch lines to the Chinese Eastern Railway, nor any loan contract agreement relating to the same. Such agreements as were negotiated through the Chinese Eastern Railway Company related to such subjects as terminal connections, interlineal traffic arrangements, telegraphs and connections, Russian jurisdiction in the railway zone, delimitation of the railway area, and the subject of customs collection in the area traversed by the railway. A series of general arrangements with Japan, however, and these of considerable importance, was negotiated during this period, these having bearing on the general subject of the delimitation of Russian and Japanese "spheres" of railway interest in Manchuria, and on

[110] MacMurray, Vol. II, pp. 1181 ff. The Chinese political authorities, acting under instructions from Mukden, unilaterally altered and violated this agreement of 1914, when, during 1926-1927, they attempted to deprive foreigners of their treaty rights in the Harbin municipal council. Their action resulted in joint protests of several foreign consuls, including the Russian, Japanese, British and American.
[111] See Chap. XLIV, Sec. a, and Chap. LII, Sec. a.
[112] See Chap. XVI, Sec. c.
[113] See Chap. V, Sec. c, and Chap. LII, Sec. a.

the subject of mutual guarantees and cooperation between Russia and Japan and between their respective railway holdings in Manchuria.[114] As a matter of fact, neither during this period, nor during the periods following down to the present, have the Russian Government or the Chinese Eastern Railway (with the exception of a 1916 contract, and those which might have been constructed, under a 1915 agreement, in the Barga [Hailar] district in western Heilungkiang) secured any considerable concessions from China with respect to prior rights to construct railways in Manchuria. No attention is given here to the various short lines and spurs of the Chinese Eastern Railway which serve the railway's timber concessions, as especially in the timber concession at Shihtouhotzu. The timber concessions along the Chinese Eastern Railway, as well as the railway spurs leading to them, are owned principally by private Russian, Polish and Japanese concessionaires, and not by the Chinese Eastern Railway.

CHAPTER XXVI

Sino-Russian Mining and Lumbering Agreements (1905-1915)

a. SINO-RUSSIAN MINING AGREEMENTS. In pursuance of the rights given to the Chinese Eastern Railway in the agreements of 1896 and 1898 to "cut timber and mine coal for the use of the railway," the railway company entered upon certain mining projects along the railway route shortly after the construction of the main line. By virtue of a special agreement, locally negotiated, dated January 14, 1902, and applicable only to Heilungkiang province, the railway company obtained (Article 1) the "exclusive right to prospect for coal and to mine coal within not more than 30 Chinese *li* on either side of the railway line," and the prior right to be consulted in any coal mining projects "outside the 30 *li* limit." [115] In 1907, by an agreement of August 30, the railway company and the authorities of Heilungkiang province agreed that (Article 1) "the right is granted to the Chinese Eastern Railway to work the coal within certain regions of Heilungkiang Province," the exact places for such mining to "be determined by the management of the railway itself," but to be confined to a thirty *li* zone on either side of the line.[116] The

---

[114] See Chap. XXXV, Secs. a and b.

[115] MacMurray, Vol. I, p. 661.

[116] Sino-Russian (Heilungkiang Province-Chinese Eastern Railway Co.) *Agreement regarding the Operation of Coal Mines in Heilungkiang Province,* August 30, 1907. MacMurray, Vol. I, p. 658.

right was not entirely exclusive, however, as Chinese might exploit such mines which would not interfere directly with the railway mines, while Chinese and foreigners might be given concessions for mining within the limited zone with the consent of the railway and the Chinese authorities. The prior right of the railway to be consulted in mining projects outside the railway mining zone was definitely rescinded in this agreement (Article 2), exploitation to be open to all foreigners under the usual conditions imposed by Chinese authority. For every 1,000 kin (chin) of coal extracted from the mines operated by the railway the company was to pay (Article 7) into the Heilungkiang provincial treasury twelve one-hundreths of a Heilungkiang tael, and an additional shaft tax.[117]

b. SINO-RUSSIAN LUMBERING AGREEMENTS. The construction of the Chinese Eastern Railway main line following 1896 necessitated the felling of virgin forest lands along the route traversed toward Vladivostok, permission to use such timber having been conceded to the railway in the original railway agreements of 1896 and 1898, the timber cut to be "for the use of the railway." On the same date (August 30, 1907) as the Chinese Eastern Railway Company negotiated with the Heilungkiang authorities a coal mining agreement the railway also signed with the authorities of Kirin province an agreement for the felling of timber along the railway in that province.[118] The company was given (Article 1) the right to "fell all kinds of timber at three places" in the province (i.e., sections near Shihtouhotzu, Kaolingtzu, and Imienpo). For all timber cut by the railway certain license fees were to be paid valid for one year, and additionally a fixed stamp tax on the quantity cut. The Chinese Government retained the right to clear open land within the timber area for settlement by Chinese immigrants (Article 6), and to permit Chinese soldiers to enter the timber areas to capture brigands.

On April 5, 1908, the Chinese Eastern Railway Company obtained a similar agreement with reference to timber-cutting rights in Heilungkiang province.[119] Three specific timber sections were designated for the purpose (i.e., Houliaokou, Piteyi, and a section at the junction of the Ch'uan river with the Sungari). Similar

[117] An identical (mutatis mutandis) coal mining agreement was signed with the authorities of Kirin province on the same date. (MacMurray, Vol. I, p. 658.)
[118] Sino-Russian (Kirin Province-Chinese Eastern Railway Co.) Agreement for the Felling of Timber in Kirin Province, August 30, 1907. MacMurray, Vol. I, p. 671.
[119] Sino-Russian (Heilungkiang Province-Chinese Eastern Railway Co.) Agreement for the Felling of Timber in Heilungkiang Province, April 5, 1908. MacMurray, Vol. I, p. 721.

license and tax provisions were imposed for these sections as for those in Kirin province. An interesting provision reserved the right to the Chinese to enter the timber areas "for the purpose of hunting and the collection of ginseng roots."

As remarked above, the Chinese Eastern Railway timber concessions are but three in number and, while important to the railway, are less important commercially than the combined concessions held by private Russian, Polish and Japanese concessionaires near the railway, as, for example, the important concessions of Mr. Kovalsky, a Polish pioneer, who has absorbed the railway concession at Imienpo, and who now sells a great part of his product to the Japanese.

CHAPTER XXVII

Status of Customs Administration in North Manchuria
(1905-1915)

a. CUSTOMS ADMINISTRATION PERTAINING TO THE RUSSIAN (C.E.R.) RAILWAY AREAS. In the original railway contract agreement of September 8, 1896, the Russo-Chinese Bank secured the provision (Article 10) that "merchandise imported from Russia into China by the railway, and likewise merchandise exported from China into Russia by the same route, will respectively pay the import and export duty of the Chinese Maritime Customs, less one-third." [120] An additional charge of one-half the import duty was to be charged for goods destined for the interior, outside the railway area, this in lieu of *likin*. Following the Russo-Japanese war these provisions remained applicable as before for the main line of the Chinese Eastern Railway and the southern section to Changchun, Japan having obtained control of the section of the railway south of Changchun. In 1913 the Japanese Government obtained, similarly, a specific reduction of one-third of the regular maritime customs duties for goods sent by rail from Chosen (Korea) to Manchuria over the Antung-Mukden railway.[121]

The possibility that the Japanese Government might secure additional customs preferences in favor of goods entering Manchuria over the South Manchuria Railway from Dairen (Dalny), following the end of the Russo-Japanese war, prompted the declaration on the part of Russia, and the acceptance on the part of China (July 2/15, 1907), that special privileges in the matter of

120 See Chap. VI, Sec. b.
121 See Chap. XXII, Sec. b.

customs charges granted to goods conveyed into Manchuria from Dairen should also be extended to goods brought into Manchuria over the (Sino-Russian) land frontier.[122] No formal agreement, however, gave any such customs preference to goods carried from Dairen over the South Manchuria Railway.[123]

As in South Manchuria following the Russo-Japanese war there was considerable delay in the opening to residence and trade of "ports" in North Manchuria, and customs houses were not opened until 1908, the delay being intimately related to the similar delay in connection with the opening of Dairen, Antung and Mukden.[124] On July 8, 1907, the Chinese Government issued experimental regulations (to be in force for one year) for the establishment of customs houses in North Manchuria, and for the delimitation of the areas in and near the railway zone which would be entitled to import goods with a reduction of one-third from the usual maritime customs charges.[125] Within a radius of ten Chinese *li* (a little over three miles) from Harbin station, and within an area extending five *li* in both directions along the railway from the stations at Manchouli, Hailar, Tsitsihar, Kuanchengtzu and a dozen other places, goods were to be entered with a reduction of one-third, goods destined for or sent to the interior outside these areas being subject to the usual duties and other charges. A head customs house was established at Harbin, and in February, 1908, branch offices at Manchouli and Pogranitchnaya (Suifenho) for the collection of customs duties at the terminal points of the Chinese Eastern Railway main line were opened.[126] On September 6, 1912, the Russian Government abolished (after January 14, 1913) the 50-verst duty-free zone on the Russian side of the Sino-Russian frontier (established originally in the treaty of 1881), authorizing China to do the same on her side

[122] MacMurray, Vol. I, p. 650.

[123] See Chap. XXII, Secs. a and b.

[124] *U. S. Foreign Relations*, 1908, p. 128. See Chap. XXII, Sec. a.

[125] MacMurray, Vol. I, p. 648. This temporary adjustment was the product of compromise. The Russians had contended that "goods subject to this reduced import duty (two-thirds) can be transported to any point along the railway lines in Manchuria without being liable to further duty." The Chinese had claimed "that the payment of two-thirds duty only entitles such goods to pass the Chinese frontier, and that they must pay transit dues (50 per cent. additional) to clear them to points further in the country." The American Minister in Peking advised the Department of State on May 17, 1907, that "the contention of the Russians is certainly correct, and it is approved by those of my colleagues who are interested in Manchurian commercial questions." (*U. S. Foreign Relations*, 1907, Pt. I, p. 131.) This view seems to be supported by careful reference to the original railway contract agreement in question. See Article 10 of the Sino-Russian contract for the construction of the Chinese Eastern Railway, September 8, 1896. (MacMurray, Vol. I, p. 76.) See Chap. III, Sec. b, and Chap. VI, Sec. b.

[126] MacMurray, Vol. I, p. 651.

of the frontier.[127] China abolished the duty-free zone on the Chinese side shortly thereafter. Regulations for the collection of customs charges, tonnage, transit and river dues on goods entering Harbin from the Sungari river were agreed upon by Russia and China on August 8, 1910.[128] Provisions for collection of these charges along the Sungari river, for goods going to or coming from the Amur river, were also contained therein.

CHAPTER XXVIII

Sino-Russian Agreements Relating to Telegraphs (1905-1915)

a. SINO-RUSSIAN TELEGRAPH AGREEMENTS. The railway contract agreements for the construction of the Chinese Eastern Railway (1896 and 1898) had given to the Russians the right to construct and operate telegraph lines for the needs of the line. These rights from Changchun south were transferred to Japan by the treaty of Portsmouth, Russia retaining them for North Manchuria.[129] The year before the Japanese Government had entered into a formal agreement with China to effect the transfer to China of all telegraph lines controlled by Japan in Manchuria, the Russian Government had already made a similar arrangement with China, the final transfer having been effected by an agreement signed by China and the Chinese Eastern Railway Company, which had operated the Russian telegraph lines in Manchuria before 1907. This transfer agreement of May 23, 1907, enabled China to recover all the telegraph lines in North Manchuria which had been operated by the Russians outside the railway territory.[130] China agreed to pay the sum of $120,000 (Mex.) to the Chinese Eastern Railway Administration for the telegraph lines thus transferred to China. By an agreement of October 7, 1907, an operation arrangement in regard to the telegraph lines owned by China and those operated by the railway for its own use was signed.[131] The agreement specifically declared in a preamble that "the forwarding or permitting others to forward public telegraph messages within the

[127] MacMurray, Vol. I, p. 650.
[128] MacMurray, Vol. I, p. 807.
[129] See Chap. XXI, Sec. a.
[130] Sino-Russian (China-Chinese Eastern Railway Co.) *Agreement for the Transfer to China of the Telegraph Lines in Manchuria outside the Chinese Eastern Railway Territory,* May 23, 1907. MacMurray, Vol. I, p. 631.
[131] Sino-Russian (China-Chinese Eastern Railway Co.) *Agreement in regard to the Working of the Telegraph Lines of the Chinese Eastern Railway,* October 7, 1907. MacMurray, Vol. I, p. 679.

Empire of China is an Imperial prerogative" and that the concession granted to the Chinese Eastern Railway Company had been solely to enable the company to maintain telegraph lines for the use of the railway itself.   China agreed to connect the Chinese lines with those within the railway area; each system was to accept and transfer telegrams to be credited to the other; and competitive rates were not to be instituted.   These provisions in general paralleled those later agreed upon by Japan in regard to Japanese and Chinese telegraph lines in South Manchuria, but in one important respect they were strikingly dissimilar.   The Russians did not obtain the special right, conceded to Japan a year later, which gave the Japanese the right to have the service of special wires from certain treaty ports to within the Japanese railway territory and which permitted Japanese clerks to have offices in the Chinese telegraph buildings to facilitate the use of these special wires.[132]   The Chinese Eastern Railway, like the South Manchuria Railway, retained, however, their own telegraph system to be used, under the agreements, for railway services only.

[132] See Chap. XXI, Sec. a.

C. THE POSITION OF OTHER POWERS: 1905-1915

CHAPTER XXIX

Multi-Power Agreements Relating to Manchuria (1905-1915)

a. MULTI-POWER LOANS FOR MANCHURIA (1910-1913) FOUR POWER CONSORTIUM. During the period immediately before, during and following the Chinese Revolution there developed, with special bearing on Manchuria, a program of international loans to the Chinese Republic which came to be known as the "Four Power Banking Consortium" program and later, upon the inclusion of Russia and Japan, the "Six Power Banking Consortium." The Currency loan of 1911 for China, containing as it did clauses providing for loans for various purposes in Manchuria, had a dual origin, the one, being the necessity in China proper for unification of the currency system, the other, being the requirement for a loan to be used by the viceregal administration of the Three Eastern Provinces for plague prevention, and for various agricultural, industrial and mining projects in Manchuria. Owing to the Revolution the Currency loan of 1911 was never floated, although the agreement therefor continued to remain in force, while an advance of £400,000 was actually made by the Four Power Banking Group, representing American, British, German and French bankers, in connection with payments for plague prevention outlays in Manchuria and for various agricultural and industrial purposes there.[138]

On April 15, 1911, various foreign banks representing the "Four-Power Banking Consortium"—including the Banque de l'Indo-Chine (French), the Deutsch-Asiatische Bank (German), the Hongkong and Shanghai Banking Corporation, Ltd. (British), and an American group of banks, including Messrs. J. P. Morgan & Co., Messrs. Kuhn, Loeb & Co., the First National Bank, and the National City Bank of New York—negotiated with the Chinese

[138] A preliminary agreement for the Chinese currency reform and Manchurian industrial development loan had been negotiated on October 27, 1910, between an American banking group and the Chinese Government. At the instance of the American bankers the Chinese Government later consented to the participation of the British, French and German banks. (MacMurray, Vol. I, p. 851.)

Government the Chinese currency reform and Manchurian industrial development loan agreement.[134] The currency reform features of the loan agreement do not concern us especially here as do those pertaining to Manchuria. The total loan, however, was for an amount not to exceed £10,000,000 at 5 per cent., the bonds to be sold at 95. Of this amount a possible £1,000,000 (Article 8, Sec. 4) might be obtained (Article 3) "for the promotion and extension of industrial enterprises in the three Manchurian provinces," the same, when advanced, to be kept in a separate "Manchurian development account." The entire loan, however, was to be secured by and made a charge upon revenues of the Chinese Government, one-half of which was designated (Article 5) as derivable from Manchuria (i.e., 2,500,000 Kuping taels annually), from Manchurian tobacco and spirits duties, production and consumption taxes. The Manchurian section of the loan was to be used (Article 8) for expenditures in connection with the promotion of immigration, reclamation and pastoral enterprises, for forestry and other agricultural enterprises in Heilungkiang, for mining enterprises and in connection with branch mints in Manchuria, the same, and any additional amount, to be in accordance with "the principle of the promotion of industries." It is understood that the several banks thus affiliated advanced the sum of £400,000 to the Chinese Government for use in Manchuria.[135] Practically speaking, no loan advanced by any international banking group (other than Russian, Japanese or French) has ever been floated, with this one exception, for general industrial purposes in Manchuria.

b. MULTI-POWER LOANS FOR MANCHURIA (1910-1913) SIX-POWER CONSORTIUM. After the conclusion of the Chinese currency and Manchurian loan agreement of 1911 by the British, French, German and American banking groups, the Russian and Japanese Governments requested that their respective banking groups might be allowed to participate in the consortium in future general loans for China including Manchuria. In a general multilateral agreement, signed by the representatives of the various banking groups concerned in Paris on June 18, 1912, this time including the Russo-Asiatic Bank (designated in the agreement as "the Russian Bank") and the Yokohama Specie Bank, Ltd. (designated as "the Japanese Bank"), a reorganization loan for the Chinese Gov-

---

[134] International Banking Group *Loan Agreement with China for Chinese Currency Reform and Manchurian Industrial Development*, April 15, 1911. MacMurray, Vol. I, p. 841.

[135] MacMurray, Vol. I, p. 850. See Willoughby, W. W., *Foreign Rights and Interests in China*, (Revised edition), Vol. II, p. 988.

ernment was arranged.[136] In the negotiations for the same the Russian and Japanese banking groups asserted what amounted to a reservation to protect their "special interests" claimed in parts of China, including Manchuria, the reservation being included in the minutes of one of the Paris meetings, dated June 19, 1912.[137] The Russian and Japanese banking groups thus asserted the right to disapprove of any loan under the general arrangement, the right to withdraw from the consortium arrangement being granted in case the consortium, or any banking group included, undertook to offer a loan or loans "contrary to the interests of Russia or Japan." The British, German, French and American groups stated that they were not in a position to express their views upon these declarations on the ground that they were not competent to deal with political questions. The next year the American banking group withdrew from the consortium, reserving their rights to further participation, by virtue of the declaration of the Department of State of the United States that "the conditions of the loan seem to us to touch very nearly the administrative independence of China itself, and this Administration does not feel that it ought, even by implication, to be a party to those conditions," and concluding "our interests are those of the Open Door—a door of friendship and mutual advantage. This is the only door we care to enter." [138] The non-participation of the German and Russian groups following the outbreak of the war left only the British, French and Japanese groups for participation. The consortium, however, while still including the nominal active participation of all groups except the American, signed on April 26, 1913, the "Chinese Government 5 Per Cent. Reorganization Gold Loan Agreement" by virtue of which £25,000,000 was paid as the first instalment to the Chinese Government.[139]

c. Project for Neutralization and Multi-Power Finance of Manchurian Railways, 1909. During 1902, while

[136] International Banking Group *Reorganization Loan Agreement with China.* June 18, 1912. MacMurray, Vol. II, p. 1021. See Chap. XLIV, Sec. b, for the new consortium negotiations in 1918 following. See Chap. XIX, Sec. d, for Japanese railway loan agreements with China.

[137] MacMurray, Vol. II, p. 1024.

[138] *Statement of the United States Government,* March 18, 1913. MacMurray, Vol. II, p. 1025. The United States Government, however, although withdrawing their support from the American bankers on March 18, 1913, reserved their right to consider future projects for participation by the American bankers in a subsequent Chinese currency reform loan, as indicated by the statement of the United States Government on October 20, 1917. (MacMurray, Vol. I, p. 852.)

[139] International Banking Group *Chinese Government Five Per Cent. Reorganization Gold Loan Agreement,* April 26, 1913. MacMurray, Vol. II, p. 1007. See Willoughby, Vol. II, p. 999.

the negotiations for the construction of the Chinchow-Aigun railway in Manchuria were under way between China and American and British banking interests, the American Secretary of State, Philander C. Knox, advanced a plan for the neutralization of Manchurian railways, this to be accomplished through the purchase with funds, advanced to China by multi-power and bilateral loan arrangements, of all foreign controlled railways in Manchuria, including the Chinese Eastern Railway and the South Manchuria Railway.[140] The Chinchow-Aigun railway project, which was, in a way, the origin and a phase of the "Knox plan," was to constitute the initial basis for American and British participation in the neutralization of the Manchurian railways.

The plan of Mr. Knox was first submitted to the British Government in a memorandum dated November 9, 1909, forwarded to the British Foreign Office.[141] The memorandum called attention to the fact that the Chinese Government had approved by an imperial decree the project for American and British finance of the Chinchow-Aigun railway (to Tsitsihar), and asserted that the Government of the United States was inclined to favor the ultimate participation in this project of such other powers as might be agreeable to China. In order to effect a "practical application of the policy of the open door and equal commercial opportunity" in Manchuria the Knox program, as then outlined, looked toward the bringing of the Manchurian railways "under an economic and scientific and impartial administration by some plan vesting in China the ownership of the railroads through funds furnished for that purpose by the interested Powers willing to participate," this to be accomplished through a multi-power loan to China.

The British Government replied on November 25, 1909, declaring themselves in accord with the "general principle" of the plan, favoring the application of the same to the end of "preservation of the Open Door policy and equal commercial opportunity," and declaring it "adapted to securing to China full control of Manchuria," but declaring, nevertheless, that the Government believed it "undesirable to consider the question of another international loan for China's railway undertakings" at the time, hence disapproving of "the first scheme" proposed.[142] The British Foreign Minister later suggested that Japan be invited to participate in the Chinchow-Aigun project. This suggestion secured the official

---

[140] See Chap. XXXI, Sec. a.
[141] *U. S. Foreign Relations*, 1909, p. 211; also 1910, p. 234.
[142] *U. S. Foreign Relations*, 1910, p. 235; also 1910, p. 242.

approval of the United States, but the matter was allowed to drop. On January 21, 1910, the American *Chargé d'Affaires* at Peking reported that the approval of the Chinese Government to the neutralization plan had been secured.[143]

Disapproval of the "Knox plan" for the neutralization of the Manchurian railways was given by both the Russian and Japanese Governments on the same date, January 21, 1910, the Russian *aide-mémoire* asserting that inasmuch as "nothing appears at the present time to threaten either this sovereignty or the open door policy in Manchuria," the Russian Government "cannot discover in the present condition of Manchuria any reason necessitating the placing on the order of the day of the questions raised by the United States Government," and therefore "must declare with absolute frankness that the establishment of an international administration and control of the Manchurian railroads as proposed by the Federal Government would seriously injure Russian interests, both public and private, to which the Imperial Government attaches capital importance." The Russian Government declared the "exploitation of its [Manchuria's] natural resources" by means of the Chinese Eastern Railway to be "of capital importance to Russia." Regarding the Chinchow-Aigun railway project the Russian Government declared that because "its accomplishment will open up a new route giving access from the south not only to the Chinese Eastern Railroad, but directly to Russian possessions at Aigun," the project had distinct "strategic and political importance," and would effect the interests of the Chinese Eastern Railway. So also with "any future project concerning a financial participation in the construction of railroads in Manchuria," the Russian *aide-mémoire* concluded, and hence the Russian Government considered "that it must reserve the privilege of examining every project of this kind from a double standpoint of its political and strategical interests and of the interests of the Chinese Eastern Railroad."[144] A month later the Russian Government informed the United States that such a railroad as the Chinchow-Aigun project "would be exceedingly injurious both to the strategic and to the economic interests of Russia," that "China in 1899 engaged not to build railroads to the north of Peking with foreign capital other than Russian, and Russia could be willing not to insist on the execution by China of this obligation only under the conditions that railroads built with capital provided by international syndicates should not be an evident

[143] *U. S. Foreign Relations,* 1910, pp. 240, 248.
[144] *U. S. Foreign Relations,* 1910, pp. 249-252.

menace to the security of the Russian frontier and should not injure the interests of Russia's railroad enterprise in Manchuria." [145]

The reply of the Japanese Government to the "Knox plan" was also in the negative. In a note of January 21, 1910, on the same date as the Russian Government replied, the Japanese Government presented its bases for objection.[146] "The most serious objection to the proposal in question lies in the fact that it contemplates a very important departure from the terms of the Treaty of Portsmouth," declared the note, because "that treaty was designed to establish in Manchuria a permanent order of things" which the "Knox plan" would upset. The plan proposed was declared to be unnecessary and undesirable, unwarranted by conditions in Manchuria. The "open door" policy, to which the Japanese Government again announced its adherence, was declared to possess "in its application to Manchuria a more comprehensive signification than it has elsewhere in China" since the treaty of Portsmouth (Article 8) pledged both Japan and Russia to use their railways exclusively for commercial and industrial purposes. In the interest of economy and efficiency of management the substitution of an international for national control of railways in Manchuria would be disadvantageous and undesirable, said the Japanese note, while the vested interests of the Japanese railways in Manchuria were such that it was only through the continuance of the present Japanese policy that protection could be extended to private Japanese undertakings in Manchuria. Both the Japanese and Russian Governments shortly thereafter addressed the Chinese Government protesting against the Chinchow-Aigun railway project, and requiring that China first consult them if railways were to be constructed with foreign capital in Manchuria.[147] France and Great Britain, thereupon, declined to give support to the plan for the construction of the Chinchow-Aigun railway, France asserting that Russia should be consulted by China before granting concessions for railways in North Manchuria, Great Britain taking the view that an account of the Anglo-Russian agreement of 1899, the British Government also considered it proper to consult Russia.[148]

The "Knox plan" for the neutralization of Manchurian railways through acquisition by the Chinese Government by means of loans

[145] *U. S. Foreign Relations,* 1910, p. 261. See Willoughby, Vol. I, p. 181. See Chap. III, Sec. e, for the Anglo-Russian and the Sino-Russian agreements of 1899. See Chap. VII, Sec. b, for the British official waiver of railway rights in Manchuria.
[146] *U. S. Foreign Relations,* 1910, p. 251. ·
[147] *U. S. Foreign Relations,* 1910, p. 257.
[148] *U. S. Foreign Relations,* 1910, pp. 256, 268.

advanced by participating foreign syndicates failed of adoption by the governments of the powers whose bankers were interested in railway finance in China, and was defeated especially by Russia and Japan. The Chinchow-Aigun railway project, an Anglo-American plan with Chinese approval, likewise failed of fruition, and was never revived in that form, though sections of that projected railway have now been constructed by the Chinese Government themselves.[149]

CHAPTER XXX

The Position of Great Britain (1905-1915)

a. BRITISH SYNDICATE PROJECT FOR HSINMINTUN-FAKUMEN RAILWAY, 1907. In 1898 a British financial organization, the Hongkong and Shanghai Banking Corporation, Ltd., had negotiated in behalf of the British and Chinese Corporation, Ltd., a railway loan agreement which authorized, in addition to the main line mentioned therein, the construction by that corporation of "branch lines or extensions" connecting with the Shanhaikwan-Newchwang-Hsinmintun railway system.[150] This right was transferable to any British firm. The Anglo-Russian exchange of notes of April 28, 1899, specifically recognized the prior rights of the British and Chinese Corporation, Ltd., under the above agreements of 1898 as an exception to the agreement then made between the two governments by which the British Government waived the right of the British Government or their nationals to seek any railway concessions north of the Great Wall, i.e., including Manchuria.[151] The Russian Government, moreover, had recognized the validity of this prior right of the British and Chinese Corporation, Ltd., as well as the binding force of the Anglo-Russian exchange of notes of 1899, in the convention signed with China of April 2, 1902.[152] The same convention, however, gave Russia the right to be consulted with regard to future construction of any or all extensions or branches of the Shanhaikwan-Newchwang-Hsinmintun railways, and by pledge from China, dated June 1, 1899, had secured the right to be consulted and to have the prior right of finance in any case of construction of a railway by China.[153]

[149] See Chap. XXXI, Sec. a, for the Anglo-American private project for the Chinchow-Aigun railway.
[150] See Chap. VII, Sec. a.
[151] See Chap. VII, Sec. b.
[152] See Chap. III, Sec. e.
[153] See Chap. III, Sec. e.

Moreover, the Japanese Government had asserted in 1906 that in certain "protocols" attached to the Sino-Japanese treaty of Peking and the additional agreement of December 22, 1905, there was contained a provision, presumed to be enforceable, to the effect that the Chinese Government would not construct "any main line in the neighborhood of and parallel to" the South Manchuria Railway, "or any branch line which might be prejudicial to the interest of the above mentioned railway." [154]

When Hsü Shih-chang became Viceroy of the Three Eastern Provinces (appointed April 20, 1907) he immediately undertook the development of railways in the provinces with an aim of projecting a new system of lines connecting North China with Kirin and the Tumen river area, and also lines connecting North China with Tsitsihar and Aigun. In November, 1907, the Chinese Government entered into an agreement with Pauling and Company, a British firm, for the construction of a short section of the western system thus projected, the line to be built from Hsinmintun to Fakumen, this to run practically parallel with the South Manchuria Railway, to the west. [155] The construction of such a line, however, was opposed and frustrated by the Japanese Government which, in a series of official protests during 1907, asserted that the construction of such a line by a British firm was contrary to the provisions said to be contained in the "protocols" attached to the Sino-Japanese treaty of December 22, 1905. The Chinese Government replied with the statement that the Japanese declaration at that time that "Japan would do nothing to prevent China from any steps she might take in the future for the development of Manchuria" was interpreted as sufficient justification for the granting of the contract, especially in view of the fact that the Japanese Government had refused to permit a definition in terms of a specific

---

[154] See Chap. XVI, Sec. c.

[155] Hsü Shih-chang, *Collection of Documents concerning the Three Eastern Provinces* (*Tung San Sheng Cheng Lueh*, Chinese title), Book II, p. 46. Cited by Hsü Shu-hsi in *China and Her Political Entity*, p. 294.

Lord ffrench, who represented Pauling and Company, and J. O. P. Bland, who represented in China the British and Chinese Corporation, Ltd., "secured early in November a concession to finance and build the proposed extension from Hsinmintun forty-seven miles north to the town of Fakumen." Williard D. Straight, who was very familiar with these negotiations, wrote in his diary: "ffrench signed his contract today (November 8, 1907) at about 5 o'clock, and was as pleased as punch. It provides for 50 miles at £6,500 per mile, £20,000 to be devoted to stations, telephones, telegraphs and the like. He has a supplementary and secret arrangement for the completion of the sections from Tsinanfu ['Tsinanfu' apparently an error, perhaps for Hsinminfu] to Tsitsihar. Total 400 miles to be built as soon as possible. Money for the road probably to be secured from Bland." (Croly, Herbert, *Willard Straight*, p. 243.)

distance of what constituted a "parallel" line to the South Manchuria Railway.[156] But the Japanese opposition was sufficient to prevent the construction of the line by the British firm, the preliminary loan contract agreement for the same being permitted to lapse, to be absorbed later in the Chinchow-Aigun project. It seems that in February, 1908, the Japanese Government proposed that China should promise to extend the Hsinmintun-Fakumen railway to Tiehling or some other station on the South Manchuria Railway. China refusing this proposal suggested that the matter be submitted to the Hague Court of Arbitration, which proposal was in turn rejected by Japan. On September 4, 1909, in a Sino-Japanese agreement concerning mines and railways in Manchuria, the Japanese Government secured the promise (Article 1) from China that "the Government of China engages that in the event of its undertaking to construct a railway between Hsinmintun and Fakumen, it shall arrange previously with the Government of Japan." [157]

British interests were also involved in the Chinchow-Aigun railway project, since this project absorbed the interest of the British firm in the Hsinmintun-Fakumen proposal, but, as in the case of the Hsinmintun-Fakumen project, the British Government was disinclined to support their nationals in any claim which was interpreted by Japan, and by Russia, as contrary to certain interests of the latter two countries in Manchuria. Great Britain was at this time allied with Japan under the terms of the Anglo-Japanese Alliance of 1905, and was also mindful of the Anglo-Russian agreement of 1899 pertaining to railway construction north of the Great Wall.[158]

CHAPTER XXXI

The Position of the United States (1905-1915)

a. ANGLO-AMERICAN PROJECT FOR CHINCHOW-AIGUN RAILWAY, 1908-1910. During the years 1907, 1908 and 1909 a project

[156] Hsü Shih-chang, *op. cit.*, quoted by Hsü Shu-hsi, p. 295. The *North China Herald* (Shanghai) reported in its issue of April 10, 1909, that the Japanese Government refused to submit the Hsinmintun-Fakumen railway question to the Hague Court of Arbitration for settlement by arbitration. See Chap. XVI, Sec. c.

[157] Sino-Japanese *Agreement Concerning Mines and Railways in Manchuria,* September 4, 1909. MacMurray, Vol. I, p. 790.

[158] See Chap. XXXI, Sec. a, and Chap. XXXIII, Sec. a. The British Foreign Office refrained from supporting the claims of the British firm, Pauling and Company, principally because of the opposition of the Japanese and Russian Governments to the Hsinmintun-Fakumen railway project. (*British Parliamentary Debates,* March 3, 1908, Vol. 185, p. 527; *U. S. Foreign Relations,* 1910, p. 269.)

for the construction of a long Chinese Government railway between Chinchow (on the Peking-Shanhaikwan-Hsinmintun railway north of the port of Hulutao) and Aigun (on the right bank of the Amur river in Heilungkiang province) *via* Tsitsihar (adjoining the Chinese Eastern Railway) was being advanced for construction by joint American and British financial and railway groups. In fact, the plan was to absorb the interests of the British firm (Pauling and Co.) in the Hsinmintun-Fakumen project. The plan looked to the possible inclusion of Russian participation through the Russo-Asiatic Bank, but did not contemplate the inclusion of Japanese finance.[159] A preliminary agreement for the financing, construction and operation of this railway was signed on October 2, 1909, by the Viceroy of Manchuria and the representative of the American banking group and Pauling and Company, the British firm which was to be the actual contractor for the construction.[160] The preliminary agreement bound the Chinese Government (Article 1) "to borrow from the banks [i.e., J. P. Morgan and Co., Kuhn, Loeb and Co., The First National Bank, and The National City Bank of New York] the sum necessary to construct the railway from Chinchow to Aigun," with interest at 5 per cent., the loan to be guaranteed "by the Imperial Government" of China with the railway itself as security, the first bonds to be issued for the construction of the section from Chinchow to Tsitsihar. Construction was to be undertaken by the British firm, Pauling and Company (Article 4), with its own chief engineer, who was to be under the control of the Chinese Board of Communications and the company thus formed. On equal terms Chinese materials were to be given preference (Article 3). Operation was to be in the hands of the company under the control of the Board of Communications (Article 5). This preliminary agreement provided that only Chinese, American and British interests were to be permitted (Article 6) participation in the company, the Chinese to have majority interest in control.

Shortly thereafter (October 6, 1909) the representative of the American banking group signed with Pauling and Company the memorandum of an agreement to secure the investment of the American bankers who were to finance the undertaking. By virtue of this memorandum it was provided that the American bankers should be assured of $2\frac{1}{2}$ per cent., that at least one-half of the

[159] Croly, Herbert, *Willard Straight*, p. 307; *U. S. Foreign Relations*, 1910, p. 260.
[160] Anglo-American Group *Preliminary Agreement with China Providing for the Financing, Construction and Operation of the Chinchow-Aigun Railway*, October 2, 1909. MacMurray, Vol. I, p. 800.

materials purchased abroad for the line should come from the United States, and that American engineers should also be employed by Pauling and Company, the contractors.[161]

The outcome of the Chinchow-Aigun railway project has been treated in connection with the plan of Secretary Knox of the United States for the neutralization of the Manchurian railways.[162]   The preliminary agreement signed by the representative of the American banking group was neither final nor irrevocable on the part of either signatory, the representative of the American group not having been given full powers to conclude a final and irrevocable agreement.[163]   The agreement, however, received sanction by an imperial edict of China on January 20/21, 1910, and was not revoked by the Chinese Government.[164]

Although the preliminary agreement for the construction of the Chinchow-Aigun railway was never actually repudiated by the American bankers, the fulfillment of it was allowed to remain in abeyance. When the Japanese, through the Yokohama Specie Bank, in December, 1915, signed a contract with China for the construction of the Ssupingkai-Chengchiatun railway (traversing a portion of the route of the proposed Chinchow-Aigun project) the United States Government, on the representation of the American bankers, communicated to the Chinese Government, under date of October 13, 1916, a statement reserving the rights accruing to the American group which had signed the original contract for the construction of the Chinchow-Aigun railway, calling attention to the fact that the final agreement for the same had been signed by the Viceroy of Manchuria under authority from the Chinese Government on April 26, 1910, and that the original contract agreement had been ratified by the Chinese Government on January 20, 1910. A similar statement was sent to the Japanese Government through the Japanese Minister in Peking on January 3, 1917. The American Government likewise reserved the prior rights of the American financiers when the Russo-Asiatic Bank in 1916 signed the contract with China for the construction of the Harbin-Heihofu (Pin-Hei) railway which was projected to traverse the northern portion of the original Chinchow-Aigun route to the Amur river. In fact, however, the Chinese Government has considered the latter contract to have lapsed, and has granted to a private Chinese company the construction rights for the Hulan-Hailun railway which has now been built in great part, running

161 MacMurray, Vol. I, p. 802.
162 See Chap. XXIX, Sec. c.
163 Croly, pp. 305-306.
164 MacMurray, Vol. I, p. 802.

north and west from a point opposite Harbin on the Sungari river. The Ssupingkai-Chengchiatun line has been extended to Taonan and to Angangchi, opposite Tsitsihar, to connect with the main line of the Chinese Eastern Railway.[165]

b. AMERICAN TREATY RIGHTS AND INTERESTS IN MANCHURIA. During the period from 1905 to 1915 American interests in Manchuria, aside from those connected with ordinary commercial transactions in the Manchurian market, and those involved in the Chinchow-Aigun railway project, were concerned mainly with a general endeavor to secure the further application of the "open door" policy as enunciated and developed following 1898.[166] In 1908 the United States entered into the Root-Takahira agreement with Japan which, besides recognizing the *"status quo"* in their "outlying insular possessions in the region of the Pacific Ocean" and in "the Far East," committed the two signatories again to support by pacific means "the independence and integrity of China and the principle of equal opportunity for commerce and industry of all nations in that Empire." [167] The principle of the "open door," as shown above, was likewise involved in the Knox plan for the neutralization of the Manchurian railways which failed of support by the other powers, especially by Japan and Russia. The Chinchow-Aigun railway project, closely associated with the Knox plan itself, looked to the inclusion of British, and perhaps Russian finance, but apparently not Japanese.[168] Later, following the outbreak of the Great War, the Department of State, like the British Foreign Office, sought to circumscribe the area of hostilities in the Far East, thus to preserve the territorial integrity of China.[169]

[165] For the reservation of American rights in the Chinchow-Aigun railway project see *U. S. Foreign Relations,* 1917, pp. 168-169. See also Chap. XXXIX, Sec. b, for the Japanese contract for the Ssupingkai-Chengchiatun railway (1915), and Chap. XLIII, Sec. b, for the Russo-Asiatic bank contract for the Pin-Hei railway (1916).

[166] See Chap. XXXI, Sec. a, and Chap. XXXIV, Sec. a.

[167] See Chap. XXXIV, Sec. a.

[168] See Chap. XXXI, Sec. a.

[169] See Chap. XXXVIII, Sec. a.

D. TREATIES AND AGREEMENTS OF ALLIANCE, COOPERATION AND GUARANTEE: 1905-1915

CHAPTER XXXII

Sino-Japanese Agreements (1905-1915)

a. SINO-JAPANESE AGREEMENTS ESTABLISHING JAPANESE TREATY RIGHTS IN MANCHURIA. The governments of Japan and China entered into no treaties of alliance or cooperation with reference to Manchuria during this period from 1905 to 1915. The bilateral arrangements signed by the two countries concerned themselves almost exclusively with the subject of Japanese treaty rights pertaining to railways in Manchuria, including the treaty and additional agreement of Peking of 1905 validating the transfer of the Kwantung leased territory (Liaotung) and the South Manchuria Railway to Japan, and subsequent treaties, conventions and agreements which were related, in the main, to the right of the Japanese to have prior consideration in the matter of constructing new railways in Manchuria.[170]

CHAPTER XXXIII

Anglo-Japanese Treaties of Alliance and Guarantee (1905-1915)

a. THE SECOND ANGLO-JAPANESE ALLIANCE, 1905. The first Anglo-Japanese treaty of alliance of January 30, 1902, was to terminate five years from the date of signature.[171] Before its expiration the governments of Japan and Great Britain renewed the alliance and included in the treaty, signed on August 12, 1905, while the Russo-Japanese war was still in progress, several provisions differing from the first treaty of alliance.[172] The treaty had for its declared object (Preamble), besides the maintenance of the general peace of the Far East, "the preservation of the common interests of all Powers in China by insuring the independence and integrity of the Chinese Empire and the principle of

170 See Chaps. XVI, and XIX to XXII inclusive.
171 See Chap. XIII, Sec. a.
172 Anglo-Japanese *Treaty of Alliance*, August 12, 1905. MacMurray, Vol. I, p. 516.

equal opportunities for the commerce and industry of all nations in China" and "the maintenance of the territorial rights" of the contracting parties in Eastern Asia and India, together with "the defence of their special interests in the said regions." This declaration was not, however, in the treaty proper, but in the preamble. To secure these ends Japan and Great Britain agreed to take common measures in their defence, in case of unprovoked attack "on the part of any other Power or Powers" (Article 2), each to come to the aid of the ally. Great Britain recognized the "paramount political, military, and economic interests" of Japan in Korea and the right of Japan "to take such measures of guidance, control, and protection in Corea [Korea] as she may deem proper and necessary to safeguard and advance those interests," to be commensurate, however, with the maintenance of equal opportunities for commerce and industry. Japan, in turn, recognized (Article 4) similar rights for Great Britain in India, particularly to the end of protecting the frontier. Great Britain agreed (Article 6) that she would maintain neutrality in the Russo-Japanese war then waging, unless some other power or powers should join in hostilities against Japan. The agreement made no specific mention of Manchuria. The treaty was to come into effect on signature and remain in force for ten years.[173]

b. THE THIRD ANGLO-JAPANESE ALLIANCE, 1911. The declared purpose of the third Anglo-Japanese treaty of alliance of July 13, 1911, was not dissimilar to that contained in the preamble to the second alliance.[174] Nor were the provisions of the treaty dissimilar to those of the treaty of 1905, except for the exclusion of the sections dealing with Korea (Korea having been annexed to Japan as Chosen in 1910), and except for the fact that (Article 4) neither country had any obligation to go to war against the power with whom it had entered into a treaty of arbitration.[175] The body of the treaty, however, contained no clause guaranteeing the territorial or administrative integrity of China or undertaking to maintain equality of opportunity for the commerce and industry of all nations, the same being, however, a declared object as stated in the preamble. The treaty provided (Article 1) that in case the

[173] See Chap. XXXVI, Sec. a, for Franco-Japanese agreement of 1907.

[174] Anglo-Japanese *Treaty of Alliance*, July 13, 1911. MacMurray, Vol. I, p. 900. For a complete account of the negotiations see: *British Documents on the Origins of the Great War*, 1898-1914, Vol. IV, Chap. 24, pp. 120 ff.

[175] It was anticipated by the parties to the treaty of alliance that a treaty of arbitration would be signed and ratified between Great Britain and the United States contemporaneously. Such a treaty of arbitration, however, was not finally concluded at the time.

rights and interests of either power were in jeopardy the two would come to an understanding as to what action should be taking mutually to safeguard them, and that (Article 2) "if by reason of an unprovoked attack or aggressive action, wherever arising, on the part of any Power or Powers," either party should be involved in "a war in defence of its territorial rights or special interests mentioned in the preamble," then the other would "at once come to the assistance of its ally." The treaty came into effect on signature, to remain in force for ten years.[176]

CHAPTER XXXIV

American-Japanese Agreement of 1908

a. THE ROOT-TAKAHIRA AGREEMENT OF 1908. On November 30, 1908, the United States and Japan, through Elihu Root, American Secretary of State, and K. Takahira, Japanese Ambassador at Washington, entered into an agreement through an exchange of notes which is generally known as the Root-Takahira agreement.[177] The Japanese Government in its note declared that the two governments were "animated by a common aim, policy, and intention" in the region of the Pacific Ocean, and that, therefore, that government asserted that (Article 2) "the policy of both Governments, uninfluenced by any aggressive tendencies, is directed to the maintenance of the existing status quo in the region above mentioned and to the defense of the principle of equal opportunity for commerce and industry in China." The Japanese note continued (Article 3) to say that "they are accordingly firmly resolved reciprocally to respect the territorial possessions belonging to each other in said region," and (Article 4) that "they are also determined to preserve the common interest of all powers in China by supporting by all pacific means at their disposal the independence and integrity of China and the principle of equal opportunity for commerce and industry of all nations in that Empire." The Japanese statement further (Article 5) asserted that "should any event occur threatening the status quo as above described or the principle of equal opportunity as above defined, it remains for the two Gov-

[176] The Anglo-Japanese treaty of alliance of 1911 was terminated by Article 4 of the Four Power Treaty of December 13, 1921, signed at the Washington Conference. See Chap. LVI, Sec. a.
[177] American-Japanese *Exchange of Notes Declaring Their Policy in the Far East*, November 30, 1908. MacMurray, Vol. I, p. 769.

ernments to communicate with each other in order to arrive at an understanding as to what measures they may consider it useful to take." A confirmation of this "common aim, policy, and intention" with respect to "the region of the Pacific" was given in the American reply.[178] The articles of agreement were repeated from the Japanese note indicating an identical attitude and commitment toward the same. Both countries, therefore, undertook to reaffirm their adherence to the policy of preserving the territorial and administrative integrity of China and of maintaining equality of opportunity for commerce and industry in China. It was, additionally, a guarantee of the *status quo* in the Pacific region.[179]

CHAPTER XXXV

Russo-Japanese Treaties and Agreements (1905-1915)

a. RUSSO-JAPANESE CONVENTION AND TREATY OF 1907. Prefatory to a detailed epitome and analysis of the specific Russo-Japanese diplomatic agreements of this period it may be said in summary that on three distinct occasions, namely, in 1907, in 1910 and in 1912, the Russian and Japanese Governments entered into bilateral agreements which were directed especially to their interests in Manchuria and Mongolia. The publication during 1918-1921 of the secret Russo-Japanese treaty of alliance of 1916 served to establish that, attached to the published political conventions of 1907 and 1910, there were contemporaneously signed by the two governments two separate secret treaties of cooperation and guarantee which undertook additionally to define in specific terms the respective "spheres of interest" of Russia and Japan in Manchuria. Also in 1921 there was published a version of the Russo-Japanese secret treaty of 1912 with respect to Mongolia and Manchuria.

Russo-Japanese Convention of 1907. Shortly after the conclusion of the Franco-Japanese agreement of June 10, 1907, for the declared purpose of preserving the peace in the Chinese Empire and in Asia generally, the governments of Russia and Japan entered into a political convention, dated July 30, 1907, by virtue of which they agreed (Article 1) mutually to respect the "actual territorial integrity of the other, and all the rights due now both

---

[178] MacMurray, Vol. I, p. 770.
[179] See Chap. XLVII, Sec. a, for the so-called Lansing-Ishii agreement of 1917.

parties by virtue of treaties, conventions and contracts now in force between them and China" in so far as these rights were not incompatible with "the principle of equal opportunity." Both countries agreed (Article 2) to recognize "the independence and territorial integrity of the Empire of China and the principle of equal opportunity for the commerce and industry of all nations in that Empire, and engage to uphold and support the maintenance of the *status quo* and respect for the said principle by all pacific means at their disposal." [180]

Russo-Japanese Secret Treaty of 1907. Simultaneously the Japanese and Russian Governments negotiated and signed a separate treaty supplementary to the open convention, it being specifically enjoined that the terms should not be published. No official version of this secret treaty has as yet been published by authority of the Japanese Government though the fact of the existence of such a treaty seems well established in consequence of the subsequent publication of the Russo-Japanese secret treaty of 1910 and of that of 1916 both of which refer specifically to the "secret treaty" of July 17/30, 1907. The exact terms of this secret treaty of 1907, however, have not been disclosed in complete detail, though it is known that the treaty contained supplementary articles as well as the treaty proper, the combined arrangement being of such a character as to define more specifically the respective interests of the two powers in Manchuria. "Japan promised not to seek railway or telegraph concessions north of a line approximate to the course of the River Nonni as it flowed east, and Russia, on the other hand, agreed to refrain from seeking railway or telegraph concessions south of that line." [181] The secret treaty appears to have contained a mutual recognition of the respective "spheres of interest" of the two powers in Manchuria, in addition to including a recognition of Japan's special interests in Korea and certain interests of Russia in Mongolia.

[180] *U. S. Foreign Relations,* 1907, Pt. II, p. 765 (official English translation handed to the U. S. Department of State by the Japanese Embassy at Washington, August 14, 1907); also printed in MacMurray, Vol. I, p. 657, being a slightly different translation, but identical in substance.

[181] Quoted from Dennis, A. L. P., *The Anglo-Japanese Alliance,* p. 28. But Dr. Dennis does not quote his source. The existence of this secret Russo-Japanese treaty of July 17/30, 1907, seems to have been well established, especially through the subsequent publication of the text of the draft treaty of July 4, 1910, by Captain George Abel Schreiner, correspondent of the Associated Press during the Great War, and Count B. de Siebert, formerly Secretary of the Imperial Embassy of Russia at London and Washington, their volume being titled: *Entente Diplomacy and the World: Matrix of the History of Europe,* 1909-1914 (p. 17). For detailed attention to the authenticity and texts of this secret Russo-Japanese treaty of 1907, and to those of 1910, 1912 and 1916 see Appendices C and D.

b. RUSSO-JAPANESE CONVENTION AND TREATY OF 1910. Following the disapproval in January, 1910, of the American plan for neutralization of the Manchurian railways the two countries especially opposed to that plan and to the Chinchow-Aigun railway project, i.e., Japan and Russia, entered into the second of the open political conventions negotiated between them since the treaty of Portsmouth. This Russo-Japanese convention in regard to Manchuria, dated July 4, 1910, provided (Article 1) that the contracting parties would "lend each other their friendly cooperation with a view to the amelioration [development?] of their respective railway lines in Manchuria and the improvement of the connecting service at the junctions of the said railways and to refrain from any competition inimical to the accomplishment of that purpose." [182] They agreed (Article 2) "to maintain and respect the *status quo* in Manchuria as resulting from all the treaties, conventions, or other arrangements concluded up to this date either between Russia and Japan or between those two powers and China." This political convention was designed to further that of 1907 and went farther by (Article 3) adding that "should any event arise likely to threaten the above-mentioned *status quo* the two high contracting parties will in every case open communications between themselves so as, to agree upon such measures as they may deem necessary to take for the maintenance of the said *status quo.*" Thus the open convention did little more than guarantee the *status quo*. The secret treaty of the same date went farther, however, by renewing the secret treaty of 1907 and including new provisions.

Russo-Japanese Secret Treaty of 1910. Accompanying this open political convention of July 4, 1910, was a more important document simultaneously signed with the injunction (Article 6) that it was to be kept "strictly secret by both Governments." Because of the special importance of this secret treaty between Japan and Russia and its bearing on an adequate interpretation of the events of the period respecting Manchuria it has been deemed wise to include here the entire text as given in the Russian draft of the treaty conveyed through the Russian Ambassador at London to the British Foreign Minister (Sir Edward Grey):

"To confirm and further develop the provisions of the Secret Treaty of June 17/30, 1907, the Russian and Japanese Governments agree to the following provisions:

[182] *U. S. Foreign Relations,* 1910, p. 835 (official English translation handed to the U. S. Department of State by the Russian Ambassador at Washington, June 28/July 11, 1910); also printed in MacMurray, Vol. I, p. 803.

"Article 1. Russia and Japan recognize, as the boundary of their specific spheres of interest in Manchuria, the line of demarcation as defined in the supplementary article to the Secret Treaty of 1907.

"Article 2. The two contracting parties agree mutually to recognize their special interests in the areas set forth below. Each of them may also, each within its own sphere of interest, take such measures as shall be deemed necessary for the maintenance and protection of these interests.

"Article 3. Each party undertakes to place no obstacle of any kind in the way of the confirmation and future development of the special interests of the other party within the boundary lines of such spheres of interest.

"Article 4. Each of the contracting parties undertakes to refrain from all political action within the sphere of interest of the other party in Manchuria. Furthermore, it has been decided that Russia shall seek no privileges or concessions in the Japanese zone, and Japan none in the Russian zone, that might be injurious to the special interests of either party, and that both Governments are to recognize the rights acquired in their spheres of interest, as defined in Article 2 of the Public Treaty of to-day's date.

"Article 5. To ensure the working of the mutual stipulations, both parties will enter into an open and friendly exchange of opinion on all matters concerning their special interests in Manchuria. In case these special interests should be threatened, the two Governments will agree on the measures that may become necessary for common action or mutual support in order to protect these interests.

"Article 6. The present Treaty will be kept strictly secret by both Governments." [183]

c. RUSSO-JAPANESE SECRET TREATY REGARDING MONGOLIA AND MANCHURIA, 1912. Following the overthrow of the Manchu dynasty in China and the establishment of the Chinese Republic under Yuan Shih-k'ai as president, the question of recognition of the republic and of the government of President Yuan confronted the powers, that is, especially during the early months of 1912. The change of government in Peking made it apparent that certain of the foreign powers concerned would use the opportunity to attempt to settle outstanding issues with China. The interests of Russia were divided between Mongolia and Manchuria. In response to a desire of the Russian Foreign Minister (M. Sazonov) to arrive at an understanding with Japan with respect to the interests of Russia in Mongolia and Manchuria, the governments of the two countries signed on June 25, 1912, a secret treaty

[183] *Draft Text of the Secret Russo-Japanese Treaty of July 4, 1910.* Siebert and Schreiner, *op. cit.,* p. 17. See Appendix C for various texts of this secret treaty and for the authentication and characterization of the same.

with respect to their mutual interests.[184] The preamble declared that the purpose of the secret treaty was "to determine more exactly and to complete the provisions of the Secret Treaties of July 17/30, 1907, and June 21/July 1 [July 4], 1910, and to prevent the possibility of any misunderstanding with regard to their special interests in Manchuria and Mongolia." Except for the confirmation contained in the treaty of the respective "spheres of interest" of Japan and Russia in Manchuria (as provided in the secret treaty of 1907), the treaty related in the main to Inner and Outer Mongolia. Inner Mongolia was divided (Article 2) into two distinct parts, roughly by a meridial line running north from Peking, that portion thus falling to the east and adjoining Manchuria being recognized as an area in which Japan had "special interests." [185]

CHAPTER XXXVI

Franco-Japanese Agreement of 1907

a. FRANCO-JAPANESE AGREEMENT RELATING TO CHINA, 1907. After the Japanese Government had entered into the Anglo-Japanese treaty of alliance of 1905, and about the same time as a political convention with Russia was negotiated, the Japanese Government entered into a general agreement with the French Government, dated June 10, 1907, which pertained to the maintenance of their positions and interests in China.[186] By this arrangement Japan and France undertook "to respect the independence and integrity of China, as well as the principle of equal treatment in that country for the commerce and subjects or citizens [ressortissants, those subject to jurisdiction] of all nations." They declared that inasmuch as they both had "a special interest in having order and a pacific state of things guaranteed especially in the regions of the Chinese Empire adjacent to the territories where they have the rights of sovereignty, protection or occupation" they engaged "to support each other for assuring the peace and security in those regions, with a view to maintaining the respective situa-

[184] *Draft Text of the Secret Russo-Japanese Treaty of 1912* with respect to Manchuria and Mongolia. Siebert and Schreiner, *op. cit.*, pp. 39-40. See Appendix C for the statements of M. Sazonov, Russian Foreign Secretary, authenticating this document.
[185] As in the case of the secret treaties of 1907 and 1910 the governments of France and Great Britain were alone informed of the existence of this secret treaty of 1912. (Siebert and Schreiner, p. 39.) See Chap. XLVI, Secs. a and b, for the Russo-Japanese convention and secret treaty of 1916.
[186] Franco-Japanese *Agreement in regard to China and the Continent of Asia,* June 10, 1907. MacMurray, Vol. I, p. 640.

tion and the territorial rights of the two High Contracting Parties in the Continent of Asia." [187]

CHAPTER XXXVII

Commitments of the Powers to the "Open Door" in Manchuria (1905-1915)

a. SUMMARY STATEMENT OF COMMITMENTS TO THE "OPEN DOOR" POLICY. During the period from 1895 to 1905 each of the principal powers having interests in Manchuria, including the United States, Great Britain, Germany, France, Russia and Japan, declared themselves by various means as committed to the policy of guaranteeing equality of opportunity for commerce and industry in China and to that of maintaining the territorial and administrative integrity, or at least the "sovereignty," of China. [188] During the period which followed there was no new and different interpretation by the United States of the "open door" policy as applied to China. In the absence of specific denunciations of the former commitments of the powers, therefore, it follows that the "open door" as enunciated in 1899 and following by the United States, to which the powers had adhered, was approved and binding upon the powers following the treaty of Portsmouth.

The commitments of the powers during 1905 to 1915 to the policy of guaranteeing equality of opportunity for commerce and industry in Manchuria and to the policy of maintaining the territorial and administrative integrity of China in Manchuria were numerous and definite on the part of all the principal powers concerned, including Japan, Russia, France, Great Britain and the United States. These commitments have been considered in some detail in the foregoing sections, but it may be serviceable to summarize the commitments of the powers most concerned with Manchurian diplomacy at this time. The Russian commitments were included in the treaty of Portsmouth (1905) and in the political convention of 1907 with Japan. The Japanese commitments were included in the treaty of Portsmouth (1905), the political convention of 1907 with Russia, and the exchange of notes with the

[187] See Chap. XXXIII, Sec. a, for the Anglo-Japanese treaty of alliance of 1905; Chap. XXXIV, Sec. a, for the Root-Takahira agreement of 1908; Chap. XXXV, Sec. a, for the Russo-Japanese convention and treaty of 1907.

[188] See Chap. XV, Sec. c, for original commitments of the powers to the policy of the "open door" with respect to China, including Manchuria; Chap. XLIX, Sec. a, for a summary statement of the commitments of the powers to the "open door" policy during 1915-1921.

United States in 1908. Japan, moreover, declared in the preambles to the Anglo-Japanese treaties of alliance of 1905 and 1911 (as did Great Britain), that one of the purposes of the alliances was to insure "the independence and integrity of the Chinese Empire and the principle of equal opportunities for the commerce and industry of all nations in China." The United States with Japan in the Root-Takahira agreement of 1908 undertook to observe the same principles. If, however, a guarantee of the *status quo* in an international agreement which binds the signatories to observe the "open door" policy is tantamount to a recognition of all existing treaty rights, then it must be obvious that the recognition of these treaty rights operates to qualify the general statement of diplomatic policy. Treaty rights, however valid *per se*, may be in derogation of a previous or contemporaneous commitment to observe the "open door."

PART III
THE THIRD PERIOD: 1915-1921

CONTENTS

PART III. THE THIRD PERIOD: 1915-1921

SUMMARY OF THE THIRD PERIOD

THE Russian period of paramount influence in Manchuria ended in 1905 with the treaty of Portsmouth. During the period that followed until 1915 Japan laid the foundation in Manchuria for her position which was then strengthened by the Sino-Japanese treaty and exchanges of notes of 1915 with respect to South Manchuria and Eastern Inner Mongolia. The far-reaching effect of this treaty and exchanges of notes of 1915 upon the international relations of Manchuria is obvious from the fact that the Japanese lease of the Kwantung leased territory was extended, along with Japanese control of the South Manchuria and Antung-Mukden railways, to ninety-nine years. Japanese policy, thereafter, was closely related to the further extension of their interests, especially with respect to railway building in Manchuria, several railway loan contracts being negotiated from 1915 to 1921 on the basis of the preliminary agreements signed with China during the period after 1905. The Japanese Government, during the period of political unsettlement in the Russian Far East following the Russian Revolution, made a definite effort to extend their influence over the Chinese Eastern Railway, but participated with the Allied powers in the multi-power intervention in Siberia and in supervision of the Trans-Siberian and Chinese Eastern Railway systems. The development of Japanese interests in the form of recognition given by Russia in the bilateral treaties and agreements of 1907, 1910 and 1912, continued in the further recognition by Russia of Japan's "special interests" in Inner Mongolia in 1916. Japan sought, through the so-called Lansing-Ishii agreement of November 2, 1917, and in the attempt during the negotiations preceding the signing of the China consortium agreement of 1920, to secure a recognition on the part of the United States and Great Britain, particularly, of her claim to "special interests" which would be of a kind to insure for Japan a general superiority of position in such matters as future railway construction in Manchuria, if not political preponderance.

But the period from 1915 to 1921 saw the development of a

new and more vital interest of Great Britain and the United States
in Manchuria than had been characteristic of the period before
1915 when private and independent British and American financial
companies and banks had sought to finance the construction of
the Hsinmintun-Fakumen and Chinchow-Aigun railway projects.
This new and more vital interest was that which was expressed
through the formation of the international banking consortium in
1918 and following, as perfected in the China consortium agreement of 1920, which body of international bankers representing
the United States, Great Britain and France (in addition to
Japan) successfully opposed the attempt of the Japanese financiers
and the Japanese Government to exclude Manchuria from the
scope of operations of the consortium. In the diplomatic correspondence between the foreign offices of Japan, on the one hand,
and of Great Britain and the United States, on the other, which
characterized the relations of the powers to Manchuria at the very
time when the powers were cooperating in Inter-allied intervention in Siberia and in supervision of the management of the Chinese
Railway, more realism may be found with respect to the policies
of the powers with respect to Manchuria than in the general
phraseology of such documents, for example, as the so-called
Lansing-Ishii agreement. This correspondence shows clearly that
Japan sought first to exclude South Manchuria and Eastern Inner
Mongolia entirely from the scope of operations of the international
banking consortium. Failing this, the Japanese Government sought
to obtain a recognition of their "special rights and interests" in
these regions by reserving, first, the right to take such steps in
these regions as they saw fit to safeguard their national welfare,
political and economic. Failing the acceptance by Great Britain
and the United States of the Japanese formula which sought to
reserve the right to veto all loans prejudicing Japan's national
welfare as she defined it, the Japanese Government withdrew the
proposed formula on condition that the powers reaffirm the general
assurances given previously that they (Great Britain and the United
States) would not countenance any operations on the part of
their bankers, members of the consortium, which would be actually
prejudicial to the national defence and economic welfare of Japan
as an independent state. Such assurance was given by Great
Britain and the United States in general terms. Having secured
this assurance the Japanese Government sought to obtain the right
to veto the construction of any railway which would connect the
proposed Taonanfu-Jehol railway with the Chinese Eastern Rail-

way in North Manchuria, i.e., the right to veto the construction by the consortium of a railway which would traverse generally the same route as that projected for the Chinchow-Aigun railway, which during 1909 and 1910 had been successfully opposed by Russia and Japan. The British Government (and similarly the United States) declared that they could not adhere to the proposed reservation that the Japanese Government be given the right to veto the construction of such a railway which did not appear to be prejudicial to the national welfare or economic existence of Japan. The Japanese Government then waived this specific request for a reservation with respect to the line to the Chinese Eastern Railway, relying on the general assurances of Great Britain and the United States that they would countenance no activity on the part of their bankers prejudicial to the economic life and national defence of Japan. Japan failed entirely to secure a reservation to exclude the Taonanfu-Jehol railway and the branch line to the seacoast from the scope of operations of the consortium. The British Government, in particular, in spite of the existence of the Anglo-Japanese alliance (which was referred to in the diplomatic correspondence), opposed the granting of reservations of particular regions from the consortium's operations on the ground that such would amount to the development, if not the actual sanction, of "spheres of interest" in particular parts of China. Especially did the British Government contest the view that Japan had any just claim to "special interests" in Eastern Inner Mongolia. The consortium negotiations, however, secured for Japan a definite recognition of the exclusion from the consortium's operations of the South Manchuria Railway and its then present branches, and of the proposed Kirin-Huining, Chengchiatun-Taonanfu, Changchun-Taonanfu, and Kaiyuan-Kirin railways, and of the lines in operation including the Kirin-Changchun, Hsinminfu-Mukden and Ssupingkai-Chengchiatun railways. Moreover, the international banking consortium was not to interfere with the "vested proprietary rights" in Manchuria, in railways and mines, nor effect the operation of the options granted, as indicated above, for the specific lines designated.

The diplomatic negotiations, therefore, which preceded the signing, without textual reservations, of the China consortium agreement of 1920, were of a character to give a practical interpretation of the "special interests" which the United States recognized Japan to possess in Manchuria under the terms of the so-called Lansing-Ishii agreement which had been signed on November

2, 1917. In this exchange of notes, which did not have the status of a formal treaty, the United States had given formal recognition to the principle, declared contemporaneously by way of interpretation to the Chinese Government, that Japan actually possessed, by virtue of geographical propinquity, certain special advantages which universally follow from proximity. The Washington Conference which followed, during the next period to be studied, by virtue of the nine power treaty concerning principles and policies to be followed in matters concerning China, secured the adoption of certain treaty provisions, signed by Japan along with the United States, which in their intrinsic character gave a new orientation to the declared policies of the powers with respect to Manchuria. The Lansing-Ishii agreement was formally terminated by an exchange of notes on April 14, 1923.

Except for the negotiations of the Russo-Asiatic Bank contract for the construction of the Harbin-Heihofu (on the Amur river) railway in 1916, the Russian Government made few efforts to secure further railway or industrial concessions in Manchuria during the period from 1915 to 1921. The fact of the Russian Revolution and the consequent disorder resulting from the rivalries between "Red" and "White" Russian forces in the Russian Far East and in Manchuria operated to prevent the Russian Government from presenting a strong front to the Chinese Government and to the powers concerning Manchurian questions. The year 1917, therefore, marked the beginning of the decline of Russian influence in North Manchuria, particularly also of the Russian control of the Chinese Eastern Railway. Chinese participation in control was admitted in the Russo-Asiatic Bank agreement of 1920 with respect to the Chinese Eastern Railway, and the years which have followed, except for temporary reassertion of authority, have seen the gradual assumption by the Chinese Government (usually exercised by the Chinese faction in power in Mukden) of certain of the functions which once were exercised exclusively by the Russian administration of the railway.

To revert, then, to the Japanese position in Manchuria from 1915 to 1921, it is evident that the preoccupation of the powers in the Great War and the incapacitation of Russian diplomacy during the war and immediately thereafter gave Japan an opportunity for building on the foundation of Sino-Japanese treaties and agreements made during the period from 1905 to 1915. The Sino-Japanese treaty and exchanges of notes of May, 1915, in a manner relaid that foundation by extending the lease of the Kwantung territory, which would otherwise have expired in 1923, to 1997, an entire period of ninety-nine years. Likewise, the railway rights of Japan in Manchuria were strengthened by the extension of the term for Japanese control of the South Manchuria Railway to 2002, and of the Antung-Mukden railway to 2007. Further treaty provisions and commitments of China in the exchanges of notes of the same date gave Japan certain jurisdictional rights not theretofore possessed, and additionally the right in principle to Japanese subjects to lease land in South Manchuria and Eastern Inner Mongolia, as well as the right to secure a fundamental revision of the Kirin-Changchun loan agreements between China and Japan, the right to develop certain coal and iron mines in Kirin and Fengtien provinces, the right to have Japanese advisers employed if foreign advisers were to be appointed by the Chinese Government, and the right to be first consulted for a loan in any case where the Chinese Government proposed to build with foreign capital any railway in South Manchuria and Eastern Inner Mongolia. This latter preferential right, as we have noted above, was successfully contested by the powers concerned in the international banking consortium with respect to certain railways in western Manchuria and Eastern Inner Mongolia. Building on this new foundation, as it were, the Japanese Government, operating through the South Manchuria Railway Company, a government institution, secured the right to construct, or to finance the construction of, several railways in Manchuria, including the Ssupingkai-Chengchiatun railway and its extension lines, the Kirin-Huining railway, and those included in the "Four Manchurian and Mongolian Railways" loan agreement of 1918, certain of these latter lines being the ones in question in the international banking consortium negotiations of 1918 to 1920. Beyond the jurisdictional rights granted to Japan under the terms of the Sino-Japanese treaty and notes of 1915 no further important provisions were conceded Japan by China with respect to increased administrative or civil and criminal jurisdictional rights in Manchuria.

Of the bilateral treaties of alliance, cooperation and guarantee signed by the powers during this period with special bearing on Manchuria the following are the more important: (1) the Russo-Japanese political convention and secret treaty of 1916 respecting the "spheres of interest" of Japan and Russia in Mongolia and Manchuria; (2) the so-called Lansing-Ishii agreement of 1917 between the United States and Japan; and (3) the Sino-Japanese agreements of 1918 of military alliance and cooperation, which related in part to the question of control of the Chinese Eastern Railway.

During this period, as formerly, the commitments of the several powers to the policy of preserving the territorial and administrative integrity of China and of maintaining in China, including Manchuria as a part of China, complete equality of opportunity for commerce and industry of the nationals of all countries, were both numerous and specific. When the United States called to the attention of Japan and Russia that the Russo-Japanese political convention of 1916 did not contain textually a reassertion of the principle of the "open door," both powers replied to the Department of State that the recognition of that policy by each of them was to be taken for granted. The year before, the United States had declared that the American Government "cannot recognize any agreement or undertaking which has been entered into or which may be entered into between the Governments of Japan and China, impairing the treaty rights of the United States and its citizens in China, the political or territorial integrity of the Republic of China, or the international policy relative to China commonly known as the open door policy." Moreover, the so-called Lansing-Ishii agreement in specific terms bound the United States and Japan to observe the policy of preserving "the independence or territorial integrity of China," and the signatories declared that "they always adhere to the principle of the so-called 'Open Door' or equal opportunity for commerce and industry in China."

But the same period saw the development of claims on the part of Japan, particularly, and less articulately on the part of Russia, to "special interests" in defined parts of Manchuria, "special interests" which, as asserted in practice by Japan, were not synonymous with those recognized by the United States. Russia and Japan mutually agreed to respect the "spheres of interest" defined in their former treaties and conventions with respect to Manchuria. Both, as early as 1912, through the reservations of their banking groups at Paris, had sought to exclude the "Six Power Consortium" from loan operations in Manchuria asserted to be prejudicial to their respective interests. The same conflict between the general adherences to the policy of the "open door" and the policy as expressed in exclusive and prior rights to finance the construction of railways in Manchuria appeared again during this period. The Japanese Government, in the negotiations preceding the signing by the banking groups of the China consortium agreement of 1920, secured a definite recognition of their "vested proprietary rights," as well as of prior rights to finance the construction of certain railways in Manchuria. Practical considerations, such as the obvious primacy possessed by one or more powers in control of arterial railways and in possession of semi-government financing mediums and steamship transportation facilities, operated during the period from 1915 to 1921 to give special advantages to the nationals of Japan, though not in apparent violation of the letter of the commitments to the "open door" policy.

A. THE POSITION OF JAPAN: 1915-1921

CHAPTER XXXVIII

Manchuria and the Sino-Japanese Treaty and Notes of 1915

a. SINO-JAPANESE TREATY AND NOTES OF 1915 REGARDING SOUTH MANCHURIA. Japan entered the war against Germany by formal declaration on August 23, 1914, following the despatch of an ultimatum to Germany on August 15 demanding the delivery into Japanese hands of the Kiaochow leased territory in Shantung province "with a view to eventual restoration of the same to China." China, however, did not enter the war until after the entrance of the United States by declaration on April 6, 1917, China having severed diplomatic relations with Germany, however, on March 14, 1917. China's actual declaration of war was made by presidential proclamation on August 14, 1917. In the meantime, i.e., on November 7, 1914, Tsingtao in the Kiaochow leased territory had capitulated to the Japanese.

From January to May, 1915, the Japanese Minister in Peking carried on negotiations with the Chinese Government looking toward the acceptance on the part of China of five groups of demands, commonly known as the "Twenty-one Demands." Both the Chinese and Japanese texts of these proposals submitted by the Japanese Government indicate the far-reaching character of the provisions which the Japanese Government sought to have written into treaty form to strengthen the Japanese position in Shantung province, in the Yangtze valley, in South Manchuria and Eastern Inner Mongolia, and in connection with the Chinese Government in Peking generally.[1] Of the five groups of demands only Group II related particularly to South Manchuria and Eastern Inner Mongolia, this group containing five articles which were, in the main, included in the treaty of May 25, 1915 (and the exchanges of notes of the same date), though with some exceptions, as in the case of the demand, successfully opposed by China, to permit

[1] *The Sino-Japanese Negotiations of 1915*, pp. 2-8. (Carnegie Endowment for International Peace, Washington, 1921.) This publication gives the official English translations of the Japanese and Chinese versions of the various documents attending the negotiations which eventuated in the Sino-Japanese treaties and exchanges of notes of May 25, 1915.

136

Japanese to *own* (in addition to *lease*) land in South Manchuria and Eastern Inner Mongolia, and the original demands of Japan for the employment of Japanese advisers in these regions, as well as the demand for the right of the Japanese Government to exercise a preliminary veto on the construction of railways by foreign nationals in these same areas.[2] Before the delivery of the Japanese ultimatum, which required that the Chinese Government accept the terms of the "Twenty-one Demands" as modified in the twenty-five conferences which had been held, China had consented to several of the demands with respect to South Manchuria and Inner Mongolia. China, however, opposed joint administration of the police in South Manchuria, the right of Japanese to *own* (in addition to *lease*) land in South Manchuria and Inner Mongolia, several jurisdictional rights which Japan desired in these areas, and the unqualified right to lease the Kirin-Changchun railway to Japan for a period of ninety-nine years.[3]

In the treaty and exchanges of notes of May 25, 1915, the more important of the provisions sought by the Japanese Government with respect to South Manchuria and Inner Mongolia were acquired. Slight discrepancies appear between the English translations of the Chinese and Japanese texts of the treaty, though in the main they are identical in substance. The Japanese text is somewhat more complete and, therefore, has been used as the basis for analysis which follows. This treaty itself, which was signed by the President of China but not ratified by Parliament, contained eight principal articles which may be epitomized as follows:

Article 1. China consents to extend the term of the lease of Port Arthur and Dairen (used for Kwantung leased territory), and the term of the Japanese possession of the South Manchuria Railway, as well as the Antung-Mukden railway, to ninety-nine years respectively. (The exchanges of notes of the same date fixed the following dates as the definite time for the expiration of these rights: The Leased Territory, 1997; the South Manchuria Railway, 2002; and the Antung-Mukden railway, 2007.)

Article 2. "The subjects of Japan shall be permitted in South Manchuria to lease land necessary either for erecting buildings for various commercial and industrial uses or for agricultural purposes." (The Chinese text says that Japanese subjects "may, by negotiations," lease land, etc.) (The term "lease" was defined in an exchange of notes to mean a long-term lease up to thirty years, unconditionally renewable.) [4]

[2] *Ibid.*, pp. 44 ff.; MacMurray, Vol. II, pp. 1220 ff.
[3] The Sino-Japanese Negotiations of 1916, pp. 68-73.
[4] It appears that the Mukden authorities, relying in the Chinese text, have prevented the general execution of this provision with regard to permitting leasing of land, as no detailed regulations for the same have ever been issued.

Article 3. "The subjects of Japan shall have liberty to enter, travel and reside in South Manchuria and to carry on business of various kinds—commercial, industrial and otherwise."

Article 4. "The Government of China shall permit joint undertakings in Eastern Mongolia of the subjects of Japan and the citizens of China, in agriculture and industries auxiliary thereto."

Article 5. Japanese subjects are to produce passports, to submit to local police regulations and to pay taxes to the Chinese authorities where they are in Manchuria under the provisions of the above three articles. In civil and criminal suits where a Japanese subject is the defendant in a mixed case he is entitled to trial by the Japanese consul; if a Chinese subject be a defendant in a mixed case he is entitled to trial by a Chinese authority, though the Japanese consular officer may be present or represented at the trial to watch the proceedings if a Japanese is involved. In land disputes (civil cases) the case is to be tried by a joint tribunal, but under Chinese law. (An exchange of notes required that the Chinese authorities consult the Japanese consular officers before putting police and tax regulations into effect as against the Japanese.) [5]

Article 6. China agrees to open to international residence and trade "suitable cities and towns in Eastern Inner Mongolia." (The exchange of notes provided that the exact commercial "ports" to be opened would be decided by the Chinese Government after consultation with the Japanese Minister in Peking.)

Article 7. China agrees to an immediate and fundamental revision of the Kirin-Changchun railway agreements in force between China and Japan, this revision to be in accordance with a standard set by previous and similar arrangements between China and other powers. Revision may be required by Japan in future to enable Japan to receive terms as advantageous as those given to other powers.[6]

Article 8. "Except as otherwise provided in this Treaty, all existing treaties between Japan and China with respect to Manchuria shall remain in force."

By several exchanges of notes of the same date (May 25, 1915) greater precision was given to the terms of the general treaty, as shown parenthetically above, and several additional provisions were agreed to by Japan and China, including the following:

1. China concedes to Japanese nationals the right to prospect for and work certain coal and iron mines in designated regions in Fengtien and Kirin

[5] Concerning this article as to Japanese jurisdiction in South Manchuria, and Article 3, concerning liberty of travel and residence, a controversy arose immediately, especially in their bearing on the status of Koreans in the Chientao district. Japan claimed after 1915 that the new treaty applied to the Koreans, but this was denied by China, continuing to exercise jurisdiction under the Sino-Japanese agreement of September 4, 1909. (*U. S. Foreign Relations*, 1915, pp. 204-206.) See Chap. XXIII, Sec. b.

[6] See Chap. XXXIX, Sec. c.

provinces, including new areas in Penhsihu, Hailung, Tunghua and the Anshan districts in Fengtien province, and certain others in Kirin province.

2. China concedes to Japanese capitalists the right to be first consulted for a loan in any case where the Chinese Government proposes to build railways in South Manchuria and Eastern Inner Mongolia with foreign capital. Also, whenever China proposes to raise a loan abroad on the security of the taxes of South Manchuria and Eastern Inner Mongolia (with the exception of the salt gabelle and the customs) they will first consult Japanese capitalists.

3. China concedes to Japan that if, in future, the Chinese Government desire to employ foreign advisers and instructors on "political, financial, military and police affairs in South Manchuria," preference will be given to Japanese.[7]

CHAPTER XXXIX
Sino-Japanese Railway (Loan) Agreements regarding Manchuria (1915-1921)

a. MANCHURIAN RAILWAYS AND THE TREATY AND NOTES OF 1915. The most important provision of the treaty and exchanges of notes of May 25, 1915, respecting railways in South Manchuria and Inner Mongolia was that which extended the period of Japanese possession of the South Manchuria Railway and the Antung-Mukden railway to ninety-nine years respectively, the former to expire in 2002, the latter in 2007. The right of the Chinese Government to redeem the South Manchuria Railway by purchase in 1939 (thirty-six years after opening of traffic over the whole line), or to receive it without payment in 1983 (eighty years after opening of traffic), was specifically revoked. So also was the right of China to recover the Antung-Mukden railway in 1923-1924 revoked by the provision extending the period of Japanese control to 2007.[8]

A second important provision of these agreements bearing on railways was that which was contained in an exchange of notes to the effect that, in case foreign capital were required by China in future for the construction of railways in South Manchuria and Inner Mongolia, China "will negotiate first with Japanese capitalists for a loan" (or "may negotiate," according to the Chinese text).[9]

---

[7] This provision was objected to by the United States Government if it were to be interpreted as granting a preference to Japan in the matter of advisers for China. The United States declared that they understood that "the Chinese Government will not discriminate unfairly in their selection" of such advisers. (*U. S. Foreign Relations,* 1915, p. 110.)

[8] See Chap. XXXVIII, Sec. a.

[9] See Chap. XXXVIII, Sec. a.

This provision amounted to the granting of a prior right to Japanese capitalists to be considered in any case where the Chinese Government sought to construct with foreign capital a railway in these regions, a provision which in application has been modified by the voluntary declaration of the Japanese delegation to the Washington Conference to the effect that the Japanese Government would not in future insist on this prior right but "is ready to throw open to the joint activity of the international financial consortium" the right of option granted Japanese capital in the case of railway construction in South Manchuria and Inner Mongolia.[10]

Further, with regard to the railway provisions of the treaty and notes of 1915, the Japanese Government obtained the concession (Article 7) in the treaty that China permit at once a "fundamental revision of the Kirin-Changchun Railway Loan Agreement."[11] This loan agreement was to expire in 1934, but by virtue of the treaty of 1915 and the loan agreement of 1917 was altered in such a way as to permit the South Manchuria Railway Company actually to take over practical control of the Kirin-Changchun railway under an additional loan to run for thirty years, thus to mature in 1947.[12]

b. SSUPINGKAI-CHENGCHIATUN RAILWAY LOAN AGREEMENT, 1915. In 1913 the Japanese Government had obtained from China, by virtue of an exchange of notes dated October 5, the right to finance the construction of five railways in Manchuria, three to be branch or connecting lines of the South Manchuria Railway, of which one was the Ssupingkai-Chengchiatun railway project.[13] The final loan agreement for this railway, which now runs from Ssupingkai on the South Manchuria Railway toward Inner Mongolia to the west, and has been extended to Paiyintalai (Tungliao) and to Taonan and Angangchi, was signed on December 27, 1915, by the Yokohama Specie Bank and the Chinese Government.[14] By

[10] See Chap. XLIV, Sec. b, and Chap. L, Sec. c.
[11] The Sino-Japanese Negotiations of 1915, p. 46.
[12] See Chap. XIX, Sec. b, and Chap. XXXIX, Sec. c.
[13] See Chap. XIX, Sec. d.
[14] Sino-Japanese (China-Yokohama Specie Bank) Agreement for the Building of the Ssupingkai-Chengchiatun Railway, December 27, 1915. MacMurray, Vol. II, p. 1249.

Under date of October 13, 1916, the American Minister in Peking communicated to the Acting Chinese Minister for Foreign Affairs a statement in which the United States reserved the rights accruing to the American financial group which originally signed the preliminary agreement of October 2, 1909, with China for the financing of the Chinchow-Aigun railway project. The final agreement for this construction contract had been signed in April, 1910, by the Viceroy of Manchuria under authority of the Chinese Government, though the execution of the contract had been postponed, "yet the rights accruing to the American Group under these arrangements

virtue of this agreement the Yokohama Specie Bank agreed to advance (Article 1) the sum of 5,000,000 yen at 5 per cent. for the construction of the line; the term of the loan was fixed (Article 5) at forty years, the same to be met by semi-annual payments derived from the profits of the line itself, the loan being secured (Article 9) on the property and revenues of the line. Article 16 provided that "the building of the road and the management of the road will be entirely in the hands of the [Chinese] Government," actual construction, however, to be under a Japanese chief engineer with a mixed staff, the Japanese chief engineer to be responsible for purchasing construction materials. Preference was to be given to Japanese materials, whether for construction or rolling stock, in case they were to be acquired from abroad. The traffic manager was also to be a Japanese. Policing or guarding of the line was to be a prerogative of the Chinese authorities (Article 17), the number of guards, however, to be a subject for agreement between the Yokohama Specie Bank and the Chinese authorities. Japan further obtained (Article 20) the right to finance the construction of an extension or branch line in case such were projected in future, and in case foreign capital were to be required. In accordance with this latter provision the Japanese have likewise financed the construction, under the supervision of Japanese engineers, of an extension of the Ssupingkai-Chengchiatun line to Taonan, and later to Angangchi, across the Chinese Eastern Railway from Tsitsihar.[15]

c. KIRIN-CHANGCHUN RAILWAY LOAN AGREEMENT OF 1917. Attention has been given elsewhere to the first Japanese loan arrangements of 1905, 1907 and 1908 for the construction of the Kirin-Changchun Railway, a line which branches from the South Manchuria Railway at Changchun.[16] In the Sino-Japanese treaty of 1915 regarding South Manchuria the Chinese Government

have never been relinquished, but . . . have been expressly reserved and continued." (*U. S. Foreign Relations,* 1917, pp. 168-169; also 1916, p. 189.) A similar statement was made by the American Government to Japan on January 3, 1917. (*U. S. Foreign Relations,* 1917, p. 169.) See Chap. XXXI, Sec. a, for the original American (and English) agreements for the Chinchow-Aigun railway. See Chap. XLIII, Sec. b, for the Russo-Asiatic Bank contract for the Pin-Hei railway, of March, 1916, and the reservation of American rights on that occasion.

[15] With regard to the financing of the Ssupingkai-Chengchiatun line and the extensions from Chengchiatun to Taonan and from Chengchiatun to Paiyintalai, it may be noted that the rights of the Yokohama Specie Bank, Ltd., to finance the construction of the extensions beyond Chengchiatun were in 1919 absorbed by the South Manchuria Railway Company which undertook to finance them. The S.M.R. Co., therefore, financed the construction of the remainder of the line to Taonan, as also to Angangchi and Tsitsihar under separate loan agreements with China. See Chap. LI, Sec. a, for the construction agreement of 1924 for the Taonan-Angangchi railway.

[16] See Chap. XIX, Sec. b.

agreed to a fundamental revision of the loan agreement of 1908 to the end of permitting greater Japanese control of the line.[17] On October 12, 1917, the South Manchuria Railway Company entered into an agreement with the Chinese Government which transferred the management of the Kirin-Changchun railway to the South Manchuria Railway Company, the line to remain, however, a part of the Chinese Government Railways.[18] "In view of the [South Manchuria Railway] Company's successful administration of the South Manchuria Railway" the Chinese Government commissioned this Japanese company (Article 3) "to direct the affairs of the Railway" during the period of the new loan agreement which provided (Article 1) for the advance by the South Manchuria Railway Company of 6,500,000 yen (deducting the amount then in arrears to the South Manchuria Railway under the old loan arrangement, i.e., about 2,000,000 yen). The term of the loan was thirty years (to mature in 1947), the interest, 5 per cent., redemption of the loan not to be permitted until the expiration of the full period. The property and receipts of the railway itself were to be security for the loan, while the Chinese Government guaranteed the payment of principal and interest. Twenty per cent. of the annual profits of the line were reserved for payment of the loan. Japanese management and control of the Kirin-Changchun railway, effected through the South Manchuria Railway Company, were to be established through selection by the company of three Japanese directors (General Affairs, Traffic and Accounting) who were to consult with the Chinese chief of administration in such matters as freight rates and general railway regulations. Preference was to be given to Chinese materials for the line, and it was provided (Article 12) that "the rights of policing, administration, jurisdiction, and taxation on the Railway and on land used by the Railway are naturally vested in the [Chinese] Government," the Chinese railway police to be paid from the receipts of the railway itself. By virtue of this Sino-Japanese railway loan agreement, therefore, the South Manchuria Railway Company obtained general control and management, for a term of thirty years (to 1947), of the Kirin-Changchun railway, the line, however, to remain a Chinese Government line.

d. KIRIN-HUINING (KAINEI) RAILWAY LOAN AGREEMENT, 1918. The Kirin-Huining (Kainei in Japanese) Railway, which had been constructed as far as Tunhua by 1927, is projected in

[17] See Chap. XXXIX, Sec. a.
[18] Sino-Japanese (China-South Manchuria Railway Co.) Agreement for a Loan for the Kirin-Changchun Railway, October 12, 1917. MacMurray, Vol. II, p. 1390.

order to complete the new railway approach from Chosen to Kirin, Changchun and Harbin, and therefore has exceptional importance. Originally, the right to participate in the financing of such a line from Kirin to Korea, should foreign capital be needed, was given to Japanese financiers under the terms (Article 3) of the Sino-Japanese convention of April 15, 1907, regarding the Hsinmintun-Mukden and the Kirin-Changchun railways.[19] Two years later (September 4, 1909) a more specific reference to this projected line was included in the Sino-Japanese agreement relating to the Chientao region, the right to construct such a line from the Kirin-Changchun Railway "to the southern boundary of Yenchi (*Chientao*, so-called), and to connect it at Hoiryong (*Huining* or *Kainei*, in Korea) with a Korean railway" being conceded (Article 6) to the Chinese Government "upon consultation with the Government of Japan." [20] But previous to the Sino-Japanese treaty and notes of 1915 regarding Manchuria there appear to have been no specific loan or contract agreements authorizing the Japanese to proceed with construction of such a railway. The blanket provision in one of these exchanges of notes of 1915 to the effect that "if foreign capital is required [for railway construction in South Manchuria] China may [or shall] negotiate for a loan with Japanese capitalists first," in the case of this Kirin-Huining project was but declaratory of a right already conceded to Japan in earlier agreements.

In 1918, however, by means of a preliminary loan agreement of June 18, three Japanese banks (Industrial Bank of Japan, Bank of Chosen, and Bank of Taiwan) obtained the contract for the construction of such a line from Kirin to Huining, near the border in Chosen.[21] This preliminary loan agreement, however, looked forward to a formal agreement for a loan in which the specific amount would be indicated, the detailed agreement to be signed within six months. The preliminary agreement, however, did undertake to fix the interest, to provide for redemption of the loan forty years after the eleventh year following the initial issue of the bonds), the property and earnings of the line were to be security for the loan, while, in general, the Tientsin-Pukow Railway loan agreement (January 13, 1908) was to be the basis for further particulars. This preliminary agreement provided (Article 9) that the sum of

[19] See Chap. XIX, Secs. a and b.
[20] See Chap. XIX, Sec. d.
[21] Sino-Japanese (China-Japanese Banking Syndicate, Bank of Chosen, etc.) *Preliminary Agreement for a Loan for the Construction of the Kirin-Huining Railway,* June 18, 1918. MacMurray, Vol. II, p. 1430.

$10,000,000 was to be paid to the Chinese Government upon the conclusion of the agreement. The Chinese Minister of Communications, in an official report sanctioned by the President of China on June 29, 1918, acknowledged that "in pursuance of this condition, $10,000,000 were paid into the Tokyo office of the Sino-Japanese Exchange Bank on the nineteenth of June (1918) to the credit of the Peking Government who are at liberty to use it without condition." [22] The same Chinese official report reaffirmed the original Sino-Japanese agreements of 1907 and 1909 pertaining to the future construction of a line from Kirin to Korea.

With respect to the legal rights of Japanese financiers in connection with the construction of a line from Kirin to Korea it may be said that they rest on the documents analyzed above (1907, 1909 and 1918), that an advance of $10,000,000 was made in 1918 to the Peking Government without limitation as to its use by China, and that, if the Chinese Government desire to continue the construction of such a line, they are legally bound to observe the conditions of these preliminary agreements. A strict reading of the above agreements, however, conveys the impression that, except for the necessity of consulting with Japan (which does not mean with respect to loans necessarily), the Chinese Government were at liberty to construct railways from Kirin to the Korean border independently of Japanese capital. It appears that Japanese rights to participate in financing such construction might only be invoked if and when the Chinese Government desired to build them with foreign capital, in whole or in part. The first section of this railway, from Kirin to Tunhua, was completed, however, in 1927, under a separate and detailed contract agreement between the Japanese contractors and the Chinese Government.[23]

e. FOUR MANCHURIAN AND MONGOLIAN RAILWAYS LOAN AGREEMENT, 1918. In 1913, by means of an exchange of notes dated October 5, the Chinese and Japanese Governments agreed that Japanese financiers were to have prior right to advance the funds necessary for the construction of five railways in Manchuria and Inner Mongolia, these lines to include three branches to the South Manchuria Railway (i.e., Ssupingkai-Chengchiatun railway (and extension to Taonan, etc.), Kaiyuan-Hailungcheng railway, and Changchun-Taonan railway), and to include also two others (i.e., Taonan-Jehol railway and Kirin-Hailungcheng railway).[24]

[22] MacMurray, Vol. II, p. 1432.
[23] See Chap. LI, Sec. b.
[24] See Chap. XIX, Sec. d.

In this exchange of notes of 1913 the Chinese Government agreed to make a loan from Japanese capitalists for the construction of all the lines mentioned, though with respect to the Kirin-Hailung-cheng line it was specifically stated that a Japanese loan would be permitted only in case it were necessary to borrow foreign capital for the construction. China thus reserved the right to construct that line herself with her own capital.

Attention has already been given to the Ssupingkai-Chengchiatun railway and its proposed extensions to Taonan and farther, this line having been dealt with by China and Japan separately from the other four projects.[25] The Changchun-Taonan and the Taonan-Jehol lines have never been built; while the Kaiyuan-Taolu light line has been built as the first section of the line which originally was projected to Hailungcheng. The Chinese themselves have undertaken the construction of the Kirin-Hailungcheng railway against the protest of the Japanese Government.[26]

On September 28, 1918, the Chinese Government signed a preliminary loan agreement with the Industrial Bank of Japan (representing a syndicate composed also of the Bank of Chosen and the Bank of Taiwan) in which the Chinese Government agreed (Article 1) that the Japanese banks would have the right to finance the construction of the following lines:

(1) Taonan-Jehol railway.
(2) Changchun-Taonan railway.
(3) Kirin-Kaiyuan railway.
(4) A railway from a point on the Taonan-Jehol railway to a certain seaport (on the Gulf of Pechihli) to be decided on by consultation between China and the banks.

This agreement being but preliminary, it was left for subsequent negotiation to decide in particular the specific loan advances for the construction of each line. General provisions only were established: the term of the loans was to be forty years after eleven years following the first bond issue; the security was to be the property and profits of the lines. Upon conclusion of this preliminary agreement the Japanese banks agreed to advance 20,000,000 yen to the Chinese Government without limitation as to its use.[27]

Except for subsequent detailed arrangements for the building of

[25] See Chap. XIX, Sec. d, and Chap. XXXIX, Sec. b.
[26] See Appendix F.
[27] Sino-Japanese (China-Japanese Banking Syndicate, Bank of Chosen, *etc.*) *Preliminary Agreement for a Loan for Railways in Manchuria and Mongolia*, September 28, 1918. MacMurray, Vol. II, p. 1448.

the relatively unimportant section of the Kaiyuan-Kirin railway (that from Kaiyuan to Taolu and Hsian), it does not appear that detailed loan agreements have been signed by China and Japanese financiers with respect to the construction of these other lines, though the Japanese financiers reserve their rights in connection therewith, except for the statements of the Japanese Government and financiers in the negotiations during the initiation of the international banking consortium in 1919-1920, and the statements of the Japanese delegation to the Washington Conference. Although the Taonan-Jehol railway has not been built, the diplomatic negotiations and the conversations of the international bankers during 1919 and 1920 clearly demonstrated the importance of the project for the construction of such a line, and of extension lines toward North Manchuria.[28]

CHAPTER XL

Sino-Japanese Industrial and Provincial Loans (1915-1921)

a. MANCHURIAN MINING, LUMBERING AND PROVINCIAL LOAN AGREEMENTS. During the period from 1905 to 1915 the Japanese Government and Japanese private financiers entered into a series of agreements with China by virtue of which the South Manchuria Railway obtained possession of the Fushun and Yentai collieries, the firm of Okura and Company acquired control of the Penhsihu collieries, and Japanese financiers obtained the right to exploit the Yalu timber reserves on the Chinese side of the Korean (Chosen) border through the formation of the Sino-Japanese Timber Company.[29] By an exchange of notes of May 25, 1915, between China and Japan the Chinese Government conceded that Japanese subjects were to enjoy the right to "investigate and select mines in the mining areas in South Manchuria" specified in the agreement, and the right "to prospect or work the same."[30] The districts specified included additional areas near the Penhsihu collieries, and others about Hailungcheng, Tunghua and elsewhere in Fengtien province as well as certain districts in Kirin province.

On October 16, 1916, the provincial government of Fengtien signed with Okura and Company a contract for the extension of a loan for 1,500,000 yen to the provincial authorities to extend the loan for that amount which was declared to have expired on

[28] See Chap. XLIV, Sec. b.
[29] See Chap. XX, Secs. a and b.
[30] See Chap. XXXVIII, Sec. a.

October 16, 1916.[31] The new agreement cancelled the former and extended the loan to one year, and as security for the extended loan the new provisions (Article 7) included all the shares of Fengtien province in the Penhsihu Iron Works and the shaft-head tax, all the royalties and shaft-head taxes of the Fushun Collieries, and all the shares of Fengtien province in the Antung Lumber Company. The agreement continued Okura and Company in charge of management of the Penhsihu collieries, a control which began shortly after the Russo-Japanese war and was formally recognized by China in 1910.

. On April 22, 1918, the provincial government of Fengtien signed with the Bank of Chosen a second loan agreement, this time providing for an advance of 3,000,000 yen to be paid over in full within seven days after signature.[32] The purpose of the loan was declared (Article 2) to be "solely for the readjustment of the reserve of the Provincial Government Bank of Manchuria" and was "not to be used for other purposes." The bearing of this loan on the control of coal mines in Manchuria appears in the fact that (Article 8) "all the shares held by Fengtien province in the Penhsihu Colliery Company" were designated as security offered the Japanese bank which advanced the loan.

Gold mining and lumbering in Heilungkiang and Kirin provinces were incidentally involved in the terms of an agreement for a loan advance of 30,000,000 yen by a Japanese banking syndicate to the Government of China (Peking), signed on August 2, 1918, by a Japanese representative of the syndicate and by the Ministers of Finance and of Agriculture and Commerce of China. The Japanese syndicate which advanced the loan included the Bank of Chosen, the Bank of Taiwan and the Exchange Bank of China, whose managing director was a Japanese. The loan agreement itself contained only very general provisions as to the application of the advances for gold mining and forestry development in Heilungkiang and Kirin provinces, though these were the declared purpose of the loan.[33] As security for the loan, however, the gold mines and national forests in these provinces, and the revenue of the Chinese Government from those mines and national forests were

[31] Sino-Japanese (Fengtien Provincial Government—Okura and Co.) *Contract for the Extension of a Loan*, October 16, 1916. MacMurray, Vol. II, p. 1335.

[32] Sino-Japanese (Fengtien Provincial Government—Bank of Chosen) *Agreement for a Loan for the Readjustment of the Reserves of the Provincial Government Bank of Manchuria*, April 22, 1918. MacMurray, Vol. II, p. 1416.

[33] Sino-Japanese (China—Japanese Banking Syndicate, Exchange Bank of China, etc.) *Agreement for a Loan for Gold Mining and Forestry in the Provinces of Heilungkiang and Kirin*, August 2, 1918. MacMurray, Vol. II, p. 1434.

hypothecated (Article 8). In a subsequent declaration of the Japanese syndicate the purpose of the loan was admitted to be "to render assistance to your [Chinese] Government in financial re-adjustment," this provision being the principal immediate purpose of the loan, rather than that of "improvement of gold mining and forestry," or the encouragement of Sino-Japanese joint enterprises as declared in other communications of the Japanese syndicate to the ministries in Peking.[34] As a matter of fact, Japanese financiers and industrialists have not participated to any great extent in the development of gold mining in North Manchuria and such of participation as there is of Japanese private business interests in the forestry industry of North Manchuria, as along the line of the Chinese Eastern Railway, is in other hands than the Japanese syndicate which negotiated the Heilungkiang and Kirin "gold mining and forestry" loan. Japanese participation or control in mining and forestry enterprises in Manchuria, aside from certain Japanese enterprises in Kirin province and along the Chinese Eastern Railway, consists mainly of the Japanese interests in the Fushun and Yentai collieries, the Penhsihu coal and iron works, the Anshan iron works and the Yalu timber industry.

CHAPTER XLI

The South Manchuria Railway and the Kwantung Government (1915-1921)

a. THE SOUTH MANCHURIA RAILWAY AND THE KWANTUNG GOVERNMENT. The establishment of the South Manchuria Railway Company by the Japanese Government in 1906, the organization of the Government General of Kwantung province at approximately the same time, and the interrelation of the railway and the provincial government of Kwantung have been considered in detail in a previous section.[35] The South Manchuria Railway Company

[34] MacMurray, Vol. II, p. 1439. This loan negotiated by the Sino-Japanese Exchange Bank of China and other Japanese banks, including the Bank of Chosen, was one of the group commonly characterized as "the Nishihara loans." In this particular class of loans to China the Yokohama Specie Bank, Ltd., did not participate. The Chinese Minister of Finance, Tsao Ju-lin, later is said to have made the statement in a communication to Military Governor Meng En-yuan of Kirin province that the so-called gold mining and forestry loan of August 2, 1918, was made for the sole purpose of raising money for the Peking Government at a time when that government was involved in military engagements with South China, and that the loan was classed as an "industrial" in order to preclude the participation of the Six Power Banking Group. (*Far Eastern Review*, August, 1918, p. 336.)
[35] See Chap. XVII, Sec. a, and Chap. XVIII, Sec. a.

has continued in a form of organization without significant alteration down until the present, except for the fact that in practice the
posts of Governor General of Kwantung province and of President
of the South Manchuria Railway Company have at times been
held jointly by the same incumbent. Minor changes in the man-
agerial organization of the railway company have been made, as
that effected by Imperial Ordinance (No. 89) on July 31, 1917,
when the office of president and of vice-president of the railway
were consolidated for a time into that of chairman of the board
of directors.[36] By Imperial Ordinance (No. 90) also of the same
date, the railway company was authorized to take charge of the
operation of the Chosen State Railways.[37] This arrangement was
cancelled, however, in 1925.

As to the form of organization of the government of Kwantung
province, that was changed but slightly in 1917, at the same time
as the South Manchuria Railway Company was authorized to
operate additionally the Chosen State Railways, when by Imperial
Ordinance (No. 82) of July 31 the functions of the Governor General were somewhat more clearly defined.[38] A more thorough reorganization of the government of Kwantung was effected on
April 12, 1919 (Imperial Ordinance No. 94), when, in place of the
Government General (*Totoku Fu*) which had existed since 1906,
there was established the new organization to be henceforth called
the Kwantung Government (*Kwanto Cho*), over which a Governor
(*Chokan*) was to have highest authority, who was not required
to be a military officer. A distinctly civil administration, instead of
an administration presided over by a high military officer, was thus
established in 1919. The civil administrative functions of the government were thus to be exercised by the Governor, while the military were to be under the Commander of the Kwantung Garrison,
except when the Governor was himself a military officer, in which
case the Governor was to assume the command of the Kwantung
army. The functions of the civil governor remained essentially the
same as before, except for the command of the army, the governor
having jurisdiction over the province or leased territory and also
power to "supervise the business of the South Manchuria Railway
Company," and to take charge of policing the railway area. A
fairly clear differentiation was thus made between the civilian police,
who both in the leased territory and in the railway zone were placed

[36] MacMurray, Vol. I, p. 563.
[37] *Ibid.*
[38] *Ibid.*, p. 569.

under the jurisdiction of the civil Governor, and the railway guards who were soldiers, and who, along with the regular troops in the leased territory, were placed under the command of the military head of the Kwantung Garrison.

In administrative matters the Governor was responsible (Article 4) to the Prime Minister (as also for his appointment); in foreign affairs he was responsible to the Minister for Foreign Affairs; and if the Governor of Kwantung were a military officer he, in the capacity of Commander of the Kwantung Garrison, would be responsible (Article 3) to the General Staff. The President of the South Manchuria Railway was to be "adviser for communications" to the Kwantung Government. To conduct ordinary civil affairs the Governor was given order-making (local ordinance) power, and might *request* (Article 7) the Commander of the Garrison for the use of military forces. Instead of the previous three civil administrative districts into which Kwantung was divided, the number was reduced to two with head offices in Dairen and Port Arthur. The Governor was to be of *shinnin* rank, i.e., to be appointed directly by the Emperor.

All Japanese consuls in Manchuria were in 1919 made additionally (Article 15) "secretaries" in the Kwantung Government, the consul general at Mukden becoming *ex officio* Chief of the Section of Foreign Affairs, Chief of the Section of Civil Affairs, and Chief Secretary of the Kwantung Government. By virtue of the fact that the Japanese consuls in Manchuria (who technically have charge of their own consular police) are also "secretaries" in and, therefore, a part of the Kwantung Government, the police authorities of the Kwantung Government may be placed at their disposal, these having jurisdiction as consular police beyond the railway zone but within Japanese consular jurisdiction. The consular police and "railway guards," moreover, may be at times identical, while the troops of the Japanese garrison, or gendarmes, may be used as a "supplementary" police force.[39] The official organization of the Kwantung Government has been altered only slightly since 1919, especially in June, 1921, and in December, 1923.[40]

[39] *Twentieth Anniversary History of the Kwantung Government* (in Japanese), pp. 274 ff., (published by the Kwantung Government *(Kwanto-cho)*, at Port Arthur, August, 1926.)
[40] *Ibid.* See Chap. L, Sec. d, for the subject of Japanese troops in Manchuria at the Washington Conference.

CHAPTER XLII

The Position of Japan in Manchuria (1915-1921)

a. THE GENERAL POSITION OF JAPAN IN MANCHURIA: 1915-
1921. The position of Japan in Manchuria following the outbreak of the Great War and until the Washington Conference on
Naval Disarmament and Pacific and Far Eastern Questions can
only be adequately appreciated by reference to the previous sections dealing with the important Sino-Japanese treaty and exchanges of notes relating to South Manchuria and Inner Mongolia
in 1915, and to the sections which deal with Sino-Japanese railway, industrial and loan agreements of the period. The Japanese
Government and Japanese financiers, moreover, were vitally concerned in the negotiations attending the formation and the delimitation of the scope and character of the activities of the international
banking consortium, a subject which is dealt with in a subsequent
section.[41] During the period of Inter-allied control of the Chinese
Eastern Railway the interests of Japan were demonstrated in the
various parleys and arrangements developing therefrom, as at the
Washington Conference. The period also saw the signing by the
Japanese Government of a series of bilateral agreements, a very
important one with Russia in 1916, and a military and a naval
convention with China in 1918, as well as the American-Japanese
(Lansing-Ishii) agreement of 1917 affecting Manchuria and
Japan's interests there. Japan by virtue of these bilateral arrangements attained to a position in Manchuria which in the field of concrete activities expressed themselves in the several railway, industrial and loan contracts and agreements obtained by the Japanese
Government from the Peking Government or the local Manchurian
authorities, especially during 1916 to 1918.

b. JAPANESE POLICE JURISDICTION AND THE CHENGCHIATUN
INCIDENT: 1916-1917. In consequence of a fracas between Chinese
and Japanese soldiers which occurred at Chengchiatun (west of
Ssupingkai, near Inner Mongolia) in January, 1916, the Japanese
Government demanded the punishment of the Chinese soldiery concerned and submitted to the Chinese Government several demands
and "desiderata" which were advanced to increase the scope of
jurisdiction of Japanese "police" in Manchuria outside the zone
of the South Manchuria Railway. These included the right to
station Japanese police officers in South Manchuria and Eastern

[41] See Chap. XLIV, Secs. a and b; also Chap. L, Sec. c, and Chap. LII, Sec. a.

Inner Mongolia (outside the railway zone) without limitation as to their numbers, the right to have Japanese military advisers employed by the Chinese Government in case foreign advisers were to be employed in South Manchuria, and the right to have Japanese military officers employed as instructors in Chinese military cadet schools.[42] The right to have Japanese military advisers employed by the Chinese Government in case foreign advisers were to be employed in connection with "political, financial, military and police affairs in South Manchuria" had, in fact, been conceded in principle by the Chinese Government by an exchange of notes of May 25, 1915. The Chinese Government, however, in their reply of January 12, 1917, declared that, while acknowledging the concession of 1915, China reserved the right not to employ any foreign advisers at all in South Manchuria (although a Japanese military officer was then employed as adviser at Mukden), and also declared that they had no intention for the present to employ any foreigner in the military cadet schools in South Manchuria. As to the establishment of Japanese police stations in South Manchuria the Chinese Government declared that there was "no necessity to station Japanese police officers" there, and that the functions which Japan sought to have recognized for such Japanese police officers were properly the prerogative of the Chinese police, not a necessary corollary of the right of extraterritoriality or of the right of residence and trade.

The outcome of the question raised by the Japanese Government was embodied in the above exchanges of notes and in that of January 22, 1917, which gave the Japanese no further jurisdictional rights in South Manchuria than they already possessed, but did provide for the punishment of the Chinese military officers and soldiers involved in the Chengchiatun incident and the payment of a small indemnity.[43]

[42] MacMurray, Vol. II, pp. 1347 ff.
[43] Ibid., p. 1347. See Chap. L, Sec. d.

B. THE POSITION OF RUSSIA: 1915-1921

CHAPTER XLIII

The Position of Russia and the Chinese Eastern Railway
(1915-1921)

a. RELATION OF RUSSIA TO THE CHINESE EASTERN RAILWAY:
1915-1921. The Russian Revolution in Europe in 1917 resulted in
temporary control of the Chinese Eastern Railway in Manchuria
by anti-Bolshevik factions in the Russian Far East, disorganization
of the management of the line resulting from the uncertainties of
the situation and the incapacity of the agencies placed in charge
of the system. In fact, ever since the outbreak of the Great War
in 1914 the Russian Government was more or less preoccupied with
political and military affairs in Europe, this situation leading to
forced neglect of Russian interests in the Far East and Manchuria.
Due to the disorganization of the Chinese Eastern Railway it was
suggested by the representatives of the Allied Powers in Peking in
1918 that the Chinese Government replace the former Russian
administration of the railway and take charge of policing the
system. The Japanese Government, however, opposed this arrangement on the ground that the existence of a Sino-Japanese military agreement of March 25, 1918, gave Japan certain rights with
reference to transportation of their troops over the Chinese Eastern
Railway.[44] A supplementary Sino-Japanese military agreement of
September 6, 1918, provided that (Article 4) "the transportation
of troops over the Chinese Eastern Railway shall be in the hands
of the organization having charge of the railway." [45] A joint Sino-
Japanese bureau was to be established for the purpose of making
arrangements" for the transportation of Chinese, Japanese and
Czecho-Slovak forces over the railway," with the provision that
other Allied Powers were to be permitted to participate in this
proposed bureau. Although these agreements were devised
ostensibly to permit Chinese control of the Chinese Eastern Railway, this was not entirely secured, the situation resulting in policing
of the railway by both Chinese and Japanese troops. The multi-

[44] MacMurray, Vol. II, pp. 1407 ff. See Chap. XLIV, Sec. a, and Chap. XLVIII,
Sec. a.
[45] MacMurray, Vol. II, p. 1413.

power agreement of January 9, 1919, for Inter-allied control of the Chinese Eastern Railway followed.[46]

At the Washington Conference, a report of the Technical Sub-Committee appointed to make a statement on the status and problem of management and control of the Chinese Eastern Railway declared that the "trusteeship" assumed under the 1919 Inter-allied agreement continued in force at the time.[47] Although that agreement was for but temporary control of the railways "with a view to their ultimate return to those in interest without the impairing of any existing rights" it was, in fact, difficult to determine the exact status of the railway in view especially of the agreement of October 2, 1920, between the Chinese Government and the reorganized Russo-Asiatic Bank (purporting to represent the bondholders of the railway).[48] This latter agreement had provided for a larger Chinese membership on the Board of Management, while the preamble authorized the Chinese Government, "in view of the situation created by the complete political disorganization in Russia, rendering temporarily impossible for the said company [C.E.R.] the maintenance of regular operation," to take "supreme control" over the railway "by virtue of the contract and of the regulations in force."

This agreement of 1920 between the Russo-Asiatic Bank (formerly the Russo-Chinese Bank, the original contractors for the Chinese Eastern Railway) and the Chinese Government had further importance in its other detailed provisions of which the following are noteworthy. The Chinese Government was given (Article 2) the right to appoint, in addition to the President, four members of Chinese nationality upon the Board of Management (i.e., five of the ten members); likewise, the Chinese Government was given the right (Article 4) to appoint two Chinese to the Committee of Audit (5 members), the president of the committee, selected from the committee itself, to be of Chinese nationality. A quorum of the Board of Management necessary to transact business was fixed (Article 3) at seven. The Chinese Eastern Railway Company recognized (Article 1) "that it should pay to the Chinese Government," the original advance (plus interest) of the Chinese Government, i.e., a sum of 5,000,000 Kuping taels (plus interest) which should have been paid to the Government by the Company beginning with the day of the opening of the said line to operation, in accord-

[46] See Chap. XLIV, Sec. a, which deals in detail with Inter-allied control from 1919 to 1922.
[47] See Chap. LII, Sec. a.
[48] *Manchuria Treaties and Agreements*, p. 210. See Chap. XLIV, Sec. a, Chap. XLV, Sec. a, and Chap. LII, Sec. a.

ance with Article 12 of the original contract." [49] The Chinese Government and the Russo-Asiatic Bank failed to come to an agreement with regard to China's request to purchase one-half of the original shares in the Chinese Eastern Railway, but it was provided (Annex 8) that "the Chinese Government, in signing the contract of October 2, 1920, declares that it does not forego its right hereafter to take up this question." In view of the various purposes for which the Chinese Eastern Railway had been used since 1896, Article 6 is particularly important:

"The rights and the obligations of the Company will henceforth be in every respect of a commercial character: every political activity and every political attribute will be absolutely forbidden to it. To this end, the Chinese Government reserves the right to prescribe restrictive measures of any character and at any time."

This agreement, it should be noted, was negotiated by the reorganized Russo-Asiatic Bank and the Chinese Government. It was signed, in fact, ten days after the Tsarist Minister in Peking had been requested to leave, recognition having been withdrawn by China. The new Soviet Government refused to recognize the agreement signed by the Russo-Asiatic Bank for the reason that that government had nationalized all banks in Russia, including the Russo-Asiatic Bank. But a reorganization of the bank had been effected in Paris in an attempt to protect French financial interests, and the management which negotiated the agreement with the Chinese Government in October, 1920, was distinctly opposed to the Soviet régime. The Russo-Asiatic Bank, in fact, after representations from China seeking to elicit reliable information as to the exact status of the bank, replied that it was "not connected with any political party in Russia," and further declared "that no other nation than Russia and China has an interest in the Chinese Eastern Railway." This would seem anomalous were it not for the fact that the Chinese Government had not recognized the Soviet Government at that time, and hence were sceptical of possible connections of the bank with the Communist party in Russia, and for the fact that no *government* other than China and Russia ever had a vested proprietary interest in the Chinese Eastern Railway. The Russo-

[49] *Ibid.*, p. 213. The Russo-Asiatic Bank and the Chinese Government differed as to what date should be taken as that for the opening of the Chinese Eastern Railway, the former contending it was 1907, the latter asserting that it was 1903. The issue was left open at the time. It is, of course, a fact that the whole of the C.E.R. system was open and in operation at the end of 1903, before the war with Japan. See Chap. LII, Sec. a.

Asiatic Bank (as the Russo-Chinese Bank) had been financed partly by private French financing institutions whose agents took this opportunity in 1920 to assert ownership of all the shares in the Chinese Eastern Railway, though the published correspondence attending these negotiations gives no financial statement of the bank or the railway company, while it is very questionable if the Russo-Asiatic Bank, as reorganized in Paris, could lay any legitimate claim to a vested proprietary interest in the Chinese Eastern Railway.

b. RUSSO-ASIATIC BANK CONTRACT AGREEMENT FOR A HARBIN TO THE AMUR RAILWAY, 1916. No important long-distance branch railway has ever been constructed by the Chinese Eastern Railway Company or the Russo-Asiatic Bank to connect with the main or the southern branch from Harbin. It is of importance, however, to consider the terms of an agreement between the Russo-Asiatic Bank and the Chinese Government, signed on March 27, 1916, by virtue of which the bank was given the construction contract for a projected railway to proceed north from Harbin to the Amur river to a point called Sahalian (Heihofu), opposite the town of Blagoveshchensk.[50] The line was termed the Pin-Hei railway

[50] Sino-Russian (China-Russo-Asiatic Bank) *Agreement for the Chinese Government Five Per Cent. Gold Loan of 1916 for the Pin-Hei Railway,* March 27, 1916. MacMurray, Vol. II, p. 1267.
Russian Rights in the Barga Region. Mention should here be made of the secession of the Buriat Mongol tribes and other inhabitants in the Barga district of western Heilungkiang province from China in 1912, and of the consequences of this revolt which affected the position of Russia and the Chinese Eastern Railway. The Barga district (also called Hulunbuir or Hailar district) is populated in large part by Mongol and other aboriginal tribes, descendants of the Tunghu. Since 1906 the Chinese have steadily encroached upon their position, both through extension of Chinese administrative machinery and through the somewhat successful encouragement of Chinese colonization there. Chafing under this advance, the Buriats and other tribes revolted during the Chinese Revolution in 1911, and in 1912 declared complete secession from China.
The Russian Government, being interested in preserving their rights in the Chinese Eastern Railway and their interests in Hailar and Manchouli, important towns in the Barga district, offered to mediate for the secessionists and China. In consequence, a Sino-Russian agreement of October 24/November 6, 1915, was signed, which was in fact a compromise on the subject of the status of Barga, giving the latter autonomy of a sort, but which also included important provisions giving Russia and the Chinese Eastern Railway prior rights to railway construction in the area. Barga (Hulunbuir) was made a special district with a local chieftain as Governor (*Fututung*), military forces to be under his command, with certain rights of protection reserved for China. Chinese were to be permitted to lease land for agricultural purposes, but not so as to interfere with the grazing industry of the natives. The Russian Government obtained the right to furnish the funds if foreign capital were required for railway construction in the special district. Russia was also to be consulted if the Chinese Government proposed to send troops into the Barga district. Barga was thus placed under a form of joint Sino-Russian protectorate.
This situation, however, was but temporary, for after the Russian Revolution the Chinese Government, by Presidential Mandate of January 28, 1920, cancelled the

(Harbin-Heihofu) and was to pass through Mergen, connecting with Tsitsihar, south of Mergen, by means of a branch line to be constructed so as to connect with the Chinese Eastern at Tsitsihar-chan. The agreement authorized the bank to float a 5 per cent. gold loan to the amount of 50,000,000 roubles, either at once or by successive issues, the same to be designated as the "Chinese Government 5 Per Cent. Gold Loan of 1916, for the Pin-Hei Railway." The bank was given a first mortgage on the line itself, its properties and its profits, and the Chinese Government was to guarantee the payment of the principal and interest of the loan. Further details of the loan contract agreement are not given because of the fact that this projected railway was never constructed by the Russo-Asiatic Bank and the construction of two sections of that line as projected has now been accomplished, or is in the process of accomplishment, by two other agencies quite independent of the Russo-Asiatic Bank. A private Chinese company has built a portion of a line shortly to be completed from Hulan (i.e., from across the Sungari river opposite Harbin) to Mergen, the Chinese Government considering the rights of the Russo-Asiatic Bank in this general railway project as having lapsed during and after the Russian Revolution.[61]

arrangement by unilaterally abrogating, over Russia's protest, the 1915 agreement with Russia. A Chinese administration was forthwith instituted in the district, which was made directly responsible to the authorities of Heilungkiang. Evidences of disaffection among the local tribes have been manifested since on several occasions, recently in 1928 and 1929. (For the Sino-Russian *Agreement concerning Hulunbuir* [Barga], October 24/November 6, 1915, see MacMurray, Vol. II, p. 1247.)

[61] See Appendix F for the building of a portion of this railway system by the Chinese. On August 24, 1916, the United States Department of State instructed the American Minister in Peking in his discretion to "call attention of Chinese Government to agreement with American Group ratified January 20, 1910, and statements of Group that their rights never formally relinquished." (*U. S. Foreign Relations*, 1916, p. 189.) In a memorandum of February 24, 1910, the Russian Government had protested to the American Secretary of State the construction of the Chinchow-Aigun railway by an American group under their contracts of 1910 with the Chinese Government. (*U. S. Foreign Relations*, 1910, p. 261; 1916, p. 199.) The American group of bankers, however, including J. P. Morgan and Co., declared to the Department of State that "they have never formally relinquished such rights as they may have under the arrangements with the Chinese Government," i.e., in the preliminary agreement of October 2, 1909 (ratified by China on January 20, 1910), and the final agreement of April 26, 1910. (*U. S. Foreign Relations*, 1916, p. 169.) The United States Government reserved the American rights in the Chinchow-Aigun railway project in a communication to the Chinese Government, dated October 13, 1916, in which it was asserted that "the rights accruing to the American Group under these arrangements have never been relinquished, but . . . have been expressly reserved and continued." (*U. S. Foreign Relations*, 1917, pp. 168-169.) A similar statement was made to the Japanese Minister in Peking on January 3, 1917. (*U. S. Foreign Relations*, 1917, p. 169.) In this connection see also Chap. XXXIX, Sec. b.

CHAPTER XLIV

Multi-Power Agreements Relating to Manchuria (1915-1921)

a. MULTI-POWER AGREEMENTS REGARDING INTER-ALLIED CONTROL OF THE CHINESE EASTERN RAILWAY. Consideration has already been given to the Sino-Russian phase of the question of ownership, control and management of the Chinese Eastern Railway following the Russian Revolution in 1917.[52] The Sino-Japanese agreements of 1918 providing for a general military alliance and cooperation, and relating more or less directly to the control of the Chinese Eastern Railway, have already been given some attention, and will again be dealt with in a subsequent section.[53] Brief reference must again be made to them here. The Japanese Government objected to the assumption of complete control over the Chinese Eastern Railway in 1918 on the strength of the previous commitment of China contained in the Sino-Japanese military agreement of March 25, 1918, permitting a measure of Japanese influence in establishing the conditions under which Japanese and other troops might be transported over the system. This Sino-Japanese military alliance had been preceded in late 1917 by an attempt of local Russian partisans to take charge of Harbin in behalf of the Soviet Government. A supplementary Sino-Japanese military agreement of September 6, 1918, provided for the establishment of a Sino-Japanese bureau to effect the organization of the railway necessary to carry into effect the provisions of the former general agreement, though not to be such as to exclude other powers from participating through membership in this bureau.[54] The Japanese Government took the view that under the terms of these agreements their action in stationing Japanese troops along the Chinese Eastern Railway in Manchuria was justified.

The signing of the Armistice of November 11, 1918, which terminated the Great War, did not end the Inter-allied intervention in the areas traversed by the Trans-Siberian Railway in Eastern Asia,

[52] See Chap. XLIII, Sec. a.
[53] See Chap. XLIII, Sec. a, and Chap. XLVIII, Sec. a.
[54] See Chap. XLVIII, Sec. a.

which had been instituted partly to permit the egress of the Czecho-
Slovak prisoners. In fact, the Armistice was but a prelude to the
signing of the Inter-allied agreement of January 9, 1919, for the
supervision of the Siberian railway system, including the Chinese
Eastern Railway, by virtue of which (Article 1) a special Inter-
allied Committee, composed of representatives of each of the
allied powers having military forces in Siberia at the time was
set up to supervise the railways in that zone.[55] This general
agreement, signed by the several powers including Japan and
the United States, provided for the institution (Article 1)
of two boards, a Technical Board and a Military Transportation
Board, the former "consisting of railway experts of the nations
having military forces in Siberia, for the purpose of administering
technical and economic management of the railways in the said
zone," and the latter "for the purpose of co-ordinating military
transportation under instructions of the proper military authorities." The Allied military forces were authorized to continue in
charge of protection of the railway system. This system of technical control of the Chinese Eastern Railway was put into effect on
March 10, 1919. John F. Stevens, an American engineer, was
made president of the Technical Board. In April, 1919, it was
decided at a meeting of the commanders of the allied expeditionary
forces in Siberia (held at Vladivostok) that Chinese troops should
be charged with the responsibility of patrolling the Chinese Eastern
Railway from Nikolsk to Manchouli, and from Changchun to
Harbin. General Horvath remained as Directing Manager of the
Chinese Eastern Railway Company until 1920, when he was dis-
placed by Boris V. Ostroumoff. The only foreign troops to be
employed *within Manchuria* were to be a garrison of one thousand
Americans at Harbin, and Japanese troops *within* the Manchurian
city of Manchouli. The arrangement was to cease "upon withdrawal of the foreign military forces from Siberia." [56]

Although the American forces were withdrawn in January, 1920,
followed shortly thereafter by those of other powers, the Japanese troops remained stationed along the Trans-Siberian railway
west of Manchouli and in the Maritime Province, while Japanese gunboats moved up and down the Amur river, the northern
boundary of Manchuria. Complete Japanese withdrawal from the

[55] *Multi-Power Agreement regarding Inter-Allied Supervision of Siberian Railway
System,* January 9, 1919. MacMurray, Vol. I, p. 82.
[56] *Ibid.,* p. 83.

Maritime Province did not take place until after the Washington Conference. The Inter-allied Technical Board, under John F. Stevens, continued to function in Harbin, however, until the end of October, 1922. The Washington Conference itself dealt with the question of the control and management of the Chinese Eastern Railway, recognizing that "the trusteeship thus assumed [under the Inter-allied agreement of 1919] continues in force."[57] At the conference, furthermore, the Japanese Delegation took occasion to state the reasons why Japan did not immediately withdraw her troops from Siberia.

b. MULTI-POWER NEGOTIATIONS AND AGREEMENT REGARDING THE INTERNATIONAL BANKING CONSORTIUM: 1918-1920. The negotiations between the various banking groups and the several foreign offices which eventuated in the China consortium agreement of October 15, 1920, serve to contrast the national interests of the powers in Manchuria. The plan for the formation of a new international banking consortium, originally broached by the American group of bankers to the Department of State on July 8, 1918, looked to the pooling of the various national banking groups for the purpose of offering loans to the Chinese Government, the loans to be such as not to prejudice, but rather to assist in the "maintenance of Chinese sovereignty and the preservation of the 'open door.'"[53] The final consortium agreement was not signed by the banks, however, until October 15, 1920, after numerous exchanges of views between the Japanese banking group and the American and British groups, and between the Japanese Government and those of the United States and Great Britain. Inasmuch as it was the attempt of the Japanese Government to exclude South Manchuria and Inner Mongolia from the scope of operation of the consortium (on the ground that Japan had "special rights and interests" in these regions of such a nature as to involve the question of national security, economic and strategic), and the attempt of that government to secure a recognition of these declared "special rights and interests" of Japan, that were the principal issues in these negotiations, it seems important to summarize the positions of Japan, Great Britain and the United States as set forth in those discussions.

Declarations of Japan. In the negotiations preliminary to the

[57] See Chap. LII, Sec. a.
[58] *The Consortium: The Official Text of the Four-Power Agreement for a Loan to China and Relevant Documents,* p. 2. (Carnegie Endowment for International Peace, Washington, 1921.)

signing of the China consortium agreement of 1920 the Japanese Government first sought to exclude South Manchuria and Eastern Inner Mongolia from the scope of operation of the international banking consortium, but later modified their position by successive steps, reserving first the right of taking steps in that region necessary to guarantee Japan's national welfare, then withdrawing this formula but retaining its substance, and, finally, asserting their right of option to construct certain railways in Manchuria and especially to veto the construction of a railway north from the proposed Taonanfu-Jehol railway.[58a] The question of the exclusion of this proposed connecting railway between the Taonanfu-Jehol line (not yet constructed) and the Chinese Eastern Railway, perhaps at Tsitsihar-chan (Tsitsihar station), was the outstanding issue in the negotiations during 1920. The Japanese Government eventually expressed their willingness to accept the general assurances of the American and British Governments that they would not countenance operations of their banking groups in the consortium inimical to Japan's economic life and national defence in Manchuria and Mongolia and, therefore, Japan waived specific acceptance by these two governments of the special reservations which the Japanese Government had proposed. The Japanese Government placed on record their interpretation of the question for future reference, though the subsequent declaration of the American banking group, that the projected Taonanfu-Jehol railway and one from that proposed line to the seacoast (not the northern line to the Chinese Eastern Railway) were to be included within the terms of the consortium agreement, was accepted by Japan. Direct statements of the Japanese Government and the Japanese financial group follow.

The initial attempt of Japan to exclude South Manchuria and Eastern Inner Mongolia from the scope of operations of the consortium agreement was contained in a letter of June 18, 1919, sent by the Japanese financial representative (M. Odagiri) to the representative of the American group (Thomas W. Lamont).[59] The letter declared that:

"We have been instructed by our principals in Japan that all the rights and options held by Japan in the regions of Manchuria and Mongolia, where Japan has special interests, should be excluded from the arrangements for pooling provided for in the proposed agreement."

[58a] Taonanfu, here spelled as in the document, is identical with Taonan, previously mentioned.

[59] *The Consortium*, p. 19.

The letter further asserted that the reservation of the Japanese bank on June 18, 1912, at a meeting of the "Six Power Consortium," constituted a statement of the Japanese position, i.e., that:

"Nothing connected with the projected loan should operate to the prejudice of the special rights and interests of Japan in the regions of South Manchuria and of the Eastern portion of Inner Mongolia adjacent to South Manchuria."

The first official statement of the Japanese Government in regard to the issue was set forth in a memorandum of the Japanese Embassy at Washington, August 27, 1919, accepting the resolutions adopted at the Paris meeting of the bankers, but excluding Manchuria and Mongolia from the scope of operations of the consortium.[60]   The memorandum declared that:

"The acceptance and confirmation of the said resolution shall not be held or construed to operate to the prejudice of the special rights and interests possessed by Japan in South Manchuria and Eastern Inner Mongolia."

After the refusal of the American and British Governments to accept this proviso the Japanese Government set forth their position in greater detail in a memorandum of March 2, 1920, to the United States, declaring that:

"From the nature of the case, the regions of South Manchuria and Eastern Inner Mongolia which are contiguous to Korea stand in very close and special relation to Japan's national defense and her economic existence. Enterprises launched forth in these regions, therefore, often involve questions vital to the safety of the country.   This is why Japan has special interest in these regions and has established there special rights of various kinds. . . . Furthermore, the recent development of the Russian situation, exercising as it does an unwholesome influence upon the Far East, is a matter of grave concern to Japan. . . . Now South Manchuria and Mongolia are the gate by which these direful influences may effect their penetration into Japan and the Far East to the instant menace of their security."[61]

The same memorandum contained a statement of certain of the "vested proprietary interests" of Japan in South Manchuria, including the railways built and the mines in operation, and additionally asserted the right of option which Japan possessed with regard to the construction of several other railways, including the Taonanfu-Jehol projected railway and a railway connecting it with

[60] *The Consortium*, p. 30.
[61] *Ibid.*, p. 34.

the seacoast (Gulf of Pechihli), concluding with a statement of the formula they sought to have accepted, i.e., that:

"In matters, however, relating to loans affecting South Manchuria and Eastern Inner Mongolia which in their opinion are calculated to create a serious impediment to the security of the economic life and national defense of Japan, the Japanese Government reserve the right to take the necessary steps to guarantee such security."

Failing the acceptance of this formula by the American and British Governments the Japanese Government communicated a memorandum to the American Department of State on April 3, 1920, indicating their willingness to accept the general assurances already given by the United States and Great Britain and not to insist on specific acceptance of the formula proposed.[62] They indicated their willingness to accept "a scheme of making these two railways (the Taonanfu-Jehol railway and the branch to the sea) a joint enterprise of the new Consortium," but proposed that:

"In the event of the new Consortium projecting in future a scheme of extending the Taonanfu-Jehol Railway to the north with a view to connection with the Eastern Chinese Railway, the assent of the Japanese Government thereto must be obtained beforehand through the Japanese group, inasmuch as such an extension being tantamount to a renewal of the so-called Chinchou-Aigun railway scheme against which a protest was lodged by Japan when the question was motioned some years ago, is calculated to have a serious effect upon the South Manchuria Railway."

The same memorandum proposed that, in case the other three powers associated in the consortium were reluctant to finance the construction of the Taonanfu-Jehol line and the branch to the seacoast, the Japanese group be then permitted to undertake the construction of the same alone. A similar memorandum was communicated to the British Government on April 14, 1920.[63]

Both the British and American Governments declined to concede to the Japanese Government the right to veto the construction of a railway running north from the Taonanfu-Jehol railway, whereupon the Japanese Government replied to the American Government under date of May 8, 1920, withdrawing their condition as to the right to veto the construction of a line connecting the proposed Taonanfu-Jehol line with the Chinese Eastern Railway but declaring that:

[62] *Ibid.,* p. 46.
[63] *Ibid.,* p. 48.

"It was simply in order to avoid future misunderstanding that the point was raised as one of the actual examples of enterprises prejudicial to Japan's vital interests which formed the subject matter of the general assurances given by the American Government. The Japanese Government feel confident that as the question involved in this case comes within the scope of the general assurances, the Governments of the Powers interested in the Consortium will, in the spirit of mutual trust and friendliness, readily appreciate Japan's point of view. . . .

"The Japanese Government, holding as they do the views as above enunciated, have no intention whatever of insisting upon obtaining the explicit assurances or consent of the American Government in regard to the two points above referred to." [64]

It appears, from the statements of the American and British Governments which follow, that the Japanese Government obtained from these two governments general assurances that they would countenance no operation inimical to the economic life and national defence of Japan, but nothing more. The right asserted by Japan to veto the construction of a railway connecting the proposed Taonanfu-Jehol railway with the Chinese Eastern Railway was not specifically conceded by Great Britain and the United States, while the Taonanfu-Jehol project and that from the seacoast to that line were to be included within the scope of the consortium's operations, Japan to be permitted to construct both of them in the event that the consortium did not desire to undertake the same. As a matter of fact, the Chinese Eastern Railway at Tsitsihar-chan has now been connected with Taonanfu by a Japanese-financed railway, the Taonanfu-Angangchi (or Tsitsihar) railway, completed to Angangchi in 1926, and to Tsitsihar in 1928.

Declarations of Great Britain and the United States. The American and British Governments, while recognizing that the "vested proprietary rights" of Japan in South Manchuria were not to be prejudiced by the operations of the consortium, and giving general assurances that the economic life and national defense of Japan would not be menaced by the consortium's program, refused to admit the proposition of the Japanese Government that the whole of South Manchuria and Eastern Inner Mongolia be excluded from the scope of operations of the international consortium. Further, the British and American Governments conceded Japan's right of option in the construction of certain railways in Manchuria, among them the Kirin-Huining, the Chengchiatun-Taonanfu, the Changchun-Taonanfu, the Kaiyuan-Kirin (*via* Hailungcheng) railways,

[64] *The Consortium,* p. 56.

and admitted that certain others already constructed by Japanese capital were outside the scope of the consortium. The Taonanfu-Jehol railway and one to connect the same with the seacoast were specifically included within the scope of the consortium's operations, while the right of Japan to veto the construction of a railway from the Taonanfu-Jehol line to the Chinese Eastern Railway was not conceded by the British and American Governments, though they gave Japan general assurance that the operations of the consortium in connection therewith would be in a spirit of mutual cooperation.

To the initial letter of the Japanese financial representative (M. Odagiri) of June 18, 1919, the representative of the American financial group (Thomas W. Lamont) replied on June 23 that:

"Mongolia and Manchuria are important parts of China, and any attempt to exclude them from the scope of the Consortium must be inadmissable. The 'special interests' to which you allude have, in our opinion, never had to do with economic matters." [65]

Consequently the matter was referred to the Department of State for consideration as a political question beyond the competence of the consortium for attention.

The Department of State addressed a memorandum to the Japanese Embassy at Washington on July 30, 1919, protesting against a blanket exclusion of South Manchuria and Inner Mongolia from the scope of operations of the consortium, stating:

"The Imperial Japanese Government will readily understand that the Government of the United States could not consistently consent that the American bankers agree to the reservation proposed, for the reason that it is believed to be an essential prerequisite to the proper functioning of the Consortium that all Chinese business of the classes proposed as appropriate for the activity of the Consortium be available for it. Reservations of regions can only impair its usefulness as an instrument for good, and limitations on its activity can only detract from its utility as a means for promoting international cooperation among those most interested in China." [66]

The British Foreign Office, in a memorandum of August 11, 1919, took a like stand with respect to Japan's attempt to exclude South Manchuria and Eastern Inner Mongolia from the scope of operations of the consortium, and further declared in clear terms its opposition to "special claims in particular spheres of interest," declaring:

[65] Ibid., p. 20.
[66] Ibid., p. 26.

· "One of the fundamental objects of the American proposals as accepted by the British, Japanese and French Governments, is to eliminate special claims in particular spheres of interest and to throw open the whole of China without reserve to the combined activities of an International Consortium. . . . Manchuria and Mongolia are important provinces of China and any attempt to exclude them from the scope of the Consortium would constitute a direct negation of the principle on which the Consortium is based, would provoke the revival of similar claims on the part of other nations and thus perpetuate the very difficulties which the Consortium is designed to obviate." [67]

To the memorandum of the Japanese Government of August 27, 1919, the United States Department of State replied on October 28, 1919, declaring themselves "unable to assent to the proviso in reference to South Manchuria and Eastern Inner Mongolia" on the ground that the proposal of Japan was tantamount to "an intermixture of exclusive political pretensions in a project which all the other Governments and groups have treated in a liberal and self-denying spirit." [68] The Department of State made it clear that they had no intention to countenance action of the consortium which would impair the "existing rights and interests" of Japan in Manchuria, i.e., those in the nature of vested proprietary rights.

The British Foreign Office replied to the Japanese communication of September 1, 1919, with one of November 19, 1919, taking a position almost identical with that taken by the United States, but reiterating its opposition to "spheres of interest" and special claims therein, declaring that "the admission of such a claim to a monopoly of commercial interests in a large geographical area of China would be a direct infringement of the fundamental idea underlying the creation of the Consortium." [69] In particular the British Government was disinclined to accept the Japanese view that Eastern Inner Mongolia should be excluded from the consortium's operations because there, "although options for railways have been granted to Japan, no work has yet been begun." Such a claim as that of Japan, because of the proximity of Eastern Inner Mongolia to Peking could not be reconciled with "the maintenance of the independence and territorial integrity of China which Japan has so often pledged herself to observe."

Replying to the Japanese memorandum of March 2, 1920, which had requested adherence to a specific formula for the reservation of Japanese rights, the Department of State of the United

[67] *The Consortium*, p. 28.
[68] *Ibid.*, p. 31.
[69] *Ibid.*, p. 33.

States stated on March 16, 1920, that it had taken cognizance of the "disavowal by Japan of any claim to exclusive economic or political rights with respect to South Manchuria and Eastern Inner Mongolia" and were compelled to reject the Japanese formula. The American memorandum, however, reasserted the assurance given to Japan in the Lansing-Ishii agreement of November 2, 1917, that "the right of national self-preservation is one of universal acceptance in the relations of States," and stated that there would be no reason to apprehend on the part of the consortium any activities inimical to the economic life or national defence of Japan. But the note declared that the Government of the United States "finds it difficult to believe that in order to meet the necessities of Japanese economic or political security it is essential for Japan alone to construct and control a railway line of such a character as the one projected from Taonanfu to Jehol and thence to the seacoast." [70] The British Foreign Office replied to the Japanese memorandum of March 16, 1920, with one dated March 19, expressing in substance the same attitude. [71]

When the Japanese Government sought to secure the sanction of Great Britain and the United States to Japan's asserted right to veto the construction of a railway from the Taonanfu-Jehol line to the Chinese Eastern Railway, the British and American Governments replied, refusing the concession, their replies dated respectively, April 28 and 29, 1920. The British reply stated that "Japan practically asks for a right to veto construction by the Consortium of a line from Taonanfu to join the Chinese Eastern Railway, on the ground that such an extension would be tantamount to a renewal of the so-called Chinchou-Aigun Railway scheme, against which Japan had lodged a protest some years ago," but that, although the British Government had "no wish to do anything which would conflict with the vital interests of their ally," they could not adhere to Japan's assertion of right with respect to the railway into North Manchuria. The British Government, however, did waive their former objection to the exclusion from the consortium of the projected lines from Taonanfu to Changchun, and from Taonanfu to Chengchiatun. [72] The American Government similarly suggested a compromise. [73]

It was in reply to these British and American statements that the Japanese Government made the declarations of May 8 and 10 that as to the projected railway to connect Taonan with the Chinese

[70] Ibid., p. 38.
[71] Ibid., p. 44.
[72] Ibid., p. 52.
[73] Ibid., p. 54.

Eastern Railway they were prepared to withdraw their request for specific reservation from the scope of the consortium, relying on the general assurances given by the British and American Governments that they would countenance no activities of the consortium inimical to the economic life and national defense of Japan.[74] The right of Japan to veto the construction of the proposed line from Taonanfu to the Chinese Eastern Railway was not conceded by Great Britain and the United States, while the Taonanfu-Jehol line and that to the sea were specifically included within the scope of the consortium.   On May 11, 1920, the representative of the American financial group (Thomas W. Lamont), then in Japan, replied to a letter from the Japanese financial representative (N. Kajiwara) of the same date, which indicates the outcome of these negotiations:

"Inasmuch as some questions have arisen during our discussions as to the status of specific railway enterprises contemplated or actually begun in Manchuria and Mongolia, we hereby confirm that we have agreed with you as follows:

1. That the South Manchurian Railway and its present branches, together with the mines which are subsidiary to the railway, do not come within the scope of the Consortium;

2. That the projected Taonanfu-Jehol Railway and the projected railway connecting a point on the Taonanfu-Jehol Railway with a seaport are to be included within the terms of the Consortium Agreement;

3. That the Kirin-Huining, the Chengchiatun-Taonanfu, the Changchun-Taonanfu, the Kaiyuan-Kirin (via Hailung), the Kirin-Changchun, the Hsinminfu-Mukden and the Ssupingkai-Chengchiatun Railways are outside the scope of the joint activities of the Consortium." [75]

The text of the final China consortium agreement of October 15, 1920, contains no reservations as to South Manchuria and Eastern Inner Mongolia, except such as have general application elsewhere in China, as, for example, the exclusion of "existing agreements relating to industrial undertakings upon which it can be shown that substantial progress has been made." [76]   The scope of operations of the consortium was clearly defined, as especially in Article 2, which follows:

"This Agreement relates to existing and future loan agreements which involve the issue for subscription by the public of loans to the Chinese Gov-

[74] *The Consortium*, pp. 56, 58.
[75] *Ibid.*, p. 61.
[76] *Ibid.*, p. 67.

ernment or to Chinese Government Departments or to Provinces of China or to companies or corporations owned or controlled by or on behalf of the Chinese Government or any Chinese Provincial Government or to any party if the transaction in question is guaranteed by the Chinese Government or Chinese Provincial Government but does not relate to agreements for loans to be floated in China. Existing agreements relating to industrial undertakings upon which it can be shown that substantial progress has been made may be omitted from the scope of this Agreement."

It should be kept in mind that the consortium agreement did not preclude, but actually specified (Article 5) and sanctioned, individual activities of each national banking group with respect to such loans as designated, provided (Article 7) that each participated only within its own market, and provided (Article 5) that "so far as possible" any national banking group was to "come to an understanding" with the entire consortium membership and float loans on a parity with those floated in other markets in a similar case. The purpose of the consortium was defined in the preamble which indicated that the organization had been formed to eliminate undesirable competition, "to assist China in the establishment of her great public utilities and to these ends to welcome the cooperation of Chinese capital." To this end the respective governments were to extend their support. The consortium agreement was to continue in force for five years. During the period from 1920 to 1925 the consortium undertook to float no loan with respect to financing the construction of any railway or other enterprise in Manchuria.

CHAPTER XLV

The Position of the Powers Other than Japan and Russia
(1915-1921)

a. THE GENERAL POSITION OF THE UNITED STATES, GREAT BRITAIN AND FRANCE. Detailed attention having been given in the previous sections to the combined interests of the United States, Great Britain and France in the four power international banking consortium negotiations and agreement, and to their bearing on Manchuria, as also to the combined interests of the several powers in the agreement for Inter-allied control and management of the Chinese Eastern Railway, it remains but to summarize the positions of each of these three powers with respect to their more specific interests and the treaty provisions bearing thereon.

The United States, in a communication of the Secretary of

State to the Japanese Ambassador at Washington, dated March 13, 1915, raised several questions with regard to the exact character of the proposals submitted by Japan for ratification by China in the negotiations of 1915. The American Government in that communication raised no objections to the articles which proposed to recognize Japan's "special position" in South Manchuria and Eastern Inner Mongolia, nor to those providing for the extension of the term of the lease of Kwantung and of the term of the South Manchuria Railway, but did state definite objections to the proposal that Japanese political, financial and military advisers be employed exclusively by China, and asserted that, under the most favored nation clauses of the American treaties with China, the United States would be entitled "to claim from China the same rights as those which Japan now seeks to have granted exclusively to her subjects" in commercial matters. This same communication, however, did contain the statement that "the United States frankly recognizes that territorial contiguity creates special relations between Japan and these districts" (Shantung, South Manchuria and "East Mongolia").[77] The latter phrase was repeated in part in the Lansing-Ishii agreement of November 2, 1917. On May 11, 1915, the Department of State instructed the American Ambassador at Tokyo to inform the Japanese Minister for Foreign Affairs that the American Government "cannot recognize any agreement or undertaking which has been entered into or which may be entered into between the Governments of Japan and China, impairing the treaty rights of the United States and its citizens in China, the political or territorial integrity of the Republic of China, or the international policy relative to China commonly known as the open door policy." The instructions were received and followed on May 13, 1915.[78]

The British participated, as did the French, in the Inter-allied control and management of the Chinese Eastern Railway and their bankers (the Hongkong and Shanghai Banking Corporation, Ltd., and Banque de l'Indo Chine) signed the China consortium agreement in 1920, after the British Government had taken an active part in securing the withdrawal of certain of the Japanese proposed reservations with respect to South Manchuria and

[77] U. S. Foreign Relations, 1915, pp. 105-111. See Chap. XLVII, Sec. a.
[78] U. S. Foreign Relations, 1915, p. 146.

Eastern Inner Mongolia.[79] The fact of the existence of the Anglo-Japanese treaty of alliance of 1911 did not prevent the British Government from contesting certain of the claims of Japan with reference to exclusion of South Manchuria from the sphere of operations of the consortium.

The French Government had a particular interest in the arrangements for Inter-allied management of the Chinese Eastern Railway by virtue of the fact that originally it had been the Paris bankers who had advanced loans to the Russian Government, part of which was used for the organization and finance of the Russo-Chinese Bank, which became the Russo-Asiatic Bank after fusion with the Banque du Nord. After the Russian Revolution the Soviet Government nationalized all Russian banks, and as the Russo-Asiatic Bank (originally the Russo-Chinese Bank) had been incorporated under Russian law, the Soviet Government took charge of its head offices in Petrograd. The bank, inasmuch as some of the bonds were held by the French, was reorganized in Paris, a procedure permissible under the statutes, thus coming under the protection of the French Government. It was following this reorganization that the Russo-Asiatic Bank entered into the agreement with China of October 2, 1920, ten days after the promulgation of the Chinese presidential mandate withdrawing recognition from the Tsarist representative, Prince Koudacheff, in Peking. Later in 1924, when China and Russia signed the agreements of May extending recognition to the Soviet Government and establishing a provisional basis for the management of the Chinese Eastern Railway to the exclusion of the interests of other parties, the French

[79] Having important bearing on the subject of Japan's position at the Peace Conference at Paris in 1919 and her interests in China, particularly with respect to the ultimate disposal of the former German rights in Shantung, but indirectly with respect also to the general commitments of the powers as to Manchuria, is the group of commitments which Japan received in 1917 from Great Britain, France, Russia and Italy with regard to Shantung. In order to obtain the assistance of Japan after January, 1917, in an effort to counteract the German blockade the British Government agreed, in an exchange of notes dated February 16/21, 1917, to support the claims of Japan to the former German rights in Shantung when the matter should come up for settlement in the peace conference at the end of the war. A further commitment was made at the same time that Great Britain would support Japan's claims to the German possessions in the islands north of the equator. France, for different reasons, made a similar commitment in the note of March 1, 1917, to the Japanese Government. On February 20, 1917, the Russian Government made a similar commitment. Italy gave a similar, but verbal promise. These arrangements between Japan and the four powers mentioned were kept secret until the Paris Peace Conference; and the United States was, therefore, not informed of their existence when Secretary Lansing and Viscount Ishii signed the agreement of November 2, 1917. See Chap. XLVII, Sec. a. (MacMurray, Vol. II, pp. 1167-1169.)

Government, calling attention to the changed status of the Russo-Asiatic Bank, protested and refused to recognize the latter arrangement. It is not evident, however, that either the French Government or French financiers have any vested proprietary rights in the Chinese Eastern Railway, or any claims in the original Russo-Chinese Bank other than such as may be recoverable directly from the Russian Government.

D. TREATIES AND AGREEMENTS OF ALLIANCE, COOPERATION AND GUARANTEE: 1915-1921

CHAPTER XLVI

Russo-Japanese Convention and Treaty of 1916

a. RUSSO-JAPANESE CONVENTION OF 1916. On July 3, 1916, the Russian and Japanese Governments, just before the Russian Revolution, signed two agreements, the one an open political convention, the other a secret treaty or convention which sought to reaffirm the three previous secret treaties of 1907, 1910 and 1912. The political convention, signed at Petrograd, provided in general terms for cooperation of Russia and Japan in the Far East, stipulating (Article 1) that neither would be a party to any arrangement or political combination directed against the other; that (Article 2) "in case either the territorial rights or the special interests in the Far East of one of the Contracting Parties, recognized by the other Contracting Party, should be menaced, Russia and Japan will confer in regard to the measures to be taken with a view to mutual support or cooperation for the safeguarding and defense of these rights and interests." [80] Inasmuch as this convention was supplemented by a secret treaty of the same date it was couched in general terms.

b. RUSSO-JAPANESE SECRET TREATY OF 1916. The fact that a secret treaty of separate articles was signed at Petrograd (by Sazonov and Motono) simultaneously with the open political convention of cooperation above characterized seems now to have been well established. The Trotsky-Lenin Government in Russia published in 1918 in official form the text of this Russo-Japanese secret treaty of July 3, 1916, and an English version was initially published in the *Manchester Guardian* on February 1, 1918.[81] This

[80] Russo-Japanese *Convention in regard to Cooperation in the Far East,* July 3, 1916. MacMurray, Vol. II, p. 1327.

[81] The authenticity of this secret Russo-Japanese treaty of 1916 with respect to Manchuria and Mongolia seems to have been well established, especially by the fact that the texts, as found in the archives of the Tsarist Foreign Office, were in 1917 published by the revolutionary government. For a discussion of this entire subject see Appendix D. An English translation of the text of the treaty was printed in the *Manchester Guardian* for February 1, 1918, another in the *New York Evening Post* on March 2, 1918, and may be found in the texts referred to in the appendix to which attention is called.

secret treaty or convention established in the preamble the authenticity of the Russo-Japanese secret treaties of July 17/30, 1907, of June 21/July 4, 1910, and of June 25/July 8, 1912. It provided (Article 1) that Russia and Japan recognized the "vital interests" of each other in China and bound them to come to an understanding for cooperative action in case the actions of any third power should bring about a state of affairs which would prejudice these declared interests. Therefore, it was provided (Article 2) that if, in consequence of the development of a situation as characterized in Article 1, there should result a declaration of war against either Russia or Japan, "the other party, at the first demand of its Ally, must come to its aid," and to continue that support until peace were established. The conditions of such active assistance in war were to be decided (Article 3) by the proper authorities. But armed aid was to be given conditional (Article 4) upon the obtaining of guarantees from the Allies (in the Great War) that the latter would give the assisting party aid "corresponding in character to the importance of the approaching conflict." The importance of this article may be found in the fact that at that time neither the United States nor China had become one of the Allied Powers in the Great War against Germany. The treaty of alliance (Article 5) was to remain in force until July 1/14, 1921, but to continue in force for another year unless there were a specific declaration of intention to terminate the treaty one year before the date set for expiration, i.e., July 1/14, 1921. The treaty of alliance was to be kept (Article 7) secret from all powers other than the signatories.[82] The Russian Revolution, however, resulted in a denunciation of this treaty along with others, and the

[82] *Sale of a Portion of the Chinese Eastern Railway to Japan.* In connection with the signing of the Russo-Japanese political convention and the secret treaty of alliance it appears that there was simultaneously signed a preliminary agreement for the sale of the southern section of the Chinese Eastern Railway, from Kuan-chengtzu to Laoshaokou, to Japan, for a consideration of 10,000,000 roubles (about $3,000,000 at the time). The section to be sold was about seventy-five miles in length (or fifty miles if only to the Sungari river) and was to extend to the Sungari river and beyond, the crossing to be arranged by Japan through separate agreement with China. It appears that the completion of the transaction was thus actually frustrated by the Chinese Government which took umbrage at the sale of this section of the Chinese Eastern Railway to Japan. The existence of such a preliminary agreement for the sale of the line, however, was admitted by the Japanese Government at the time and is supported by circumstantial evidence in the fact that the Japanese Department of Agriculture and Commerce made a statement to the press on July 9, 1916, recognizing the transaction and commenting on the commercial value of the acquisition. Baron Ishii informed the British Ambassador at Tokyo that a preliminary agreement of that nature had been signed with Russia during July, 1916, but that difficulties arose in connection with the arrangements to be made with the Chinese Government for traffic over the Sungari river and in connection with the question of Japanese navigation

fact of its existence was made known through the publication by the Trotsky-Lenin régime in Petrograd in 1918.

CHAPTER XLVII

American-Japanese Agreement of 1917 ✓

a. THE LANSING-ISHII AGREEMENT OF 1917. The immediate antecedents of the particular exchange of notes of November 2, 1917, which has become generally known as the Lansing-Ishii agreements have an important bearing on the interpretation of that mutual declaration of policy of the United States and Japan. During January, 1917, the British and Japanese Governments indicated their willingness to have the American bankers renew their active participation in offering with the other powers loans to China through the Six Power Consortium. The rumor that American banking interests desired to participate along with Japan and other countries in offering loans for railway construction in Manchuria led the Japanese Ambassador at Washington to inquire of the American Secretary of State on January 25, 1917, if such were contemplated, to which the Secretary replied that "the Ambassador must be aware that the American Government recognized that Japan had special interests in Manchuria. Although no declaration to that effect had been made by the United States yet this Government had repeatedly shown a practical recognition of the fact and did not desire to do anything there to interfere with Japan's interests. . . . The Secretary called the attention of the Ambassador in this connection to the difference between

rights on the Sungari. The American Ambassador at Tokyo communicated to the Department of State under date of July 18, 1916, that: "We now have confidential information that these matters have been finally agreed to and the conventions signed, subject, however, to some settlement with China as to navigation rights on the Sungari river." The Japanese Foreign Office declared during August that these arrangements had not been finally perfected. It was generally understood in Tokyo that the manner of payment for the section purchased would be in the form of war materials to be supplied to the Russians. (*U. S. Foreign Relations*, 1916, p. 436; pp. 438; 440-446.) Finally, it is evident that the Japanese Government have not acquired possession and assumed management of the section of the Chinese Eastern Railway in question, and its exact status is not clear. The Russian Revolution occurred in 1917, whereupon, after the attempted pro-Bolshevik *coup d'état* in Harbin in the late autumn of that year, General Horvath became General Manager of the Chinese Eastern Railway, the Chinese members of the Board of Directors taking no significant part in the management of the line. The character of the relations which followed between the Japanese General Staff and General Horvath and later Ataman Semenov is a subject beyond the scope of this study, but is mentioned here only to draw attention to some of the reasons for the failure of the complete transfer to Japan of this the most extreme southern section of the Chinese Eastern Railway.

Manchuria, where Japan's special interests were conceded, and Shantung where no such special interests were recognized." [83] In response to an inquiry from the American Minister in Peking the State Department further explained their interpretation of the statements made to the Japanese Ambassador on January 25, 1917, to this effect:

"In my conversation with the Japanese Ambassador I had in mind nothing more than to point out the difference between conditions in Shantung and those in Manchuria, and, in using the phrase 'special interests,' I had reference only to such specific concessions as the lease of the Kwantung Peninsula and the lease of the South Manchuria and other railways with the right to maintain railway guards, et cetera.

"The assumption of the Legation, therefore, is correct, that the 'special interests' of Japan, in the view of the Department, are to be understood as confined to those specific rights and privileges which were obtained by the Japanese Government from China and from Russia by way of international agreement." [84]

On June 13, 1917, Viscount Ishii Kikujiro was appointed by the Japanese Government Ambassador Extraordinary and Plenipotentiary to the United States at the head of a mission which was to proceed to Washington to arrive at an understanding with the American Government with regard to outstanding international questions bearing on the relations of the two countries in the Far East, especially with reference to China. The mission arrived in the United States in August, and following preliminary conversations and exchanges of views the representatives of Japan and the United States signed the so-called Lansing-Ishii agreement of November 2, 1917, the same being in the nature of an exchange of notes, and not in any sense a treaty.

Two days after the appointment of Viscount Ishii to his mission (June 15) the then Japanese Ambassador at Washington read a paper to the American Secretary of State in which he asserted that, on account of recent rumors emanating from Peking concerning the alleged involvement of the American Government in "the present political crisis" in China, and due to the then recent representations of the American Government to the Chinese Government in Peking (counseling China to establish a responsible and united central government by composing internal political

[83] U. S. Foreign Relations, 1917, pp. 116-118. Secretary Lansing to Ambassador Guthrie (Tokyo).
[84] U. S. Foreign Relations, 1917, p. 187. Secretary Lansing to Minister Reinsch (Peking).

differences) "without previously consulting Japan," there had been "generated in the minds of a certain part of the people (of Japan) a feeling of uneasiness." The Ambassador, therefore, requested that the United States take appropriate means to reassert "its friendly attitude toward Japan in respect of Chinese problems." [85]

On June 22, 1917, the Secretary of State, after acknowledging the appointment of Viscount Ishii as envoy to the United States at the head of a mission, stated to the Japanese Ambassador then at Washington that:

"The American Government is pleased to remove any doubts which may arise as to its purpose by reaffirming the statements made in the note of Secretary Bryan to Viscount Chinda, dated March 13, 1915." [86]

The American Secretary of State called attention to the details of that statement of Secretary Bryan, in particular to the lengthy declaration of the unqalified adherence of the United States to the policy of preserving the territorial and administrative integrity of China, and of maintaining equality of opportunity for commerce and industry in China, and drew attention further to the fact that Secretary Bryan in that note of March 13, 1915, had declared that the inclusion in any Sino-Japanese treaty or agreement of a provision making obligatory upon China the recogni-

[85] *U. S. Foreign Relations,* 1917, p. 259. It may be admitted that the exact reasons which prompted the sending of the Ishii Mission to the United States at that time, and which prompted the United States to enter into the agreement with Japan, may not yet be known publicly. The recent publication of *United States Foreign Relations* for 1917, however, serves to throw new light on the rôle which purely Chinese questions played in the arrangement then made. It is for this reason that special emphasis has been placed on these new materials. This new evidence substantiates the assertion that, whatever may have been the influence of the desire to enter into an arrangement on naval matters (though the United States was not then informed of the secret naval agreements between Japan, on the one hand, and Great Britain, France and Italy, on the other), and whatever may have been the real importance of the alleged effort to dispel rumors spread by German propaganda concerning Japanese and American motives in China, there were influences germane to China and Manchuria which were of special importance.

Three additional factors, therefore, appear to have played a combined rôle of some importance in bringing about the exchange of notes between Mr. Lansing and Viscount Ishii: (1) the rumor which reached Japan that American bankers were seeking to launch loans for railway construction in Manchuria; (2) the American declaration to the Chinese Government urging the various Chinese factions to compose their differences and support a unified government; and (3) the Japanese misgivings with regard to the activities of the late Dr. Paul S. Reinsch, American Minister at Peking. Evidence to this effect may be found in the diplomatic correspondence published in *United States Foreign Relations,* 1917, for the months of January to June, important portions of which are quoted in context above. In the light of this correspondence there is little evidence to support the statement that "this agreement was only another of the many measures of expediency imposed by the political exigencies of the War," a certain British view.

[86] *U. S. Foreign Relations,* 1917, p. 261. Secretary of State to Japanese Ambassador.

tion of a preferential and exclusive right to have Japanese advisers, political, military and police, appointed by the Chinese Government was "derogatory to the political independence and administrative entity of that country." [87]   The Secretary of State further declared in that statement of June 22, 1917, that he was willing to reaffirm the statement of Secretary Bryan on March 13, 1915, to the effect that the United States Government "recognizes that territorial contiguity creates special relations between Japan and these districts," the latter having been used by Secretary Bryan (as stated in his communication of March 13) to apply solely to Shantung, South Manchuria and "East Mongolia," and not to China generally.   He declared to the Japanese Ambassador:

"I desire to direct your excellency's attention to the fact that, while Mr. Bryan's note thus expressed the views of the United States in regard to international relations in the Far East, I do not find that it anywhere went to the extent of stating or recognizing that Japan has special or close relations, political as well as economic, with China as a whole, as your excellency stated at our interview on June 15 last.   Mr. Bryan merely said that the United States recognized that territorial contiguity creates special relations between the districts of Shantung, Southern Manchuria and East Mongolia, but he did not admit that the United States might not in the future be justified in expressing its views in regard to Chino-Japanese relations involving these districts." [88]

The American Secretary also took exception to the representation of the Japanese Ambassador to his home government that the Secretary had referred to Japan's interests as "paramount," asserting that the term used was "special" interest.

The outcome of these preliminary exchanges of views between the then Japanese Ambassador at Washington and the American Secretary of State was the understanding with regard to the same general question arrived at between Viscount Ishii, after his arrival in August, and the Department of State.   The formal agreement, commonly known as the Lansing-Ishii agreement of November 2, 1917, was in the form of an exchange of notes and as such did not receive, and did not need to receive, the consent of the United States Senate to be binding.   Consequently, the status of the agreement was distinct from that of a treaty formally approved by the Senate for ratification. [89]   The exchanges of notes of November 2 declared that they embodied the "desires

[87] U. S. Foreign Relations, 1917, p. 261.   Secretary of State to Japanese Ambassador.
[88] Ibid.
[89] The text of the so-called Lansing-Ishii agreement of November 2, 1917, was published on November 6 in the United States and on November 7 in Japan, although

and intentions" of the two powers "with regard to China." The text of the American note of November 2, as acknowledged and confirmed by Viscount Ishii Kikujiro on the same date, declared:

"The Governments of the United States and Japan recognize that territorial propinquity creates special relations between countries, and, consequently, the Government of the United States recognizes that Japan has special interests in China, particularly in the part to which her possessions are contiguous.

"The territorial sovereignty of China, nevertheless, remains unimpaired and the Government of the United States has every confidence in the repeated assurances of the Imperial Japanese Government that while geographical position gives Japan such special interests they have no desire to discriminate against the trade of other nations or to disregard the commercial rights heretofore granted by China in treaties with other powers.

"The Governments of the United States and Japan deny that they have any purposes to infringe in any way the independence or territorial integrity of China and they declare, furthermore, that they always adhere to the principle of the so-called 'Open Door' or equal opportunity for commerce and industry in China.

"Moreover, they mutually declare that they are opposed to the acquisition by any Government of any special rights or privileges that would effect the independence or territorial integrity of China or that would deny to the subjects or citizens of any country the full enjoyment of equal opportunity in the commerce and industry of China." [90]

The body of the notes as exchanges in identic terms thus contained both a recognition of the fact that "territorial propinquity creates special relations between countries, and consequently, the Government of the United States recognizes that Japan has special interests in China, particularly in the part to which her possessions are contiguous" and, in three other paragraphs of each note, a very clear reassertion of the declared policy of each of the two governments with respect to observance of the principle of recognizing "the territorial sovereignty of China," "the independence or territorial integrity of China," and "the principle of the so-called 'Open Door' or equal opportunity for commerce and industry in China." [91]

the texts of the agreement had been released in Tokyo and Peking prematurely. The official text was published in: *U. S. Treaty Series*, No. 630 (Washington, 1919), under the title: "Agreement Effected by Exchange of Notes between the United States and Japan: Mutual Interest relating to the Republic of China." Also to be found in MacMurray, Vol. II, pp. 1394-1396; *U. S. Foreign Relations*, 1917, pp. 264-265.

[90] *U. S. Foreign Relations*, 1917, pp. 264-265.

[91] The somewhat controversial point as to whether or not the United States drew a distinction, in the negotiations preliminary to the signing of the so-called Lansing-Ishii agreement, between Shantung and Manchuria is considered at some length in Appendix E.

Bearing on the interpretation of the so-called Lansing-Ishii agreement is the note of November 8, 1917, sent by the United States Department of State for transmission through the American Legation in Peking and at once communicated to the Chinese Foreign Office. The statement declared that the Japanese Government had proclaimed in the exchange of notes of November 2 that "the policy of Japan as regards China is not one of aggression," that Japan had "no intention to take advantage commercially or indirectly of the special relations to China created by geographical position," and that "the Governments of the United States and Japan again declare their adherence to the Open Door Policy and recommit themselves, so far as these two Governments are concerned, to the maintenance of equal opportunity for the full enjoyment by the subjects or citizens of any country in the commerce and industry of China." This statement of the American Government declared further that "Japanese commercial and industrial enterprises in China manifestly have, on account of the geographical relation of the two countries, a certain advantage over similar enterprises on the part of citizens or subjects of any other country," that "the statements in the Notes require no explanation," but that "they not only contain a reaffirmation of the Open Door Policy but introduce a principle of non-interference with the sovereignty and territorial integrity of China, which, generally applied, is essential to perpetual international peace." [92]

On November 9, 1917, the Chinese Foreign Office replied to the above statement of the United States (the replies given to the American Minister in Peking and by the Chinese Minister at Washington to the Department of State) to the effect, *inter alia,* that "the Chinese Government will not allow herself to be bound by any agreement entered into by other nations." [93] In the conversations between the Chinese Minister at Washington and the American Secretary of State on November 12, 1917, the Secretary gave a detailed explanation of his use of the term "special interests" in the agreement with Viscount Ishii of November 2, asserting that the recognition of Japan's "special interests" particularly in the part (of China) to which her possessions are con-

[92] *U. S. Foreign Relations,* 1917, p. 268; also in MacMurray, Vol. II, p. 1396. For a discussion of the rendering of the terms "special interests" and "special advantage" into Chinese see Appendix E.
[93] MacMurray, Vol. II, p. 1396.

tiguous was but "the statement of an axiom," capable, under current international practice, of universal application.[94]

For the American interpretation of the terminology of the so-called Lansing-Ishii agreement of November 2, 1917, the statements of the Department of State preceding the signing by the international banking groups of the China consortium agreement of October 15, 1920, have direct application. The United States Government throughout the correspondence with the Japanese Government adhered to its statement of July 30, 1919, to the Japanese Embassy at Washington that "the Government of the United States could not consistently consent that the American bankers agree to the reservation proposed" by the Japanese financial group that "Manchuria and Mongolia, where Japan has special interests, should be excluded from the arrangements for pooling provided for in the proposed agreement." [95] That the interpretation by the Japanese Government of the so-called Lansing-Ishii agreement differed from that of the United States has been frequently asserted. As no subsequent statement of mutual agreement as to the interpretation of the so-called Lansing-Ishii agreement has been published under the joint signatures of the representatives of the two governments it is reasonable to assume a different interpretation by the Japanese Government, though the texts of the notes exchanged on November 2, 1917, were in the English language. When the United States Government, however, called attention to the fact, in a communication to the Japanese Embassy on March 16, 1920, that the notes exchanged between Secretary Lansing and Viscount Ishii on November 2, 1917, contained an implicit statement that "the right of national self-preservation is one of universal acceptance in the relations between States," the Japanese Government replied (April 3, 1920) accepting that statement and offering no differing interpretation of the so-called Lansing-Ishii agreement.[96]

The new and more comprehensive definition of the "open door" policy contained in the nine-power treaty of the Washington Conference (February 6, 1922) relating to principles and policies to be followed in matters concerning China, by incorporating into a

[94] For a quotation at length from the statement of the American Secretary of State to the Chinese Minister at Washington (November 12, 1917) explaining his interpretation of the agreement with Japan see Appendix E. (*U. S. Foreign Relations*, 1917, p. 273.)

[95] See Chap. XLIV, Sec. b, for a discussion of the American-Japanese exchanges of notes preceding the signing of the China consortium agreement of 1920.

[96] *The Consortium* (Official Texts and Documents), pp. 46-47. See Chap. XLIV, Sec. b. See Appendix E for a note on the Japanese interpretation.

formal treaty, signed by the powers including Japan and the United States, a series of provisions among which was the commitment not to seek "any general superiority of rights with respect to commercial or economic development in any designated region of China," actually was of a nature to supersede any such arrangement as contained in the Lansing-Ishii exchange of notes of 1917.[97] The Lansing-Ishii agreement was not, however, specifically abrogated or repudiated at the Washington Conference or in the treaties pursuant thereto. The agreement was formally terminated by an exchange of notes of April 14, 1923, between the American Secretary of State (Charles Evans Hughes) and the Japanese Ambassador at Washington (Hanihara Masanao) in which it was stated that "in the light of the understandings arrived at by the Washington Conference on the Limitation of Armament, the American and Japanese Governments are agreed to consider the Lansing-Ishii correspondence of November 2, 1917, as cancelled and of no further force or effect." [98]

Before concluding the subject of the so-called Lansing-Ishii agreement it is pertinent to recall that the recognition of certain kinds of "special interests" of Japan in "the regions of the Chinese Empire adjacent to the territories where they [Japan and France] have rights of sovereignty, protection, or occupation" was declared as early as 1907 in the Franco-Japanese agreement, and that even earlier Great Britain in the Anglo-Japanese treaties of alliance of 1902 and 1905, and again in 1911, recognized that Japan had "special interests" in Eastern Asia including China. The Russo-Japanese treaties and conventions of 1907, 1910 and 1912, as well as those of 1916 went farther by recognizing that Japan had a "sphere of interest" (especially with respect to railways) in South Manchuria.[99] From the texts of the various agreements of Japan with the foreign powers it is obvious that the Japanese "interests" recognized by Russia, Great Britain and France were broader in scope and character than those recognized by the United States.

[97] For the statement of the President of the United States (Warren G. Harding) before the Senate Foreign Relations Committee (March 7, 1922) on the occasion of the transmission of the texts of the Lansing-Ishii agreement to that body, see Appendix E.

[98] *American Journal of International Law*, Vol. 17 (1923), pp. 510-512; *U. S. Treaty Series*, No. 667.

[99] For the recognition by other foreign powers of Japan's "special interests" in certain districts of China, see: for the French, Chap. XXXVI, Sec. a; for the British, Chap. XXXIII, Secs. a and b; for the Russian, Chap. XXXV, Secs. a, b and c, and Chap. XLVI, Secs. a and b.

CHAPTER XLVIII

Sino-Japanese Military and Naval Agreements of 1918

a. Sino-Japanese Military Cooperation Agreements and Manchuria, 1918.   In pursuance of an exchange of notes between the Japanese Minister for Foreign Affairs and the Chinese Minister at Tokyo, dated March 25, 1918, the Japanese and Chinese Governments signed two agreements, one for military cooperation, dated May 16, 1918, and one for naval cooperation, dated May 19, 1918, both negotiated at Peking.   Before the publication of these agreements of military and naval cooperation (which was authorized by the two governments on March 14, 1919) the Japanese Minister for Foreign Affairs, on May 30, 1918, made the official statement that as the accords were in the nature of military agreements their immediate publication was undesirable, but that the agreements "only embody concrete arrangements as to the manner and conditions under which the armies and navies of the two countries are to cooperate in common defence against the enemy." [100]   The statement scouted the assumption that they contained provisions by which "Japan will take the control of Chinese railways," *etc.*   As previously noted, this military alliance was signed shortly after an attempted Soviet Russian *coup d'état* in Harbin (November, 1917).

The terms of these two agreements refer, in the main, to the character which cooperation between Japan and China should assume and have only indirect bearing on Manchuria, except for certain provisions noted hereafter.   The agreement for military cooperation (May 16, 1918) provided that (Article 1) in view of the realization "that the gradual extension of enemy influence towards the East may jeopardize the peace of the two countries," China and Japan agree to "take concerted action against the common enemy." [101]   This article had particular bearing on the matter of Sino-Japanese cooperation in Siberia, as shown by the terms of the supplementary military agreement of September 6, 1918, in which the first article provided that this cooperation should be directed to aiding the Czecho-Slovak forces "in the two Siberian provinces of Trans-Baikalia and Amur." [102]   The provi-

---

[100] MacMurray, Vol. II, p. 1408.
[101] Sino-Japanese *Military Agreement*, May 16, 1918. MacMurray, Vol. II, p. 1411.
[102] Sino-Japanese *Supplementary Military Agreement*, September 6, 1918. Mac-Murray, Vol. II, p. 1413.

sions of the naval agreement (May 19, 1918) are not germane to this study, except indirectly.[103]

The provisions of the Sino-Japanese military agreement of May 16, 1918, and of supplementary agreement expanding the same, have especial bearing on Manchuria and the position of Japan in those sections which refer to the transportation of military troops over the Manchurian railways, and in particular in those articles which apply to the Chinese Eastern Railway. The military agreement of May 16, 1918, provided (Article 8) that "when military transportation necessitates the use of the Chinese Eastern Railway, the provisions in the original treaty regarding the management and protection of the said railway shall be respected. The methods of transportation shall be decided upon at the time."[104] The supplementary military agreement of September 6, 1918, expanded this clause by providing that (Article 4) "the transportation of troops over the Chinese Eastern Railway shall be in the hands of the organization having charge of the railway. China and Japan shall establish a joint bureau for the purpose of making proper arrangements with the railway organization for the transportation of Chinese, Japanese and Czecho-Slovak forces over the railway. Should other Allied countries later desire to carry on military operations in this region, they shall be permitted to participate in this bureau."[105]

On the strength of these Sino-Japanese military agreements of 1918 the Japanese General Staff sought to have Japanese military forces in Manchuria take control of the Chinese Eastern Railway. After the opening of the main Trans-Siberian line by the Czecho-Slovak forces, and in pursuance of the Inter-allied agreement of 1919, the Japanese troops occupied the Trans-Baikal railway area as far west as Chita. The Japanese forces actually policed a part of the Chinese Eastern Railway for a period, before General Horvath was deposed, their partial control of the railway ceasing, however, some time after the Japanese Government signed with the other Allied powers the agreement of January 9, 1919, providing for Inter-allied control and management of the Chinese Eastern Railway under the Technical Board and the Military Transportation Board thus established.[106]

By a Sino-Japanese supplementary military agreement of February 5, 1919, it was provided that the original military agree-

[103] MacMurray, Vol. II, p. 1412.
[104] Ibid.
[105] Ibid., p. 1413.
[106] See Chap. XLIV, Sec. 2.

ment of May 16, 1918, should terminate on the end of the war
with Germany and Austria, this to mean when the peace treaty was
signed by Japan and China, and when Chinese and Japanese troops
stationed outside Chinese territories shall have been withdrawn
"simultaneously with the troops of the various Allied countries
stationed in the same territories." [107] It would appear, therefore,
that the Sino-Japanese military agreement of May 16, 1918, did
not actually terminate until the withdrawal of Japanese troops from
Siberia and the Maritime Province after the Washington Conference.[108]

CHAPTER XLIX

Commitments of the Powers to the "Open Door" Policy in Manchuria (1915-1921)

a. SUMMARY STATEMENT OF COMMITMENTS TO THE "OPEN
DOOR" POLICY: 1915-1921. The commitments of the several
powers to the policy of the "open door" in China, which had been
made originally in 1899 and following, were not revoked by any
single power during the period from 1915 to 1921. That several powers, however, entered into agreements which qualified in
practice the statements of general foreign policy, simultaneously or
otherwise made, is obvious. Moreover, the bilateral agreements
of the powers guaranteeing the *status quo* in the Far East, and in
Manchuria, if such agreements are tantamount to bilateral recognition of specific treaty rights, actually were of a nature to modify
in practice the general statement of adhesion to the policy of preserving the territorial and administrative integrity of China and of
maintaining equality of opportunity for commerce and industry
in Manchuria. During this period the question of general recognition of the "vested proprietary rights" of Japan, particularly,
in Manchuria was raised in the negotiations preceding the signing
of the China consortium agreement of 1920.

To the general policy of the "open door," i.e., to the policy of
preserving the territorial and administrative integrity of China and
of maintaining equality of opportunity for commerce and industry
in China, including Manchuria, each of the principal powers concerned with Manchurian affairs committed itself during this period,
reaffirming previous declarations of adherence. On May 11, 1915,
the Department of State of the United States instructed the Amer-

---

[107] MacMurray, Vol. II, p. 1414.
[108] See Chap. XLIV, Sec. a.

ican Ambassador at Tokyo to inform the Japanese Minister for Foreign Affairs that the American Government "cannot recognize any agreement or undertaking which has been entered into or which may be entered into between the Governments of Japan and China, impairing the treaty rights of the United States and its citizens in China, the political or territorial integrity of the Republic of China, or the international policy relative to China commonly known as the open door policy." [109]   On March 13, 1915, the American Secretary of State had communicated to the Japanese Ambassador at Washington a statement recognizing "that territorial contiguity creates special relations between Japan and these districts" among which he specifically included Manchuria.   But the same communication reasserted the traditional American policy of the "open door" and declared, with respect to the provision eventually included in part in a Sino-Japanese exchange of notes of 1915 regarding South Manchuria and which provided that Japanese advisers, political, military and police, should be employed by China if foreign advisers were required, that "these proposals, if accepted by China, while not infringing the territorial integrity of the Republic, are clearly derogatory to the political independence and administrative entity of that country."   The note declared that "the United States could not regard with indifference the assumptions of political, military or economic domination over China by a foreign Power, and hopes that your excellency's Government will find it consonant with their interests to refrain from pressing upon China an acceptance of proposals which would, if accepted, exclude Americans from equal participation in the economic and industrial development of China and would limit the political independence of that country." [110]

In view of the fact that the two provisions of the Russo-Japanese convention of 1916 providing for cooperation in the Far East did not specifically reaffirm the previous declarations of the two governments to preserve the territorial and administrative integrity of China and to maintain equality of opportunity for commerce and industry in China, the United States Government communicated to both of those governments inquiries on the point.   Under date of August 16, 1916, the Department of State instructed the American Ambassador at Tokyo to inquire of the Japanese Foreign Office if there had been any change in their previous policy of observing the "open door" policy, to which the Japanese Foreign

109 *U. S. Foreign Relations,* 1915, p. 146. See Chap. XLV, Sec. a.
110 *Ibid.,* pp. 105-111.

Office replied on September 13 that they had not "entertained for a moment any intention to depart from the policy to which they have avowedly committed themselves respecting the maintenance of the independence and territorial integrity of China as well as the principle of equal opportunity for the trade of all nations in that country." [111]   A like assurance was given by the Russian Foreign Office to the United States on August 23, 1916.[112]

In the Lansing-Ishii agreement of November 2, 1917, the Japanese and American Governments reaffirmed their intentions to adhere to the policy preserving "the independence or territorial integrity of China, and they declare, furthermore, that they always adhere to the principle of the so-called 'Open Door' or equal opportunity for commerce and industry in China." [113]   This same agreement, however, recognized that "territorial propinquity creates special relations between countries, and, consequently, the Government of the United States recognizes that Japan has special interests in China, particularly in the part to which her possessions are contiguous."   A partial explanation of the latter commitment was made to China in the American note of November 8, following which it declared with regard to those "special interests" of Japan: "Japanese commercial and industrial enterprises in China manifestly have, on account of the geographical relation of the two countries, a certain advantage over similar enterprises on the part of citizens or subjects of any other country." [114]   The same communication, however, declared that "the Governments of the United States and Japan again declare their adherence to the Open Door Policy and recommit themselves, as far as these two Governments are concerned, to the maintenance of equal opportunity for the full enjoyment by the subjects or citizens of any country in the commerce and industry of China" and, additionally, "introduce a principle of non-interference with the sovereignty and territorial integrity of China."

In response to the attempts of the Japanese Government to secure reservations to the China consortium agreement of 1920 and to exclude South Manchuria and Eastern Inner Mongolia from the scope of operations of the international banking consortium on the ground that Japan possessed "special interests" in these regions, the British and American Governments declared to Japan

[111] *U. S. Foreign Relations,* 1916, p. 446. Japanese Department of Foreign Affairs to the American Embassy.

[112] *Ibid.,* p. 445.

[113] See Chap. XLVII, Sec. a.

[114] See Chap. XLVII, Sec. a.

that "Mongolia and Manchuria are important provinces [parts] of China, and any attempt to exclude them from the scope of the Consortium would constitute a direct negation of the principle on which the Consortium is based." [115] The British Government declared on November 19, 1919, that the exclusion of Inner Mongolia could not be reconciled with "the maintenance of the independence and territorial integrity of China which Japan has so often pledged herself to observe." The American Government declared on July 30, 1919, that "reservations of regions can only impair its [the consortium's] usefulness as an instrument for good." The final China consortium agreement of October 15, 1920, signed by representatives of the American, British, French and Japanese banking groups, declared that the several national groups were "prepared to participate on equal terms in such undertakings as may be calculated to assist China in the establishment of her great public utilities and to these ends welcome the cooperation of Chinese capital." It is evident from the position of the United States Government, as taken in the negotiations preceding the signing of the China consortium agreement of 1920, that the "special interests" which the United States Government recognized as possessed by Japan in China, "particularly in the part to which her possessions are contiguous," were not such as would in any way preclude the participation of American or other foreign capital in the development of Manchuria. Only "vested proprietary rights" in specific railways and mining enterprises already in operation, and designated prior options to finance certain railway construction in Manchuria, were specifically exempted from the scope of operations of the international banking consortium. The essential purpose of the consortium and the declared policies of the several governments concerned were served in the final consortium agreement which was ratified in consonance with the statement of the American banking group at the outset of the negotiations (July 8, 1918) that "through cooperation of England, France, Japan and the United States much can be accomplished for the maintenance of Chinese sovereignty and the preservation of the 'open door.' " [116]

[115] See Chap. XLIV, Sec. b.
[116] See Chap. XLIV, Sec. b.

CONTENTS

PART IV. THE FOURTH PERIOD: 1921-1929

SUMMARY OF THE FOURTH PERIOD

THE superior position of Japan in Manchuria, which was established by the Sino-Japanese treaty and notes of 1915 with respect to South Manchuria and Eastern Inner Mongolia, and, in fact, was reconstructed on a firmer and broader foundation by those agreements, has not been materially altered since that time. The Washington Conference, while unquestionably the most significant international event of the period from 1921 to 1929 in its bearing on the international relations of Manchuria, did not shake the foundations of Japan's position there. The Conference failed to give decisive consideration to the intrinsic validity of the Sino-Japanese treaties and exchanges of notes of 1915, and, consequently, left the status of the Kwantung leased territory and of the South Manchuria and Antung-Mukden railways intact. Nor did the Conference materially alter the position of Japan with respect to prior rights to construct specific railways under agreements with China, the Japanese declarations going *in fact* no farther than reassertion of the rights which Japan had conceded her during the negotiations attending the formation of the international banking consortium. The Japanese Delegation did, however, withdraw the reservation made in 1915 to the effect that the Japanese Government reserved the right to insist on the performance of certain obligations (i.e., with respect to the employment of Japanese advisers by the Chinese Government in South Manchuria) contained in Group V of the original Japanese demands, and, with specific reference to South Manchuria, contained in the exchange of notes of May, 1915. No concrete program for the removal of foreign troops or "railway guards" from any part of Manchuria was formulated at the Conference, the entire subject of foreign troops, railway guards and police in China (with exceptions specified in areas *outside of Manchuria* being left open for subsequent attention by a commission of inquiry which should proceed only upon a request of China for its constitution. With regard to Japanese postal agencies in Manchuria the Conference took no action, except to adopt a resolution specifically *excepting* postal agencies in leased territories (i.e., in Kwantung leased territory), and those which had been "specifically provided for by treaties," from the application of the general declaration that all foreign postal agencies in China should be abolished *conditionally.* In other words, if it be accepted that no specific treaty provision justifies the maintenance of postal agencies in the South Manchuria Railway zone, then the Japanese Delegation agreed, by approval of the resolution, that such postal agencies would be abolished, but abolished *under conditions* specified in the resolution. The declarations of the Chinese Delegation that Japan possessed and operated wireless stations in Manchuria outside the railway zone without adequate treaty right were successfully contested by the Japanese Delegation. As to wireless installations in the Kwantung leased territory or in the South Manchuria Railway zone, the Conference specifically exempted them from the application of the provision in the radio resolution that foreign radio stations in China should be limited as to their use in transmission of messages. To this resolution, however, the Chinese Delegation made a reservation. As to wire telegraphs in Manchuria the Conference did nothing, except to permit an exchange of views between China and Japan.

From these facts alone it would appear that the Washington Conference could not justifiably be characterized as "unquestionably the most significant international event of the period from 1921 to 1929," as above described. Justification for this characterization rests primarily on the more definite character and international legal status given to the principles of the "open door" policy or doctrine in regard to China as found in the nine power treaty relating to principles and policies concerning China, signed by the several countries, including China, on February 6, 1922. Nor were the exchanges of views as to the interpretation of that treaty of little import. Some importance, furthermore, attaches to the several resolutions adopted which were related both to the undertakings of the powers to observe strictly the territorial and administrative integrity of China, and to maintain equality of opportunity in commercial matters. Finally, the indirect effect of the nine power treaty referred to upon the variant interpretations which in some circles were placed upon the so-called Lansing-Ishii agreement of 1917 is significant. The Conference prepared the way for the categorical termination of that agreement which was accomplished in the following year. The categorical termination of the Anglo-Japanese alliance of 1911 in the four power treaty in regard to the insular possessions of the powers in the Pacific ocean, signed December 13, 1921, had a distinct bearing upon Manchuria. The Anglo-Japanese alliances of 1902, 1905 and 1911 had played a not unimportant rôle in the international relations of Manchuria in matters where British interests were concerned, though the existence of the alliance had not prevented the British Government from contesting the proposed reservations of the Japanese Government to the China consortium agreement of 1920.

The period from 1921 to 1929 saw a continuation of the development of Japanese railway interests in both South and North Manchuria. Construction of the Japanese-financed railway system, connecting the South Manchuria Railway at Ssupingkai with Chengchiatun (and Paiyintalai), Taonan, Angangchi and recently Tsitsihar, continued throughout this period. The specific contract agreement for Japanese financing and construction of the Taonan-Angangchi railway, which now has been extended so as to cross the Chinese Eastern Railway at Tsitsihar-chan, i.e., on to Tsitsihar, the provincial capital of Heilungkiang, was signed in 1924 with the Chinese Government. This new system, which remains legally a Chinese Government railway system, gives the South Manchuria Railway a new approach to North Manchuria, thus enabling it to be less dependent upon the southern section of the Chinese Eastern Railway. There are, to be sure, qualifications to the facilities which the South Manchuria Railway will derive from this system, especially those to be found in the lack of interlineal traffic agreements over the various segments of the system, and the obvious desire of the Chinese eventually to route the goods traffic to a Chinese port outside of Japanese control, i.e., to avoid Dairen.

The other important railway contract agreement acquired by Japan during this period is that for the financing and construction of the extension of the Kirin-Changchun railway, i.e., the Kirin-Tunhua line, an extension of which to the Chosen border is now the subject of negotiation between the Japanese Government and the Chinese authorities in interest. The Kirin-Tunhua railway has been built with Japanese direction in pursuance of a series of Sino-Japanese agreements beginning with 1907; the specific contract agreement, however, was not formulated and signed until October, 1925. The importance of this railway, and especially of the projected new railway approach to Changchun over this route from Chosen is too evident to need elucidation, except to emphasize that such a railway

system for Japan would have both economic and strategic advantages.

An interesting and not unimportant phase of railway development in Manchuria during this period from 1921 to 1929 is that
which concerns itself with the endeavor of the Chinese to build
railways in Manchuria entirely independent of foreign capital
and control. Particularly since 1925 has this phase been evident.
The period has seen a rejuvenation of interest in the development
of a new Chinese port, as, for example, Hulutao, on the Gulf of
Pechihli, which, during 1907 to 1910, was a subject of particular
interest to the Manchurian viceregal and provincial authorities.
From the Peking-Mukden Railway, which in 1921 was the only
important railway in Manchuria exclusively under Chinese control,
the Chinese have already built branch lines toward Inner Mongolia,
the Tahushan-Paiyintalai (Tungliao) line having now been completed to connect with the extension of the Ssupingkai-Chengchiatun
line at Paiyintalai. Through traffic of a sort was inaugurated entirely over Chinese-owned railways from Angangchi (practically on
the Chinese Eastern Railway) to the Peking-Mukden line at
Tahushan during 1929. Whether, in view of the obligations of the
Chinese authorities to the South Manchuria Railway Company,
which financed the construction of the connecting links, this Chinese
railway system will be enabled to remain independent of Japanese
financial assistance and control remains to be seen. Neither the
financial condition of the Chinese Government (either Nanking
or Mukden), nor that of the specific Chinese railway companies
in question, is at present such as to enable this new western Manchurian railway system to be operated efficiently without Japanese
or other financial assistance. The payments on the Japanese advance for the construction of the Taonan-Angangchi line are now,
on the authority of the South Manchuria Railway Company, in
arrears.

But this Chinese interest in construction of independent Chinese
railways in Manchuria has been characteristic also of Kirin province, east of the South Manchuria Railway line, and also of North
Manchuria, in Heilungkiang province above Harbin. In Kirin
province the Chinese since 1925 have constructed the Mukden-
Hailungcheng railway which has recently been completed to Kirin,
thus to form a line geographically parallel with the Kirin-Changchun railway which is under Japanese management, though Chinese-
owned. The building of the Mukden-Kirin railway was undertaken by the Chinese without Japanese or other foreign financial

assistance, though not without official protests from the Japanese Government in view of the obvious possibility of the effect which interlineal connections between this new line and the Peking-Mukden Railway would have upon the goods traffic of the South Manchuria Railway. In North Manchuria, the Hulan-Hailun line has been constructed from a river port opposite Harbin, extending *via* Suihua, through one of the finest wheat belts of all Manchuria, on toward Hailun, with the ultimate object of continuation to Mergen, and then perhaps to the Amur river. The Hulan-Hailun railway has been constructed by a Chinese registered company with capital entirely Chinese, though the line was built under the technical supervision of Boris V. Ostroumoff, former Manager of the Chinese Eastern Railway. It is evident that the completion of these several railway systems in Manchuria, i.e., the Hulan-Hailun line, the Taonan-Tsitsihar line, the extensions of these lines to Mergen and beyond, the Tahushan-Paiyintalai line, and perhaps a new short-cut from Paiyintalai to Taonan, would serve to effectuate the system which was projected by American and British financiers in the memorable Chinchow-Aigun railway project of 1909 and 1910. In this connection it is pertinent to remark that the international banking consortium has not undertaken to finance the construction of a single railway in Manchuria since the time of its formation in October, 1920.

The severing of diplomatic relations—already bound by only a fragile thread—between the Soviet and Chinese Governments, which was announced on July 17, 1929, from Moscow, and which followed immediately upon the temporary failure of diplomatic interchanges between Moscow and Nanking over the Chinese *coup d'état* directed against the Chinese Eastern Railway, drew attention to the importance of the question of that dangerous anamoly in the international relations of Manchuria. The question of the Chinese Eastern Railway was little affected by the Washington Conference, while Inter-allied supervision of the operation of the railway terminated finally in October, 1922, when John F. Stevens left Harbin. The most important recent documents bearing on the status of the Chinese Eastern Railway are the following: (1) the Russo-Asiatic Bank agreement with the Chinese Government in 1920; (2) the Soviet Government's agreements of May 31, 1924, with the Peking Government; and (3) the Soviet Government's agreement with the Mukden Government of September 20, 1924, the latter being in most respects identical with the agreement negotiated with the Peking Government on May 31. The first agreement was negotiated by the Russo-Asiatic Bank after reorganization of that bank in Paris, following nationalization of the banks in Russia; hence the French Government is concerned, especially as the Chinese Eastern Railway was built originally with capital partly French. The Soviet Government have refused to recognize the 1920 agreement. The French Government, on the other hand, have refused to recognize their exclusion from participation in the settlement of the Chinese Eastern Railway question which was specifically provided in the Soviet Russian agreements with Peking and Mukden in 1924. Those agreements of 1924 were provisional arrangements for management of the Chinese Eastern Railway, and looked toward a more formal and specific arrangement subsequently—which has so far failed to eventuate. They provided in principle for, and sought to establish in fact, equality of representation as between Chinese and Soviet Russian nationals in the management of the railway—which has equally so far failed to eventuate. Policy control in the hands of the Soviet Russians, and police control in the hands of the Chinese have been responsible for numerous, almost continuous, incidents of which the most important until 1929 was the Chinese troop transportation incident precipitated by the action of the Russian Manager, Mr. Ivanoff. That incident of January, 1926, was not dissimilar in some respects to that which brought on the severing of diplomatic relations between Russia and China in July of 1929. Each arose out of a question of jurisdiction, and each was the natural product of fundamentally different political interests and policies with respect to the railway, as between the Chinese and Soviet Governments.

In the face of such realism it would be perhaps but distracting to do more than draw attention to the commitments of the powers to the "open door" policy as contained in the nine power pact regarding principles and policies to be followed concerning China—except to note that all the powers vitally concerned in Manchuria, excluding Russia, are bound by that treaty. Russia's *renunciations* and positive commitments with respect to China, including Manchuria, contained in the Sino-Russian agreements of 1924, are at once both *more* and *less* far-reaching than the nine power treaty of 1922.

A. THE POSITION OF JAPAN: 1921-1929

CHAPTER L

Manchuria and the Washington Conference: Effect on Japan's Position

a. EFFECT ON THE STATUS OF THE SINO-JAPANESE TREATY AND NOTES OF 1915. Except for the fact that the Chinese Delegation at the Washington Conference reserved the right for China to "seek a solution, on all future appropriate occasions, concerning those portions of the Treaties and Notes of 1915 which did not appear to have been expressly relinquished by the Japanese Government" it may be said, in a phrase, that the Washington Conference did not alter the status of the Sino-Japanese treaty and notes of 1915 with respect to South Manchuria and Eastern Inner Mongolia. The Chinese Delegation did seek, however, to question the validity of those treaties and exchanges of notes in the thirteenth meeting (December 7, 1921) of the Committee on Pacific and Far Eastern Questions, and again in the thirty-first meeting of the Committee (February 3, 1922), on which latter occasion the Chinese case was based on four points, i.e., (1) that Japan offered no *quid pro quo* in return for the concessions obtained from China; (2) that the agreements were intrinsically in violation of treaties between China and other powers; (3) that the agreements were inconsistent with principles relating to China adopted at the Conference; and (4) that, for practical reasons of expediency, they should be the subject of impartial examination with a view to revision or abrogation.[1]

The Japanese Delegation succeeded in preventing the Conference from going into the question of the validity of these treaties and exchanges of notes of 1915 by definitely stating that Japan had no intention to permit the Conference to consider what was a question for consideration by China and Japan alone, declaring that "the Japanese Delegation cannot bring itself to the conclusion that any useful purpose will be served by research and re-examination at this Conference of old grievances which one of the nations represented here may have against another. It will be

[1] *Conference on the Limitation of Armament,* Washington, 1921-1922 (Washington, 1922), pp. 1558, 1084.

more in the line with the high aim of the Conference to look forward to the future with hope and with confidence." [2]   At the
same time, in this, the thirtieth meeting of the Committee (February
2, 1922), the Japanese Delegation reasserted the validity of the
treaties and notes of 1915, declared that China's request for cancellation was tantamount in itself to a recognition of the binding
force of the same, that an "exceedingly dangerous precedent will
be established, with far-reaching consequences upon the stability of
the existing international relations in Asia, in Europe and every-
where" if it were allowed that "the rights solemnly granted by
treaty may be revoked at any time on the ground that they were conceded against the spontaneous will of the grantor," and, therefore,
that the Washington Conference was no proper occasion for re-
consideration of the subject of the validity of the Sino-Japanese
treaties and notes of 1915.[3]   Japan declared that the Conference
clearly recognized concessions "made by China *ex contractu,* in the
exercise of her own sovereign rights" as not inconsistent with the
principles adopted by the Conference.   To this the Chinese Delegation replied that "a still more dangerous precedent will be established with consequences upon the stability of international relations which cannot be estimated, if, without rebuke or protest
from other Powers, one nation can obtain from a friendly, but, in
a military sense, weaker neighbor, and under circumstances such
as attended the negotiation and signing of the Treaties of 1915,
valuable concessions which were not in satisfaction of pending controversies and for which no *quid pro quo* was offered." [4]   China,
therefore, reserved the right to seek a solution of the general question "on all future appropriate occasions."

Of the other powers represented at the conference only the
United States made a definite statement as to its position in regard

[2] *Conference on the Limitation of Armament,* pp. 1508-1510. Also Mr. Hanihara's
statement that the question of the "Twenty-one Demands" was "one to be taken up
between Japan and China, if it were to be taken up at all, and not at this Conference,"
p. 1160.

[3] *Ibid.,* pp. 1508-1510. These statements of the Japanese and Chinese Delegations
to the Conference were inserted into the records of the plenary sessions of the
Conference.

[4] *Ibid.,* pp. 1556-1560. In connection with this reservation of rights of the Chinese
Delegation in behalf of the Chinese Government it may be noted that the Peking
Cabinet addressed a note to the Japanese Government, dated March 10, 1923, demanding the abrogation of the Sino-Japanese treaties of 1915, and the return of
the Kwantung leased territory. The Japanese Government replied with a categorical
refusal. (*China Year Book,* 1924, p. 864.) In the absence of the 1915 treaties and
exchanges of notes, the lease of the Kwantung territory would have expired on
March 27, 1923, i.e., twenty-five years after the original Sino-Russian lease convention
of 1898. See Chap. IV, Sec. a, for the original lease convention.

to the Sino-Japanese treaties and exchanges of notes of 1915. At
the thirty-first meeting of the Committee (February 3, 1922) the
American Delegation declared that the Department of State had
made the position of the United States clear in the communication
of May 13, 1925, to the Japanese Government, in which the American Government declared that they "cannot recognize any agreement or undertaking which has been entered into or which may be
entered into between the Governments of China and Japan impairing the treaty rights of the United States and its citizens in China,
the political or territorial integrity of the Republic of China, or
the international policy relation to China commonly known as the
open door policy." [5]   The United States Delegation further declared that they were gratified to be advised by the Japanese Delegation (as stated in the Committee meetings) that Japan was ready
to withdraw the reservation which she made in 1915 "to the effect
that Group V of the original proposals of the Japanese Government—namely, those concerning the employment of influential
Japanese as political, financial and military advisers," etc., would
be postponed for future negotiations.   Specifically, with respect
to the treaty and notes of 1915 concerning South Manchuria and
Eastern Inner Mongolia, the American Delegation was gratified
to accept the statement of the Japanese Delegation that "Japan
has no intention of insisting on a preferential right concerning the
engagement by China of Japanese advisers or instructors on political, financial, military or police matters in South Manchuria."   So
also was the American Delegation gratified to accept the statement
of the Japanese Delegation in regard to the scope of operations of
the international banking consortium.[6]   In regard to the right
to lease land, granted to Japanese in the treaty and notes of 1915,
the United States Government declared that they "will, of course,
regard it as not intended to be exclusive, and, as in the past, will
claim from the Chinese Government for American citizens the
benefits accruing to them by virtue of the most favored nation
clauses in the treaties between the United States and China."   The
American Delegation refrained from taking any definite position
regarding the intrinsic validity of the treaty and notes of 1915, declaring the same a question apart from the treaty rights of the
United States, and reasserting that, in any case, the United States
would follow, and seek the cooperation of other powers in follow-

[5] *Ibid.*, pp. 1560 ff. See Chap. XLV, Sec. a, for this statement of American policy
in context.
[6] *Ibid.*, p. 1562.

ing, the traditional policy of maintaining the territorial and administrative integrity of China and the policy of insuring equality of opportunity for the commerce and industry of all nationals in China. The positions of each of these three powers were written into the record of the sixth plenary session of the Conference.[7]

b. Effect on the Status of the Kwantung Leased Territory. It naturally follows from the foregoing that the Washington Conference did not alter the legal status of the Kwantung leased territory, which, under the Sino-Japanese treaty and notes of 1915 regarding South Manchuria and Eastern Inner Mongolia, had been extended to remain in Japanese possession for a total period of ninety-nine years, i.e., until 1997. The Chinese Delegation attempted, through the raising of the question of the validity of the treaties of 1915 and through the introduction of the question of the leased territories of the several powers in China, to secure an alteration in the status of the Kwantung leased territory in Manchuria. The Chinese Delegation at the outset raised the general question of leased territories in the twelfth meeting of the Committee (December 3, 1921) without special attention to the Kwantung leased territory. That statement, however, brought forth the detailed statement of the Japanese Delegation in the same Committee meeting that "it is characteristic of Japan's leased territories that she obtained them, not directly from China, but as successor to other Powers at considerable sacrifice in men and treasure," in the case of Kwantung leased territory succeeding Russia only after the Russo-Japanese war.[8] In view of the fact that Japan had declared on several occasions that the Japanese Government would restore Kiaochow (in Shantung), and that negotiations to that end were actually under way during the Conference, there remained only Kwantung leased by Japan. The Japanese Delegation then made this important statement with regard to the same:

"The only leased territory, therefore, which remains to be discussed at the Conference, so far as Japan is concerned, is Kwantung Province, namely, Port Arthur and Dairen. As to that territory, the Japanese Delegation desire to make it clear that Japan has no intention at present to relinquish the important rights she has lawfully acquired and at no small sacrifice. The territory in question forms a part of Manchuria—a region where, by reason of its close propinquity to Japan's territory, more than anything else, she has vital interests in that which relates to her economic life and national safety." [9]

[7] *Conference on the Limitation of Armament,* p. 324 ff.
[8] *Ibid.,* pp. 1064 ff.
[9] *Ibid.*

The Japanese Delegation further declared that there were then 65,000 Japanese in the leased territory and that the commercial and industrial interests of Japanese established therein had attained a magnitude which made them an "essential part of the economic life" of Japan. The Delegation asserted that the vital interests of Japan in South Manchuria had been recognized by the powers in the negotiations preceding the formation of the international banking consortium.[10]

To this detailed statement of the Japanese, Dr. Koo, speaking for the Chinese Delegation, replied that he could understand the attitude of Japan, and while not able to accept all of the statements of the Japanese delegate (Mr. Hanihara), found the Japanese position perfectly intelligible. Dr. Koo merely declared that the Chinese Delegation received with regret Japan's statement that she had no intention of giving up her lease in Manchuria, but that the Chinese Delegation had no desire to press the question at that particular moment.[11] The matter of the legal status of the Kwantung lease was thus left untouched by the Conference.

c. EFFECT OF THE WASHINGTON CONFERENCE ON JAPANESE RAILWAY RIGHTS. The fact that the Washington Conference brought about no change in the status of the Sino-Japanese treaty and notes of 1915 with respect to South Manchuria and Eastern Inner Mongolia, except for the Japanese declarations at the Conference to the effect that Japan would not insist on the perform-

---

[10] *Ibid.* Mr. Balfour declared at this time that in his earlier statement in the Committee he had "never intended to imply that any action Great Britain might take with regard to Weihaiwei would be determined or guided by the disposition of the Manchurian question; that he had not had Dalny (Dairen) in mind at all, but had been thinking of the Shantung peninsula, in which Weihaiwei is situated." *Ibid.*, p. 1070.

[11] *Ibid.*, p. 1072. In the next (thirteenth) meeting of the Committee of the Whole, Dr. Koo made the following important statement with respect to the importance of the Kwantung leased territory for China: "Both Port Arthur and Dalny are situated in Manchuria, which is an important part of Chinese territory. Not only does the national safety of China rely upon the safeguarding of Manchuria, as an integral portion of the Chinese Republic, because these three Eastern Provinces, as the Chinese people call Manchuria, have been the historic road of invasion into China throughout the past centuries, but also the security of the economic life of the Chinese people depends in a very vital measure upon the conservation and development, with the surplus capital of the world, of the natural and agricultural resources in Manchuria—a region where to-day an abundance of raw material and food supplies are already accessible to all nations, on fair terms and through the normal operation of the economic law of supply and demand. Moreover, Manchuria is an important outlet for the surplus population from the congested provinces in other parts of China."

"In view of the foregoing facts, it is clear that China has such truly vital interests in Manchuria that the interests of any foreign Power therein, however important they may be in themselves, can not compare with them. The fact of close propinquity of Manchuria to Korea, if it justifies any claim to consideration, can be equitably appealed to only on the condition of reciprocity." (*Ibid.*, p. 1084.)

ance by China of certain of the provisions as contained in the exchanges of notes pertaining to the prior right of Japanese capitalists to finance the construction of all railways in South Manchuria for which foreign capital was to be used by China and pertaining to the right to have Japanese advisers employed in South Manchuria, naturally continued in force the provisions of the Sino-Japanese treaty of 1915 with respect to the extension of the terms of Japanese control of the South Manchuria and Antung-Mukden railways. The South Manchuria Railway was to remain under Japanese control for the full ninety-nine years, i.e., until 2002; the Antung-Mukden Railway similarly until 2007. In the general discussion between the Chinese and Japanese Delegations at the Conference pertaining to the validity of the treaties of 1915 the matter of the extension of the period for Japanese control of the South Manchuria and Antung-Mukden railways was but incidentally touched upon.

China had agreed in the Sino-Japanese treaty of 1915 regarding South Manchuria to effect with Japan an immediate and fundamental revision of the Kirin-Changchun railway agreements. Such revision had been secured by Japan in 1917 and the matter was not touched upon by the Washington Conference.[12] China had also conceded, in an exchange of notes attending the negotiations in 1915 with respect to South Manchuria, the right of Japanese capitalists to be first consulted for a loan in any case where the Chinese Government desired to construct in South Manchuria and Eastern Inner Mongolia a railway with the use of foreign capital.[13] In the thirtieth meeting (February 2, 1922) of the Committee on Pacific and Far Eastern Questions the Japanese Delegation declared, in view of the changes since 1915, that:

"Japan is ready to throw open to the joint activity of the International Financial Consortium recently organized, the right of option granted exclusively in favor of Japanese capital, with regard, first, to loans for the construction of railways in South Manchuria and Eastern Inner Mongolia, and, second, to loans to be secured on taxes in that region; it being understood that nothing in the present declaration shall be held to imply any modification or annulment of the understanding recorded in the officially announced notes and memoranda which were exchanged among the Governments of the countries represented in the Consortium and also among the national financial groups composing the Consortium, in relation to the scope of the joint activity of that organization."[14]

[12] See Chap. XXXIX, Sec. c.
[13] See Chap. XXXVIII, Sec. a, and Chap. XXXIX, Sec. b.
[14] *Conference*, pp. 1510-1512. See Chap. XLIV, Sec. b, for the international banking consortium.

This important statement, while indicating the willingness of Japan to permit the general waiver of the provisions found in the Sino-Japanese exchange of notes of May 25, 1915, with respect to the prior rights to be given Japanese capitalists to finance the construction of railways in South Manchuria and Eastern Inner Mongolia, merely reaffirmed, on the part of Japan, the position which the Japanese Government and financiers had been constrained to take, and which had been sustained by the other powers in the negotiations attending the formation of the China consortium agreement of 1920. The importance of those negotiations and the commitments of the powers contained therein is thus obvious.[15]

d. EFFECT OF THE WASHINGTON CONFERENCE ON JAPANESE TROOPS AND POLICE. At an early meeting of the Committee on Pacific and Far Eastern Questions (ninth meeting, November 29, 1921) the Chinese Delegation raised the whole question of foreign troops and police in China, along with the question of foreign wireless and telegraph stations. China presented a detailed statement of the number and character of Japanese troops and police in Manchuria and made the assertion that the Chinese Government had not sanctioned the provisions of the treaty of Portsmouth (1905) by which Japan and Russia agreed to limit the number of troops in the form of "railway guards" which they would employ to patrol their respective railways in Manchuria.[16] The Chinese Delegation declared, furthermore, that:

"Since 1905, police stations and branch stations have been established along the South Manchuria Railway, in violation of both law and treaty. In 1915, in virtue of the new treaty between China and Japan, sentry boxes of police stations belonging to the South Manchurian Railway were established in such unopened points ["ports"] as K'aip'ing, T'aolu, Pamien-ch'eng, Ch'angt'u, and Chengchiatun, with Japanese police. In addition, there are numerous *gendarmerie* under the command of the Commander-in-Chief of the Kwantung Leased Area, also special police of the South Manchurian Railway Company, who exercise functions similar to those of the Japanese police. As in Japanese consulates in Manchuria, there are attached to the Japanese consulates in Manchuria, secret police. Finally, there are also Korean police officers under the immediate jurisdiction of the Governor General of Korea." [17]

[15] See Chap. XLIV, Sec. b. The Japanese Delegation also presented a statement of their government's position in connection with the non-withdrawal of their troops from the Maritime Province following Inter-allied intervention in 1919. (*Conference,* pp. 1394 ff.) To this statement the American Delegation replied in a lengthy declaration drawing attention to the divergence of policy between the American and Japanese Governments with respect to their respective military forces in Siberia in 1919 and following. (*Ibid.,* pp. 1406 ff.) Both statements were entered into the records of the plenary sessions of the Conference. (*Ibid.,* pp. 340 ff.)

[16] *Conference,* pp. 988 ff.

[17] *Ibid.,* pp. 994 ff.

To this declaration of the Chinese Delegation, which had concluded with the proposal that the foreign troops and police in China (with certain exceptions) be removed, the Japanese Delegation replied in the same meeting of the Committee, stating in succinct terms the reasons for the stationing of Japanese troops in various parts of China, including Manchuria. After speaking briefly as to the reasons for stationing railway guards in Shantung the Japanese Delegation stated that:

"The maintenance of troops along the South Manchurian Railway stands on a different footing. This is conceded and recognized by China under the Treaty of Peking of 1905. (Additional Agreement, Article II.) It is a measure of absolute necessity under the existing state of affairs in Manchuria—a region which has been made notorious by the activity of mounted bandits. Even in the presence of Japanese troops, those bandits have made repeated attempts to raid the railway zone. In a large number of cases they have cut telegraph lines and committed other acts of ravage. Their lawless activity on an extended scale has, however, been effectively checked by Japanese railway guards, and general security has been maintained for civilian residents in and around the railway zone. The efficiency of such guards will be made all the more significant by a comparison of the conditions prevailing in the railway zone with those prevailing in the districts remote from the railway. The withdrawal of railway guards from the South Manchurian Railway will no doubt leave those districts at the mercy of bandits, and the same conditions of unrest will there prevail as in remote corners of Manchuria. In such a situation it is not possible for Japan to forego the right, or rather the duty, of maintaining railway guards in Manchuria, whose presence is duly recognized by treaty." [18]

The Japanese Delegation further stated that the stationing of Japanese troops along the Chinese Eastern Railway since 1919 was in accordance with the Inter-allied agreement concluded at Vladivostok in 1919, and that these troops had the duty of maintaining communications between the Japanese contingents in Siberia and South Manchuria.[19]

To these assertions of the Japanese the Chinese Delegation replied that China would be glad to be informed later from the Japanese Delegation as to the time when the troops would be withdrawn. At a later meeting (eleventh, December 2, 1921) of the Committee the Chinese Delegation questioned the Japanese interpretation of the Sino-Japanese treaty and additional agreement of December 22, 1905, asserting that under the treaty of Portsmouth

[18] *Conference*, pp. 1004-1006.
[19] See Chap. XLIV, Sec. a, for Inter-allied control of the Chinese Eastern Railway.

(Article 3) Japan agreed "to evacuate completely and simultaneously Manchuria except the territory affected by the lease of the Liaotung Peninsula," and "to restore entirely and completely to the exclusive administration of China all portions of Manchuria now in occupation or under the control of the Japanese or Russian troops, with the exception of the territory above mentioned."[20] Inasmuch as Russia had withdrawn her troops, declared the Chinese Delegation, Japan ought now to do the same thing. The Chinese Delegation did not, however, question the Japanese interpretation of the particular clause to which the Japanese Delegation referred as the legal justification for the presence of Japanese troops along the South Manchuria Railway. They concluded this statement with a minimizing of the bandit situation in Manchuria, as portrayed by the Japanese, and declared that "China asks to be given an opportunity to show that she can maintain order along the South Manchurian Railway. The opportunity can only be granted if Japan will withdraw her forces, which China asks be done for the reasons given." The Chinese Delegation in this statement had also taken issue with the necessity which Japan alleged for stationing Japanese troops along the Chinese Eastern Railway.[21]

In view of the fact that the essential issue seemed to be whether China actually could offer the protection for foreign interests which she declared she desired to exhibit, the Chairman (Mr. Hughes) appointed a Subcommittee to deal with the details. In the thirteenth meeting of the Committee of the Whole (December 7, 1921), however, the Japanese Delegation replied to the Chinese statement considered above with the declaration that "in all frankness" the stationing of Japanese troops and police in some parts of China was "solely due to our instinct for self-protection." They declared the Chinese statement as to the interpretation of the Sino-Japanese treaty and agreement of December 22, 1905, "unconvincing" and that the fact that Russia had withdrawn her troops temporarily from the Chinese Eastern Railway was for reasons which did not give Japan assurance that that situation would be permanent.[22] Nor could it be defended, the declaration continued, that anything like a state of tranquillity actually prevailed in Manchuria of a nature to justify the withdrawal of Japanese troops at that time. "As for the contention that China should be given an opportunity of proving her ability to maintain peace and order in Man-

[20] *Conference*, p. 1040. See Chap. XVI, Sec. a., b. and c.
[21] *Ibid.*, p. 1042.
[22] *Ibid.*, pp. 1088 ff.

churia, the reply is obvious," declared the Japanese Delegation: "Japanese interests and Japanese security are matters of such importance that she [Japan] can not afford to take obvious risks" or "pander to a sentimental idea at the risk of creating grave international difficulties in a region which has already been the source of a life-and-death struggle on the part of Japan." The Japanese Delegation therewith presented a detailed statement in an appendix regarding the actual state of affairs in Manchuria, emphasizing that conditions in North Manchuria were even worse than in South Manchuria.[23]

No concrete program for the removal from China of foreign troops in the form of "railway guards" was adopted at the Washington Conference, except for specific areas, as Shantung, and none for Manchuria, except generally in connection with the Chinese Eastern Railway. The Conference in the fifth plenary session (February 1, 1922) adopted a general Resolution, as prepared by the Subcommittee on Drafting and adopted in the Committee of the Whole on January 5, 1922, to the effect that the nine powers represented at the conference agreed to appoint representatives to a commission of inquiry to go into the whole matter of armed forces, including police and railway guards in China, the same to be appointed "whenever China shall so request."[24] Except for the general airing of the issue of Japanese troops and police in South Manchuria the Washington Conference made no alteration in fact in their status or jurisdiction.

e. Effect of the Washington Conference on Japanese Post Offices, Telegraphs and General Jurisdiction. Shortly after the Japanese acquired the Kwantung leased territory and the South Manchuria Railway their Government had put into effect along the line of the railway and in the leased territory a Japanese postal system. The raising of the question of foreign postal agencies in China thus affected the Japanese system in Manchuria. In the sixth meeting of the Committee of the Whole (November 25, 1921) the Chinese Delegation proposed that "the Powers assembled in the Conference agree at once to abolish all postal services now maintained by them in China."[25] The question of Japanese post offices in South Manchuria was not separately dealt with at the Conference, but along with the general question in the whole of China. The Japanese Delegation declared in the seventh

[23] *Conference*, p. 1090.
[24] *Ibid.*, pp. 184 ff.
[25] *Ibid.*, pp. 940 ff.

meeting of the Committee (November 26, 1921) that Japan had no desire to perpetuate the system of foreign postal agencies in China, but at the same time they declared that "the safety of communication in China was not assured," and that as Japanese nationals in particular would be involved, because of the large number of Japanese in China, it was necessary that China offer guarantees before any general withdrawal of Japanese postal agencies in China (and therefore in Manchuria) could be expected. The general question was then referred to a Subcommittee to draft a resolution on the subject.[26] This Subcommittee reported a resolution which, in its final form, was adopted at the fifth plenary session of the Conference (February 1, 1922) to the effect that the powers concerned agreed to abolish their postal agencies in China conditionally by January 1, 1923, and excepting those in leased territories or "specifically" provided for by treaties.[27] On the ground that the conditions proposed have not been satisfied with respect to Manchuria, the Japanese Government still continues to maintain Japanese post offices in South Manchuria throughout the South Manchuria Railway system. The Japanese Delegate in the Subcommittee which dealt with the framing of the general Resolution pertaining to foreign postal agencies in China took the position that Japan's right to maintain a postal system in the South Manchuria Railway area was contained in the terms of the treaty of Portsmouth, i.e., in pursuance of the original provisions of the Sino-Russian agreements which rights were acquired by Japan in 1905, and which gave Japan every kind of political authority in the railway zones including the right of taxation and postal administration. This view of the Japanese Delegate in the Subcommittee was not affirmed by the Subcommittee's report, but, from the effect of the general resolution adopted by the fifth plenary session of the Conference, foreign post offices maintained in China "specifically" provided for by treaty were excepted.[28] The Washington Conference, therefore, did not alter the status of the Japanese postal system in the Kwantung leased territory, and excepted from the resolution adopted with regard to foreign postal agencies in China such as were established in conformity with authority "specifically provided by treaty." There is, in fact, no specific grant in the treaty of Portsmouth, or in the Sino-Russian agreements antecedent thereto, *specifically* granting to Japan (or to Russia) the right to establish post offices in South

[26] *Ibid.*, p. 966.
[27] *Ibid.*, pp. 182-184.
[28] Willoughby, W. W., *China at the Conference* (Baltimore, 1922), pp. 134-135.

Manchuria, or anywhere in Manchuria outside of the Kwantung leased territory.

Japanese Wireless and Telegraphs in Manchuria. The Chinese Delegation at the Conference, in presenting a list of foreign wireless installations in China, specified several in Manchuria which were alleged to have been established by Japan without the consent of China. This statement declared that Japan had wireless stations at Harbin and Manchouli, in addition to those in the Kwantung leased territory and the South Manchuria Railway zone.[29] The same statement alleged that of wire telegraphs Japan had "thirty-four stations along the South Manchurian Railway," and others at Changchun, Hunchun and Yenchi (Chientao). The Chinese Delegation, after asserting that "all the arguments that have been presented in favor of immediate abolition of foreign postal stations apply with equal force to the abolition or surrender to the Chinese Government of these foreign electrical means of communication," declared that "there is thus no need for the maintenance in China by other countries of wire or wireless installations."

The Japanese Delegation replied by asserting that there were two types of such wire and wireless installations in China, those based on treaty rights, and those not thus provided for. As to the latter they declared that "the withdrawal or abolition of the foreign troops, railway guards, police stations, and telegraphic and wireless installations should not be immediately decided simply because the Chinese authorities have not given their express consent. There are specific reasons for the existence of such institutions in each special case."[30] The Japanese Delegation also corrected the statement of the Chinese Delegation that Japan had wireless installations at Harbin and Manchouli, by stating that the wireless station at Harbin was not under Japanese control, and that there was no wireless station at all at Manchouli.[31]

In the resolution adopted in the fifth plenary session of the conference with regard to radio stations in China (February 1, 1922) it was specifically provided that "if any question shall arise as to the radio stations in leased territories, in the South Manchurian Railway Zone" (or in the French Concession at Shanghai) they shall be regarded as matters for discussion between China and the Governments concerned.[32] The matter of the status of Japanese

[29] *Conference*, pp. 990-992.
[30] *Ibid.*, p. 1000. See Chap. XXI, Sec. a, for Sino-Japanese telegraph and cable agreements.
[31] *Ibid.*, p. 1028.
[32] *Ibid.*, pp. 196 ff.

wireless stations in Manchuria was left, in that manner, untouched by the Conference, except that the Chinese Delegation in the Committee of the Whole (twenty-seventh meeting, January 27, 1922) made the reservation that the Chinese Government "does not recognize or concede the right of any foreign power or of the nationals thereof to install or operate, without its express consent, radio stations in leased territories" (and other designated places). The Conference adopted no resolution specifically relating to wire telegraphs in China, hence leaving the matter of Japanese telegraphs along the South Manchuria Railway *in statu quo.*[33]

CHAPTER LI

Sino-Japanese Railway Agreements (1921-1929)

a. AGREEMENT FOR JAPANESE CONSTRUCTION OF THE TAONAN-ANGANGCHI LINE, 1924. Since 1921 the Japanese Government and financiers, especially the South Manchuria Railway Company, have been interested primarily in the construction with Japanese capital of two principal railway extensions in Manchuria. Of immediate importance is the Taonan-Angangchi railway, which, in fact, has now been extended across the Chinese Eastern Railway at Tsitsihar-chan to the city of Tsitsihar, the provincial capital of Heilungkiang. Of perhaps greater ultimate importance is the extension of the Kirin-Changchun railway from Kirin to Tunhua, this extension having been completed to Tunhua with the anticipation of its eventual extension to Huining (Kainei) in Chosen. Each of these railway extensions has been financed by Japanese capital under separate construction contract agreements.

The Taonan-Angangchi-Tsitsihar railway is an extension of the Ssupingkai-Chengchiatun-Taonan railways which, as now completed, connects the South Manchuria Railway at Ssupingkai (between Mukden and Changchun) directly with the Chinese Eastern Railway in North Manchuria at Tsitsihar-chan (Tsitsihar Station), from which railway junction the line has now been completed to Tsitsihar itself, the provincial capital of Heilungkiang. Definite plans have been made to extend the system north to Mergen. It

---

[33] In the drafting committee created by the Committee of the Whole, however, Dr. Koo affirmed that, in the railway zones, Japan had by treaty only ordinary business administrative rights for the operation of the railways, and that while Japan might, therefore, have the right to operate telegraph lines required for the use of the railway, this did not carry with it the right to operate radio stations. (Willoughby, *China at the Conference*, p. 162.)

will be recalled that in 1913 by the "Five Manchurian Railways Loan Agreement" the Japanese obtained the right to finance the construction of five railways in Manchuria and Eastern Inner Mongolia. Subsequently, the Ssupingkai-Chengchiatun line was excluded from these five and was dealt with separately, the Sino-Japanese railway loan agreement of December 27, 1915, being the basis for the construction of this line.[34] This latter contract contained a provision (Article 20) permitting the Yokohama Specie Bank to finance the construction of an extension or branch line in case such were projected in future, and in case foreign capital were required. In pursuance of this preliminary loan agreement of 1915, which contract was taken over by the South Manchuria Railway Company, the Japanese financed the construction of most of the line from Chengchiatun to Taonan, the last segment in that extension having been opened to traffic in November, 1923.

For the construction of a further extension from Taonan to Angangchi the Sino-Japanese loan contract agreement was signed at Mukden on September 3, 1924, between the South Manchuria Railway Company (Director Y. Matsuoka, until recently vice president of the South Manchuria Railway Company) and the Mukden Government (the late Marshal Chang Tso-lin, commander-in-chief for the armies of the Three Eastern Provinces, and Wang Yung-chiang, then acting Civil Governor of Fengtien province).[35] No official version of this loan contract agreement for the Taonan-Angangchi extension has previously been published in English; the epitome of the provisions of the agreement here given are taken from the official text as communicated to the writer by the Head Office of the South Manchuria Railway Company in Dairen for initial publication in English.

This contract agreement for the construction of the Taonan-Angangchi line provided that the line should be constructed by Japanese engineers under a chief engineer (Mr. Fujine, then chief of the Railway Department of the South Manchuria Railway, and now a member of the Board of Directors of the South Manchuria Railway). The South Manchuria Railway Company supplied a part of the materials in the form of rails, station equipment,

[34] See Chap. XXXIX, Sec. b.

[35] The provisions of the Sino-Japanese loan contract agreement of September 3, 1924, as analyzed in the above section, are taken from the text of the agreement as communicated officially to the writer by the Head Office of the South Manchuria Railway Company in Dairen, South Manchuria, with the authorization for publication. This official version confirms, in the main, the general analysis of the provisions of this agreement (published without the date of the agreement or the negotiators) to be found in *The China Year Book*, 1928, p. 264.

engines and rolling stock for the construction and operation of the line, the engines and rolling stock being loaned by the South Manchuria Railway Company for a specific figure. The contract provided that, if available, Chinese materials were to be given preference. Parenthetically, it may be noted that the United States Steel Corporation supplied rails for the new extension to an amount estimated at nearly a half million yen. The Japanese contractors were to advance the sum of 12,920,000 Japanese yen to cover construction cost, that sum being liable to change by negotiations.[36] The contract agreement provided that this entire sum was to be repaid to the Japanese contractors within six months after the completion and transference of the entire line. Failing payment within that period the same amount was to be converted into a formal loan secured by the line itself and its profits, on which interest at the rate of 9 per cent. was to be paid annually.[37] Redemption of the loan was to take place through annuity payments over a period of thirty years beginning at the eleventh year after transference of the line, though payment of the loan might be made at an earlier date. During the currency of the loan a Japanese adviser with several assistants are to be engaged by the railway authorities, the railway itself to remain, however, legally a Chinese government railway, under the general management of a Chinese Director General. Construction of the Taonan-Angangchi extension began on May 28, 1925; by spring of 1926 the Nonni river had been crossed; in July construction had been extended to the terminus, Angangchi, though the stations and relaying of portions of the line were not

[36] In August, 1926, the Japanese Chief Engineer (Mr. Fujine, now a member of the Board of Directors of the South Manchuria Railway) stated to the writer that the total expenditure on account of rails and construction cost, and charged to the railway on account of outlay for lease of rolling stock from the South Manchuria Railway Company, was 12,920,000 yen. For a discussion of the territory traversed by the line and its relation to the Manchurian railway system see the writer's articles: "Economic Bases for New Railways in Manchuria," in the *Chinese Economic Journal*, Vol. I, No. 4 (April, 1927); (Published by the Chinese Government Bureau of Economic Information, Peking.) The same was translated into Japanese and published by the Department of Railways (Traffic Bureau), Tokyo as "Manshū Shinsetsu-tetsudō-no Keizai-teki Konkyo" in *Gai-koku-tetsudō-chōsa-Shiryo*, Vol. I, No. 3 (June 20, 1927). Also: "Railway Politics in Manchuria," *The China Weekly Review* (Shanghai), Vol. XL, No. 7 (April 16, 1927), and Vol. XL, No. 8 (April 23, 1927).

[37] On April 10, 1929, a communication from the Head Office of the South Manchuria Railway Company (Dairen) to the writer stated that the contract money advanced to the Chinese for the construction of the Taonan-Angangchi railway was then in arrears, and that, although negotiations were then under way for fixing the amount of the loan to be placed on the railway, no definite new loan contract had been agreed upon at the time.

completed until December 1, 1926, the entire length of the Taonan-Angangchi line being 142 miles.[38]

International interest has attended the construction with Japanese capital of the Taonan-Angangchi railway extension principally because it is the realization of a portion of the Chinchow-Aigun railway project which Anglo-British interests had sought to construct in 1909 and 1910.[39] Due to the official opposition of the Japanese and Russian Governments in 1909 and 1910 the original American contract agreement of October 2, 1909, with the Chinese Government has remained in abeyance. In 1916 the United States Government reserved the rights accruing to the American financiers who had contracted for the construction of the Chinchow-Aigun railway after the Yokohama Specie Bank had obtained from the Chinese Government the right to finance the construction of the Ssupingkai-Chengchiatun railway and after the Russo-Asiatic Bank had obtained the right to finance the construction of the Harbin-Heihofu railway, with branch lines from Mergen to Tsitsihar.[40] In 1919 and 1920 during the negotiations attending the formation of the China consortium agreement of 1920 the Japanese Government sought to exclude from the scope of operations of the international banking consortium any railway line which might be projected to connect the proposed Taonanfu-Jehol railway with the Chinese Eastern Railway. The United States and Great Britain, while refraining from conceding the specific exclusion of such a project from the scope of operations of the consortium, gave Japan general assurances that their bankers would not be supported in operations which were interpreted by their governments to be obviously prejudicial to the vital interests of Japan.[41]

b. AGREEMENT FOR JAPANESE CONSTRUCTION OF THE KIRIN-TUNHUA LINE, 1925. The second important Chinese railway which the South Manchuria Railway has financed in Manchuria since the Washington Conference is the extension of the Kirin-

---

[38] It appears that an extension of the Taonan-Angangchi line across the Chinese Eastern Railway at Tsitsihar-chan to Tsitsihar, the provincial capital of Heilungkiang, was completed on December 8, 1928, and opened to traffic on December 11. Through traffic from Tahushan on the Peking-Mukden line (over the Chinese-built Tahushan-Paiyintalai [Tungliao] line), via Chengchiatun and the Chengchiatun-Taonan railway to Tsitsihar, was inaugurated shortly thereafter. (*The Japan Weekly Chronicle,* January 24, 1929, p. 93.) For the Russian opposition to the extension of the Taonan-Angangchi line to cross the Chinese Eastern Railway see the writer's article: "Economic Bases for New Railways in Manchuria" (*Chinese Economic Journal,* April, 1927); reprinted in *The Far Eastern Review* (Shanghai), May, 1927.
[39] See Chap. XXXI, Sec. a, and Chap. XXIX, Sec. c.
[40] See Chap. XXXIX, Sec. b, and Chap. XLIII, Sec. b.
[41] See Chap. XLIV, Sec. b.

Changchun railway from Kirin to Tunhua in Kirin province. Originally the right of the Japanese to participate in financing the construction of such a line, should foreign capital be required, was conceded to Japan in the Sino-Japanese convention of April 15, 1907, regarding the Hsinmintun-Mukden and the Kirin-Changchun railways.[42] In the Sino-Japanese agreement relative to Chientao (September 4, 1909) the right to construct such a line "to the southern boundary of Yenchi [Chientao, so-called], and to connect it at Hoiryang [Huining or Kainei] with a Korean railway" was conceded to Japan in indefinite terms by the Chinese Government. In 1918, by means of a preliminary loan agreement of June 18, three Japanese banks (Industrial Bank of Japan, Bank of Chosen and Bank of Taiwan) obtained the contract for the construction of such a line from Kirin to Huining (Kainei). This contract agreement, however, was but preliminary, but it was agreed that the sum of $10,000,000 was to be advanced at once to China on the conclusion of the agreement. That sum was paid to the (Peking) Chinese Government.[43] Construction of the line, however, did not begin until June, 1926, due to the fact that the final and detailed contract agreement for construction and possible loan to be secured by the line itself had not been negotiated with Peking.

The final and detailed contract agreement for financing the construction of the Kirin-Tunhua extension from Kirin was signed in Peking on October 24, 1925, by the Chinese Government (Yeh-Kung-ch'o, then Minister of Communications) and the South Manchuria Railway Company (Y. Matsuoka, then a director of the South Manchuria Railway Company and until recently vice-president).[44] The fact of the signing of this contract agreement was at once reported in the Peking press, but no authentic and official version of the actual provisions of the agreement had been published in English.[45] The analysis of the contract agreement which follows is taken from an official text communicated to the writer by the Head Office of the South Manchuria Railway Company in Dairen.

The provisions of the loan contract agreement for the construction of the Kirin-Tunhua railway extension are similar in most

<hr>

[42] See Chap. XXXIX, Sec. d.
[43] See Chap. XXXIX, Sec. d.
[44] The provisions of the Sino-Japanese loan contract agreement of October 24, 1925, as analyzed above, are taken from the text of the agreement as communicated officially by the Head Office of the South Manchuria Railway Company (Dairen) to the writer, with the authorization for publication. This official version confirms the general provisions of the agreement which were published (without date) in *The China Year Book*, 1928, p. 265.
[45] Bearing on the status of this contract agreement of October 24, 1925, for the

respects to those of the contract of 1924 for the construction with Japanese capital of the Taonan-Angangchi railway. The original rights of the three Japanese banks which signed the preliminary agreement of 1918 for the construction of the entire line projected from Kirin to Huining (Kainei) have been absorbed by the South Manchuria Railway Company. The agreement of 1925 provided that the sum of 18,000,000 (later increased to 24,000,000) Japanese yen would be advanced by the South Manchuria Railway for the cost of constructing the line to Tunhua, the original sum having been liable to change on negotiation should the exigencies of construction require. A Japanese chief engineer was to be employed to supervise the construction. Chinese construction materials were to be given preference. The Chinese Government were to redeem the entire amount advanced for construction cost immdiately upon the date of completion and transference of the line to Chinese management. On transference, the line was to be under the control of a Chinese Director General. Failing payment in full within one year after transference, the amount unpaid by China was to be converted into a formal loan with annual interest at 9 per cent., the same to be redeemed within thirty years from the annual revenues of the line which were to be deposited in Japanese and Chinese banks. Earlier redemption was to be permitted if the Chinese Government desired to recover the line before the expiration of the thirty-year period. As security for the loan, as in the case of the Taonan-Angangchi line, a lien was placed on the line while the revenues were hypothecated. During the currency of the loan, or any portion of it, a Japanese chief accountant with his several Japanese assistants were to be employed by the railway administration. The line, however, was to remain under the management of the Chinese Director General. Actual construction began on June 1, 1926; tunneling and construction of a bridge over the Sungari river occupied part of 1927; the entire line was completed on October 10, 1928.

It is evident from the terms of this final contract agreement of October 24, 1925, that it includes only the section from Kirin to

construction of the Kirin-Tunhua railway the following is pertinent: "When Marshal Chang Tso-lin's satellites in Peking were removed during the period of Kuominchun hegemony in the capital, the new ministry, less favorable to Japan's aspirations in Manchuria than the former, on January 7, 1926, formally repudiated the then unpublished agreement. Japan protested, and when the exigencies of civil war (the next in chronological order in this part of China) introduced a new cabinet slate, the legality of the Ki-Kai [i.e., the portion from Kirin to Tunhua] construction contract was declared to be reestablished." From the writer's article: "Railway Politics in Manchuria" in *The China Weekly Review*, Vol. XL, No. 7 (April 16, 1927), pp. 186-187.

Tunhua, i.e., a total segment of approximately 130 miles, and that a definitive loan agreement for the construction of the remainder of the Kirin-Huining project to Chosen is not included therein.[46] In passing, it may be noted that the entire Kirin-Huining project was definitely excluded from the scope of operations of the international banking consortium in the negotiations between the Japanese Government, on the one hand, and the British and American Governments, on the other.[47]

The status of the Taonan-Angangchi and the Kirin-Tunhua railways, while being legally Chinese-owned lines under Japanese supervision during the currency of the loans attached to each, is different from the status of the several purely Chinese owned and constructed lines which have been built in Manchuria since the Washington Conference, including the Mukden-Hailungcheng-Kirin railway and the Tahushan-Paiyintalai railway. Both of these latter have been built by the Chinese without Japanese or other foreign capital, and both have been the object of protests by the Japanese Government. The Chinese have also built the Hulan-Hailun railway *via* Suihua, which runs north from a point opposite Harbin on the Sungari river to Suihua, and then to the northwest to Hailun, with the intention of eventual extension to Mergen, where it would connect with a proposed extension of the Taonan-Angangchi-Tsitsihar line to Mergen. A line northeast to the Amur, perhaps to Aigun, would complete the original Chinchow-Aigun railway project of 1909 and 1910, but not in the form of a single system built and operated under a uniform management.[48]

[46] Negotiations have been under way for over a year between the Japanese authorities and the Mukden Government in connection with a definitive loan contract agreement for the construction of the remainder of the Kirin-Huining (Kainei) line, i.e., from Tunhua to a Chinese city on the Manchurian side of the Korean border near the Korean city of Kainei (Hoiryang or Huining). The *Asahi* (Osaka) reported in May, 1929, that negotiations to this end had been conducted between Japan (represented by a director and another official of the South Manchuria Railway Company) and the Mukden Government (represented by the late Marshal Chang Tso-lin, along with Chang Tso-hsiang, then *tuchun* of Kirin). Failing a definite arrangement, negotiations were again instituted by the Japanese railway officials in the spring of 1928, which the *Asahi* reported to have resulted in the conclusion of a secret agreement under which all preliminary arrangements for beginning construction were to be completed by May 11, 1929. Following the death of Marshal Chang Tso-lin in June, the matter was taken up with General Chang Tso-hsiang and Marshal Chang Hsueh-liang, son of Chang Tso-lin, at which time the Chinese sought to repudiate the secret agreement on the ground that there had been a flaw in the procedure of drawing up the original agreement. It is evident that as soon as such a definite agreement is established the continuation of the Kirin-Tunhua line to the Chosen border will be undertaken. (*The Japan Weekly Chronicle*, May 2, 1929, p. 507.)

[47] See Chap. XLIV, Sec. b.

[48] This interesting phase of recent railway developments in Manchuria is considered in some detail in Appendix F dealing with independent Chinese lines.

B. THE POSITION OF RUSSIA (1921-1929)

CHAPTER LII

Russia and the Chinese Eastern Railway (1919-1929)

a. THE CHINESE EASTERN RAILWAY AND THE WASHINGTON CONFERENCE. It will be recalled that the Russian Revolution in 1917 resulted in the general ineffectiveness of Russian diplomacy with respect to Manchuria, and in 1919 brought about Inter-allied supervision of the Chinese Eastern Railway, as well as the assertion of Japan's right to station troops along that railway in pursuance of the Sino-Japanese military agreements of 1918.[49] Also, during the period immediately preceding the Washington Conference, the Chinese Government and the reorganized Russo-Asiatic Bank had entered into the agreement of October 2, 1920, which had authorized the Chinese Government, "in view of the situation created by the complete political disorganization in Russia, rendering temporarily impossible for the said company [C.E.R.] the maintenance of regular operation," to take over "supreme control" of the Chinese Eastern Railway.[50] This was admittedly on the part of China a temporary arrangement, this fact being reaffirmed by the Chinese Delegation at the Washington Conference.

When the subject of the Chinese Eastern Railway came up for discussion at the Washington Conference, the Chairman (Mr. Hughes) in the Committee of the Whole on Pacific and Far Eastern Questions suggested that its complexity counseled its immediate submission to a Subcommittee of Technical Advisers, representing the various national delegations involved in the question. This Subcommittee proposed, after prolonged consideration of the question, the adoption of a report pertaining to the status and future financing, operation and policing of the line. This Subcommittee reported in part as follows:

"The Chinese Eastern Railway being an indispensable factor in the economic development of Siberia, as well as Northern Manchuria, and constituting an essential link in a transcontinental railway system of international importance, the nations represented at this Conference are interested in its

[49] See Chap. XLII, Sec. a, Chap. XLIV, Sec. a, and Chap. XLVIII, Sec. a.
[50] See Chap. XLIII, Sec. a.

preservation, its efficient operation, and its maintenance as a free avenue of commerce, open to the citizens of all countries without favor or discrimination.

"The status of the Chinese Eastern Railway is determined by the contract concluded in 1896 between China and the Russo-Chinese (Russo-Asiatic) Bank and the contract concluded in 1898 between China and the Chinese Eastern Railway Company, and subsequent contracts between China and that Company. The necessary funds for its construction were furnished by the Russian Government and it was built under the direction and supervision of that Government, acting through the Chinese Eastern Railway Company. The Railway is in effect the property of the Russian Government. China has certain reversionary rights which are provided for in the original contract of 1896.

"The absence of a recognized Russian Government since 1917 has made imperative, for some time past, certain measures providing for the preservation and continued operation of the Railway. Early in 1919—as a consequence of assistance which had been given to Russia, at her request, in the operation of the entire Trans-Siberian system, including the Chinese Eastern Railway—certain Powers, which are represented at this Conference, undertook to continue this assistance upon definite terms. An agreement was concluded in January, 1919, between the United States and Japan, under the terms of which China, France, Great Britain and Italy subsequently cooperated. The fundamental purpose of the arrangement thus brought about was explicitly declared to be the temporary operation of the Railways in question, with a view to their ultimate return to those in interest without the impairing of any existing rights.

"The trusteeship thus assumed continues in force. Changes which have intervened since 1919 render necessary readjustments in this mode of operation." [51]

The Subcommittee of Technical Advisers proposed, therefore, a plan which would deal with the three principal problems of finance, operation and police. As to finance, it was recommended that, in order to obtain funds from bankers interested in financing the line, there should be established in Harbin an inter-power Finance Committee to replace the so-called Inter-allied Committee and the so-called Technical Board, provided for in the 1919 agreement among the powers. This Financial Committee was to restrict its functions to financing the line and to be "entrusted with the exercise of the trusteeship which was assumed in 1919," until the "general recognition by the Powers of a Russian Government." As to operation, it was recommended that, in order to refrain from disturbing the normal situation, the Chinese Eastern Railway Company should

[51] *Conference on the Limitation of Armaments*, pp. 1376-1378.

be entrusted with actual control in technical matters. As to protection of the line, it was proposed that "as the Railway Zone lies in Chinese territory," this function should devolve upon a Chinese *gendarmerie,* but, as a temporary and exceptional measure, "justified alike by existing conditions and the precedent of a Russian guard," policing of the railway zone should remain in the hands of the Chinese Eastern Railway Company itself, which should control and provide for the payment of the railway guards.[52]

The above report of the Subcommittee of Technical Advisers was not accepted by the Chinese representative (Dr. Hawkling Yen) and consequently failed of adoption by the Committee of the Whole, and, therefore, was not considered by the plenary sessions of the Conference. The matter was instead referred to a subcommittee of the Subcommittee of Technical Advisers for report. Dr. Hawkling Yen's statement of "observations and reservations" to the report just characterized contained a detailed declaration of the Chinese position in which he asserted that China could not accept the proposals pertaining especially to the constitution of a Finance Committee to have charge of the railway's finances, nor to the provision for policing of the Chinese Eastern Railway with a Chinese *gendarmerie* under a "mixed Committee," when the function of policing the line should be definitely a concern of the Chinese Government itself. He asserted that "the precedent of a Russian guard has no legal ground as it was expressly stipulated in the Agreement of 1896 that it was the Chinese Government which was to take measures to assure the safety of the Railway and of the persons in its service." [53] He further drew attention to the fact that although the Chinese Government had paid the sum of 5,000,-000 Kuping taels to the Russo-Chinese Bank, and the Railway Company was to repay the same amount upon the completion of the line, that amount had never been paid to China. China had entered into the agreement of 1920 with the Russo-Chinese Bank, he declared, in order "to assume the responsibilities on behalf of Russia respecting the Railway," and that "in doing so China did not intend to seek an undue advantage from the present situation in Russia but rather to exercise the rights of a sovereign State within whose territory the Railway runs and because of her deep interest therein." The Inter-allied agreement of 1919 was admittedly, on the part of the powers, a temporary agreement, to come to an end on withdrawal of their military forces from Siberia.

[52] *Conference on the Limitation of Armaments,* pp. 1376-1378.
[53] *Ibid.,* pp. 1378-1380.

In offering the report of the subcommittee of the Subcommittee of Technical Advisers the Chairman (Mr. Root) declared that the committee had been "wrestling" with the subject for a long time and that all that was possible to report in the form of a resolution was the one presented. That latter report was then adopted (thirtieth meeting, February 2, 1922) by the Committee of the Whole and later reported to and adopted by the sixth plenary session of the Conference.[54] That resolution (XII) left the difficult question of the status and supervision of the Chinese Eastern Railway almost entirely untouched by the Conference, except for the observations and reservations made in committee meetings, by briefly declaring:

"That the preservation of the Chinese Eastern Railway for those in interest requires that better protection be given to the Railway and the persons engaged in its operation and use; a more careful selection of personnel to secure efficiency of service, and a more economic use of funds to prevent waste of the property;

"That the subject should immediately be dealt with through the proper diplomatic channels."

From the materials presented as to the question of the status and supervision of the Chinese Eastern Railway at the Washington Conference it is obvious that this matter was left practically *in statu quo*. The final withdrawal of Japanese troops from the Maritime Province took place shortly after the Washington Conference and the Inter-allied agreement of 1919 for multi-power supervision came to a close when the Technical Board ceased functioning at Harbin in the autumn of 1922.[55]

b. STATUS OF THE CHINESE EASTERN RAILWAY: 1919-1929. The status of the Chinese Eastern Railway during the years which have ensued since the Washington Conference has been a difficult question for solution as between the Chinese and Russian Governments particularly. The French Government, moreover, due to the fact that that government in 1919 and following had extended national protection to the Russo-Asiatic Bank, as reorganized in

---

[54] *Ibid.*, pp. 316-318. A separate Resolution (XIII) adopted by the Conference declared that the powers "reserve the right to insist hereafter upon the responsibility of China for performance or non-performance of the obligations towards the foreign stockholders, bondholders and creditors of the Chinese Eastern Railway Company, which the Powers deem to result from the contracts under which the Railroad was built and the action of China thereunder and the obligations which they deem to be in the nature of a trust resulting from the exercise of power by the Chinese Government over the possession and administration of the Railroad." (*Ibid.*, p. 318.) The Chinese Delegation (Mr. Sze as spokesman) made a statement of their reservations to this Resolution; nor did the Resolution call for acceptance by China, which was, therefore, not secured. (*Ibid.*, pp. 318 ff.)

[55] See Chap. XLIII, Sec. a, and Chap. XLIV, Sec. a.

Paris after the nationalization of banks in Russia, have an interest of a sort in the railway which was built originally by funds advanced in part by that bank (as the Russo-Chinese Bank), of whose bonds the French have since 1907 held a large part. When the management of the Russo-Asiatic Bank signed with the Chinese Government the agreement of October 2, 1920, that agreement had the support of the French Government. The Russian Government, on the other hand, has consistently refused to recognize the validity of the agreement.[56] That the French Government should refuse to recognize the subsequent Sino-Russian agreement of May, 1924, with respect to the provisional management of the Chinese Eastern Railway was a foregone conclusion.[57]

In the interval between the Washington Conference and the resumption of diplomatic relations in 1924 between China and Russia, the latter as the Union of Soviet Socialist Republics, the Russian Government took steps to recover principal control of the Chinese Eastern Railway. This endeavor, which characterized the period from 1918 to 1925, became especially apparent after the termination of Inter-allied control of the technical management of the railway in late 1922. Moreover, it is apparent that, in some respects the Russian interpretation of their interests in the railway was not in complete consonance with the declarations which that government and their officials in China had made during 1919 and 1920.

c. DECLARATIONS OF THE SOVIET GOVERNMENT IN 1919 AND 1920. During the negotiations held between the Russian envoy to Peking (L. M. Karakhan) and a representative of the Chinese Foreign Office (Dr. C. T. Wang) during March-November, 1923, the texts of two important "Declarations" of the Russian Foreign Office made during July, 1919, and during September, 1920, were important factors in the *pourparlers*. Both of these "Declarations" were admittedly signed by Mr. Karakhan as acting Commissar for Foreign Affairs of the Union of Soviet Socialist Republics. The first "Declaration," dated, Moscow, July 25, 1919, contained (in the form in which it was received on March 26, 1920, by the Ministry for Foreign Affairs in Peking after indirect transmission) far-reaching denunciations of the former policy of the Tsarist Government, including specific denunciation of all secret treaties of the old

---

[56] In the Sino-Russian agreement on "general principles" (May 31, 1924) these two governments declared their intention to settle the question of the Chinese Eastern Railway "to the exclusion of any third party or parties." See Chap. LII, Sec. d.

[57] See Chap. LII, Sec. d.

régime made with China, and the declarations that "the Soviet Government returns to the Chinese people without demanding any kind of compensation, the Chinese Eastern Railway, as well as all mining concessions, forestry, gold mines, and all other things which were seized from them by the government of the Tsars, Kerensky, and the brigands, Horvath, etc." [58] The same "Declaration" renounced the privileges under extraterritoriality and consular jurisdiction which accrued to Russian nationals under the old Tsarist treaties. (In fact, certain of these privileges were taken from Russians by unilateral action of the Chinese Government in 1920.)

Later, during 1922, when a Soviet envoy (Mr. Joffe) was in Peking negotiating for resumption of diplomatic relations between China and the Soviet Government, and for a working agreement in regard to the Chinese Eastern Railway, he declared in a formal note of November 11, 1922, to the Chinese Foreign Office (Peking) that, although the Soviet Government did renounce "the predatory and violent policy of the Tsar's Government" in that "Declaration" of 1919, that the Soviet Government was compelled to insist on recognition of their "rights in China" pending resumption of diplomatic relations, and in particular declared that the clause alleged to be contained in the "Declaration" of 1919 was spurious, the clause (as published in the Chinese Foreign Office translation) stating that:

"It is the intention of the Workers' and Peasants' Governments to restore to China, without any compensation, all rights and interests referring to the Chinese Eastern Railway." [59]

Mr. Joffe had declared in a note of November 6 to the *Wai Chiao Pu* that this first declaration of 1919 was merely a unilateral statement of a program phrased in general terms, and in no wise binding upon the Russian Government, asserting that:

"Even if Russia vests in the Chinese people her title to the Chinese Eastern Railway, this will not annul Russia's interests in this line which is a portion of the Great Siberian Railway and unites one part of the Russian territory with another." [60]

[58] Chinese official translation of the *Text of the Declaration* of July 25, 1919/March 26, 1920, made by Acting Commissar for Foreign Affairs (L. M. Karakhan) of the Union of Soviet Socialist Republics. *The China Year Book,* 1924, pp. 868-870. See also the *Peking and Tientsin Times,* November 13, 1922. It has been noted in context above that Mr. Joffe denied that this particular quotation was contained in the declaration of Mr. Karakhan. (Letter of November 11, 1922, to the *Wai Chiao Pu, The China Year Book,* 1924, p. 861.)

[59] *The China Year Book,* 1924, p. 861.

[60] *Ibid.*

During the Karakhan-Wang negotiations in Peking (March-November, 1923) the text of a second "Declaration" of the Soviet Foreign Office of 1920 was a subject for controversy. The latter was that of an official communication to the Chinese Foreign Office, signed by Mr. Karakhan as acting Commissar for Foreign Affairs at Moscow on September 27, 1920, and transmitted in person by a Chinese official from Moscow to Peking.[61] It was addressed "To the *Wai Chiao Pu*." This "Declaration," which contained seven articles, was to be the basis for an agreement to be signed with China. It contained, *inter alia*, according to the Soviet text, a provision (Article 3) that the Chinese Government should agree not to proffer aid to Russian counter-revolutionaries and would disarm, intern and hand them over to the Russian Government. With respect to the Chinese Eastern Railway it declared (Article 7) that the two governments should agree to sign "a special treaty on the way of working the Chinese Eastern Railway with due regard to the needs of the Russian Socialist Federated Soviet Republic." [62] Mr. Joffe declared in his letter to the *Wai Chiao Pu* of November 11, 1922, that the existence of these two articles (Articles 3 and 7) in the "Declaration" of 1920 placed definite obligations upon China.[63] Mr. Karakhan, a year later, declared in his letter of November 23, 1923, to Dr. C. T. Wang (as published by mutual consent) that:

"Never and nowhere could I have said that all the rights in the Chinese Eastern Railway belong to China. . . . I quite agree with you that the question of the Chinese Eastern Railway must be settled at a Conference, and not in the agreement which you proposed I should sign." [64]

It is evident that, while there is some reason to suppose that the Soviet "Declarations" of 1919 and 1920 were not intended by the Commissar for Foreign Affairs to be binding commitments (which, in the nature of the case, they could not be because they were but unilateral statements of policy not of a character to alter formal treaty stipulations), the "rights and interests" of the Soviet Government in the Chinese Eastern Railway appeared to that government in a somewhat altered light four and five years after the "Declarations" were made. Mr. Joffe declared in his letter of

[61] *The China Year Book*, 1924, p. 870.

[62] Soviet Russian official version of the *Text of the Declaration* of September 27, 1920, made by Acting Commissar for Foreign Affairs (L. M. Karakhan) of the Union of Soviet Socialist Republics. *The China Year Book*, 1924, pp. 870-872.

[63] *The China Year Book*, 1924, p. 861.

[64] *Ibid.*, pp. 875-876.

November 6, 1922, that these "Declarations" could not be regarded as valid forever.[65]

As to the actual management of the Chinese Eastern Railway then in existence, Mr. Joffe declared in his note of November 3, 1922, to the *Wai Chiao Pu* that the then Manager (Boris V. Ostroumoff) had been guilty of corrupt practices and demanded that he be arrested and tried, demanding further that the dispute over the Chinese Eastern Railway be submitted to a commission of inquiry to proceed to Harbin to arrange the basis for a new provisional management agreement between the Chinese and Soviet Governments.[66] No such commission, however, was appointed, and Manager Ostroumoff, who had been appointed after the Russo-Asiatic Bank agreement with China in 1920, continued in his post until after the Sino-Russian agreements of May, 1924.

As to the policing of the Chinese Eastern Railway, that function remained in the hands of the Chinese authorities from 1919 to 1924 without significant interruption, the railway guards being employed by the management of the railway (both Chinese and "White Russians") with the tacit or particular consent of Marshal Chang Tso-lin at Mukden. The American president of the Inter-allied Technical Board left Harbin in October of 1922.

d. SINO-RUSSIAN AGREEMENTS OF 1924 CONCERNING THE CHINESE EASTERN RAILWAY. There occurred in 1924 the signing of three Sino-Russian agreements with important bearing on the problem of the Chinese Eastern Railway. Two of these were signed by the Peking Government on May 31, 1924, of which one concerned itself principally with the "general principles" which were to be the bases for definitive settlements in a subsequent conference, but which also provided for the resumption of diplomatic relations between the Peking Government and the Soviet Government.[67] Important provisions of this agreement on "general principles," however, concerned themselves with the problem of the Chinese Eastern Railway. The other agreement signed on the same day was devoted exclusively to the question of the Chinese

---

[65] *Ibid.*, p. 861. A pertinent statement of the *Novosti Jizni* (Harbin) is as follows: "While Karakhan two years ago determined to relinquish the [Chinese Eastern] Railway in favor of China, in order to show the sincerity of the Soviet Government, this dramatic gesture was caused on the one hand by particular impulses on the part of the young Government, while on the other hand it had no legal force, for China could accept such a gift only from an acknowledged Government." (Quoted in *The Peking and Tientsin Times,* November 21, 1922.)

[66] *Ibid.*, p. 860.

[67] See Chap. LVIII, Sec. a, for the terms (other than those bearing on the Chinese Eastern Railway) of the Sino-Russian agreement of Peking, May 31, 1924.

Eastern Railway. The third agreement was between the Soviet Government and the Mukden Government (under Marshal Chang Tso-lin), which was signed on September 20, 1924, and this, likewise, concerned itself principally with the important subject of the Chinese Eastern Railway.

Negotiations between C. T. Wang, representing the *Wai Chiao Pu,* and L. M. Karakhan, Russian envoy at the head of a mission to Peking, had been prolonged from March to November, 1923, principally due to differences of opinion over the subject of the Chinese Eastern Railway and the question of Russian troop evacuation from Outer Mongolia.[68] Dr. V. K. Wellington Koo, the Chinese Foreign Minister, replied to the Soviet ultimatum of March 19, 1924, on April 1, refusing to ratify the draft agreement arranged between Dr. Wang and Mr. Karakhan.[69] Discussions were later resumed between Minister Koo and Mr. Karakhan, however, after the exchanges of views characterized above with respect to the "Declarations" of Russian policy made in 1919 and 1920. These eventuated in the Sino-Russian agreements of Peking, dated May 31, 1924, the one, an agreement on "general principles for the settlement of questions" between the two governments, the other, an agreement for the provisional management of the Chinese Eastern Railway." The former, which reestablished diplomatic relations between Russia and China, is characterized elsewhere, i.e., with regard to the provisions which are more or less extraneous to the Chinese Eastern Railway question.[70] Summarily, it may be said here, however, that the general provisions of the agreement contained far-reaching specific denunciations of the rights and privileges obtained by the former Tsarist Government with respect to China, and (Article 6) a provision whereby both governments agreed not to engage in propaganda "directed against the political and social systems of either contracting party." [71]

The Peking Agreement on General Principles in its Relations to the Chinese Eastern Railway. This same agreement pertaining to "general principles" also gave primary attention to the subject of the Chinese Eastern Railway. The conference, which was to be called within a month, and was to complete its work within six months, was to consider the "question of the Chinese Eastern Railway." A settlement of the question was to be based (Article 9)

[68] *The China Year Book,* 1924, pp. 864 ff.
[69] *Ibid.*
[70] See Chap. LVIII, Sec. a.
[71] *American Journal of International Law, Supplement,* Vol. 19 (1925), pp. 55-63.

on the principle of recognition of the "purely commercial" character of the railway. An important section of Article 9 provided that:

" . . . With the exception of matters pertaining to the business operations which are under the direct control of the Chinese Eastern Railway, all other matters affecting the rights of the national and the local governments of the Republic of China—such as judicial matters, matters relating to civil administration, military administration, police, municipal government, taxation, and landed property (with the exception of lands required by the said railway)— shall be administered by the Chinese authorities."

Russia agreed to a redemption of the line by China under the following terms (Article 9, Sections 2, 3 and 4):

"The Government of the Union of Soviet Socialist Republics agrees to the redemption by the Government of the Republic of China, with Chinese capital, of the Chinese Eastern Railway, as well as all appurtenant properties, and to the transfer to China of all shares and bonds of the said Railway.

"The Governments of the two Contracting Parties shall settle at a Conference as provided in Article II of the present Agreement the amount and conditions governing the redemption as well as the procedure for the transfer of the Chinese Eastern Railway.

"The Government of the Union of Soviet Socialist Republics agrees to be responsible for the entire claims of the shareholders, bondholders and creditors of the Chinese Eastern Railway incurred prior to the revolution of March 9th, 1917."

It is thus evident that while China's right to redeem and recover the railway was granted in principle, such transference was to be only in pursuance of a conference to be called for the purpose of arranging details. No specific date was set, aside from the reaffirmation of the dates established in the original 1896 contract agreement, for such redemption. The date, the amount and the conditions of redemption were not specified in the agreement. A slightly more definite provision for redemption was, however, contained in the Mukden agreement of September, 1924, but, nevertheless, indefinite as to whether immediate redemption with Chinese capital was to be permitted. The original contract of 1896 was declared to be in force, except where in conflict with the agreement then signed, the same to be in force until alteration in the proposed conference. Finally, with respect to the Chinese Eastern Railway, the two signatories to the agreement pledged that the future status of the railway would be determined "to the exclusion of any third party or parties." [12]

The Peking Agreement for Provisional Management of the Chinese Eastern Railway. The specific agreement of the same date (May 31, 1924) relating to provisional management of the Chinese Eastern Railway, pending the final solution of the question at the conference to be called in pursuance of the agreement just characterized, declared in the preamble that the Chinese Eastern Railway was built "with capital furnished by the Russian Government and constructed entirely within Chinese territory," that the line "is a purely commercial enterprise, and that, excepting for matters appertaining to its own business operations, all other matters which affect the rights of the Chinese national and local governments shall be administered to the Chinese authorities." [13] Management of the line was to be entrusted (Article 1) to a Board of Directors composed of ten members, five of each nationality to be appointed by their respective governments. From the Chinese membership the Chinese Government was to appoint one to be President of the Board, who was also to be Director General. From the Russian membership of directors the Russian Government was to designate one to be Vice President, who was concurrently to serve as Assistant Director General. The same article provided that seven should constitute a quorum, and that all decisions of the Board of Directors were to be approved by six members. The Director General and the Assistant Director General were "to jointly manage the affairs of the Board of Directors and they shall both sign all the documents of the Board." The post of Manager of the railway, however, was established as distinct from the Director General, the former, as in the past, to have (Article 3) actual direction of the details of operation of the railway. The Manager was to be a Russian national of the Union of Soviet Socialist Republics. He was to have two assistant managers, the one a Chinese, the other a Russian national, who, together with the Manager, were to be appointed by the Board of Directors, the appointments of each to be confirmed by their respective governments. Their rights and duties were to be defined by the Board of Directors. [74]

This system of equality of representation in the management of the railway was further to be made effective through the provision

[12] *American Journal of International Law, Supplement,* Vol. 19 (1925), pp. 55-63. See Appendix G for the full text of the agreement.

[13] Sino-Russian *Agreement for Provisional Management of the Chinese Eastern Railway,* May 31, 1924. Official text in *American Journal of International Law, Supplement,* Vol. 19 (1925), pp. 56-58. See Appendix G for full text of agreement.

[74] *Ibid.,* pp. 56-58.

(Article 2) that the Board of Audit, consisting of five members, should be composed of two Chinese and three Russians, appointed by their respective governments. The president of the Board of Audit, however, was to be a Chinese elected by and from the board itself. Further, all chiefs and assistant chiefs of departments were to be appointed by the Board of Directors under the provision (Article 4) that in any case where the chief of department was a national of one country, the assistant chief would necessarily be a national of the other. Finally, it was provided (Article 5) that "the employment of persons in the various departments of the Railway shall be in accordance with the principle of equal representation between the nationals of the Republic of China and those of the Union of Soviet Socialist Republics." A bilateral Declaration (No. 7) of the same date (May 31, 1924) made by Dr. Koo and Mr. Karakhan provided, in explanation of Article 5, that "the application of this principle is not to be understood to mean that the present employees of Russian nationality shall be dismissed for the sole purpose of enforcing the said principle." [75] An exchange of notes of the same date provided that the Chinese Government would "discontinue the services of all the subjects of the former Russian Empire now employed in the Chinese army and police force, as they constitute by their presence or activities a menace to the safety of the Union of Soviet Socialist Republics." [76]

As to the procedure to be followed in case of disagreement within the Board of Directors this Sino-Russian agreement of May 31 provided (Article 6) that such matters should be referred to the two governments for adjustment, i.e., by diplomacy. A very indefinite provision (Article 8) referred to the disposition of the profits of the railway by merely stating that the net profits "shall be held by the Board of Directors and shall not be used pending a final settlement of the question of the present Railway." This provisional agreement was to be effective on signature (May 31, 1924) and to terminate when the proposed conference had settled the outstanding questions. [77]

[75] *Ibid.*, p. 62. See Appendix G.

[76] *Ibid.*, p. 62.

[77] On June 2, 1924, a representative of the Russo-Asiatic Bank (as reorganized in Paris after the nationalization of banks in Russia and hence under the French flag) protested to the *Wai Chiao Pu*, ostensibly in behalf of the French bondholders whose interests had been ignored by the Soviet Government. It appears, however, that the Chinese Government refused to recognize the position taken by certain powers in diplomatic representations to the *Wai Chiao Pu* at that time, and asserted that that government could not recognize the validity of the claims to interests in the Chinese Eastern Railway which were in conflict with the Sino-Russian agreement of May 31, 1924.

The Mukden Agreement on General Principles and regarding the Chinese Eastern Railway. Recognizing the realities of the situation, which arose from the practical independence of the Mukden Government (under Marshal Chang Tso-lin) from Peking, the Soviet Government, represented by N. K. Kouznetzov, proceeded to negotiate with the Manchurian authorities an agreement which would obtain the sanction of the Mukden Government to the general arrangements made with Peking with respect to provisional management of the Chinese Eastern Railway. The negotiations were successful and on September 20, 1924, Chang Tso-lin was constrained to sign an agreement with reference to the Chinese Eastern Railway which, in its principal provisions, was practically identical with that signed by the Peking Government in the late spring of the year. The Peking agreement, however, had merely reasserted the right of China to recover the railway in accordance with the terms of the 1896 contract which was declared in force, and had contained a section recognizing *in principle* China's right to redeem the railway by purchase. The Mukden agreement provided (Article 1) that, instead of recovery at the end of eighty years following completion of the line (presumably after 1903) as provided in the 1896 agreement, recovery without payment might take place after the expiration of sixty years.[78] Moreover, the Mukden agreement provided (Article 1) specifically for a revision of the statutes of the railway within four months after signature. But, as to provision for management of the line, no new changes were made, and, hence, the Russian Manager was left with broad powers, particularly so when, in case of deadlock or non-action of the Board of Directors, the actual operation of the railway remained in his hands. This agreement reiterated the provision of the Peking agreement (May 31, 1924) in an important section with regard to spreading of propaganda by providing (Article 5) in terms identical with the Peking agreement, as follows:[79]

[78] Sino-Russian (Mukden Government—Soviet Government) *Agreement in regard to General Principles and Provisional Management of the Chinese Eastern Railway,* September 20, 1924. (Authoritative Text in the English language.) See Appendix G for the full text of the agreement. The Mukden Government had refused to recognize the validity and binding force of the Sino-Russian agreements of May 31, 1924, negotiated with the Peking Government.

[79] "On the 3rd of October, 1924, Boris V. Ostroumoff [Manager of the Chinese Eastern Railway who had been appointed after the 1920 agreement of the Russo-Asiatic Bank with the Peking Government] was dismissed by the new board of directors and placed under arrest by General Chu Ching-lan at Harbin without a warrant. He was refused bail and kept in confinement." After having been in detention for six months, Manager Ostroumoff was "handed a copy of the charges against him."

"The Governments of the two Contracting Parties mutually pledge themselves not to permit, within their respective territories, the existence and/or activities of any organizations or groups whose aim is to struggle by acts of violence against the Government of either Contracting Party.

"The Governments of the two Contracting Parties further pledge themselves not to engage in propaganda directed against the political and social systems of either Contracting Party."

The final settlement of the Chinese Eastern Railway question, which was to be undertaken in a conference to be called within one month after May 31, 1924, was deferred until August 26, 1925, and when the conference was called it consisted mainly of formal exchanges of greetings of the delegates. The Russian Ambassador had arranged to leave for Moscow on the following day. The conference was resumed without significant achievement in December, 1925, the "final settlement" of the question of the Chinese Eastern Railway being indefinitely postponed—to beyond the present time.

e. THE IVANOFF INCIDENT IN REGARD TO CHINESE TROOP TRANSPORTATION, 1926. The first important opportunity for the practical interpretation of the Sino-Russian agreements of May and September, 1924, with respect to the operation of the Chinese Eastern Railway came during the period from November, 1925, to February, 1926. During this period the Russian Manager (Mr. Ivanoff) of the railway came into constant conflict with the Chinese members of the railway's directorate over matters of policy, operation and jurisdiction. On November 10, 1925, it appears that the Russian Manager issued an order that on and after December 1, 1925, no Chinese troops would be carried over the Chinese Eastern Railway without prepayment of railway fares. At a meeting of the Board of Directors, held in Harbin on November 30, the Chinese president and members of the board protested this action, and, it appears, the Russian members of the directorate reluctantly conceded the point that Chinese railway guards might be transported over the line without prepayment.[80] The Chinese directors, how-

After trial proceedings which extended from June 4 to September 12, 1925, he was discharged by the court under the amnesty proclamation of January 1, 1925, which had been previously unenforced as against him by the local Chinese authorities. (*Report of the Commission on Extraterritoriality in China*, China No. 3 [1926], pp. 85-86. British Foreign Office Publication.) Mr. Ostroumoff was thus deposed from the position of Manager of the Chinese Eastern Railway, A. N. Ivanoff, having been placed in the position from October 3, 1924.

[80] *The Peking Leader*, December 5, 1925. The Ivanoff Incident occurred while the writer was in North China, which gave him the opportunity to make notes on the events occurring at that time in connection with an interpretation of the Sino-Russian agreements of May and September, 1924.

ever, demanded the right of the Mukden authorities to transport any and all troops over the railway without prepayment. The importance of the latter demand on the part of the Chinese was evident in the fact that during the last part of November General Kuo Sung-lin, a subordinate general of Marshal Chang Tso-lin, mutinied and issued a manifesto denouncing Marshal Chang and Lieutenant General Yang Yü-t'ing, the marshal's chief of staff.[81] The Kuo Sung-lin mutiny, in fact, brought on hostilities between his forces and those of Marshal Chang Tso-lin, which caused the Japanese Government to increase their garrison in the South Manchuria Railway zone and take certain other measures in anticipation of possible eventualities from the conflict.[82]

A crisis developed concerning the matter of troop transportation over the Chinese Eastern Railway when Manager Ivanoff, who in May had summarily dismissed a large number of "White" Russians from the employ of the railway, attempted in the middle of January to put his order of November 15 into effect. Chinese soldiers of Marshal Chang Tso-lin returning from Changchun to Harbin on the night of January 21, were prevented under the order of Manager Ivanoff from entraining without first paying their fares. In view of the fact that, as it appears, no such requirement had ever been made of Chinese soldiers of the Mukden Government since 1918 (the same being transported presumably under a deferred pay-

[81] *Manifesto* of Kuo Sung-lin. Printed in English text in full in *The Peking Leader*, December 1, 1925.

[82] In this connection it may be noted that the despatch of Japanese reenforcements to the garrison in South Manchuria, in pursuance of an order of the Japanese General Staff (December 15, 1925), brought on the protest of the Peking Government. General Shirakawa, commander-in-chief of the Kwantung Garrison troops, issued an order circumscribing the area of hostilities between the troops of Marshal Chang Tso-lin and General Kuo Sung-lin, specifically forbidding them from carrying on hostilities within twenty *li* of both termini of the South Manchuria Railway zone. These acts produced demonstrations and boycotts by Chinese in various parts of China directed against Japan. On December 31, 1925, the Japanese Minister in Peking presented a note to the *Wai Chiao Pu* declaring, *inter alia*, that "the stationing of Japanese troops in Manchuria, which is provided for in treaties, has the object of giving effective policing in the areas along the South Manchuria Railway and protection to life and interests of the Japanese people," that the disturbances in China justified the sending of troop reenforcements which "was merely for the purpose of replacement of the original Japanese garrisons there." The note specifically repudiated the prevalent assertions among Chinese characterizing "the despatch of Japanese troops to Manchuria as an expression of aggression." (*The Peking Leader*, January 13, 1926.) To this communication the Chinese Government (Peking) replied under date of January 8, 1926, that "with reference to the stationing of Japanese troops in Manchuria, it is hoped that the Japanese residents and soldiers there should strictly follow the policy of the Japanese Government of absolute neutrality. As peace and order are being now gradually restored, the additional Japanese troops sent there should be immediately withdrawn so as to avoid unwarranted suspicions." (*The Peking Leader*, January 13, 1926.)

ment arrangement), in accordance with a reputed long-standing regulation of the Board of Directors, this summary action of the Manager was interpreted by General Chang Huan-hsiang, military governor of the Chinese Eastern Railway zone and commander of the railway guards at Harbin, acting under orders from Marshal Chang Tso-lin, as a direct attempt to place obstacles in the way of the marshal's military success at the time of the crisis brought on by the mutiny of Kuo Sung-lin. General Chang Huan-hsiang, thereupon, on January 22 arrested Manager Ivanoff and three Russian members of the Board of Directors of the railway.[83] The Chinese military practically took over, for a short time, operation of the Chinese Eastern Railway with the technical assistance of the "White" Russians. A "White" Russian engineer was made temporary manager in place of Ivanoff, while the Chinese and "White" Russian Railway guards took charge of the sale of railway tickets when the trains ran.

On the same day (January 22, 1926) Mr. Karakhan, Russian Ambassador in Peking, protested strongly against the arrest of Manager Ivanoff, conveying the instructions of Chicherin to demand his immediate release, and declaring: "I reserve the right to return to the matter of this arrest and to demand satisfaction for such an unheard of violation of the Agreement of 1924."[84] On the next day Ambassador Karakhan delivered an ultimatum to the *Wai Chiao Pu* at Peking to the effect that "within three days full order on the Chinese Eastern Railway be restored, agreement fulfilled, and Mr. Ivanoff released." In response to this determined action of the Russian envoy in Peking, and following requests on the part of the Peking Government made of Chang Tso-lin, the latter released Manager Ivanoff, who was continued in his post. The so-called "settlement" of the affair on January 24, 1926, was of little importance, merely confirming the *status quo ante*. Failure of the Board of Directors subsequently to present a quorum of seven members, due to the continual absence of the Russian members, prevented the board from passing upon the action of Mr. Ivanoff. Marshal Chang Tso-lin's military quelled the mutiny of Kuo Sung-lin, and the former's position was thus strengthened with respect to the Chinese Eastern Railway until his sudden death in June, 1928.[85]

[83] *The Peking Leader*, January 24, 1926.
[84] *Ibid*. See also: *European Economic and Political Survey*, Vol. II, No. 4 (Oct. 30, 1926), pp. 105-107 (Paris).
[85] *The Peking Leader*, February 3, 1926.

It seems clear that the generality and inadequacy of the provisions of the Sino-Russian agreements of May and September,
1924, for provisional management of the Chinese Eastern Railway
are a principal cause of the constant conflict which produced the
crisis in January of 1926, and which later produced strikingly
similar controversies over jurisdiction.   The agreements of 1924
were, of course, provisional; they looked toward a working arrangement which would be perfected by a formal and detailed agreement
to be arranged through conference discussions.   Failing the latter,
the provisional arrangements have made it necessary to fall back
for legal bases, for specific authority in certain matters, on the
original contract agreement of 1896.

With regard to the issue of troop transportation over the Chinese Eastern Railway, the Russians contended, to quote the protest
of Ambassador Karakhan to the Mukden Government, that "the
Chinese military authorities have always declined any agreements,
preferring uncontrolled transportation that has only facilitated
abuses," that as early as September, 1921, the Chinese President of
the Board of Directors addressed a communication to the Mukden
Government "insisting on the obligatory payment for military transportation but without results"; that "the Chinese Eastern Railway
has never refused to transport troops, but merely insisted that such
transportation should not be free of charge," although payment
might be deferred; and that this procedure was provided for in
the established regulations of the Board of Directors of the railway.
The arrest of Manager Ivanoff by a Chinese military officer was
declared to be without legal right.[86]

The Chinese authorities of Peking, Mukden and Harbin contended, on the contrary, that the order of Manager Ivanoff to
compel prepayment for troop transportation was in direct opposition to a regulation of the Board of Directors of the railway permitting free transportation of Chinese soldiers, as well as "railway
guards"—though it appears that, in view of the deadlock in the
board meeting of November 30, no such regulation actually existed
at the time of the Ivanoff incident.   The Chinese further contended
that, in any event, the railway's Manager had no right to issue
such an order without the sanction of the Board of Directors,
particularly in view of the fact (Article 1, Section 8 of the Mukden
Agreement) that the "rights and duties" of the Manager were
to be defined by the Board of Directors.   Drawing attention
to the assumption of authority on the part of the Russian Manager

[86] *The Peking Leader,* January 22, 1926.

in the absence of decision on the part of the directors, instead of referring such matters to the governments of both countries for diplomatic settlement as provided for (Article 1, Section 11) in the Mukden agreement of 1924, the Chinese contended that the action of Manager Ivanoff was evidently an abuse of authority, taken at a time when his action was calculated to embarrass the Mukden military in important troop movements. Finally, the Chinese contended that, under the original railway contract agreement of 1896, the sovereign rights of China in her territory were specifically recognized and that, therefore, in such an emergency as existed, the Chinese not only possessed the right to transport their troops over the railway without charge, and certainly with deferred payment, but even the ultimate right to take possession of the railway itself.[87]

Without reference to whether the emergency which actually existed might have justified the latter action on the part of the Chinese, it would appear that, aside from the obvious clash of interests and policies involved in the incident, the legal issue would turn in part on whether all the formalities of procedure had been followed by Manager Ivanoff in issuing his order which was made effective December 1, 1925. Apparently, on the day before, the Board of Directors had voted to permit deferred payment for the transportation of railway guards, but that no sufficient majority of the board approved free transportation of regular Chinese troops. Whether the arrest of Manager Ivanoff and the appropriation of railway trains for troop transportation was justified as a matter of *policy* is beyond the scope of this discussion.

The practical independence of the Mukden Government from Peking, an independence made the more important in its relation to the Chinese Eastern Railway because of the increasing military strength of Marshal Chang Tso-lin, made it necessary for the Russian nationals in the management of the railway to deal directly with Mukden under difficult circumstances. No definitive agreement for the management of the railway had been perfected since the provisional agreements of May and September, 1924. During the months which followed the crisis precipitated by Manager Ivanoff in January, 1926, the Russian Manager had continued, however, to displace many "White" Russian employees, who had in some cases become naturalized Chinese subjects, filling their posts with Soviet Russian nationals. The Soviet Union of railway work-

---

[87] The above is an epitome of the Chinese contentions as represented in the contemporary press dispatches from Harbin, Mukden and Peking to have been stated by Chinese officials. See, for example, *The Peking Leader*, January 24, 27, 29, and 30, and February 3, 1926.

ers continued to insist on the filling of these posts with members of the Union. The policing of the railway, however, remained in the hands of the Chinese under the Mukden Government. This anomalous situation naturally led to continual friction between the Soviet Russian Manager and chiefs of departments and the Chinese military. Both sides alleged constant violation of both the spirit and letter of the Sino-Russian agreements of May and September, 1924.

f. STATUS OF THE RAILWAY AFTER 1925. Since 1925 the Chinese authorities, i.e., the Chinese Government of Mukden under Chang Tso-lin until his death in June, 1928, and since then under his son, Chang Hsueh-liang, have succeeded in increasing by progressive steps the amount of Chinese participation in the control of the Chinese Eastern Railway. An unsuccessful attempt had been made in 1923 to take over the land offices of the railway. But later, certain of the functions of the railway administration, such as the education department, were assumed by the local Chinese authorities. In August, 1926, the Chinese commandeered the Chinese Eastern Railway fleet of steamers on the Sungari river and created the Northeastern Navigation Company to take charge of the fleet. In February, 1926, the Chinese authorities arbitrarily set aside the 1914 Harbin municipal council agreement against the protests of the foreign consuls.

The tenure of office of the "White" Russians in various technical and subordinate posts has been precarious, as the new Manager (Mr. Emshanov) of the railway remained a national of Soviet Russia. With respect to financial administration the Chinese succeeded during 1926 and 1927 in securing greater participation in the accounting administration, and forced an arrangement whereby a portion of the receipts of the railway would be deposited in the Three Eastern Provinces Bank (under the Mukden Government, or Chang Tso-lin and Chang Hsueh-liang) at Mukden, instead of entirely in the Dalbank in Harbin or in Vladivostok. Particularly with regard to division of the profits of the railway were the clauses of the provisional agreements of May and September, 1924, inadequate.

The Chinese Eastern Railway remained under nominal joint Sino-Russian operation, with the General Manager appointed by the Soviet Russian Government, and a large technical staff principally of Russians (both "Red" and "White") who supplied the technical ability for the operation of the line. Policing of the line since 1920 has been assumed by the Chinese, i.e., by guards sanctioned by the Mukden authorities, and many "White" Russian railway guards are employed. This somewhat anomalous situation rests legally on the Sino-Russian agreements of 1924. The Russo-Asiatic Bank (which as the Russo-Chinese Bank had originally financed the Chinese Eastern Railway in 1896) went into receivership in September, 1926.[88] Attention to the legal issues involved in these controversies over the Chinese Eastern Railway should, of course, not lead to a minimizing of the relatively more important political questions involved, which are, however, beyond the scope of this discussion.

[88] For a discussion of the attempts of the Chinese authorities to take over control of certain of the enterprises and offices of the Chinese Eastern Railway Company see the writer's article titled "Railway Politics in Manchuria" in *The China Weekly Review*, April 13 and April 23, 1927. For the events of 1929 see the Introductory Chapter.

C. THE POSITION OF OTHER POWERS: 1921-1929

CHAPTER LIII

The Position of the United States (1921-1929)

a. THE POSITION OF THE UNITED STATES: 1921-1929. With respect to the Sino-Japanese treaties and exchanges of notes of 1915 pertaining in part to Manchuria the United States Delegation at the Washington Conference took occasion to reaffirm the position taken by the American Secretary of State (Mr. Bryan) in his notes of March 13 and May 13, 1925, to the Japanese Government. At the thirty-first meeting of the Committee of the Whole (February 3, 1922) Secretary Charles Evans Hughes declared that the United States Government retained the same attitude and policy with respect to China as then expressed by Secretary Bryan.[89] He further expressed gratification that the Japanese Government were ready to withdraw the reservation which had been made in 1915 to the effect that Group V of the original proposals of the Japanese Government—namely concerning the employment of influential Japanese as political, financial and military advisers, etc.—would be postponed for future negotiations. As to the treaty and notes of 1915 specifically with reference to South Manchuria, Secretary Hughes expressed gratification at the statement of the Japanese Delegation that "Japan has no intention of insisting on a preferential right concerning the engagement by China of Japanese advisers or instructions on political, financial, military or police matters in South Manchuria." He also expressed gratification at the statement of Japan that the Japanese Government would not insist on exclusive rights to finance railway construction in Manchuria, but that the international banking consortium might be permitted to participate.[90] As to the right to lease land in Manchuria the United States Delegation declared that the American Government would interpret that right, under most favored nation treatment, as not of an exclusive character in favor of Japanese subjects alone. The so-called Root Resolutions of the

[89] *Conference on Limitation of Armaments*, pp. 1560 ff. See Chap. L, Sec. a, and Chap. XLV, Sec. a.
[90] *Conference*, p. 1562.

Conference expressed in more definite terms the American policy with regard to the "open door" in China, and it was in response to these resolutions that the "open door" was defined in more specific terms in the nine power treaty relating to principles and policies to be followed in matters concerning China, which was adopted by the Conference and signed on February 6, 1922.[91]

Since the Washington Conference the United States has taken no especially active part in Manchurian diplomacy. The American president of the Inter-allied Technical Board, John F. Stevens, remained in office in Harbin until October, 1922, when Inter-allied supervision of the Chinese Eastern Railway was definitely brought to a close. The Washington Conference, however, had adopted a resolution to the effect that at that time the trusteeship assumed under the Inter-allied Agreement of 1919 continued in force. Only with respect to the Chinese Eastern Railway question has the continued interest of the United States in Manchurian affairs been particularly evidenced. That interest, however, Secretary Hughes had declared at the Washington Conference to be one of desiring to do anything in the power of the government "to promote the proper conduct of that road, as one of the greatest instrumentalities of commerce in the East." He had declared further that "the United States Government had no interest whatever in the ownership and had no desire to secure control."[92]

CHAPTER LIV

The Position of Great Britain (1921-1929)

a. THE POSITION OF GREAT BRITAIN: 1921-1929. The position of the British Government, as expressed by the British Delegation to the Washington Conference, was very similar to that of the United States. British interests, however, were more definitely concerned in Shantung. Mr. Balfour stated that the British Government did not take the position that the matter of the retrocession of Weihaiwei was dependent upon the Japanese attitude with respect to the Kwantung leased territory but that Great Britain's willingness to negotiate for a complete return of Weihaiwei to Chinese administration was related intimately with the return of the Kiaochow leased territory.[93] The termination of the

[91] See Chap. LXI, Sec. a.
[92] *Conference*, p. 1270.
[93] *Ibid.*, p. 1070.

Anglo-Japanese treaty of alliance of 1911 by specific provision in the four power treaty of December 13, 1921, relating to insular possessions and insular dominions in the Pacific ocean, released Great Britain from such obligations with respect to Manchuria as might have been contained therein.[94] The interest of the British Government in the ultimate adjustment of the question of the Chinese Eastern Railway has apparently been less articulate than that of the American Government.

CHAPTER LV

The Position of France and Germany (1921-1929)

a. THE POSITION OF FRANCE AND GERMANY: 1921-1929. German nationals, who lost their extraterritorial rights in China during the Great War, have as individuals taken a prominent part in commercial enterprises in Manchuria since 1921, but the German Government have not participated in the outstanding international questions in Manchuria, e.g., in the question of the Chinese Eastern Railway, since 1921. Except for a German-Japanese trade agreement with particular bearing on the market for Manchurian soya bean oil in Germany, the German Government have not been concerned particularly with Manchurian diplomacy since the outbreak of the Great War.

The official interests of France in Manchuria, however, are more definite, and relate themselves particularly to the French Government's interest in the Russo-Asiatic Bank which was reorganized in Paris following the nationalization of Russian registered banks, including the Russo-Asiatic Bank.[95] The Russo-Asiatic Bank contract with the Chinese Government of October, 1920, had the support of the French Government, in an effort to protect the interests of French bankers who, since the original organization of the Russo-Chinese Bank, had held certain of the bonds of the institution which had financed, in the main, the Chinese Eastern Railway Company. The French Government, therefore, protested the Sino-Russian agreements of May 31, 1924, which undertook to exclude all third parties from consideration in the ultimate settlement of the Chinese Eastern Railway question. The intimate relation between the French Government and that of the Tsarist Russian Government with respect to Manchurian affairs

[94] See Chap. LVI, Sec. a.
[95] See Chap. XLIII, Sec. a, and Chap. LII, Sec. d.

was in sharp contrast with that between the French and Soviet Governments following the Russian Revolution. Moreover, the similarity of interest of the French and Japanese Governments with respect to the Chinese Eastern Railway was demonstrated in the contemporaneous protests of those two governments upon the signing of the Sino-Russian agreements of May 31, 1924.

D. TREATIES AND AGREEMENTS OF ALLIANCE, COOPERATION AND GUARANTEE: 1921-1929

CHAPTER LVI

The Four Power Treaty in Regard to the Pacific, 1921

a. TERMINATION OF THE ANGLO-JAPANESE ALLIANCE AT THE WASHINGTON CONFERENCE. In bearing on Manchuria, the most significant provision of the four power (the United States, the British Empire, France and Japan) treaty of the Washington Conference relating to their insular possessions and insular dominions in the region of the Pacific ocean was that which terminated the Anglo-Japanese treaty of alliance of July 13, 1911. In fact, that provision (Article 4) contained in the treaty, signed December 13, 1921, was in several respects, the principal clause in the entire treaty. That article stated that:

"This Treaty shall be ratified as soon as possible in accordance with the constitutional methods of the High Contracting Parties and shall take effect on the deposit of ratifications, which shall take place at Washington, and thereupon the agreement between Great Britain and Japan, which was concluded at London on July 13, 1911, shall terminate." [96]

The treaty was to remain in force for ten years (Article 3), during which period the several signatories undertook (Article 1) to "respect their rights in relation to their insular possessions and insular dominions in the region of the Pacific Ocean," and agreed that "if there should develop between the High Contracting Parties a controversy arising out of any Pacific question and involving their said rights which is not satisfactorily settled by diplomacy and is likely to affect the harmonious accord now happily subsisting between them, they shall invite the other High Contracting Parties to a joint conference to which the whole subject will be referred for consideration and adjustment." The powers

[96] Multi-Power (the United States, the British Empire, France and Japan) *Treaty Relating to Their Insular Possessions and Insular Dominions in the Region of the Pacific Ocean,* December 13, 1921. *Conference on Limitation of Armament,* pp. 1612-1616. The supplementary treaty of the same date, which defined the term "insular possessions and insular dominions" with respect to Japan, provided that "only Karafuto [or the Southern portion of the island of Sakhalin], Formosa and the Pescadores, and the islands under the mandate of Japan" were thus included. (*Ibid.,* p. 1619.)

agreed (Article 2) to "communicate with one another fully and frankly in order to arrive at an understanding" for joint action in any case where the said rights were "threatened by the aggressive action of any other Power." Mr. Viviani, of the French Delegation, in particular drew attention to the fact that "at the moment of its ratification the Anglo-Japanese Alliance comes to an end." [97] Responding, Mr. Balfour, of the British Delegation, declared: "Now, I am perfectly well aware that the Treaty between Great Britain and Japan has been the cause of much searchings of heart, of some suspicions, of a good deal of animadversion in important sections of opinion in the United States, and I think that from the historical point of view that attitude may at first cause surprise, for certainly nothing was further from the thoughts of the original framers of the Treaty between Japan and Great Britain than that it could touch in the remotest way, either for good or for evil, the interests of the United States. The United States seemed as remote from any subject touched in the original agreement, as Chile or Peru." He concluded by stating that the British Government had arrived at the conclusion, however, in view of the misapprehensions in the United States as to the application of the Anglo-Japanese alliance, that the only way "out of this impasse" was by removing the obstacle, i.e., the treaty of alliance itself. [98]

CHAPTER LVII

Termination of the Lansing-Ishii Agreement, 1923

a. TERMINATION OF THE LANSING-ISHII AGREEMENT, 1923. The so-called Lansing-Ishii agreement of November 2, 1917, was not specifically terminated at the Washington Conference or in any of the treaties signed in pursuance of the Conference. The signing of the nine power treaty (February 6, 1922) relating to principles and policies to be following in matters concerning China, however, gave a more definite form to the commitments of the powers to the "open door" policy, while the treaty contained in its several provisions commitments which were of a nature to destroy the effectiveness of any of the provisions contained in the Lansing-Ishii exchange of notes which might have been interpreted as contrary in substance to that treaty. [99] The American-Japanese

[97] *Conference,* p. 166.
[98] *Ibid.,* pp. 170-172.
[99] See Chap. LXI, Sec. a.

commitments in the exchange of notes of November 2, 1917, were specifically terminated, however, by an exchange of notes between the American Secretary of State (Charles Evans Hughes) and the Japanese Ambassador (Hanihara Masanao) at Washington, dated April 14, 1923, which declared that "in the light of the understandings arrived at by the Washington Conference on the Limitation of Armament, the American and Japanese Governments are agreed to consider the Lansing-Ishii correspondence of November 2, 1917, as cancelled and of no further force or effect." [100]

CHAPTER LVIII

Sino-Russian Agreement of May 31, 1924

a. SINO-RUSSIAN AGREEMENT ON GENERAL PRINCIPLES, MAY 31, 1924. On May 31, 1924, the Chinese Government (Peking) and the Soviet Government signed two agreements, one pertaining especially to the Chinese Eastern Railway, the other on "general principles for the settlement of the questions between them." The latter provided for (Article 1) resumption of diplomatic relations between China and Russia and contained a provision (Article 2) looking toward the convening of a conference within one month for the adjustment of outstanding questions between them.[101]   All treaties, agreements, protocols, contracts, etc., concluded between China and the former Tsarist Government were annuled (Article 3), and, likewise, all treaties, etc., concluded between the Tsarist Government and third parties "affecting the sovereign rights or interests of China" were declared (Article 4) to be "null and void," together with (Article 10) all the "special rights and privileges relating to all concessions in any part of China acquired by the Tsarist Government under various conventions, treaties, agreements, etc."   Outer Mongolia was recognized (Article 5) as an "integral part" of China in which Russia agreed to respect China's "sovereignty."   Each signatory agreed (Article 6) not to engage in propaganda "directed against the political and social systems of either contracting party."   Russia renounced (Article 11) the Russian share of the Boxer indemnity and agreed

- [100] *American Journal of International Law,* Vol. 17 (1923), pp. 510-512. See Chap. XLVII, Sec. a.
- [101] Sino-Russian (Peking Government—Soviet Government) *Agreement on General Principles for the Settlement of Questions,* May 31, 1924. *American Journal of International Law, Supplement,* Vol. 19 (1925), pp. 55-63. Also in *The China Year Book,* 1924-1925, pp. 1192-1200. See Chap. LII, Sec. d, for the Sino-Russian agreements of 1924 bearing on the status of the Chinese Eastern Railway.

(Article 12) "to relinquish the rights of extraterritoriality and consular jurisdiction," as well as to negotiate with China (Article 13) a new commercial treaty, including the subject of customs tariff, on the basis of equality and reciprocity. The remaining provisions of the agreement related to the question of the Chinese Eastern Railway and have been considered in detail elsewhere.[102]

CHAPTER LIX

Russo-Japanese Convention of 1925

a. RUSSO-JAPANESE CONVENTION OF 1925 RECOGNIZING THE SOVIET GOVERNMENT. Shortly after the conclusion of the Sino-Russian agreements of May and September, 1924, the Japanese Government, after negotiations in Peking extending over several months, signed in the Chinese capital with the Soviet Government a convention, dated January 20, 1925. The convention, which was made effective by an exchange of ratifications at Peking on April 15, 1925, and which had been signed by K. Yoshizawa, Japanese Minister to Peking, and L. M. Karakhan, Soviet Russian Ambassador to Peking, provided (Article 1) for reestablishment of diplomatic relations between Russia and Japan by extending recognition to the Soviet Government.[103] The convention reaffirmed (Article 2) the binding effect of the treaty of Portsmouth (1905) which was declared to be "in full force," but provided that other treaties, conventions, etc., between Japan and Russia entered into before November 7, 1917, should be "reexamined at a conference to be subsequently held," to be attended by representatives of the two governments. Besides providing in other sections for (Article 3) a revision of the Russo-Japanese Fisheries Convention of 1907, for (Article 4) the subsequent negotiation of a treaty of commerce, and (Article 6) the placing of Russian

---

[102] See Chap. LII, Sec. d.

[103] Sino-Japanese *Convention of Recognition of the Soviet Government, etc.* (with attached protocols, declarations and reports), January 20, 1925. *American Journal of International Law, Supplement,* Vol. 19 (1925), pp. 78-88. Also in *The China Year Book,* 1925, pp. 788-796. In connection with the resumption of diplomatic relations between Japan and Russia provided for in the above convention it may be remarked that conferences between the Japanese Government and the Government of the Far Eastern Republic of Siberia had been held at Dairen and at Changchun during 1921 and 1922, at the last of which a representative of the Soviet Government of Russia, Mr. Joffe, was in attendance. These conferences concerned themselves principally with such subjects as the removal of Japanese troops from Siberia, commercial concessions in the Russian Far East, and related subjects, and, because only indirectly related to Manchuria, have not been considered in detail in this study. As a matter of fact these conferences were indecisive.

(presumably Siberian) natural resources in principle at the disposal
of Japan, the convention specifically provided that (Article 5) each
government was to refrain from official participation in dissemination of propaganda in the territories of the other. The protocols
attached to the convention and pertaining to Saghalien have only
indirect bearing on Russo-Japanese relations in Manchuria.

CHAPTER LX

The Resolutions of the Washington Conference (1921-1922)

a. THE RESOLUTIONS OF THE CONFERENCE IN RELATION TO
MANCHURIA. Of the thirteen principal resolutions adopted by
the several delegations to the Washington Conference, i.e., those
not definitely incorporated *in substance* into the treaties of the
Conference, several relating to Manchuria have been considered
elsewhere in context. The resolutions which were adopted and
which have bearing, more or less, on Manchurian international relations are indicated below, together with the number given to
each in the Conference minutes:

1. Resolution VI regarding Foreign Postal Agencies in China
2. Resolution VII regarding Foreign Armed Forces in China
3. Resolution VIII regarding Radio Stations in China
4. Resolution IX regarding the Unification of Railways in China, and accom-
    panying Declarations
5. Resolution XI regarding Existing Commitments of China or with respect
    to China
6. Resolution XII regarding the Chinese Eastern Railway, approved by the
    Powers including China
7. Resolution XIII regarding the Chinese Eastern Railway, approved by the
    Powers other than China.[104]

Attention has been called to the very general wording and lack
of effectiveness of several of these (notably Resolutions VI, VII,
VIII and XII) in their application to Manchuria.[105] Resolutions
IX and XI have not been considered in context. Resolution IX
merely expressed the "hope that to the utmost degree consistent
with legitimate existing rights, the future development of railways in China shall be so conducted as to enable the Chinese Government to effect the unification of railways into a railway system

[104] See Chap. LII, Sec. a, for these resolutions in regard to the Chinese Eastern
Railway.
[105] See Chap. L, Secs. d and e, and also Chap. LII, Sec. a.

under Chinese control, with such foreign financial and technical assistance as may prove necessary in the interests of that system." [106] Resolution XI, if complied with, would have especially important bearing on Manchuria. It provided that:

Sec. 1. "The several Powers other than China will at their earliest convenience file with the Secretariat General of the Conference for transmission to the participating Powers, a list of all treaties, conventions, exchanges of notes, or other international agreements which they may have with China, or with any other Power or Powers in relation to China, which they deem to be still in force and upon which they may desire to rely. . . . In any case in which the document may not have been published, a copy of the text (in its original language or languages) will be filed with the Secretariat General of the Conference.

"Every treaty or other international agreement of the character described which may be concluded hereafter shall be notified by the Governments concerned within sixty (60) days of its conclusion to the Powers who are signatories of or adherents to this Agreement."

It was further provided in this Resolution (Sec. 2) that "all those contracts between their nationals, of the one part, and the Chinese Government or any of its administrative subdivisions or local authorities, of the other part, which involve any concession, franchise, option or preference with respect to railway construction, mining, forestry, navigation, river conservancy, harbor works, reclamation, electrical communications, or other public works or public services, or for the sale of arms or ammunition, or which involve a lien upon any of the public revenues or properties of the Chinese Government or of any of its administrative subdivisions" should be filed with the Secretariat General of the Conference "at their earliest convenience, for transmission to the participating Powers." [107] In future, every such contract should be notified by the governments concerned to the several powers signatories or adherents to the above agreement. The Chinese Government (Sec. 3) agreed to notify, under the above conditions, the participating and interested powers of the conclusion of any such agreements as indicated. Other powers, not members of the conference, were to be invited to adhere. The various debates in the committee meetings pertaining to this resolution brought out some of the problems involved in its application.

As to the international legal status and binding force of such resolutions characterized above, the Chairman (Mr. Hughes) ex-

[106] *Conference on Limitation of Armament*, p. 1652.
[107] *Ibid.*, pp. 1654 ff.

pressed his opinion in the sixth plenary session (February 4, 1922) of the Conference, as follows:

"It will be observed that certain of the Resolutions adopted by the Committee, and on its recommendation adopted by the Conference, are put in treaty form, and other Resolutions are not put in that form. The distinction is that those engagements which it is deemed require the sanction of a treaty are put in the form of a treaty and proposed for execution by the Powers. In other cases, the Resolutions are of a character not requiring such sanction in the form of a treaty, and are deemed to be binding upon the Powers according to their tenor when adopted by the Conference." [108]

CHAPTER LXI

Treaty Definition of the "Open Door" Policy: Nine Power Treaty, 1922

a. TREATY DEFINITION OF THE "OPEN DOOR": COMMITMENTS OF THE POWERS. No exhaustive analysis of the debates in the Washington Conference committee meetings pertaining to the definition and binding force of the "open door" policy, or the particular policy of the "open door" as enunciated by John Hay initially in 1899, is here possible. Suffice it, at the outset, to draw attention to the original Root Resolution which was adopted by the Conference in plenary session (fourth, December 10, 1921) and which was incorporated in identical phraseology in the nine power treaty relating to principles and policies concerning China. Commenting on this resolution itself the Chairman (Mr. Hughes) declared in the plenary session:

"It is hardly necessary to point out the great importance of this declaration. It is, in truth, a charter containing an assurance to China of protection from acts in derogation of her sovereignty and independence and administrative autonomy, and also an assurance that as between the Powers there will be a careful observance of the principle of free and equal opportunity in matters relating to China, and that no one will seek special advantages or privileges at the expense of the rights of others." [109]

The general effectiveness of the original wording of the resolution as presented by Mr. Root was not destroyed by the minor amendments made in the Committee of the Whole, which discussion, however, did provide a somewhat limited basis for interpretation

[108] *Conference on Limitation of Armament,* p. 286.
[109] *Ibid.,* p. 148.

of the Resolution as adopted, and as incorporated in the treaty itself. In the discussions in the Committee of the Whole (eighteenth meeting, January 16, 1922) new clauses were added to the proposed draft of the treaty pertaining to the "open door." The French, British and Japanese Delegations took an active part in securing greater precision to the wording of the articles in the proposed treaty. Baron Shidehara, among other statements, asserted (twentieth meeting, January 18, 1922) that the policy of the "open door," as initiated by Secretary Hay, was then "limited in its scope, both as concerning its subject matter and the area of Chinese territory to which it applied," and that "the principles formulated in the draft Resolution were of an entirely different scope from the policy of the open door as conceived in 1898-99 [Sic!—1899-1900]; the draft Resolution gave, in a certain sense, a new definition to that policy." [110] Mr. Hughes, replying to this statement, asserted that while "it was quite true that in the original statement of the policy by Secretary Hay there were specific points mentioned; it was also true that the bearing of those points and the intent of the policy were very clearly presented. The general purpose in view and the real meaning of the open door policy were indicated in the communications addressed to the several Governments under instructions from Secretary Hay." [111] After reviewing the history of the application of the "open door" policy, and the general acceptance of that policy by the several powers in numerous commitments, Mr. Hughes concluded that:

"In the light of these reiterated statements which could hardly be regarded as ambiguous, the Chairman could not assume that the statement of principles recorded in the Resolution before the Committee was a new statement. He rather regarded it as a more definite and precise statement of the principle that had long been admitted, and to which the Powers concerned had given their unqualified adherence for twenty years." [112]

Mr. Hughes further reiterated his interpretation of points in the "open door" resolution before the Committee of the Whole, points which were subsequently included in the treaty, stating that "they were dealing with the open door, an avenue of opportunity, an avenue to legitimate enterprise—and not with obstacles to legitimate enterprise; and all that was embraced in the various undertakings which, to the extent of the particular rights essential to their

[110] *Ibid.*, p. 1250.
[111] *Ibid.*, p. 1250.
[112] *Ibid.*, p. 1258.

prosecution, of course monopolized a special line of endeavor in a concrete or particular case, were amply protected by the last clause of the first Article. The purpose was, however, to safeguard the principle, so that under the guise of particular undertakings there should not be an assertion of a general superiority of right or a monopoly or preference which would be in conflict with the principles to which the Powers represented on the Committee adhered."[113] The articles of the "open door" treaty which follow were not, therefore, to be interpreted as placing obstacles in the way either of acquisition on the part of the nationals of any foreign power of particular rights in the form of patents, trade-marks, copyrights, and mining permits, or of acquisition and continuation of "rights as may be necessary to the conduct of a particular commercial, industrial or financial undertaking," reservations to this effect being ultimately included within the treaty as signed by the several powers.

The definition of the "open door" policy (not necessarily of the policy as enunciated at a particular time by John Hay) which was contained in the nine power treaty relating to principles and policies concerning China, signed February 6, 1922, is too incisive in itself to permit of adequate epitome. Reference to the text of the treaty itself is made necessary by the succinct wording and general inclusiveness, as well as the qualifications, of the treaty itself.[114] It must suffice here, then, to comment briefly and to remark that the "open door" policy as defined by the treaty, and to which all powers signatories to the treaty are now bound, clearly commits all the powers (except Russia) who have major interests in the Manchurian provinces (1) "to respect the sovereignty, the independence, and the territorial and administrative integrity of China," and (2) to maintain "equality of opportunity in China for the trade and industry of all nations." As to the first postulate, the treaty (Article 1) imposes the negative obligation "to refrain from taking advantage of conditions in China in order to seek special rights or privileges," and the positive obligation "to provide the fullest and most unembarrassed opportunity to China to develop and maintain for herself an effective and stable government." As to the second postulate, the treaty (Article 1) imposes the positive obligation upon foreign powers "to use their influence for the pur-

[113] *Conference on Limitation of Armament*, p. 1266.
[114] Multi-Power (the United States, Belgium, the British Empire, China, France, Italy, Japan, the Netherlands and Portugal) *Treaty relating to Principles and Policies concerning China,* February 6, 1922. *Conference* pp. 1621-1629.

pose of effectually establishing and maintaining the principle of equal opportunity for the commerce and industry of all nations throughout the territory of China." To this end the foreign powers agreed (Article 2) not to enter into treaties or agreements of any sort which would infringe or impair the principles above stated. But more specifically, with respect to the maintenance of the principle of equality of opportunity, the treaty provided (Article 3) that the foreign powers would not seek, nor support their nationals in seeking, "any arrangement which might purport to establish in favor of their interests any general superiority of rights with respect to commercial or economic development in any designated region of China," or "any monopoly or preference" as would deprive the nationals of other powers of legitimate commercial rights—with the reservation that such "rights as may be necessary to the conduct of a particular commercial, industrial, or financial undertaking" (or trade-mark rights, etc.) should not be abridged. China agreed to apply these principles in dealing with applications for economic rights and privileges from the outside, whether from the nations signatory to the treaty or otherwise (i.e., for example, Russia). "Spheres of influence" (Article 4) were specifically denounced; the signatories agreed not to support "mutually exclusive opportunities in designated parts of Chinese territory." China agreed (Article 5) that she would not exercise or permit "unfair discrimination of any kind" with respect to "the whole of the railways in China." China's rights as a neutral were to be respected by outside powers in case of a war in which China was not a belligerent; China agreed (Article 6) to observe the obligations of neutrality when she was a neutral. And, finally, whenever a situation arises "which in the opinion of any one of them involves the application of the stipulations of the present Treaty" the powers agreed (Article 7) that "full and frank communication" between them should follow. Powers not signatories (Article 8) were to be invited to adhere, and the treaty was to take effect on exchange of ratifications, to continue in force in perpetuity.

By this important international document the policy of the "open door" with respect to China, i.e., including Manchuria also, was given a more precise and, at once, more binding international legal status than it had ever possessed previously. The general principles, however, both in regard to respecting the territorial and administrative integrity of China, and with respect to maintaining equality of opportunity for trade and industry in China, had long been established in unilateral declarations and in bilateral and legally enforceable treaties, to which, even before the Washington Conference, the governments of the United States, Great Britain, France, Russia and Japan had adhered. At the Washington Conference the Chinese Government became a participant, in a more definite sense, in the enforcement of these principles. But the interpretation given the treaty in the Committee of the Whole had elicited the statement from the Chairman (Mr. Hughes) that the treaty was not to be understood as "coercive." The treaty was presumably to be enforced, as treaties often are—or are not—by reliance on international good faith. So also with respect to the treaty's application to Manchuria.

APPENDICES

APPENDICES

APPENDIX A

The Sino-Russian (Li-Lobanoff) Secret Treaty of Alliance, 1896

The existence of the Sino-Russian secret treaty of alliance of 1896 has now been established beyond all conjecture. A telegraphic summary of the treaty was presented to the Committee of the Whole on Pacific and Far Eastern Questions by the Chinese Delegation at the Washington Conference, which summary served to authenticate the version of the same treaty which was made public at Paris during the Peace Conference in 1919. But the existence of such a secret treaty of alliance between China and Russia had been known in certain circles outside of Russia and China almost contemporaneously with its signature at St. Petersburg.

When Li Hung-chang was in St. Petersburg on the occasion of the coronation of Tsar Nicholas II, during the spring of 1896, he was approached by Count Witte, Russian Minister of Finance, with the suggestion that the two countries sign a treaty of alliance directed against possible aggression on the part of Japan, and that there be included within the text of the treaty a provision whereby the Chinese Government would concede to Russia the right to construct a railway short-cut across North Manchuria, thus to shorten the distance from European Russia to Vladivostok by obviating the circuitous route along the course of the Amur river. Although Li Hung-chang had come to Russia for the major purpose of extending China's appreciation of the rôle which Russia had played in intervening to prevent Japan from retaining the portion of Fengtien province which Japan had acquired by cession in the Treaty of Shimonoseki, and of the part which Russia had played in floating the initial loan to pay the first instalment on the indemnity to Japan, he was disinclined to permit Russia to obtain a foothold in southern Manchuria. Hence he was opposed to the construction of any southern section of such a railway toward Port Arthur. The publication by Count Witte in 1921 of his *Memoirs* has made possible a more adequate interpretation of the course of the negotiations attending the signing of this treaty.[1] Witte, to

[1] *The Memoirs of Count Witte* (translated from the original Russian manuscript and edited by Abraham Yarmolinsky, 1921).

253

quote his own *Memoirs,* "dwelt on the services which he had recently done" to China, and impressed Li Hung-chang with the importance to China of maintaining friendly relations with Russia.[2] In order to present a united front against Japan, Witte asserted that not only an alliance, but also a railway across North Manchuria toward Vladivostok, was of great mutual advantage to Russia and China. The railway would be necessary to permit of rapid transportation of Russian troops in the eventuality of provocation on the part of Japan. Although Li made objections at first, he was constrained to sign the proposed treaty of alliance. Fear of Japanese aggression in Manchuria, together with gratitude for the "placing of her first large foreign loan abroad," influenced his decision to comply.[3]

Count Witte had conducted the preliminary negotiations, but the treaty was signed by Prince Lobanoff-Rostovsky, Russian Minister for Foreign Affairs. The latter was entrusted with the final drafting of the treaty along the lines agreed upon by Witte and Li. An interesting incident occurred when the date came for the signing of the final draft. Witte informs us that on this occasion he suddenly discovered to his great surprise and dismay that in the clause binding China and Russia to go to war as allies the original Li-Witte wording had been altered, and that as drafted would have obligated Russia to come to the aid of China as against *any or all* powers, instead of Japan alone. "Twenty minutes for lunch" was declared and the secretaries corrected the wording so that the alliance was, as originally planned by Witte, directed only against aggressive action on the part of Japan.[4] These new copies were "quietly substituted" and were signed by Li Hung-chang in final form. Signature took place on May 22 (June 3, the Russian Julian calendar date), 1896.[5] Secrecy was specifically enjoined on the signatories. The treaty was to extend for a period of fifteen years (apparently from the date when, on confirmation by China of a separate contract for the construction of the Manchurian railway short-cut, the treaty should come into force, i.e., from October 20, 1896, or perhaps from September 30, 1896).[6]

[2] *The Memoirs of Count Witte,* p. 89.
[3] *Ibid.,* pp. 90-91.
[4] *Ibid.,* pp. 93 ff.
[5] That the exact date for the signing of the Li-Lobanoff treaty was June 3, 1896 (May 22, old Russian date), was stated by J. V. A. MacMurray in a memorandum to Dr. Payson J. Treat, which is quoted by Dr. Paul H. Clyde: *International Rivalries in Manchuria* (Columbus, O., 1926) p. 39.
[6] The date for the expiration of this treaty is not entirely clear, inasmuch as the text of the treaty is somewhat indefinite. The treaty was to remain in force for

The existence of such a treaty of alliance was widely rumored during 1896 and the years following. It was generally confused with what was termed the "Cassini Convention" which was supposed to have been signed by Count Cassini and certain Chinese officials before the departure of the former for St. Petersburg, i.e., on or before September 30, 1896.[1] That the "Cassini Convention" as such never existed has now been well established. The agreement for which Count Cassini was waiting with packed baggage during those weeks in Peking has been shown to be not such a treaty of alliance, but the contract for the construction and operation of the Chinese Eastern Railway, which had been signed at St. Petersburg on August 16/28, 1896, and, finally, at Berlin on September 8, 1896. Ratifications were, however, not exchanged for this agreement at Peking until October 20, 1896.[8] M. Cordier and M. Gérard have well demonstrated that the text of the so-called "Cassini Convention," which Dr. Dudgeon was supposed to have procured from the *Tsung-li Yamen,* was spurious, in fact, a badly confused and garbled attempt of fusion of both the treaty of alliance and the railway contract agreement.[9] Witte's *Memoirs* make no mention of any "Cassini Convention" and its non-existence has been conclusively proved by the authentication of the actual secret treaty of alliance signed by Li and Lobanoff at St. Petersburg.

The first more or less authentic text of the Li-Lobanoff secret treaty of 1896 was published in the London *Daily Telegraph* of February 15, 1910, under the caption: *"Manchuria—A Chinese View of the Situation"* by "An Admirer of Li Hung-chang"—which "admirer" was Li Ching-mai, Chinese Minister to the Court of St. James, the son of the great statesman, Li Hung-chang.[10] That text conforms to the telegraphic summary presented by the Chinese Delegation to the Washington Conference, but is more detailed and exact, naturally. The publication was made in 1910 by Li Ching-mai ostensibly to justify his father's action, and, as it was

fifteen years after "the day on which the contract stipulated in Article 4 [for the construction of the Manchurian railway short-cut] shall have been confirmed [i.e., by the Emperor of China]." MacMurray gives the date for the exchange of ratifications at Peking as October 20, 1896. Cordier, however, gives September 30, 1896, the exact date when Count Cassini left for St. Petersburg. (Cordier, H., *Histoire Generale de la Chine, etc.* Quatre tomes, Paris, 1920. Vol. IV, pp. 202-203.) The latter is probably in error.

[7] Version of the so-called "Cassini Convention" published in the *North China Herald,* October 30, 1896. MacMurray, Vol. I, pp. 79-81.

[8] MacMurray, Vol. I, p. 74. See Chap. III, Sec. b.

[9] Cordier, *op. cit.,* Vol. IV, pp. 202-203.

[10] MacMurray, Vol. I, p. 81. M. A. Gérard in 1918 established the substantial accuracy of the disclosure of Li Ching-mai in 1910 by publishing his: *Ma Mission*

thought, after the termination of the period of fifteen years prescribed in the treaty. It would appear, however, that the treaty had still over a year to continue before expiration.

Copies of one version of the Li-Lobanoff secret treaty were circulated at the Paris Peace Conference, and the Chinese Delegation to the Washington Conference, as noted above, presented a telegraphic summary of the treaty, which was at that time officially recognized by the Chinese Government to have been signed in 1896 and in force for fifteen years thereafter. The telegraphic summary as then presented follows:

"Article 1. The High Contracting Parties engage to support each other reciprocally by all the land and sea forces at [as against] any aggression direct by Japan against Russian territory in Eastern Asia, China or Korea.

"Article 2. No treaty of peace with an adverse party can [shall] be concluded by either of them without the consent of the other.

"Article 3. During military operations all Chinese ports shall be open to Russian vessels.

"Article 4. The Chinese Government consents to the construction of a railway across the Provinces of Amur and Kirin in the direction of Vladivostok. The construction and exploitation of this railway shall be accorded to the Russo-Chinese Bank. The contract shall be concluded between the Chinese Minister at St. Petersburg and the Russo-Chinese Bank.

"Article 5. In time of war Russia shall have free use of the railway for the transport and provisioning of her troops. In time of peace Russia shall have the same right for the transit of her troops and provisions.

"Article 6. The present treaty shall come into force from the day on which the contract stipulated in Article 4 shall have been confirmed. It shall have force for fifteen years." [11]

It is interesting to note that this secret treaty expired presumably, on October 20, 1911 (or perhaps earlier, but not before August, 1911, i.e., fifteen years after the treaty came into force), or *after*

en Chine: 1893-1897. M. Gérard was French Minister to China during the period when the Li-Lobanoff treaty was negotiated. He wrote in his memoirs: "Although the treaty was intended to remain secret, I one day had in my hands for a few minutes, during a visit which I made in the spring of 1897 to Li Hung-chang at his residence, in Peking, the copy of the document which he had signed the previous year with Prince Lobanoff." M. Gérard also declared the English versions of the so-called "Cassini Convention" apocryphal, and that "there never was, properly speaking, any 'Cassini Convention.'" (Gérard, p. 146.) The Empress Dowager Tse Hsi is said to have made an allusion to this treaty in 1900 when, in a communication to the Tsar, she is said to have declared that Li Hung-chang in 1896 "drew up on our behalf and concluded with your country a secret treaty of alliance which is duly recorded in the Imperial Archives." (Bland and Backhouse, China Under the Empress Dowager, p. 336.

[11] Conference on the Limitation of Armament, p. 1414.

the publication by Li Ching-mai of the text of the treaty, and *after* the conclusion of the third Anglo-Japanese alliance of July 13, 1911, —unless it be contended that the treaty was terminated by adverse breach during the period from 1900 to 1905, or was voidable as a result of those circumstances.

APPENDIX B

The Alleged Sino-Japanese Secret "Protocols" of December 22, 1905

The authenticity of the alleged Sino-Japanese "Secret Protocols" of December 22, 1905, is far more difficult to establish than that of the Li-Lobanoff secret treaty of alliance signed between China and Japan in 1896. This arises from the important fact that the Japanese Government have never published an *official* English version of those "protocols" in full and authoritative form, and from the fact that, apparently, the Chinese Government has never accepted the authenticity, or at least the interpretation and degree of enforceability, which the Japanese Government have on occasion sought to attribute to them. Whether attached to the formal treaty of Peking of December 22, 1905, and to the additional agreement of the same date, there were other "protocols" containing commitments on the part of China with regard to railway rights in Manchuria, commitments which were signed in due form by both parties, has long been a matter of controversy. Whether these "protocols" took the form of formal agreements or were merely the signed record of the proceedings of the conferences then held between Yuan Shih-k'ai and Baron Komura, and their fellow negotiators, may also be a matter of question. Finally, whether, if merely the signed record of proceedings these "protocols" actually contained certain provisions not then made known at once to other powers, and whether, if contained therein, they are enforceable as a part of the treaty itself, may also be subject to some question. There would have been, and there would now be, no occasion for such hesitance in giving final judgment, if the Japanese Government had published an *official* version of these "protocols" in full, above the signatures of the plenipotentiaries of both China and Japan, and if such a version were accepted by the Chinese Government, or *vice versa*. These alleged "secret protocols" have been characterized in detail in context in the previous sections and their importance, whether enforceable or not, has on numerous occasions been indicated by the course of events in connection with the history of projects for foreign-financed railways in Manchuria. Neither

258

the particular statements of the governments concerned, nor the didactic assertions of certain individuals who have held strong opinions one way or the other, have altered the writer's determination to state the facts as they are available to him.

At the outset, it should be noted that, when the ratifications were exchanged (January 23, 1906) of the Sino-Japanese treaty and additional agreement of December 22, 1905, no additional "protocols" or other commitments were at the same time included in the instrument of ratification.[1] There is, apparently, no published evidence that subsequent ratification of such "protocols" ever took place.

It has been asserted that these "protocols" were kept secret due to the desire of the Chinese Government. That this was the case is not entirely certain. That, if such "protocols" actually were signed in due form, they were kept secret for a time is obvious. The Japanese Government, in 1906 and following, evidently informed both the American and British Governments of the *existence* of such "protocols," but there is no evidence that any *text* of the same was ever transmitted *officially* to either of these governments. On January 12, 1906, Huntington Wilson, American *Chargé d'Affaires* at Tokyo, transmitted to the Department of State a communication from Kato Takaaki, Japanese Minister for Foreign Affairs, to the effect that on January 11 the *Chargé* had been informed from the Foreign Office that *none* of the documents signed on December 22, 1905, in Peking were to have been published until after the formal exchange of ratifications "but that since much of their contents had in some way become known, it had been decided to give them out informally."[2] No copy of such "protocols" seems to have been handed to the American *Chargé* at the time, though Mr. Wilson informed the Department that:

"Certain protocols, containing further arrangements of no small importance, were drawn up in conjunction with the treaty and agreement; but, as I was informed at the foreign office, these protocols are being kept secret for the present in accordance with an understanding with China."[3]

Mr. Wilson also drew attention to the fact that the treaty and additional agreement had been drafted only in the Chinese and Japanese languages and that "this is interesting as a departure

[1] MacMurray, Vol. I, p. 550. There is contained herein also an unsigned version in the form of a "Summary of alleged Secret Protocols to Sino-Japanese Treaty of December 22, 1905." (*Ibid.*, pp. 554-555.)
[2] *U. S. Foreign Relations*, 1906, Pt. II, p. 996.
[3] *Ibid.* See Chap. XVI, Sec. c.

from Japan's former practice in making treaties to have the governing text in a western language, rather than one in the relatively ambiguous Japanese or Chinese."

Mr. Kato, Japanese Minister for Foreign Affairs, evidently referred in his conversation with Mr. Wilson to the dispatch sent by the Peking correspondent of the *Asahi* (Osaka) to Japan in which a telegraphic summary of certain "protocols" was contained. Commenting on this dispatch of the *Asahi* the English editor (the late Robert Young) of the *Japan Chronicle* (Kobe) stated on January 18, 1906:

"There has been a widespread belief that in addition to the clauses of the recently published treaty between Japan and China, there existed a secret agreement between the two Powers. It was, indeed, reported that Baron Komura, addressing his countrymen at a reception given in his honour at Tientsin, had made a statement to the effect that there was a secret agreement. . . . It now transpires that the "secret agreement" consists of about half a dozen chapters of records of the proceedings at Peking between Baron Komura and the Chinese Plenipotentiaries, containing various agreements between the two Governments. These records, it is stated, will not be published, but the *Asahi* correspondent indicates their purport."[4]

The *Asahi* further stated that when the records of the negotiations at Peking were transmitted by Baron Komura to Mr. T. Kato, the Foreign Minister, the latter requested that the "secret agreement," if annexed to the treaty, be shown to him. The Japanese press then announced that this "secret agreement" was merely the record of proceedings of the conferences which contained certain commitments which, it was thought, the Foreign Minister might publish shortly after the exchange of ratifications of the treaty itself. No such *official* publication has appeared of any *complete* record of the proceedings or of any "protocol" duly signed. The *Asahi* correspondent had concluded his dispatch from Peking with the statement that no such secret understanding, in the proper sense of the word, existed between the two powers.[5]

The existence of some form of secret agreement between China and Japan, entered into at the Peking negotiations in December, 1905, seems to have been conveyed by Japan to the British Foreign Office before 1908. Sir Edward Grey stated in Parliament on

[4] *The Japan Weekly Chronicle,* January 18, 1906. What is apparently a direct quotation (though not thus indicated) from this issue of the *Japan Chronicle* is contained in Weale, B. L. Putnam, *The Truce in the East and its Aftermath* (N. Y., 1907), pp. 484-485 of the Appendices. Each of these references gives a version of the alleged "protocols" in four articles.
[5] *The Japan Weekly Chronicle,* January 18, 1906.

March 3, 1908, that the existence of such an agreement, containing a clause stipulating that parallel lines to the South Manchuria Railway should not be constructed by China in Manchuria, was not denied by the Chinese Government.[6] There appears to be no evidence, however, that the Chinese Government had *affirmed* their existence or had accepted a *particular* version of the same. Again, on March 24, 1908, Sir Edward Grey stated in Parliament that the British Government had been informed that the agreement had been signed by the Chinese representatives and that there could be no doubt as to its validity.[7] Sir Edward did not present any conclusive evidence for making the statement.

The statements of Sir Edward Grey were made in Parliament shortly after the official protests of the Japanese Government against the construction by the British firm, Pauling and Company, of the Hsinmintun-Fakumen railway, to branch from the Peking-Mukden line at Hsinmintun, and to run north to Fakumen, i.e., practically parallel geographically with the South Manchuria Railway from Mukden to Kaiyuan. During the months of 1907 the Japanese Government made a series of such protests to Peking on the ground that the construction by any foreign firm, other than Japanese, of a railway in South Manchuria which would parallel the South Manchuria Railway was forbidden to China under the terms of the "protocols" attached to the treaty of Peking of December 22, 1905. The texts of these protests are not available; that they referred to "the minutes" of the conference held in Peking is more likely than that they referred categorically to bilaterally signed "protocols," in view of the fact that the Chinese reply to one of these protests has been published, the latter commenting on Japan's reference to "the minutes of the Sino-Japanese Conference." [8] This communication from the Chinese Foreign Office drew attention to the fact that, while the Japanese plenipotentiaries had been opposed at that conference to the fixing of a definite distance in miles to indicate what was a "parallel" railway, the Chinese plenipotentiaries had sought a more definite statement. This communication *did not deny*, apparently, the existence of commitments in some form or other, but drew attention to the fact that the Chinese in 1905 "added a declaration that Japan would do nothing

[6] British *Parliamentary Debates*, March 3, 1908, Vol. 185, p. 527.
[7] *Ibid.*, March 24, 1908, Vol. 186, p. 1191.
[8] Text of the reply of the Chinese Foreign Office as quoted from Hsü Shih-chang, *Tung San Sheng Cheng Lueh (Record of the Three Eastern Provinces* in Chinese) by Hsü Shuhsi, *China and Her Political Entity* (N. Y., 1926), pp. 295-296.

to prevent China from any steps she might take in the future for the development of Manchuria." [9]

At the time of the failure of the Chinchow-Aigun railway project, due to the combined opposition of the Russian and Japanese Governments, the latter government addressed a note to the Chinese Government, under date of February 5, 1910, apparently calling attention to the commitments of China not to construct "parallel" lines to the South Manchuria Railway in Manchuria. The American *Chargé* in Peking informed the Department of State that the Chinese Foreign Office had informed him that "Japan based her claims to be consulted [in the Chinchow-Aigun railway project] on the fact that the proposed road would parallel the South Manchuria Railway." [10] This incident, however, did not bring to light an *official* and complete account of China's alleged commitments, asserted to have been made in December, 1905. In the formal statement of the Japanese Foreign Office communicated to the Department of State of the United States (January 21, 1910), which presented Japan's reasons for rejecting the so-called "Knox plan" for neutralization of the Manchurian railways, and reserving the subject of the Chinchow-Aigun railway project for subsequent attention, there was no mention of the existence of any special commitment of China concerning the interdicting of "parallel" railways in Manchuria. [11] Moreover, there is no mention of such "protocols" in any of the railway contract agreements between China and Japan made from 1905 to the present, with respect to railways asserted to have been mentioned in those "protocols." With regard to these alleged "protocols," therefore, it may be said that, until further information is available from the archives of the Japanese or other foreign offices, since the initial and indefinite reference to "certain protocols" made by the Japanese Foreign Office to Mr. Wilson at Tokyo in January of 1906, no *official* information as to the textual character of such "protocols" has been conveyed to the American Department of State. That the British Foreign Office, however, has been more adequately informed as to the exact character of these alleged "protocols" is not improbable.

Nor is the *official* attitude of the Chinese Government toward the declared existence of such "protocols" entirely clear. It is evident that both the Chinese and Japanese plenipotentiaries at the

[9] Quoted by Hsü Shushi, pp. 295-296.
[10] *U. S. Foreign Relations*, 1910, p. 257.
[11] *Ibid.*, pp. 251-252.

conference in Peking in December, 1905, agreed that the minutes of the conference were not to be published, at least until after some time. Chinese officials at the time asserted that Baron Komura actually made such a request for a bilateral interdicting of foreign-financed (i.e., other than Japanese) railways in South Manchuria.[12] The only published evidence available to the writer as to a particular *official* reference to such "protocols" by the Chinese Government is that contained in the communication quoted above with respect to the reply of China to Japan's protest in connection with the Hsinmintun-Fakumen railway project. No reference to "protocols" is there made; but there is a specific reference to "minutes of the conference," and, moreover, there appears to be contained therein no denial that China made *certain commitments* at the time—of what binding character, or of what enforceability, is not clear.

The existence of such "protocols" (which, if existent, were in fact "secret") has been repudiated, however, by T'ang Shao-yi, former Governor of Fengtien province, and one of the Chinese secretaries to the Peking conference in December, 1905. In the course of a conversation of January 28, 1908, as reported by W. W. Rockhill, T'ang Shao-yi asserted that no clause debarring China from paralleling the South Manchuria Railway existed. He further asserted that there was no secret agreement then signed, and that this fact had been made known to the legations in Peking at the time. The matter was discussed, he is reported to have said, in the conference sessions, Japan desiring such an agreement, but none such was arrived at, and none signed by the respective plenipotentiaries. Nor do the signed minutes of the conferences contain any such mutual agreement, it was asserted.[13] As to this statement it may be said that there is not conclusive evidence that T'ang Shao-yi was entirely informed as to what Yuan Shih-k'ai or some other official might have done in connection with some form of agreement with Japan on such a matter. Nor was his statement of a nature to carry the weight that an official declaration on the part

[12] *The Japan Weekly Chronicle*, December 7, 1905. Prince Ch'ing, who signed the treaty and additional agreement of December 22, 1905, was apparently not in attendance at the various conferences after the first meeting and until the conclusion of the sessions, Yuan Shih-k'ai being the principal negotiator, who was assisted by Chu Hung-chi, Minister for Foreign Affairs. See also the *Japan Chronicle* for Nov. 23 and 30; Dec. 21, 1905.
[13] Rockhill, W. W., *Treaties, Conventions, Agreements, etc., relating to China and Korea*, (Oct., 1904-Jan., 1908). (Published by the Department of State, Wash., 1908.) Rockhill's note (p. 140) following an *unofficial* text of the "protocols." (Rockhill's note also printed in Willoughby, W. W., *Foreign Rights and Interests in China*, 2 Vols., Baltimore, 1927, Vol. I, p. 172.)

of the Chinese Government itself would have. It does not appear that the Chinese Foreign Office since that time has specifically *denied* the existence of certain commitments of the character attributed in some circles to them.

As to the assertion that "the protocol is included in the diplomatic documents of Japan, accessible to all students of international relations," it may be said that, while they may exist in certain documents in Japanese, there is, to the knowledge of the writer, no available *official* text of the same in the English language. The current texts are "alleged" or "reported"; they cannot carry the weight which an official version published by the Japanese Government, and transmitted in full directly to the foreign chancelleries concerned, would carry. In the "admirable libraries" for which the United States is reputed to be famous, the writer has failed to find any *official* version of the "protocols" in question. Neither in the Japanese language collection of treaties, nor in the French and English text of Japanese treaties, *etc.*, published by the Japanese Ministry for Foreign Affairs in revised form in 1918, is there any mention of such "protocols." [14] The treaty and additional agreement of December 22, 1905, are in both—but not the "protocols."

"Although the Chinese did later deny the validity of the protocols, the case presented by them was far from convincing and until further evidence is forthcoming must lead inevitably to the conclusion that they were actually signed, and furthermore, that there was nothing secret about them." This quoted statement, in the light of evidence presented above, would seem to require more substantiation upon four points. If the Chinese and Japanese Governments were in agreement to publish the alleged "protocols" of December, 1905, in *official* form it is not impossible that the validity of the "protocols" might be established beyond peradventure. The most recent Japanese semi-official publication of one more unofficial and unsigned version of what is termed "Protocols attached to the Treaty of Peking, December 22, 1905," appears in a recent South Manchuria Railway publication.[15] This adds nothing to the authenticity of the alleged "secret protocols." Historical accuracy would better be assisted by conformity to the eleventh resolution of the Washington Conference. Until that time there

[14] Ministère des affaires étrangères, *Recueil des traités et conventions conclus entre l'empire du Japon et les puissances étrangères.* (2 tomes, Imprimerie Impériale, 1918.) One of these volumes is in Japanese, the other in foreign languages, especially French. Chinese and Japanese texts of the treaty and additional agreement of December 22, 1905, are given on pages 281 to 288 of the Japanese volume. No other "protocols" or "minutes of conferences" are attached.

[15] *Report of Progress in Manchuria: 1907-1928*, pp. 199-201.

would seem to be some justification in raising the question of the actual existence of such "protocols" and in refraining from a definite statement as to their enforceability. As for any practical and legal bearing that such would have upon the future in the international relations of Manchuria it seems apparent that since the negotiations preceding the formation of the China consortium agreement of October, 1920, and especially since the Washington Conference, they would be practically obsolete. The above review of the subject of the authenticity of the alleged "secret protocols" has been made entirely without regard to the extraneous political issues which have been involved in the official references made to them.

APPENDIX C

The Secret Russo-Japanese Treaties of 1907, 1910 and 1912

The existence of the secret Russo-Japanese treaty of July 17/30, 1907, seems now to have been well established. The publication of the texts of the draft treaties of June 24/July 4, 1910, and June 25/July 8, 1912, as well as that of July 3, 1916, all signed secretly by Russia and Japan, has indicated that the secret treaty of 1907 was basic—it being referred to in each of the subsequent draft texts mentioned. The draft texts of the secret treaties of 1910 and 1912 (which treaties were signed at the same time and place as the open conventions of those dates) were published in unofficial but, apparently, reliable versions in 1921 by Captain George Abel Schreiner, correspondent of the Associated Press during the Great War, and Count B. de Siebert, formerly Secretary of the Imperial Embassy of Russia at London and Washington, and Secretary to Count Witte, who was the head of the Russian delegation to the Portsmouth Peace Conference in 1905.[1] This work does not contain a copy of the secret treaty of 1907, but the documents published therein (those of 1910 and 1912) do contain references to such a secret treaty of July 17/30, 1907. The correspondence of Mr. Isvolsky, Russian Minister for Foreign Affairs before 1910, has served to authenticate both that secret treaty of 1907 and that of 1910.[2] Moreover, when the Chinese Delegation to the Wash-

---

[1] B. de Siebert and George Abel Schreiner, *Entente Diplomacy and the World: Matrix of the History of Europe, 1909-1914*. (N. Y. and London, 1921.) Of the Russo-Japanese secret treaty of 1907 Dr. A. L. P. Dennis (Clark University) has written: "The text of this treaty has never been published; but in view of the subsequent references to this treaty and from other sources of information it seems highly probable that these were its chief provisions" (referring to the demarcation of the Russian and Japanese "spheres of interest" in Manchuria). (*The Anglo-Japanese Alliance*, [Berkeley, Cal., 1923], p. 28.) Professors P. J. Treat (Stanford U.) and H. F. MacNair (U. of Chicago), together with Professor Dennis have accepted the authenticity of the secret Russo-Japanese treaty of 1907—as well as those of 1910, 1912 and 1916. Certain information preliminary to the actual negotiation of this treaty of 1907 is contained in Emile Laloy's work on the Tsarist documents published by the Bolsheviks in 1917. He presents evidence that Count Hayashi, Japanese Minister for Foreign Affairs, looked with favor on the negotiation of such a secret treaty, but was inclined to feel that, if made known, such would be accepted with disfavor by China. (Laloy, Emile, *Les Documents Secrets des Archives du Ministère Des Affaires Etrangères de Russia, publié par Les Bolcheviks* [Paris, 1919], p. 25.) Laloy does not contain a copy of the text of the treaty.

[2] Siebert and Schreiner, pp. 18-44.

ington Conference presented a list of inter-power agreements with reference to China, the list included the secret Russo-Japanese treaty of July 30, 1907 (as well as those of 1910, 1912 and 1916), the existence of no one of which was denied by the Japanese Delegation.[3]

As to the second (July 4, 1910) Russo-Japanese secret treaty of virtual alliance there is more available information. The draft text of this treaty was published by Siebert and Schreiner.[4] An identical version was printed in the *New York American*, April 17, 1921, by the same authors. Isvolsky, who signed the secret Russo-Japanese treaty of 1910 with Viscount Motono at St. Petersburg, is stated to have declared in a strictly confidential letter to the Russian Ambassador in London, dated June 11/24, 1910 (No. 760), that:

"Negotiations have been taking place for some time past between St. Petersburg and Tokyo Cabinets in order precisely to establish and bring into conformity, their joint interests in Manchuria, so that peace in the Far East may be further secured. An experience of three years has proved the expediency of the Russo-Japanese Treaty of July 17/30, 1907, and the two Governments have now unanimously recognized that the above-mentioned aim can be best attained by a further development to this treaty. . . . To-day both Cabinets have come to a perfect understanding and they are about to set their signatures to a public and a secret agreement. The first promotes closer joint action between Russia and Japan in the question of Manchurian railways and confirms anew the firm resolution of both Governments to maintain the *status quo* in these districts. The Secret Treaty defines more precisely the two spheres of interest, as well as the limitations to which they subject themselves in order to reinforce their mutual relations and to preserve the positions proper to them in Manchuria from all interference on the part of other Powers. . . . May I request you to bring the above to the knowledge of Sir Edward Grey and to inform him confidentially of both projects, whilst at the same time expressing the hope that he will regard these two diplomatic documents as a new guarantee of peace and quiet in the Far East."[5]

To this communication the Russian Ambassador is stated to have replied with a telegram dated June 15/28, 1910, to the effect that he had carried out the instructions of the Foreign Minister and that Sir Edward Grey was "very much gratified" at the Russo-Japanese convention and secret treaty of 1910.[6] Isvolsky is

[3] *Conference on the Limitation of Armament,* p. 1152.
[4] Siebert and Schreiner, pp. 17-18. (Also published by the same authors in the *New York American*, April 17, 1921.) See Chap. XXXV, Sec. b.
[5] Siebert and Schreiner, pp. 16-17.
[6] *Ibid.,* p. 19.

stated to have declared to the Russian Ambassador at London in a telegram of June 16/29, 1910, that the French and British Governments had both been informed of the secret treaty and that that had been done with the full knowledge of the Japanese Government.[7] Apparently, after diplomatic exchanges between St. Petersburg and Tokyo extending throughout 1909, and especially during the interval following the presentation by the American Secretary of State of the "Knox plan" for the neutralization of the Manchurian railways, a more or less definite understanding as to the desirability of signing a secret treaty with regard to Manchuria had eventuated by February and March of 1910. The Russian Ambassador at Tokyo is stated to have telegraphed Isvolsky on February 23/March 8, 1910, that Baron Komura shared Russia's views that there should be an agreement to maintain the "*status quo* in Manchuria" and "the definite demarcation of the special Russian and Japanese interests and their protection against aggression on the part of a third Power."[8]

The draft text of the secret Russo-Japanese treaty of June 25/July 8, 1912, is also printed in Siebert and Schreiner.[9] This treaty referred, in the main, to Mongolia, i.e., to Outer Mongolia, and also to that portion which, especially since 1915, has been commonly termed "Inner Mongolia," though neither a geographical nor political definition of the same is made by the Chinese Government. A line was drawn generally to follow the meridian of Peking so as to divide "Inner Mongolia" into two parts, that to the east being recognized (Article 2) as a Japanese "sphere of interest." Except for the fact that the treaty reaffirmed the provisions of the earlier treaties of 1907 and 1910 with respect to Manchuria, this secret treaty of 1912 had nothing to do with Manchuria. Pertaining to the negotiation of this secret treaty, it is stated that Mr. Sazonoff, who followed Isvolsky as Foreign Minister in 1910, telegraphed to the Russian Ambassador at London, under date of June 19/July 2, 1912 (No. 1233), the following message:

"Personal and confidential. The intention exists of signing a secret convention with Japan with regard to our spheres of interest in Inner Mongolia. In agreement with the Japanese Government we communicate the text of the projected document to the French and British representatives. The Japanese Government will send a similar note to Paris and London." (The draft text followed.)[10]

[7] Siebert and Schreiner, p. 19.
[8] *Ibid.*, p. 15.
[9] *Ibid.*, pp. 39-40. See Chap. XXXV, Sec. c.
[10] Siebert and Schreiner, p. 39.

No *official* text of any one of the above three secret treaties between Russia and Japan has been published by order of either the Russian or Japanese Governments for general dissemination. It seems evident that either the texts themselves or their general tenor were conveyed to the British and French Governments contemporaneously in each case. These documents were apparently not found by the Trotsky-Lenin searchers in the Tsarist imperial archives when, in that hasty rummaging for tell-tale documents in 1917, they discovered the secret Russo-Japanese treaty of 1916. The latter served to establish the fact of the existence of the first three above mentioned and characterized.

APPENDIX D

The Secret Russo-Japanese Treaty of 1916

The fourth Russo-Japanese secret treaty of the period from 1905 to 1917, i.e., that of July 3, 1916, seems to have been established as authentic beyond question. In fact, there is more evidence to support the authenticity of this secret treaty than of those which preceded it—except for the fact that this treaty of 1916 in itself, in its preamble, calls attention by reaffirmation to the secret treaties of 1907, 1910 and 1912. The Trotsky-Lenin Government in Russia published in the *Izvestia* in 1917, and in the *Gazette* of the Provisional Workmen-Peasants' Government of December 21, 1917, the text of the treaty as found in the archives of the Imperial Russian Foreign Office.[1] The first English translation of that secret treaty seems to have been published in the *Manchester Guardian* on February 1, 1918; a second English translation was published in the *New York Evening Post* on March 2, 1918. Subsequently, several versions, all those examined by the writer being identical in substance, were published, among them the French translation published in 1919 by Emile Laloy.[2]

The fact of the existence of the Russo-Japanese treaty of alliance of 1916 was kept secret until the following year when the text of the treaty was published by the Revolutionary Government in Russia. There was, however, a widespread feeling in certain foreign offices that in addition to the open political convention of July 3, 1916, signed by Sazonoff and Motono at Petrograd, there was

---

[1] The text of this Russo-Japanese secret treaty of alliance of 1916 was first published in *Izvestia*, in 1917. The same was published by the Revolutionary Government in the *Gazette* of the Provisional Workmen-Peasants' Government, December 21, 1917. Apparently the first English version of the text appeared in the *Manchester Guardian* on February 1, 1918, the same being a translation from *Izvestia*. The *New York Evening Post* published a similar, but not identical, translation, on March 2, 1918. The latter is the text given in MacMurray, Vol. II, p. 1328. Laloy (referred to in Appendix C) published a French version (pp. 119-121) in Paris in 1919, the date "1915" appearing therein obviously being in error. Leo Pasvolsky (*Russia in the Far East*, p. 165) published an English version in New York in 1922. The text of the same given by David Hunter Miller in *My Diary at the Conference of Paris, with documents* (22 Vols. of a limited edition of 40 sets, N. Y., 1924) is taken from the *Manchester Guardian.* '(Miller, Vol. VI, pp. 250-251.) The texts in MacMurray and in Miller are not identical, but contain no discrepancies in substance. See Chap. XLVI, Sec. b.

[2] Laloy, pp. 119-121.

simultaneously negotiated and signed a supplementary understanding which had been kept secret. The feeling was due in part to the confusion of the same with the text of still another agreement between Russia and Japan with respect to the sale of a portion of the southern section of the Chinese Eastern Railway (Changchun to Laoshaokou, or to the Sungari river) to Japan. The latter was admitted by Baron Ishii at Tokyo to have been signed in preliminary form, but was stated to have been subject in part to the attitude which the Chinese Government would take to the transfer.[3] The *Manchuria Daily News* (Dairen), however, lent assistance to the rumor of a secret political convention by declaring editorially at the time that a secret treaty, in addition to the published convention, had been signed, and that the same was in the form of "an offensive and defensive alliance."[4] To the inquiries of the Japanese Foreign Office, made by the American Ambassador at Tokyo, as to whether there were "supplementary articles" to the published convention, a reply was made in the negative.[5] The indefinite inquiry, and the indefinite answer, however, were such as to create the presumption that the Japanese Foreign Office believed the American State Department was inquiring concerning the arrangements for the purchase of the Chinese Eastern Railway section in question, and not concerning the existence of any other secret agreement.

It is interesting to note that this Russo-Japanese secret treaty of virtual alliance was to continue in force from signature until July 1/14, 1921, i.e., until one day after the termination of the Anglo-Japanese convention of alliance of 1911. The latter was subject to continuation in the absence of specific notification to terminate, given one year before the date for normal expiration. So also was the secret Russo-Japanese treaty of alliance of 1916 to continue under identical circumstances. Under the terms of the four power pact of the Washington Conference the Anglo-Japanese alliance has been terminated. So also, apparently, the secret Russo-Japanese treaty of 1916 under the terms (Article 2) of the Russo-Japanese convention of January 20, 1925.[6] By the same token it would appear that the Russo-Japanese secret treaties of 1907, 1910 and 1912, no longer have any definite binding validity.

[3] *U. S. Foreign Relations,* 1916, pp. 442-446; also p. 436.
[4] *Ibid.,* p. 434.
[5] *Ibid.,* pp. 442-446.
[6] See Chap. LIX, Sec. a.

APPENDIX E

Interpretation of the Lansing-Ishii Agreement of 1917

Bearing on the interpretation of the American-Japanese exchange of notes of November 2, 1917, which was effected by Robert Lansing, Secretary of State, and Viscount Ishii, Japanese special envoy to the United States at the head of a mission, certain matters are considered below which, in order not to encumber the manuscript, have not been dealt with in the body of the section dealing with the so-called Lansing-Ishii agreement.[1] It has frequently been stated that there were two distinct interpretations placed upon the agreement, in particular upon the term "special interests," by the American and Japanese Governments. Whatever may be the justification for that assertion, it appears that, on the contrary, there is more evidence readily available to justify an opposite view. By "interpretation" one refers legally to that contained in diplomatic or otherwise officially declared documents. Of special importance in any matter of interpretation of an international legal document is the exchange of views in the form of specific definitions of terms, and in the nature of specific reservations, made in the negotiations attending that document. The enforceability of such definitions and reservations can best be determined by reference to specific cases.

Attention has been given in the body of the section dealing with the Lansing-Ishii agreement to the preliminary negotiations which resulted in the exchange of notes of November 2, 1917. The very evident distinction between "paramount" and "special" interests was then made clear, the former being specifically repudiated by Secretary Lansing.[2] It is not clear that the Japanese Minister in Peking in November, 1917, presented to the Chinese Foreign Office in *official* and *written* form any interpretation of the term "special interests" other than such as might have been inferred from a particular Japanese translation of the text of the notes themselves. The notes may have been "paraded in the Chinese Foreign Office

[1] See Chap. XLVII, Sec. a.
[2] *U. S. Foreign Relations*, 1917, p. 261. Mr. Lansing's testimony before the Senate Foreign Relations Committee. (*Hearings* before the Committee on Foreign Relations of the United States Senate, *Treaty of Peace with Germany*, pp. 139-253. Washington Gov't. Printing Office, 1919.)

as yielding important concessions from the United States," but to *parade* an international legal document is one thing; to place a specific legal *interpretation* upon it is another.[3] Moreover, it is not unlikely that Viscount Motono did say to the Russian Ambassador at Tokyo in 1917 that if differences arose in future as to the interpretation of "special interests," Japan "would have at her disposal better means for applying in practice her interpretation, than would the United States."[4] There apparently is no evidence that the Japanese Government ever sought subsequently to secure a legal interpretation of the Lansing-Ishii from the United States which could conform with such an opinion as to desirable *policy*. On the contrary, during the negotiations attending the organization of the international banking consortium from 1918 to 1920, the Japanese Government at no time placed any specific and declared interpretation upon the terms of the Lansing-Ishii agreement which was in any way irreconcilable with that placed upon the same agreement by the United States, either at the time of those negotiations or in those attending the signature of the Lansing-Ishii agreement.[5] President Warren G. Harding declared furthermore in March, 1922, before the Senate Foreign Relations Committee, as to the American interpretation of the agreement and its reconcilability with the "open door,"

[3] The quotation is from Paul S. Reinsch: *An American Diplomat in China*, p. 308. (N. Y., 1922.) There is, however, some evidence that an attempt was made by the Japanese Minister in Peking to secure from the American Minister an acceptance of the Japanese version, and that the American Minister declined. No *official* evidence of this, however, has been available to the writer. If such were true, it would mean that the interpretation to be placed on the rendering into Chinese of the phrase "special interests" would be of the character analyzed elsewhere in this Appendix. It would appear that even the acceptance of that Japanese rendering into Chinese would not necessarily be irreconcilable with the interpretation placed upon it by the United States.

[4] Quoted by Leo Pasvolsky (*Russia in the Far East*, Appendix 1, pp. 168-169) from the *Gazette* of the Provisional Workmen-Peasants' Government, December 2 (15), 1917.

[5] The fact that M. Odagiri, in his letter of June 18, 1919, to Thomas W. Lamont, *drew attention* to the Lansing-Ishii exchange of notes in the same letter in which he asserted that Japan possessed "very special relations" geographically and historically in Manchuria and Mongolia was in no wise an official interpretation of the Lansing-Ishii agreement. However much Mr. Odagiri may have been the mouthpiece of the Japanese Government, he was not a representative of the Japanese Government. Nor did the letter do more than *draw attention* to the existence of the exchange of notes: it did not declare that the United States was understood to have conceded in the Lansing-Ishii agreement that Japan had "very special relations" of a political or even an economic character in Manchuria. (*The Consortium*, pp. 19-20.) In the *official* correspondence concerning the consortium, it was the United States Government which first mentioned the Lansing-Ishii agreement (March 16, 1920), in reply to which the Japanese Government, instead of presenting a counter interpretation, inferentially accepted the American Government's interpretation—and withdrew (in the same paragraph) the formula which had previously been offered to secure a right of veto, in certain cases, to the operations of the consortium in South Manchuria and Eastern Inner Mongolia. (*The Consortium*, pp. 46-47.) See Chap. XLIV, Sec. b.

"That this was not an erroneous construction appears from the meaning ascribed to the phrase 'special interests in China,' which is found in the final statement made on behalf of Japan at the recent conference. The phrase was interpreted to mean that propinquity gave rise to an interest differing only in degree, but not in kind, as compared with the interests of other powers." [6]

Secretary Lansing made clear in the negotiations with Viscount Ishii that, while recognizing that Japan had "special interests" in territory contiguous to hers, such was "only the special interest that comes from being contiguous to another country whose peace and prosperity were involved"; that such "special interests" were not different from those of the United States in Mexico or Canada, for example; that the American recognition was "absolutely not" tantamount to any endorsement of the so-called "Twenty-one Demands"; that the agreement did not in any way endorse the commitments of Great Britain, France, Russia and Italy in their secret agreements made with Japan in 1917 with reference to the ultimate disposition of the former German rights in Shantung [for those secret agreements were not known to the Department of State at the time]; and that the United States did not recognize that Japan possessed any *political* interests in Manchuria or elsewhere in China. The term "special interest" was not used to convey the idea of "paramount interest," said Mr. Lansing to the Senate Foreign Relations Committee. He did state, however, that the "special interests" which the United States recognized Japan to possess in China related to China as a whole.[7] The text of the exchanged notes conveys the latter impression. To the Japanese Ambassador, however, Secretary Lansing had stated on January 25, 1917, that there was a difference between Manchuria "where Japan's special interests were conceded" and Shantung "where no such special interests were recognized." [8] On June 22, 1917, he had declared to the Japanese Ambassador that the United States did not recognize that Japan had "special or close relations, political as well as economic, with China as a whole." [9]

The significance, or insignificance, of the "special interests" which the United States recognized Japan to possess in China was lucidly explained in a memorandum of Secretary Lansing to the Chinese Minister at Washington on November 21, 1917, as follows:

[6] *U. S. Senate Document*, No. 150, 67th Congress, 2nd Session.
[7] *Hearings* before the Committee on Foreign Relations of the U. S. Senate, *Treaty of Peace with Germany*, pp. 139-253.
[8] *U. S. Foreign Relations*, 1917, pp. 116-118.
[9] *Ibid.*, 1917, p. 261.

"He [the Chinese Minister] asked what 'special interests' meant. I said it was the statement of an axiom; that it was a statement which could not be successfully denied and could be universally applied and that, in view of declaration in last clause of note signed by Ishii, it was advantageous to China for both Governments declared themselves opposed to 'any government' infringing China's independence and territorial integrity, a declaration which applied to the parties to the understanding as well as to others; that such a bargain seemed decidedly in China's favor; further in reply to his inquiry I stated that I believed phrase 'territorial propinquity' applied alike to Japan, Russia, France and England and that China might also apply it. Further, that I believed Chinese Government had acted wisely in presenting memorandum above but that no reservation or caveat could change the natural consequence of propinquity." [10]

Turning now to the confusion which arose at once over the rendering of the terms "special interests" and "a certain advantage" (the latter contained in the State Department's note of November 8, 1917, to the Chinese Foreign Office) into the Chinese and Japanese languages, it should be remarked at the outset that *unofficial* translations into those languages have no bearing on legal interpretation of the notes exchanged between Mr. Lansing and Viscount Ishii. A fundamental factor also is that the notes were exchanged in the English language, which is, therefore, the authentic version in any question of interpretation. The factors which legally have bearing on the interpretation of the English texts, likewise have identical bearing on the intepretation of any foreign-language text.

That the original Japanese official translation of the texts into Chinese, as handed to the Chinese Foreign Office, erred on the side of greater inclusiveness than the legitimate translation has been frequently asserted, as by the then American Minister at Peking, Dr. Reinsch. [11] There is, perhaps, no adequate justification for this view. The term apparently used by the Japanese translation into Chinese (i.e., *t'e-pieh li-yi*) does not intrinsically, nor in its frequent use, convey anything more than "special advantage," which is practically identical with the term "a certain advantage" used by the State Department in its note of November 8 to the Chinese Foreign Office. It does not necessarily convey, therefore, the meaning "special position"—whatever that is—attributed to it by Dr. Reinsch. [12] If the term used in the Japanese translation into Chinese

[10] *U. S. Foreign Relations*, 1917, p. 273.

[11] Reinsch, *op. cit.*, p. 309.

[12] *Ibid.* Dr. Reinsch here also says: "The Department authorized me to deliver an explanatory note to the effect that the interests referred to were of an economic, not a political, nature." It is interesting to note that Dr. Reinsch here also quotes the

(i.e., *t'e-pieh li-yi*) be interpreted to mean "vested proprietary interests," it may be well to recall that the "vested proprietary interests" of Japan in South Manchuria were later specifically recognized by the United States (and by Great Britain) in the negotiations leading up to the signing of the China consortium agreement in October, 1920.[13] It thus appears that whether the term used by the Japanese to render "special interests" (i.e., *t'e-pieh li-yi*) in Chinese be interpreted one way or the other, in neither case is the meaning so altered as to convey the idea of "sphere of interest" (*li-yi fan-wei*), or "sphere of influence" (*shih-li fan-wei*), the term "sphere" (*fan-wei*), which connotes more or less exclusive rights or interests, not being included in either the Chinese, Japanese or English texts. In presenting testimony before the Senate Foreign Relations Committee (in the hearings on the treaty of peace with Germany) Dr. John C. Ferguson, a well-reputed sinologist, asserted that the characters (*t'e-pieh li-yi*), used by the Japanese to translate the term "special interests" into Chinese, was a legitimate rendering and that they did not convey the term of "paramountcy."[14] He added that the term might be used to convey a different shade of meaning than "special interests" and more than might be inferred from mere geographical propinquity or contiguity, but asserted that the distinction was unimportant one way or the other, "the English text being the official text as communicated to the Chinese Government." He did not state that the Japanese translation into Chinese was necessarily incorrect. Finally, it may be said, however, that the rendering of the term "special interests" into Chinese may perhaps most accurately be accomplished through the use of the Chinese characters *"t'e-pieh kuan-hsi,"* i.e., "special concern" or "special importance," or its practical synonym, "special interests." In the light of the interpre-

Japanese Minister at Peking who said that just as "several other countries have territory that borders on China" which gives them "a special interest in these parts of China which they touch," so also "in exactly the same way, Japan has special rights in China." That is also exactly what the American Government interpreted the term "special interests" to mean, as shown by Secretary Lansing's repeated statements. The statement of the Japanese Minister, quoted by Dr. Reinsch, gives no justification for the American Minister's assertion that the Japanese Minister "evidently saw in the notes an endorsement of the principle of spheres of influence."

[13] The Department of State, in its memorandum of October 28, 1919, to the Japanese Government, declared that it was not the intention of the United States or of the consortium to encroach upon the "existing vested Japanese interests in the region indicated"; the wording of the consortium agreement (Article 1) "plainly excludes those enterprises which are already developed and thus constitute vested proprietary interests." (*The Consortium*, p. 32.)

[14] *Hearings* before the Committee on Foreign Relations of the U. S. Senate, *Treaty of Peace with Germany, Sen. Doc.* 106, 66th Cong. 1st Sess., p. 595 *et seq.* Quoted by W. W. Willoughby in *Foreign Rights and Interests in China*, Vol. I, pp. 366-367.

tation placed upon the term "special interests" in the negotiations attending the signing of the Lansing-Ishii agreement that would seem to be the correct rendering, and that was the rendering used in the translation which the American Government submitted to the Chinese Foreign Office.

In concluding this section on the official interpretation of the Lansing-Ishii exchange of notes of November 2, 1917, it may be especially pertinent to quote in detail the statements of the late Warren G. Harding, President of the United States, made before the Senate Foreign Relations Committee on March 7, 1922:

"In the light of the other declarations of the notes in question, it has been the view of the Government of the United States that this reference to special interests in China did not recognize any right or claim inconsistent with the sovereignty or political independence of China or with our "open-door" policy.

"That this was not an erroneous construction appears from the meaning ascribed to the phrase "special interests in China," which is found in the final statement made on behalf of Japan at the recent conference. The phrase was interpreted to mean that propinquity gave rise to an interest differing only in degree, but not in kind, as compared with the interests of other powers.

"The negotiation of this treaty [the nine power pact of February 6, 1922, relating to principles and policies to be followed concerning China] is in itself the most formal declaration of the policy of the Executive in regard to China, and supersedes any Executive understanding or declaration that could possibly be asserted to have any contrary import.

"My answer, then, to your first question is that the so-called Lansing-Ishii agreement has no binding effect whatever, either with respect to the past or to the future, which is in any sense inconsistent with the principles and policies explicitly declared in the nine power treaty to which I have referred." [15]

As has been noted elsewhere, however, the nine power pact did not in itself terminate the so-called Lansing-Ishii agreement; it did make that exchange of notes of little practical importance. The agreement was specifically terminated by an exchange of notes of April 14, 1923, between Secretary Charles Evans Hughes and Ambassador Hanihara Masanao.[16]

[15] U. S. *Sen. Doc.* 150, 67th Cong. 2nd Sess.
[16] *American Journal of International Law,* Vol. 17 (1923), pp. 510-512; *U. S. Treaty Series,* No. 667.

APPENDIX F

The Chinese Position in Manchuria: Construction of Independent Chinese Railways (1925-1929)

An interesting and not unimportant new phase of the railway situation in Manchuria appears in the fact that since the Washington Conference, and especially since 1925, the Chinese have themselves undertaken the construction with Chinese capital of several important railways in Manchuria. These include the Tahushan-Paiyintalai (Tungliao) line, the Mukden-Hailungcheng-Kirin line, and the Hulan-Hailun line. Other lines of lesser importance, either branches of the above, or separately constructed, are now completed, in process of completion, or projected.

Hulan-Hailun Railway. This new railway has now been completed from Hulan, opposite Harbin on the Sungari river, *via* Suihua to Hailun running north and northwest from Hulan. The last section to Hailun was completed and opened to traffic in December, 1928. This line (Hu-Hai) was built with Chinese capital supplied principally by the Tsitsihar Provincial Bank (formerly controlled by General Wu Chun-sheng, late *tuchun* of Heilungkiang) but under the technical supervision of Boris V. Ostroumoff, formerly General Manager of the Chinese Eastern Railway Company. The construction company, called *Ju Yi Kung Ssu* in Chinese, is registered under Chinese law and is entirely financed by Chinese capital, technical assistance only being supplied by the Russian construction engineers. The operation of the line, from the date of completion of the several segments constructed, is in charge of the Chinese. Rails for the line have been purchased through Suzuki and Company, a Japanese firm, which in turn purchased rails to the value of over a half million yen from the United States Steel Products Company, for delivery to the Hulan-Hailun railway.[1]

[1] The subject of new Chinese railways in Manchuria is dealt with in an article by the writer, titled: "Economic Bases for New Railways in Manchuria" in the *Chinese Economic Journal*, Vol. I, No. 4 (April, 1927), published by the Chinese Government Bureau of Economic Information, Peking. The same was reprinted in the *Far Eastern Review* (Shanghai), May, 1927. The same was translated into Japanese and published by the Department of Railways (Traffic Bureau), Tokyo, as "*Manshū Shinsetsu-tetsudō-no Keizai-teki Konkyo*" in *Gai-koku-tetsudō-chōsa-Shiryō*, Vol. I, No. 3 (June 20, 1927). (The original article as published contained a map of new Manchurian railways and their relation to natural and agricultural resources.)

Construction was begun in 1926; the section to Suihua was completed by 1927; the entire line to Hailun was completed and opened to traffic in December, 1928.[2] The Chinese company intends to continue construction northwest to Mergen (Nungkiang) on the upper Nonni river, from which point plans have already been made to construct the line northeast to the Amur river, to Aigun and/or Heihofu.

Aside from the commercial importance of the line, the Hulan-Hailun railway and its proposed extensions to Mergen and Heihofo or Aigun has particular interest internationally in view of the fact that the extensions contemplated would traverse much the same route as that portion of the proposed Chinchow-Aigun railway in which Anglo-American interests were involved in 1909 and 1910. Moreover, it will be recalled that the Russo-Asiatic Bank obtained a contract for the construction of such a line actually from Harbin to Mergen and Tsitsihar in 1916. There is evidence that at that time the Russo-Asiatic Bank actually made an initial advance to the Chinese Government in connection with the construction of such a line and that that amount has never been repaid. (M. Gravé, Mukden representative of the Russo-Asiatic Bank, informed the writer in Mukden in the summer of 1926 that such was the case.) The Chinese, however, have interpreted the non-activity of the Russo-Chinese Bank in connection with implementing the terms of their contract of 1916—a situation produced by the unsettlement in North Manchuria during and after the Russian Revolution—as sufficient grounds for declaring the 1916 contract agreement abrogated. The Hulan-Hailun railway has been built by a purely Chinese company on that assumption. It is interesting to note that the Hu-Hai line has been built with the standard gauge characteristic of the Chinese Government Railways and those other new Chinese lines of Manchuria, in this respect differing from the Chinese Eastern Railway broad gauge, but identical with gauge of the South Manchuria Railway system.

Tahushan-Paiyintalai Railway. The completion of this Chinese railway during 1927 brought to fruition what amounts to the southern portion of the railway system projected by Viceroy Hsü Shih-chang, and later by Viceroy Hsi Liang from 1908 to 1910, and which was to be built by the Anglo-American group as a part of the Chinchow-Aigun railway system. Originally, construction was

[2] *The Japan Weekly Chronicle,* January 24, 1929, p. 93. The writer's article, titled "Railway Politics in Manchuria" published in two parts in the *China Weekly Review* (Shanghai), April 16 and 23, 1927, deals with some of the political questions involved in the new railway developments in Manchuria.

completed northwest to Changwu from where an extension to Chengchiatun was planned. In 1927, however, this plan was altered, and the Chinese company financing the line continued construction northwest to Tungliao (Paiyintalai) instead, thus to connect with the western terminal of the spur of the Ssupingkai-Chengchiatun extension to Tungliao. A form of through traffic was inaugurated from Tahushan (on the Peking-Mukden line) *via* Tungliao, Changchiatun and Taonan to Angangchi in December, 1928, although interlineal traffic agreements between these distinct lines have not been perfected as yet. The Chinese who have financed and constructed the Tahushan-Paiyintalai line are considering an extension north from Paiyintalai to Taonan so as to obviate routing traffic from North Manchuria *via* Chengchiatun over the line which has been constructed with Japanese capital.

The construction of the Tahushan-Paiyintalai line has repeatedly been protested by the Japanese Government, and Japanese interests have sought to participate in financing the construction of the line, especially as this new western Manchurian railway system when completed would offer serious competition to the South Manchuria Railway system with respect to certain regions in western and northwestern Manchuria. The development of the Chinese port of Hulutao, long contemplated and actually started several years ago, would furnish an outlet on the Gulf of Pechihli which might, in the course of years, attain a position of importance, though perhaps not of a nature to endanger the exceptional position of Dairen.

Mukden-Hailungcheng-Kirin Railway. This purely Chinese financed and built railway runs from Mukden *via* Hailungcheng to Kirin to connect Kirin city on the Kirin-Changchun line (under Japanese management) with the Peking-Mukden line (a Chinese Government Railway), and the South Manchuria Railway. The line to Hailungcheng, commonly termed the Feng-Hai line, was opened to through traffic in November, 1928, while the remainder of the line to Kirin was completed in 1929. The line runs north of the Japanese-controlled Fushun collieries but connects with a Chinese coal mine near the same. This railway has been constructed by officials of the Mukden Government in cooperation with the Kirin provincial authorities, official funds having been defrayed for the purpose, as well as funds supplied by interested officials privately. A portion of the funds has been raised by private loans. It is not clear if the line can be operated without resorting to borrowing foreign capital, in the nature of the case, from the Japanese.

The Japanese Government has protested the construction by the Chinese of this the Mukden-Hailungcheng-Kirin line on several occasions, as in January, 1927, when Consul General Yoshida (Mukden) objected to the completion of the line to Kirin, on the ground that the construction of the line violated the Sino-Japanese agreement of 1913, commonly referred to as the "Five Manchurian and Mongolian Railways" loan agreement, and the Sino-Japanese railway loan agreement of 1918, commonly called the "Four Manchurian and Mongolian Railways" loan agreement, both of which were represented as giving Japanese financial interests certain rights to participate in the construction of such a line.[3] As a matter of fact, however, it is not clear that the 1913 agreement gave Japanese financiers the right necessarily to participate in the construction of a branch line from Kirin to Hailungcheng. The agreement indicates that such an option exists only on condition that foreign capital were to be borrowed for the purpose. That agreement, in the form of an exchange of notes of 1913, further gave Japanese financiers the right to participate in such a case in the construction of a line from Kaiyuan *via* Hailungcheng to Kirin, as did also the loan agreement of 1918. Neither agreement specifies the Mukden-Hailungcheng-Kirin line, and it does not appear that there would be valid grounds for protesting, on the basis above indicated, the construction by Chinese independent capital *unless* foreign capital were to be required, or *unless* it be contended that the construction of the line serves to obviate the construction of the Kaiyuan-Hailungcheng-Kirin line (which has been constructed in the form of a narrow gauge line as far as Taolu). The construction with Japanese capital of each of the lines mentioned in the Sino-Japanese agreement of 1918 in question appears to be *permissive* on the part of the Chinese, not *mandatory*. Until foreign capital is required for the Mukden-Hailungcheng-Kirin line it would appear that the Chinese are within their rights in constructing it independently of Japanese capital. Whether it is possible, in the present state of Manchurian, and in particular of Mukden Government, finances, to operate the line without outside, presumably Japanese, financial assistance is another matter.

As a matter of fact, the Mukden-Hailungcheng-Kirin line was completed despite Japanese protests. During the early months of 1928 relations between Tokyo and Peking were somewhat strained over the issues presented by the fact that the Mukden-Hailungcheng Railway sought to enter into a through-

---

[3] The writer's article in the *Chinese Economic Journal, op. cit.,* p. 332.

traffic arrangement with the Chinese Peking-Mukden Railway, and also transferred rolling stock from the Taonan-Angangchi Railway, which, in fact, had been obtained from the South Manchuria Railway Company for use evidently only on the Taonan-Angangchi line. A through-traffic arrangement had also been made with the South Manchuria Railway Company for routing goods to Dairen. The Chinese sought to avoid the latter agreement and connect with the Peking-Mukden line at Mukden. This action, together with the transfer of the rolling stock, caused the Japanese Minister (Mr. Yoshizawa) to protest during March, 1928, to the Peking Government.[4] The late Marshal Chang Tso-lin was then in power in Peking. The Peking Government apparently demurred and cancelled the through-traffic agreement with the South Manchuria Railway Company, whereupon the latter obstructed the linking of the Mukden-Hailungcheng line with the Peking-Mukden line at Mukden by refusing to permit a crossing of the South Manchuria Railway right of way. Finally, it may be noted that a branch line of the Mukden-Hailungcheng-Kirin railway from Hailungcheng southeast to Fusung is now being surveyed by the Chinese administration of the railway.[5]

[4] The writer's article, titled "Sino-Japanese Interests and Issues in Manchuria" in *Pacific Affairs* (Published by the Institute of Pacific Relations, Honolulu), December, 1928, pp. 12-13.
[5] *The Japan Weekly Chronicle*, January 24, 1929, p. 93.

APPENDIX G

Official Texts of the Sino-Russian Agreements of 1924

(1)

Agreement on General Principles for the Settlement of Questions between the Republic of China and the Union of Soviet Socialist Republics, Peking, May 31, 1924.[1]

The Republic of China and the Union of Soviet Socialist Republics, desiring to reestablish normal relations with each other, have agreed to conclude an Agreement on general principles for the settlement of the questions between the two countries, and have to that end named as their Plenipotentiaries, that is to say:

His Excellency the President of the Republic of China: Vi Kyuin Wellington Koo,

The Government of the Union of Soviet Socialist Republics: Lev Mikhailovitch Karakhan,

Who, having communicated to each other their respective full powers, found to be in good and due form, have agreed upon the following Articles:

ARTICLE I. Immediately upon the signing of the present Agreement, the normal diplomatic and consular relations between the two Contracting Parties shall be reestablished.

The Government of the Republic of China agrees to take the necessary steps to transfer to the Government of the Union of Soviet Socialist Republics the Legation and Consular buildings formerly belonging to the Tsarist Government.

ARTICLE II. The Governments of the two Contracting Parties agree to hold, within one month after the signing of the present Agreement, a conference which shall conclude and carry out de-

[1] Sino-Russian (Peking Government—Government of the Union of Soviet Socialist Republics) *Agreement on General Principles for the Settlement of Questions between Them,* Peking May 31, 1924. *Official Text* printed in the *American Journal of International Law, Supplement,* 1925, Vol. 19, pp. 53-56. This also contains the several declarations and an exchange of notes, as well as the *Agreement for the Provisional Management of the* Chinese Eastern Railway, signed on the same date. Also published in the *Russian Review* (Washington), Vol. III, No. 20 (October 15, 1925) pp. 414-419.

tailed arrangements relative to the questions in accordance with the principles as provided in the following Articles.

Such detailed arrangements shall be completed as soon as possible and, in any case, not later than six months from the date of the opening of the conference as provided in the preceding paragraph.

ARTICLE III. The Governments of the two Contracting Parties agree to annul at the conference, as provided in the preceding article, all conventions, treaties, agreements, protocols, contracts, *et cetera,* concluded between the Government of China and the Tsarist Government and to replace them with new treaties, agreements, *et cetera,* on the basis of equality, reciprocity and justice, as well as the spirit of the Declarations of the Soviet Government of the years of 1919 and 1920.

ARTICLE IV. The Government of the Union of Soviet Socialist Republics, in accordance with its policy and Declarations of 1919 and 1920, declares that all treaties, agreements, *et cetera,* concluded between the former Tsarist Government and any third party or parties affecting the sovereign rights or interests of China, are null and void.

The Governments of both Contracting Parties declare that in future neither Government will conclude any treaties or agreements which prejudice the sovereign rights or interests of either Contracting Party.

ARTICLE V. The Government of the Union of Soviet Socialist Republics recognizes that Outer Mongolia is an integral part of the Republic of China and respects China's sovereignty therein.

The Government of the Union of Soviet Socialist Republics declares that as soon as the questions for the withdrawal of all the troops of the Union of Soviet Socialist Republics from Outer Mongolia—namely, as to the time-limit of the withdrawal of such troops and the measures to be adopted in the interests of the safety of the frontiers—are agreed upon at the conference as provided in Article II of the present Agreement, it will effect the complete withdrawal of all the troops of the Union of Soviet Socialist Republics from Outer Mongolia.

ARTICLE VI. The Governments of the two Contracting Parties mutually pledge themselves not to permit, within their respective territories the existence and/or activities of any organizations or groups whose aim is to struggle by acts of violence against the Governments of either Contracting Party.

The Governments of the two Contracting Parties further pledge themselves not to engage in propaganda directed against the political and social systems of either Contracting Party.

ARTICLE VII. The Governments of the two Contracting Parties agree to redemarcate their natural boundaries at the conference as provided in Article II of the present Agreement, and pending such redemarcation, to maintain the present boundaries.

ARTICLE VIII. The Governments of the two Contracting Parties agree to regulate at the aforementioned conference the questions relating to the navigation of rivers, lakes and other bodies of water which are common to their respective frontiers, on the basis of equality and reciprocity.

ARTICLE IX. The Governments of the two Contracting Parties agree to settle at the aforementioned conference the question of the Chinese Eastern Railway in conformity with the principles as hereinafter provided:

(1) The Governments of the two Contracting Parties declare that the Chinese Eastern Railway is a purely commercial enterprise.

The Governments of the two Contracting Parties mutually declare that, with the exception of matters pertaining to the business operations which are under the direct control of the Chinese Eastern Railway, all other matters affecting the rights of the national and the local Governments of the Republic of China—such as judicial matters, matters relating to civil administration, military administration, police, municipal government, taxation, and landed property (with the exception of lands required by the said railway)—shall be administered by the Chinese Authorities.

(2) The Government of the Union of Soviet Socialist Republics agrees to the redemption by the Government of the Republic of China, with Chinese capital, of the Chinese Eastern Railway, as well as all appurtenant properties, and to the transfer to China of all shares and bonds of the said railway.

(3) The Governments of the two Contracting Parties shall settle at the conference as provided in Article II of the present Agreement, the amount and conditions governing the redemption as well as the procedure for the transfer of the Chinese Eastern Railway.

(4) The Government of the Union of Soviet Socialist Republics agrees to be responsible for the entire claims of the shareholders, bondholders and creditors of the Chinese Eastern Railway incurred prior to the revolution of March 9, 1917.

(5) The Governments of the two Contracting Parties mutually agree that the future of the Chinese Eastern Railway shall be determined by the Republic of China and the Union of Soviet Socialist Republics, to the exclusion of any third party or parties.

(6) The Governments of the two Contracting Parties agree to draw up an arrangement for the provisional management of the Chinese Eastern Railway pending the settlement of the question as provided under Section (3) of the present Article.

(7) Until the various questions relating to the Chinese Eastern Railway are settled at the conference as provided in Article II of the present Agreement, the rights of the two Governments arising out of the contract of August 27th/September 8th, 1896, for the construction and operation of the Chinese Eastern Railway, which do not conflict with the present Agreement and the Agreement for the Provisional Management of the said Railway and which do not prejudice China's rights of sovereignty, shall be maintained.

ARTICLE X. The Government of the Union of Soviet Socialist Republics agrees to renounce the special rights and privileges relating to all concessions in any part of China acquired by the Tsarist Government under various conventions, treaties, agreements, et cetera.

ARTICLE XI. The Government of the Union of Soviet Socialist Republics agrees to renounce the Russian portion of the Boxer Indemnity.

ARTICLE XII. The Government of the Union of Soviet Socialist Republics agrees to relinquish the rights of extraterritoriality and consular jurisdiction.

ARTICLE XIII. The Governments of the two Contracting Parties agree to draw up simultaneously with the conclusion of a commercial treaty at the conference as provided in Article II of the present Agreement, a customs tariff for the two Contracting Parties in accordance with the principles of equality and reciprocity.

ARTICLE XIV. The Governments of the two Contracting Parties agree to discuss at the aforementioned conference the questions relating to the claims for the compensation of losses.

ARTICLE XV. The present Agreement shall come into effect from the date of signature.

In witness whereof, the respective Plenipotentiaries have signed the present Agreement in duplicate in the English language and have affixed thereto their seals.

Done at the City of Peking this Thirty-First Day of the Fifth

Month of the Thirteenth Year of the Republic of China, which is, the Thirty-First Day of May One Thousand Nine Hundred and Twenty-Four.

V. K. WELLINGTON KOO   [Seal]

L. M. KARAKHAN   [Seal]

Agreement for the Provisional Management of the Chinese Eastern Railway, Peking, May 31, 1924.[1]

The Republic of China and the Union of Soviet Socialist Republics mutually recognizing that, inasmuch as the Chinese Eastern Railway was built with capital furnished by the Russian Government and constructed entirely within Chinese territory the said Railway is a purely commercial enterprise and that, excepting for matters appertaining to its own business operations, all other matters which affect the rights of the Chinese National and Local Governments shall be administered by the Chinese Authorities, have agreed to conclude an Agreement for the Provisional Management of the Railway with a view to carrying on jointly the management of the said Railway until its final settlement at the conference as provided in Article II of the Agreement on General Principles for the Settlement of the Questions between the Republic of China and the Union of the Soviet Socialist Republics of May 31, 1924, and have to that end named as their Plenipotentiaries, that is to say:

His Excellency the President of the Republic of China: Vi Kyuin Wellington Koo,

The Government of the Union of Soviet Socialist Republics: Lev Mikhailovitch Karakhan,

Who, having communicated to each other their respective full powers, found to be in good and due form, have agreed upon the following Articles:

ARTICLE I. The Railway shall establish, for discussion and decision of all matters relative to the Chinese Eastern Railway, a Board of Directors to be composed of ten persons, of whom five shall be appointed by the Government of the Republic of China and five by the Government of the Union of Soviet Socialist Republics.

The Government of the Republic of China shall appoint one of

---

[1] Sino-Russian (Peking Government—Government of the Union of Soviet Socialist Republics) *Agreement for the Provisional Management of the Chinese Eastern Railway,* Peking, May 31, 1924. *Official Text* printed in the *American Journal of International Law,* Supplement, 1925, Vol. 19, pp. 55-58. The declarations and exchange of notes of the same date follow, pp. 58-63. Also published in the *Russian Review* (Washington), Vol. III, No. 21 (November 1, 1925), pp. 439-440, but without the declarations and exchange of notes.

the Chinese Directors as President of the Board of Directors, who shall also be the Director-General.

The Government of the Union of Soviet Socialist Republics shall appoint one of the Russian Directors as Vice-President of the Board of Directors, who shall be the Assistant Director-General.

Seven persons shall constitute a quorum, and all decisions of the Board of Directors shall have the consent of not less than six persons before they can be carried out:

The Director-General and Assistant Director-General shall jointly manage the affairs of the Board of Directors and they shall both sign all the documents of the Board.

In the absence of either the Director-General or the Assistant Director-General, their respective governments may appoint another Director to officiate as the Director-General or the Assistant Director-General (in the case of the Director-General, by one of the Chinese Directors, and in that of the Assistant Director-General, by one of the Russian Directors).

ARTICLE II. The Railway shall establish a Board of Auditors to be composed of five persons, namely two Chinese Auditors, who shall be appointed by the Government of the Republic of China and three Russian Auditors who shall be appointed by the Government of the Union of Soviet Socialist Republics.

The Chairman of the Board of Auditors shall be elected from among the Chinese Auditors.

ARTICLE III. The Railway shall have a Manager, who shall be a national of the Union of Soviet Socialist Republics, and two Assistant Managers, one to be a national of the Republic of China and the other to be a national of the Union of Soviet Socialist Republics.

The said officers shall be appointed by the Board of Directors and such appointments shall be confirmed by their respective Governments.

The rights and duties of the Manager and the Assistant Managers shall be defined by the Board of Directors.

ARTICLE IV. The Chiefs and Assistant Chiefs of the various Departments of the Railway shall be appointed by the Board of Directors.

If the Chief of Department is a national of the Republic of China, the Assistant Chief of Department shall be a national of the Union of Soviet Socialist Republics, and if the Chief of Department is a national of the Union of Soviet Socialist Republics, the

Assistant Chief of Department shall be a national of the Republic of China.

ARTICLE V. The employment of persons in the various departments of the Railway shall be in accordance with the principle of equal representation between the nationals of the Republic of China and those of the Union of Soviet Socialist Republics.

ARTICLE VI. With the exception of the estimates and budgets, as provided in Article VII of the present Agreement, all other matters on which the Board of Directors cannot reach an agreement shall be referred for settlement to the Governments of the Contracting Parties.

ARTICLE VII. The Board of Directors shall present the estimates and budgets of the Railway to a joint meeting of the Board of Directors and the Board of Auditors for consideration and approval.

ARTICLE VIII. All the net profits of the Railway shall be held by the Board of Directors and shall not be used pending a final settlement of the question of the present Railway.

ARTICLE IX. The Board of Directors shall revise as soon as possible the statutes of the Chinese Eastern Railway Company, approved on December 4, 1896, by the Tsarist Government, in accordance with the present Agreement and the Agreement on General Principles for the Settlement of the Questions between the Republic of China and the Union of Soviet Socialist Republics of May 31, 1924, and in any case, not later than six months from the date of the constitution of the Board of Directors.

Pending their revision, the aforesaid statutes, in so far as they do not conflict with the present Agreement on General Principles for the Settlement of the Questions between the Republic of China and the Union of Soviet Socialist Republics, and do not prejudice the rights of sovereignty of the Republic of China, shall continue to be observed.

ARTICLE X. The present Agreement shall cease to have effect as soon as the question of the Chinese Eastern Railway is finally settled at the conference as provided in Article II of the Agreement on General Principles for the Settlement of the Questions between the Republic of China and the Union of Soviet Socialist Republics of May 31, 1924.

ARTICLE XI. The present Agreement shall come into effect from the date of signature.

In witness whereof, the respective Plenipotentiaries have signed the present Agreement in duplicate in the English language and have affixed thereto their seals.

Done at the City of Peking this Thirty-First Day of the Fifth Month of the Thirteenth Year of the Republic of China, which is, the Thirty-First Day of May One Thousand Nine Hundred and Twenty-Four.

V. K. WELLINGTON KOO [Seal]

L. M. KARAKHAN [Seal]

Declarations attached to the Sino-Russian Agreements of Peking, May 31, 1924:[2]

Declaration (I)

The Government of the Republic of China and the Government of the Union of Soviet Socialist Republics declare that immediately after the signing of the Agreement on General Principles between the Republic of China and the Union of Soviet Socialist Republics of May 31, 1924, they will reciprocally hand over to each other all the real estate and movable property owned by China and the former Tsarist Government and found in their respective territories. For this purpose each Government will furnish the other with a list of property to be so transferred.

In faith whereof, the respective Plenipotentiaries of the Governments of the two Contracting Parties have signed the present Declaration in duplicate in the English language and have affixed thereto their seals.

Done at the City of Peking this Thirty-First Day of the Fifth Month of the Thirteenth Year of the Republic of China, which is, the Thirty-First Day of May One Thousand Nine Hundred and Twenty-Four.

V. K. WELLINGTON KOO [Seal]

L. M. KARAKHAN [Seal]

Declaration (III)

The Government of the Republic of China and the Government of the Union of Soviet Socialist Republics jointly declare that it is understood that with reference to Article IV of the Agreement on General Principles between the Republic of China and the Union

[2] Of the several declarations attached to the Sino-Russian agreements of May 31, 1924, only those are included here which have particular bearing on Manchuria.

of Soviet Socialist Republics of May 31, 1924, the Government of the Republic of China will not and does not recognize as valid any treaty, agreement, *et cetera*, concluded between Russia since the Tsarist régime and any third party of parties, affecting the sovereign rights and interests of the Republic of China. It is further understood that this expression of understanding has the same force and validity as a general declaration embodied in the said Agreement on General Principles.

In faith whereof, the respective Plenipotentiaries of the Governments of the two Contracting Parties have signed the present Declaration in duplicate in the English language and have affixed thereto their seals.

Done in the City of Peking this Thirty-First Day of the Fifth Month of the Thirteenth Year of the Republic of China, which is, the Thirty-First Day of May One Thousand Nine Hundred and Twenty-Four.

V. K. WELLINGTON KOO   [Seal]
L. M. KARAKHAN   [Seal]

Declaration (IV)

The Government of the Republic of China and the Government of the Union of Soviet Socialist Republics jointly declare that it is understood that the Government of the Republic of China will not transfer either in part or in whole to any third Power or any foreign organization the special rights and privileges renounced by the Government of the Union of Soviet Socialist Republics of May 31, 1924. It is further understood that this expression of understanding has the same force and validity as a general declaration embodied in the said Agreement on General Principles.

In faith whereof, the respective Plenipotentiaries of the Governments of the two Contracting Parties have signed the present Declaration in duplicate in the English language and have affixed thereto their seals.

Done at the City of Peking this Thirty-First Day of the Fifth Month of the Thirteenth Year of the Republic of China, which is, the Thirty-First Day of May One Thousand Nine Hundred and Twenty-Four.

V. K. WELLINGTON KOO   [Seal]
L. M. KARAKHAN   [Seal]

Declaration (VII)

The Government of the Republic of China and the Government of the Union of Soviet Socialist Republics, having signed the Agreement on General Principles between the Republic of China and the Union of Soviet Socialist Republics on May 31, 1924, hereby agree, in explanation of Article V of the Agreement for the Provisional Management of the Chinese Eastern Railway of the same date, which provides for the principle of equal representation in the filling of posts by citizens of the Republic of China and those of the Union of Soviet Socialist Republics, that the application of this principle is not to be understood to mean that the present employees of Russian nationality shall be dismissed for the sole purpose of enforcing the said principle. It is further understood that access to all posts is equally open to citizens of both Contracting Parties, that no special preference shall be shown to either nationality, and that the posts shall be filled in accordance with the ability and technical as well as educational qualifications of the applicants.

In faith whereof, the respective Plenipotentiaries of the Governments of the two Contracting Parties have signed the present Declaration in duplicate in the English language and have affixed thereto their seals.

Done at the City of Peking this Thirty-First Day of the Fifth Month of the Thirteenth Year of the Republic of China, which is, the Thirty-First Day of May One Thousand Nine Hundred and Twenty-Four.

V. K. WELLINGTON KOO   [Seal]

L. M. KARAKHAN   [Seal]

Exchange of Notes

Peking, May 31, 1924.

MR. L. M. KARAKHAN,

Extraordinary Plenipotentiary Representative of the Union of Soviet Socialist Republics to the Republic of China. Peking.

DEAR MR. KARAKHAN:

On behalf of my Government, I have the honor to declare that, an Agreement on General Principles for the Settlement of the Questions between the Republic of China and the Union of Soviet Socialist Republics having been signed between us to-day, the Government of the Republic of China will, in the interests of friendship between the Republic of China and the Union of Soviet Socialist Republics, discontinue the services of all the subjects of the former Russian Empire now employed in the Chinese army and police force, as they constitute by their presence or activities a menace to the safety of the Union of Soviet Socialist Republics. If you will furnish my Government with a list of such persons, the authorities concerned will be instructed to adopt the necessary action.

I have the honor to remain,

Yours faithfully,

V. K. WELLINGTON KOO,

Minister for Foreign Affairs of the Republic of China.

Peking, May 31, 1924.

DEAR MR. KOO:

I have the honor to acknowledge the receipt of the following note from you under this date:

"On behalf of my Government, I have the honor to declare that, an Agreement on General Principles for the Settlement of the Questions between the Republic of China and the Union of Soviet Socialist Republics having been signed between us to-day, the Government of the Republic of China will, in the interests of friendship between the Republic of China and the Union of Soviet Socialist Republics, discontinue the services of all the subjects of the farmer Russian Empire now employed in the Chinese army and police force, as they constitute by their presence or activities a menace to the safety of the Union of Soviet Socialist Republics. If you will furnish my government with a list of such persons, the authorities concerned will be instructed to adopt the necessary action."

In reply, I beg to state, on behalf of my government, that I have taken note of the same and that I agree to the propositions as contained therein.

I have the honor to be,

Very truly yours,

L. M. KARAKHAN,

Extraordinary Plenipotentiary Representative of the Union of Soviet Socialist Republics to the Republic of China.

Agreement between the Government of the Autonomous Three Eastern Provinces of the Republic of China and the Government of the Union of Soviet Socialist Republics, Mukden, September 20, 1924.[1]

The Government of the Autonomous Three Eastern Provinces of the Republic of China and the Government of the Union of Soviet Socialist Republics, desiring to promote the friendly relations and regulate the questions affecting the interests of both Parties, have agreed to conclude an Agreement between the two Parties, and to that end named as their Plenipotentiaries, that is to say:

The Government of the Autonomous Three Eastern Provinces of the Republic of China:

Cheng Tsian, Lui Yung-huan and Chung Shih-ming

The Government of the Union of Soviet Socialist Republics:

Nikolai Kirillovich Kouznetzov

Who, having communicated to each other their respective full powers, found to be in good and due form, have agreed upon the following Articles:

Article I. The Chinese Eastern Railway

The Governments of the two Contracting Parties agree to settle the question of the Chinese Eastern Railway as hereinafter provided:

---

[1] Sino-Russian (Mukden Government—Government of the Union of Soviet Socialist Republics) *Agreement on General Principles and for the Provisional Management of the Chinese Eastern Railway*, Mukden, September 20, 1924. The text printed here is the *official version* as communicated by Chinese official sources to the representatives of foreign governments immediately after the conclusion of the agreement in Mukden. A preliminary draft text of this agreement was issued through the Rosta News Service from Peking, October 7, 1924, and has been published in the South Manchuria Railway publication: *Report of Progress in Manchuria: 1907-1928*, pp. 234-238. This latter version is of the preliminary and unsigned draft, the date attributed to the agreement therein being in error. The version, however, is generally correct except for one or two important inaccuracies. What purported to be a text of this agreement was published in *The China Year Book*, 1925, pp. 797-800. While this latter version is generally correct in substance, the arrangement is so confused as to justify the statement that it is a badly garbled version from preliminary drafts, entirely unreliable for purposes of quotation.

(1) The Governments of the two Contracting Parties declare that the Chinese Eastern Railway is a purely commercial enterprise.

The Governments of the two Contracting Parties mutually declare that, with the exception of matters pertaining to the business operations which are under the direct control of the Chinese Eastern Railway, all other matters affecting the rights of the National and the Local Governments of the Republic of China, such as judicial matters, matters relating to civil administration, military administration, police, municipal government, taxation and landed property (with the exception of lands required by the Chinese Eastern Railway for itself) shall be administered by the Chinese Authorities.

(2) The time-limit as provided in the Article XII of the Contract for the Construction and Operation of the Chinese Eastern Railway of August 27th/September 8th, 1896, shall be reduced from eighty to sixty years, at the expiration of which the Government of China shall enter gratis into possession of the said Railway and its appurtenant properties.

Upon the consent of both Contracting Parties, the question of a further reduction of the said time-limit, that is, sixty years, may be discussed.

From the date of signing the present Agreement, the Union of Soviet Socialist Republics agrees that China has the right to redeem the Chinese Eastern Railway. At the time of redemption, the two Contracting Parties shall determine what the Chinese Eastern Railway had actually cost, and it shall be redeemed by China with Chinese capital at a fair price.

(3) The Government of the Union of Soviet Socialist Republics agrees in a Commission to be organised by the two Contracting Parties to settle the questions of the obligations of the Chinese Eastern Railway Company in accordance with Section 4 of Article IX of the Agreement on General Principles for the Settlement of the Questions between the Republic of China and the Union of Soviet Socialist Republics signed on May 31st, at Peking.

(4) The Governments of the two Contracting Parties mutually agree that the future of the Chinese Eastern Railway shall be determined by China and the Union of Soviet Socialist Republics to the exclusion of any third party or parties.

(5) The Contract for the Construction and Operation of the Chinese Eastern Railway of August 27th/September 8th, 1896, shall be completely revised, in accordance with the terms specified in this Agreement, by a Commission of the two Contracting Parties

in four months from the date of signing the present Agreement. Pending the revision, the rights of the two Governments arising out of this Contract, which do not conflict with the present Agreement and which do not prejudice China's right of sovereignty, shall be maintained.

(6) The Railway shall establish, for discussion and decision of all matters relating to the Chinese Eastern Railway, a Board of Directors to be composed of ten persons, of whom five shall be appointed by China and five by the Union of Soviet Socialist Republics.

China shall appoint one of the Chinese Directors as President of the Board of Directors, who shall be ex-officio the Director-General.

The Union of Soviet Socialist Republics shall appoint one of the Russian Directors as Vice-President of the Board of Directors, who shall be ex-officio the Assistant Director-General.

Seven persons shall constitute a quorum, and all decisions of the Board of Directors shall have the consent of not less than six persons before they can be carried out.

The Director-General and the Assistant Director-General shall jointly manage the affairs of the Board of Directors, and they shall jointly sign all the documents of the Board.

In the absence of either the Director-General or the Assistant Director-General, their respective Governments may appoint another Director to officiate as the Director-General or the Assistant Director-General (in the case of the Director-General, by one of the Chinese Directors, and in that of the Assistant Director-General, by one of the Russian Directors).

(7) The Railway shall establish a Board of Auditors to be composed of five persons, namely, two Chinese Auditors, who shall be appointed by China, and three Russian Auditors, who shall be appointed by the Union of Soviet Socialist Republics.

The Chairman of the Board of Auditors shall be elected from among the Chinese Auditors.

(8) The Railway shall have a Manager, who shall be a national of the Union of Soviet Socialist Republics, and two Assistant-Managers, one to be a national of the Republic of China, and the other to be a national of the Union of Soviet Socialist Republics.

The said officers shall be appointed by the Board of Directors, and such appointments shall be confirmed by their respective Governments.

The rights and duties of the Manager and the Assistant Managers shall be defined by the Board of Directors.

(9) The Chiefs and the Assistant Chiefs of the various depart-

ments of the Railway shall be appointed by the Board of Directors.

If the Chief of a department is a national of the Republic of China, the Assistant Chief of that department shall be a national of the Union of Soviet Socialist Republics, and if the Chief of a department is a national of the Union of Soviet Socialist Republics, the Assistant Chief of that department shall be a national of the Republic of China.

(10) The employment of persons in the various departments of the Railway shall be in accordance with the principal of equal representation between the nationals of the Republic of China and those of the Union of Soviet Socialist Republics.

(NOTE:—In carrying out the principle of equal representation, the normal course of life and activities of the Railway shall in no case be interrupted or injured, that is to say, the employment of the people of both nationalities shall be in accordance with the experience, personal qualifications and fitness of the applicants.)

(11) With the exception of the estimates and budgets as provided in Section 12 of Article I of the present Agreement, all other matters on which the Board of Directors cannot reach an agreement, shall be referred to the Governments of the Contracting Parties for a just and amicable settlement.

(12) The Board of Directors shall present the estimates and budgets of the Railway to a joint meeting of the Board of Directors and the Board of Auditors for consideration and approval.

(13) All the net profits of the Railway shall be held by the Board of Directors and shall not be used pending a final settlement, in a joint Commission, of the question of its distribution between the two Contracting Parties.

(14) The Board of Directors shall make a complete revision, as soon as possible, of the Statutes of the Chinese Eastern Railway Company approved on December 4th, 1896, by the Tsarist Government in accordance with the present Agreement and not later than four months from the date of constitution of the Board of Directors.

Pending their revision, the aforesaid Statutes, insofar as they do not conflict with the present Agreement and do not prejudice the rights of sovereignty of the Republic of China, shall continue to be observed.

(15) As soon as the conditions of the redemption by China of the Chinese Eastern Railway are settled by both Contracting Parties, or as soon as the Railway reverts to China upon the expiration of the time-limit as stipulated in Section 2 of Article I of the

present Agreement, all parts of this Agreement concerning the same shall cease to have effect.

ARTICLE II. Navigation

The Governments of the two Contracting Parties agree to settle, on the basis of equality, reciprocity and the respect of each other's sovereignty, the question relating to the navigation of all kinds of their vessels on those parts of the rivers, lakes, and other bodies of water, which are common to their respective borders, the details of this question to be regulated in a Commission of the two Contracting Parties within two months from the date of signing the present Agreement.

In view of the extensive freight and passenger interests of China on the lower Amur River into the sea, and the extensive freight and passenger interests of the Union of Soviet Socialist Republics on the River Sungari up to and including Harbin, both Contracting Parties agree, on the basis of equality and reciprocity, to take up the question of securing the said interests in the said Commission.

ARTICLE III. Boundaries

The Governments of the two Contracting Parties agree to redemarcate their boundaries through a Commission to be organised by both Parties, and, pending such redemarcation, to maintain the present boundaries.

ARTICLE IV. Tariff and Trade Agreement

The Governments of the two Contracting Parties agree to draw up a Customs Tariff and conclude a Commercial Treaty in a Commission to be organised by the said Parties on the basis of equality and reciprocity.

ARTICLE V. Propaganda

The Governments of the two Contracting Parties mutually pledge themselves not to permit within their respective territories the existence and/or activities of any organization or groups whose aim is to struggle by acts of violence against the Government of either Contracting Party.

The Governments of the two Contracting Parties further pledge themselves not to engage in propaganda directed against the political and social systems of either Contracting Party.

ARTICLE VI. Commissions

The Commissions as provided in the Articles of this Agreement shall commence their work within one month from the date of signing this Agreement, and shall complete their work as soon as possible and not later than six months. This does not apply to those Commissions, whose time-limits have been specified in the respective Articles of this Agreement.

ARTICLE VII

The present Agreement shall come into effect from the date of signature.

In witness whereof, the respective Plenipotentiaries have signed the present Agreement in duplicate in the Chinese, Russian and English languages, and have affixed thereto their seals.

In case of dispute, the English text shall be accepted as the standard.

Done at the City of Mukden this Twentieth Day of the Ninth Month of the Thirteenth Year of the Republic of China, which is the Twentieth Day of September, One Thousand Nine Hundred and Twenty-Four.

Signed:

CHENG TSIAN	[Seal]
LUI YUNG-HUAN	[Seal]
CHUNG SHIH-MING	[Seal]
KOUZNETZOV	[Seal]

DOCUMENTARY SOURCES

In the brief list of documentary sources which follows no effort has been made to include any but those which are of principal value for the student who wishes to obtain the original texts of documents analyzed and epitomized in the foregoing chapters. Many references are mentioned in footnotes in the text which are not included below, as, for example, newspaper and periodical materials, and certain books which have usually been cited in connection with a commentary on interpretation of isolated documents. The arrangement which is used below is intended to be essentially practical.

MacMurray, J. V. A., *Treaties and Agreements with and concerning China, 1894-1919.* 2 vols., New York, Oxford University Press, 1921.

Manchuria Treaties and Agreements. Pamphlet Series of the Carnegie Endowment for International Peace, No. 44. Washington, The Endowment, 1921.

Rockhill, W. W., *Treaties and Agreements with or concerning China and Korea, 1895-1904.* Washington, Government Printing Office, 1904.

Rockhill, W. W., *Treaties, Conventions, Agreements, etc., relating to China and Korea,* October, 1904-January, 1908. Washington, Department of State, 1908.

Korea Treaties and Agreements. Pamphlet Series, Carnegie Endowment for International Peace. Washington, The Endowment, 1921.

Sino-Japanese Negotiations of 1915. Pamphlet Series, Carnegie Endowment for International Peace. Washington, The Endowment, 1921.

The Consortium: the official text of the four-power agreement for a loan to China and relevant documents. Pamphlet Series, Carnegie Endowment for International Peace. Washington, The Endowment, 1921.

Ministère des affaires étrangères, *Recueil des traités et conventions conclus entre l'empire du Japon et les puissances étrangères.* 2 vols., one being the Japanese and Chinese texts, the other containing the foreign texts, usually French. Tokyo, Imprimerie Impériale, 1918.

U. S. Foreign Relations. Annual Series, volumes from 1898 down through 1917 (last volume published by 1929) used. Washington, Government Printing Office.

U. S. Treaty Series. Published by the Department of State serially. Washington, Government Printing Office.

American Journal of International Law. Journal and *Supplements,* the latter containing complete texts of certain documents. Published at Washington.

Conference on the Limitation of Armament. Official minutes of the Washington Conference on the Limitation of Armament and on Pacific and Far Eastern Questions. Published by the Government Printing Office, Washington, 1922.

Willoughby, W. W., *China at the Conference.* Unofficial publication which, however, contains notes on the Washington Conference, including certain records of committee and subcommittee meetings not otherwise published. Baltimore, The Johns Hopkins University Press, 1922.

Willoughby, W. W. *Foreign Rights and Interests in China.* 2 vols., revised edition. A standard work containing extensive quotation and commentaries relating to diplomatic documents and negotiations. Baltimore, The Johns Hopkins University Press, 1927.

British Documents on the Origins of the Great War, 1898-1914. 4 vols. This new work is especially useful in connection with a study of the Anglo-Japanese Alliances. Published at London, British Foreign Office, various dates.

Siebert and Schreiner (B. de Siebert and George Abel Schreiner), *Entente Diplomacy and the World: Matrix of the History of Europe,* 1909-1914. Contains draft texts of the secret Russo-Japanese treaties of 1910, 1912 and 1916. New York and London, 1921.

Laloy, Emile, *Les Documents Secrets des Archives du Ministère des Affaires Etrangères de Russie, publié par les Bolcheviks.* Paris, 1919.

Miller, David Hunter, *My Diary at the Conference of Paris.* 22 vols. of a limited edition of 40 sets. New York, 1924.

The China Year Books. Issued annually by the *Peking and Tientsin Times,* under the editorship of Mr. Woodhead. Tientsin, China.

The Japan Year Books. Issued annually by The Japan Year Book Office, Tokyo, Japan.

Minor sources, cited for an occasional document and of little general importance pertaining to Manchuria, have been omitted from the above classification.

INDEX

For references to major events, treaties and agreements the reader is referred to the detailed tables of contents (for the period 1895-1905, page 1; for 1905-1915, page 45; for 1915-1921, page 127; for 1921-1929, page 191). Concerning the scope of the Index, see page xvi.

America, *see* United States

American interests in Manchuria and the "open door," before 1905, 29, after 1905, *see* United States; reservation of rights in Chinchow-Aigun railway contract, 114

Amur, *see* Harbin-Heihofu railway

Anglo-German agreement (1900), 41

Anglo-Japanese alliances, 116-118, 240-241, 271

Anshan iron works, Japanese interests in, 148

Antung, opening of customs office in, 87-88

Antung-Mukden railway, customs reduction agreement for goods transported over, 87-88; extension of, 139; reconstruction of, 59, 72-73

Aoki, Viscount, reply to first "Hay note" of, 30, 38

Asakawa, K., cited, 60

Balfour, Arthur J. (later Earl), 201, 237, 241

Banks represented in Four Power Consortium, 104

Banque de l'Indo-Chine, 104, 170

Barga region, Russian relations with, 98, 156

Bezobrazoff, Alexander M., 80

Bland, J. O. P., 111

Boxer rising, occupation of railways during, 68; second Hay declaration on "open door" caused by, 39

British, *see also* Great Britain; loan contract agreement for Shanhaikwan-Newchwang-Hsinmintun railway, 26; loans to South Manchuria Railway, 63; rights to organize Shanhaikwan-Newchwang railway waived (1899), 27; syndicates' project for Hsinmintun-Fakumen railway (1907), 110-112

British and Chinese Corporation loan agreement with Chinese Administrator General of the Imperial Railways of North China, 26-27, 110-112

Bryan, William J., commenting on Japan's acceptance of "open door" declaration of 1900, 40; on "open door," 177-

178; Charles Evans Hughes reaffirms declaration of, 236

Bülow, Count B von, declares Anglo-German agreement non-applicable to Manchuria, 41

Cable agreements between China and Japan, 82

"Cassini Convention," 255

Chang Hsueh-liang, Marshal, 215, 234

Chang tso-hsiang, *tuchun* of Kirin, 215

Chang Tso-lin, Marshal, 210, 214, 215, 223, 230, 231

Changchun railway agreement (1902), 14

Chefoo, Japanese and Russian cables to, 82-84

Chengchiatun, extension of Chinchow-Aigun railway system projected to, 280

"Chengchiatun incident," 151-152

Chientao district, question of jurisdiction over Koreans in, 90-92, 138; railway agreement concerning, 213

China, jurisdiction over Koreans of, 138; position in Manchuria of, 278-282; troop transportation by, 229-234

Chinchou in neutral zone, 18

Chinchow-Aigun railway, project for, 107-110, 112, 163, 262, 279

Chinese Eastern Railway, crisis of 1929 over, xvii-xxviii; customs administration in Russian zone of, 25, 100-102; effect of Washington Conference (1921) on, 216-219; Inter-allied control of, 158-160; lumbering agreements with Russia of, 99-100; mining agreements with Russia of, 98-99; original contract agreements concerning, (1896) 12, (1898) 13; Peking-Moscow agreement (1924) on provisional management of, 288 ff.; Russian telegraph lines on, 83, 102-103; sale to Japan of portion of, 54, 174; status defined in Mukden agreement (1924), 296-299; status defined in Peking-Moscow agreement (1924), 285-286; status from 1919 to 1929, 219-220; status since 1925, 234-235

Chinese subjects in Kirin, jurisdiction over, 19-20